D1278885

. . . is an authorized facsimile made from the master

copy of the original book. Further unauthorized

copying is prohibited.

Books on Demand is a publishing service of UMI.

The program offers xerographic reprints of more

than 136,000 books that are no longer in print.

The primary focus of Books on Demand is academic

and professional resource materials originally pub-

lished by university presses, academic societies, and

trade book publishers worldwide.

UMI
BOOKS ON DEMAND™

UMI
A Bell & Howell Company

300 North Zeeb Road
P.O. Box 1346
Ann Arbor, Michigan 48106-1346

1-800-521-0600   734-761-4700
http://www.umi.com

Printed in 1998 by xerographic process on acid-free paper

12

Why Genocide?

THE ARMENIAN AND JEWISH EXPERIENCES

IN PERSPECTIVE

Why Genocide?

THE ARMENIAN AND JEWISH EXPERIENCES

IN PERSPECTIVE

Florence Mazian

Iowa State University Press / Ames

FLORENCE MAZIAN received her B.A. and Ph.D. degrees from
Wayne State University and is currently a member of the
faculty of The University of Michigan—Dearborn.

FIRST EDITION, 1990

INTERNATIONAL STANDARD BOOK NUMBER: 0-8138-0143-5

Library of Congress Cataloging-in-Publication Data

Mazian, Florence, 1942-
    Why genocide? : the Armenian and Jewish experiences in perspective
Florence Mazian.—1st ed.
    p. cm.
    Bibliography: p.
    Includes index.
    ISBN 0-8138-0143-5
    1. Genocide. 2. Armenian massacres, 1915-1923. 3. Holocaust, Jewish (1939-1945)—Causes.
    I. Title.
HV6542.M39 1990
304.6'63'095662—dc20   89-15268

To the memory of my dear father, Armenag,

and to my mother, Alice,

whose families were victims of the Turkish

genocide of Armenians, and

to the memory of my beloved brother, Peter

Also, I wish to dedicate this work to

my sister, Armeney, and niece, Lisa,

and Very Rev. Father Paren Avedikian,

who served as my inspiration

CONTENTS

PREFACE

THE purpose of this study is to answer a very basic question: Why is genocide, rather than any other alternative, selected by a people or state as the solution to a real or imagined problem? To answer this question the author makes use of some concepts stated in Neil Smelser's theory of collective behavior and specifically his theoretical insights into what he calls "hostile outburst."[1] By reconceptualizing some of his ideas and adding new components to them, this study develops a theory of genocide. In addition, the study applies the newly created theory to the Armenians in Turkey during World War I and, more recently, to the European Jews during World War II.

Smelser believes there are six determinants of collective behavior—factors that create a condition in which collective behavior is most likely to occur. These include *structural conduciveness, structural strain, growth and spread of generalized beliefs, precipitating factors, mobilization of participants for action, and operation of social control.*[2] By reconceptualizing some of Smelser's work, this study has incorporated parts of his analysis of collective behavior into a new framework and revised and added to his six aspects of collective behavior to create determinants that I have specifically formulated for the analysis of genocide. My six new conceptual categories serving as determinants are:

1. *Creation of "Outsiders,"* which is like structural conduciveness and incorporates structure of responsibility and precipitating factors.
2. *Internal Strife,* which is similar to Smelser's structural strain and contains his strain in social organization, that includes real or threatened deprivation and strain in norms.
3. *Destructive Uses of Communication,* which is a composite of two new categories that are related to communication and are derived from Smelser's growth and spread of generalized beliefs. They are *aggressive ideology,* which is composed of his strain in values, and

propaganda war, which is composed of his facilities and strain, generalized aggression, and spread of beliefs.

4. *Powerful Leadership with Territorial Ambitions Forming a Monolithic and Exclusionary Party*, which is a new category.

5. *Organization of Destruction*, which is formed from mobilization of participants for action, and it utilizes parts of Smelser's organization of the hostile outburst, accessibility to objects of attack, and ecology.

6. *The Failure of Multidimensional Levels of Social Control*, which is a newly formulated concept designed to address the social control of genocide. This sixth new determinant is composed almost exclusively of a new typology of social control for analyzing genocide. In this typology there are two conceptual levels of social control—*external* and *internal*, that is, methods of social control outside of the victim group's control (external) or theoretically within their realm of control (internal). External controls consist of the aggressor state and its citizenry, other nations, and religious institutions. Internal controls include interference by the victim group's ethnic state, mobilization of the victim group's agencies of self-defense, a realization of impending group annihilation, and physical ability to retaliate. With these new categories of determinants of genocide, a theory by which the mechanisms of genocide can be understood has been constructed.

To return to our original question: Why is genocide, rather than any other alternative, selected as a solution to a situation of strain? The key to answering this question, and a basis for the theory of genocide, is the concept of the *value-added process*, which permits us to view genocide as a consequence of the convergence of many factors, each adding power and vitality to one another, simultaneously limiting and reducing the use of alternatives other than genocide to decrease strain. The theoretical framework presented here posits the six previously listed determinants to explain genocide. These components of the theory are viewed in a static fashion for purposes of analysis. However, in reality, all six act in conjunction with one another in a dynamic, synergistic fashion to bring about genocide. These factors must be present and must interact with one another simultaneously for genocide to become a reality. The existence of one or two factors alone cannot result in genocide. Thus genocide is the culmination of a dynamic process in which certain factors merge and coalesce until, eventually, constructive options for dealing with strain are cast aside and genocide becomes a viable and "practical" alternative method of dealing with a "problem" group.

rather than any other alternative method been selected as a means of solving a "problem"?

Since genocide has not been the standard method of resolving group conflict but, rather, has been an anomaly, an explanation of conditions conducive to it would broaden our understanding of the phenomenon. This book delineates conditions that increase the likelihood of genocide and establishes a theoretical framework for its analysis. This theoretical framework is then applied to the Armenian genocide and Jewish Holocaust.

As the world becomes smaller and technology more sophisticated, the potential for genocide is increased. Through advanced computer technology and a sophisticated military, one can now more easily target and eliminate certain segments of the population than in the past. Hence it is important that we understand the dynamics involved in the act of genocide to better target potential genocidal situations and possibly ameliorate situations that might culminate in this egregious crime.

I

THEORETICAL INQUIRY
INTO ARMENIAN GENOCIDE

THE TURK came . . . as an alien. . . . His rule . . . has been the rule of strangers over enslaved nations in their own land. It has been the rule of cruelty, faithlessness, and brutal lust; it has not been government, but organized brigandage.

—E. A. FREEMAN

1

CREATION OF "OUTSIDERS"

PART I concerns the genocide of the Armenian people, which will be analyzed within the framework of our theory of genocide set forth briefly in the Preface. This theory involves the determinants of the value-added process—the creation of "outsiders," internal strife, powerful leadership with territorial ambitions, destructive uses of communication, the organization of destruction, and failure of multidimensional levels of social control—which will be applied to the Armenian case. What follows is an examination of social relations between Moslems and non-Moslems in the Ottoman Empire, an experience making Armenians "outsiders" in their own historic homeland during approximately five hundred years (starting with the *millet* system) of Ottoman domination preceding the 1915 genocide.

HISTORY OF INTERGROUP TENSIONS

From the inception of the Ottoman Empire, religion proved to be the most important factor for social distinctions among Ottoman subjects. All other forms of discrimination and abuse against non-

3

Moslems were legitimized, since religion provided the *legal* basis for discrimination in the Ottoman state.

The political-legal structure institutionalizing religious discrimination was known as the *millet* system. Since *millet* legitimized discrimination, a potentially dangerous situation for non-Moslems was built right into the social structure. This state of affairs ensured that Christians would be "outsiders" to the social system. During the late nineteenth and early twentieth centuries, internal strife, aggressive leadership, and a destructive ideology would create an even greater malevolent environment for non-Moslems.

The actual process leading ultimately to genocide was set into motion when the Seljuk Turks invaded northern Ararat in A.D. 1021. Armenia was overcome by the Byzantine army in 1045 and annexed to the empire. By 1080 Armenia was under Seljuk domination after Alp-Arslan led the Turks into Armenia.[1]

Yet the greatest catastrophe for the Armenians was the Mongol invasion of 1236. The state of Zacharides was subjugated by the Mongols in 1235–36, and the rest of Armenia Major was overrun in 1242–43. The subsequent 1254 census by the conquerors imposed enormous taxes on the Armenian male population.

The Mongol Ilkhanate turned Moslem in 1302, signaling a deterioration of the status of Armenians vis-a-vis their Moslem neighbors. In the following decades Armenians were to be deprived of their inherited lands, taxed heavily, and victimized by unstable and capricious rule.[2]

A violent and destructive campaign took place under "Tamerlane" (Timur-lenk) during 1386–88. Armenia was ruled in this period by two Turkoman dynasties—the "Black Rams" (*Kara-Koyunlu*) based at Van and the "White Rams" (*Ak-Koyunlu*) located at Diarbekir. In 1502 Safavid Persia took over Armenia following a battle led by Shah Ismail at Sharur, Armenia. For the next 150 years the Armenian frontier shifted as powerful Ottoman Turkey and Persia engaged in bitter wars upon Armenian soil. Their conflicts grew out of a fierce antipathy between the Shiite Moslems of Persia and the "orthodox" Sunni Moslems of Turkey.[3]

Before 1514 the Ottomans had not pushed far enough east to actually conquer part of Armenia, but in that year Sultan Selim "the Grim" defeated Shah Ismail at the Battle of Chaldiran and captured almost half of the Armenian plateau. Much of the rest of Armenia was conquered by Suleiman I, "the Magnificent," twenty years later.[4]

Millets—1453

The basis of relations between Moslems and non-Moslems was clarified in two treaties the Prophet Mohammed concluded—one with Christians of Narjan (in Arabia) and the other with Jews of Khaybar (Arabia). In essence the treaties stipulated that peoples could keep their faith and much of their possessions if they paid a tax. Non-Moslem monotheists came to be known as *ahl al-dhimma* or *dhimmis* ("protected peoples"), "gaining" this status upon payment of taxes. As Islam's armies advanced, people could either embrace Islam, pay taxes, or face death.[5]

Benjamin Braude and Bernard Lewis, in *Christians and Jews in the Ottoman Empire*, comment:

> Religiously speaking, both Christianity and Judaism were looked upon with disdain by the Ottoman state and its agencies. They were referred to as "their null and depraved contention" (*ala za'mihim al-fasid*) or "their void rites" (*batil ayyinleri*). They were regarded as different from and thus unequal to the followers of the ruling religion, basically deprived of certain rights and quite often molested and harassed. Their distinctness was consciously maintained not only out of religious considerations, but also as the best administrative means for their preservation.[6]

Non-Moslem communities were called *rayahs* (Arabic), meaning "flocks." Christopher Walker, in *Armenia: The Survival of a Nation*, contends this term was used for non-Moslems because it connotes they were "protected ones." He states that "the protection that they received . . . was in practice closer to that of a racketeer than a biblical vision."[7]

A philosophy of statecraft emphasizing government-as-art rather than government-as-principle was the ruling code for all Islamic regimes. The peoples of Central Asia (Mongols and Turks) in time spread the Islamic concept of the brotherhood of all believers and the Asian idea of empire.[8]

This model of statecraft, first elaborated by Seljuk and later Ottoman Turks in the Middle East, became an international system of public order in which many peoples of different religions and cultures were kept together for several hundred years by the supremacy of two major establishments. The first of these, basically secular in nature, was "the Ruling Institution," containing various bureaucratic departments and the armed forces. Within these two, ex-slaves or slaves assumed dominant roles. The second establishment was the "Muslim Institution," administered by *shari'a* jurists of various categories. Each of these, though theoretically independent, was joined to a representative council, the *diwan*. Supposedly neither of these agencies would obstruct the centralized despotism principle necessary to the rule of individual sultans or caliphs and their delegates, the *wazirs*—especially when the idea gained ground that a military power might constitute a valid imamate (the territory ruled by an imam, the leader of prayer in a Moslem mosque).[9]

With the rise of the *millet* system in the fifteenth century, permanent social cleavages were created in the Ottoman population—the word "*millet*" is Arabic for "religious sect."[10] When the Ottomans conquered Constantinople in 1453, the various creeds were granted certain "privileges" by Sultan Mohammed II when he issued an edict creating *millets*.[11] All Christian subject groups were organized into this structure, and Armenians thus became a subject nation of the newly ruling Osman dynasty.[12]

Adda Bozeman, in her book *The Future of Law in a Multi-Cultural World*, analyzes this development.

Under the umbrella of a nominal or defused centralism, then, organizational impulses had been channelled early into a variety of separate corporate structures, each representative of a special set of interests, callings, or commitments. In fact it was only through belonging to such a corporation that the individual, unrecognized either as a citizen or as a member of a nationality, acquired status in the Ottoman Empire. This was particularly true of his religious association with the millet, a nonterritorial communal formation encompassing the members of each officially recognized belief system; for since religion was the paramount rallying point for all Near Eastern peoples, it could be used effectively also by the imperial administration as a structuring principle in its governance of subject populations and as a control mechanism through which loyalty to the dynastic state could be assured. However, it needs to be remembered in this context that each millet was an entity in itself, having scant, if any, relations with other organized sects.[13]

Such a structure served to intensify the separation of the different nationalities. The distinct Armenian, Greek, and Syrian communities vied with one another over which should have greater privileges. Consequently, the original hostilities arising out of creed were emphasized and, intentionally or not, a custom arose whereby the sultan ruled largely by force of jealousies—in effect, a "divide and conquer" principle.[14]

One "privilege" granted the Armenians under the *millet* system was the right of their patriarch to exercise personal jurisdiction over education, social position, marriage, divorce, and other matters of his people.[15] The Armenian community was permitted to make decisions regarding a number of internal matters, including inheritance, founding of hospitals, and management of prisons. Thus each *millet* was, by and large, self-governing and retained its own institutions.[16] At the inception of the Ottoman Empire the rulers decided that Christians could maintain their language, traditions, and religion.[17] This makes the sultan's system look quite tolerant.

In 1461, eight years after Constantinople had been conquered, Hovagim, an Armenian archbishop to Constantinople, was summoned to serve as patriarch of the non-Moslems of the empire. As Walker observes,

> The Armenian Patriarchate of Constantinople was thus a creation of the Ottoman authorities, not of the Armenian church. Its jurisdiction overrode that of the establishments created by the Church itself. . . . It was a political appointment; but since the Ottoman empire was a theocracy, it was expressed in ecclesiastical terms.[18]

Note that *millets* appear to be liberal structures since they permit various peoples to retain their own language and religion. However, Viscount James Bryce points out that the *millet* system, though permitting autonomy in culture, religion, and social life for non-Moslems, was "a maimed autonomy, for it . . . jealously debarred [some peoples] from any political expression."[19]

Both economic and political considerations motivated the "tolerance" exhibited in the system. By maintaining distinct groups, the conquerors could live at the expense of non-Moslems, since the sedentary Christians had developed industry, commerce, and agriculture as opposed to their nomadic conquerors. Exploitation could be continued if the racial identity of the *rayahs* could be left intact, if they were subjected to taxation, and if they were repressed so they would remain weak and incapable of revolt.[20]

Millets created a social structure that made the Ottomans the undisputed dominant group in their heterogeneous and extensive empire by dividing the society into victor and vanquished.[21] Obviously from the start there were flaws in the Ottoman system that rendered the position of Armenians intolerable. The most serious problem was that Moslem law did not apply to non-Moslems, who had separate courts and prisons. Moslems could be assured of a fair hearing in civil cases judged among themselves. However, should a conflict erupt between a Moslem and non-Moslem, the Moslem could always receive a hearing in a religious court, the *mehkeme*, where the testimony of the non-Moslem was forbidden. Later, non-Moslems would be allowed to testify against Moslems, but their testimony would almost always be disregarded.[22]

Henry Morgenthau, American Ambassador to Turkey during World War I, reflects on some of the consequences of the *millet* system.

The sultans . . . erected the several peoples such as the Greeks and the Armenians, into separate "millets," or nations, not because they desired to promote their independence and welfare, but because they regarded them as vermin, and therefore disqualified for membership in the Ottoman state. The attitude of the Government toward their Christian subjects was illustrated by certain regulations which limited their freedom of action. The buildings in which Christians lived should not be conspicuous and their churches should have no belfry. Christians could not ride a horse in the city, for that was the exclusive right of the noble Moslem. The Turk had the right to test the sharpness of his sword upon the neck of any Christian.

According to Morgenthau, the conquered "infidels" were considered to be infinitely inferior to the followers of Allah, were held in contempt, and were considered less valuable than herds of animals.[23]

For the minorities, legal rights, participation in the mainstream of political life, and social interaction with Moslems were minimal or nonexistent. Unpredictable "toleration" resulted in segregation, accompanied by economic exploitation, prejudice, and confiscation of property.[24]

Dr. Fridtjof Nansen, a Norwegian explorer, elucidates the condition of Christians under Ottoman rule in the following statement:

To their Muhammedan "masters" the Christians were slaves and chattels, whom Allah had given to the faithful, and who were quite outside the pale of the law. The testimony of an infidel—i.e. a Christian—against a Moslem was invalid in the law courts; nor could he defend himself against violence and robbery, because no Christian was allowed to carry arms. This, of course, gave the Kurds and other marauders a pretty free hand.[25]

Taxes

In Turkey, oppression of *millets* was almost always manifested via brutal taxation. Edouard Philipee Engelhardt, in *La Turquie et le Tanzimat ou histoire des reformes dans l'Empire ottoman*, advises that exorbitant taxation was " . . . justified by this principle of the Koran: Strike the infidels until they submit and pay their taxes." Eventually, of course, Christians were impoverished by taxes. In *The People of Ararat*, Joseph Burtt contends "the rayas [sic] were crushed under the yoke of a fanatical, incapable and ignorant government, which burdened the people with taxes and made the normal development of subject races impossible."[26]

Since they were Christians, Armenians could not bear arms, leaving them at the mercy of predatory neighbors. Being unable to bear arms, they were automatically exempted from military service, which made it impossible for them to form an officer class. Christians could not go to war, since only a Moslem could draw his sword to defend Islam. Yet Christians were subject to a boy-collection (*devshirme*), wherein officials could take boy children from their families, educate them as Moslems, and enlist them in the Ottoman civil service. *Devshirme* was an established practice in some Armenian localities by the end of the sixteenth century. (The practice was discontinued by the mid-eighteenth century.)[27]

There existed another tax resulting in thousands of Christian boys between four and eight years of age being taken every year from their families, circumcised and raised as Moslems to form a standing army, which was Turkey's most formidable offensive weapon against Christians—the renowned Janissary Corps. Members of this fighting force (formed in 1430) were trained with monastic and military discipline and were taught to view the corps as their only home. They were considered the flower of the Ottoman troops; it was they who stormed Constantinople on 29 May 1453. Not only were male Christian infants taken and raised as Moslem soldiers, but also the most beautiful Christian women were taken and impressed into harems.[28]

Another tax, the *kharadj*, a "humiliatian tax," was imposed on all non-Moslem males, age fifteen to sixty-five, "for the right to live from one year to the next." And ironically, yet another tax was paid by Christian males for exemption from military service, even though they had always been rigorously excluded from service anyway.

The *rayah* were permitted life tenancy of property, but the right of ownership was reserved without usufruct to the state, which demanded rent in the form of a tithe—one-tenth of the harvest; Moslems paid this also. This land tax was collected from farmers by local authorities approved by the local government. Farmers were not permitted to begin their harvests unless fiscal authorities were present. Furthermore, farmers were forced to abide by rules that forbade improvements in agricultural techniques. After taxes, the peasant retained only one-third of the harvest.

In addition, there was a tax on herds and a customs tax, the latter being 3.5 percent for non-Moslems and 2 percent for Moslems. Special taxes existed, also, which had been enacted for one year but were never discontinued. Refusal to pay often meant loss of land or life.[29]

All Christians had to pay a property tax and a poll tax. These were collected in an unorderly fashion, with officials using extortion tactics whenever possible. Victims, of course, had no legal redress. No redress existed for an Armenian who suffered loss of limb, property, or life at the hands of a Moslem. This was not caused by carelessness on the part of law officers but by governmental corruption. Proof of this was that complainants themselves were speedily punished for having lodged a complaint against their persecutors.[30] Houses of Armenians were taxed at one-third of their assessed value a year. A 10 percent tax was applied to shops, mills, and building establishments. In addition, any man following a profession or trade was charged a 10 percent tax.[31]

Of all the Christian peoples of the empire, Armenians alone had to bear the burden of *kishlak,* or "right to quarter," which was a right of the Kurds since antiquity. *Kishlak* required that Armenians provide Kurds with free winter quarters for four to six months a year. Aside from this being a disagreeable (and dangerous) situation for the Armenians, it proved expensive, since Kurdish squatters consumed large quantities of food and animals. In effect, the Armenian community was impoverished by these taxes.[32]

By the 1890s taxes levied upon Armenians were exorbitant. Dr. Johannes Lepsius explains that "the methods employed to collect [the taxes] . . . constitute by themselves a sufficient justification for the sweeping away of Ottoman rule in Armenia." He elaborates upon different rates of taxation applied to Christians and Moslems. For example, he cites the town of Erzeroum, where 8,000 homes were inhabited by Moslems. Yet they paid only 395,000 *piastres,* but Christians, whose houses numbered but 2,000, paid 430,000 *piastres.*[33]

Lepsius points to a typical method of tax collection:

A family, for instance, is supposed to contribute, say, £5, and fulfils [sic] its obligation. The zaptiehs [government agents], however, ask for £3 or £4 more for themselves, and are met with a rash refusal. Negotiations, interlarded with violent and abusive language, ensue, and £1 is accepted. But the zaptiehs' blood is up. In a week they return and demand the same taxes over again. The Armenians wax angry, protest and present their receipt; whereat the zaptiehs laughingly explain that the document in question is no receipt but a few verses from a Turkish book. The villagers plead poverty and implore mercy. Greed, not compassion, moves the zaptiehs to compromise the matter for £3 more, but the money is not forthcoming. Then they demand the surrender of the young women and girls of the family to glut their brutal appetites, and refusal is punished with a series of tortures over which decency and humanity throw a veil of silence. Rape, and every kind of brutal outrage conceivable to the diseased mind . . . varied perhaps with murder or arson, wind up the incident.[34]

Frederick Greene, in *Armenian Crisis in Turkey,* points to three abuses the Ottoman government empowered the Kurds to perpetrate in their method of tax collection: (1) unjust and corrupt assessments, (2) injustice and severity in collecting and (3) farming of taxes. Greene's explanation of tax farming follows:

Taxes are often farmed out to the highest bidder, who usually is some powerful Kurdish chief. Either in consequence of this power, or by means of bribes, he is secure from interference on the part of the government. He collects the amount due the government and then takes for himself as much as he chooses. . . .

While he is collector for these villages they are considered as belonging to him. During the year his followers pay frequent visits to the villages. They are ignorant and brutal, and on such visits, as also when collecting taxes, they treat the villagers with the utmost severity.

. . . assessors and collectors—and they are many, a different one for each kind of tax, personal, house and land, sheep, tobacco, etc.—on their visits to the villages, take with them *a retinue of servants and soldiers, who, with their horses, must be kept at the expense of the village, thus entailing a very heavy additional burden upon them.* Soldiers and servants sent to the villagers to make collections, very naturally take things for themselves.

According to Greene, such taxation reduced nearly all Armenian villages to a condition of extreme poverty.[35]

There was no visible remedy for this situation, as under Sultan Abdul-Hamid II courts of law had become extremely corrupt. The party who paid the most was rendered a favorable verdict by the *qadis* (judge). Jury members, who shared in the booty, protected captured bandits. The judges were uneducated and poorly paid or not paid at all, so that their corruptness provided them with a livelihood. Cafes and bathhouses provided recruitment grounds for witnesses, and judges adjudicated on the basis of such invalid testimony. Reports of European consuls indicate that Christian testimony was not taken into account in courts of law.[36]

INTENSIFICATION OF AGGRESSION AGAINST OUTSIDERS

Under Sultan Abdul-Hamid II a policy known as Pan-Islamism was adopted. In reality, it was not a religious policy since men could be full Moslems before its inception. Pan-Islamism was, however, a politically expedient measure. Like many heads of state, the sultan was essentially an opportunist regarding matters of religious faith.

Pan-Islamism served to unify the Moslems against non-Moslems and could be used for reactionary or revolutionary ends. Sultan Abdul-Hamid II used it for reactionary purposes when he attempted, and largely succeeded in, ironing out differences between Kurd and Turk and Albanian and Turk by uniting them against the "threat to Islam" allegedly posed by Christian communities—the peoples of the Balkans in the west and the Armenians in the east.[37]

An emerging Moslem religious fanaticism, exploited cynically by the government, brought about a deterioration in the relations between Kurds and Armenians, and the Kurds were given free reign to commit atrocities with impunity. Yves Ternon, in *The Armenians: History of a Genocide*, indicates that "Abdul-Hamid achieved his objectives by creating between the Armenians and Kurds, who for centuries had lived on fairly amicable terms, a permanent state of suspicion, antagonism, and hatred which would only grow worse over the years."[38]

The Hamidian Cavalry

In 1891 the Sublime Porte, in a move to avoid implementation of reforms (suggested by European powers) in the treatment of Christians in the Ottoman Empire, created a cavalry composed exclusively of Kurds—the Hamidians. Some were convicts released from Turkish prisons and encouraged to rob and kill upper-class Armenians. The Hamidian Cavalry was proposed by some of the highest officials in the Ottoman Empire to drive Armenians out of borderlands, such as Alashkerd, and to replace them with Moslems. This maneuver would reduce the number of Armenians in various areas so that special reforms suggested by Europe could simply be averted. Moreover, should war break out, a Kurdish cavalry could counterbalance the force of the Cossacks.[39]

Abdul-Hamid created the Hamidian Cavalry, named after himself, by an imperial *irade* (a written decree of a Moslem ruler). He claimed the Hamidians would be used to protect border areas in Asia Minor. Marshal Zekki Pasha was appointed to command the Sixth Army Corps and organize the Hamidians. Forty-eight regiments were created, each with five to six hundred men. Regular army colonels and captains were responsible for command. Other ranks were filled by heads of gangs or tribes and bandits.

The Kurds, however, were not simply protecting border areas. Kurds poured into major cities such as Erzingan, Van, Erzeroum, Bitlis, Moush, Mardin, Diarbekir, and Sivas. They had been armed to the teeth and encouraged by the government to occupy the fertile plains of the Armenians (that Kurds had long coveted). Only the highest-ranking officers of the Hamidians were paid; the rest were supposed to live off of the Armenians. Kurds were not punished for their crimes but were, instead, rewarded. Charles S. Hampton, British Consul at Erzeroum, referred to the existing state of affairs as "organized robbery, legalized murder, [and] rewarded rape."[40] Abdul-Hamid II could only benefit by intensifying hostilities between Kurds and Armenians, who, had they revolted together, would have posed a dire threat to the Empire.

The Massacres of 1894-96

In 1894 the local governor of Sassoun, under the pretext of an Armenian rebellion, ordered the Hamidians to attack. The Armenians succeeded in defending themselves, but Abdul-Hamid II was enraged that Moslems had been killed in the fighting. The sultan sent a *firman* (decree or sanction) to his provincial governors and *not* just in Sassoun investing them "with full powers to repress the rebellion."[41]

The Sassoun outbreak served to whet their appetite for Armenian plunder, and it was soon apparent that no one would suffer negative consequences for doing so. Actually, it became well-known throughout the empire that leaders of massacres would be rewarded rather than punished. Consequently, eyes of longing were cast on Christian houses and women. Property and sex could be appropriated without danger if Armenian men could be destroyed.[42]

After Sassoun, any excuse became sufficient reason to slaughter Armenians, even an argument in a bazaar:

Armed with bludgeons and with hatchets, with yataghans and knives the rabble poured out into the street to murder indiscriminately any Armenian in sight. Churches, hitherto respected by Moslem law, were desecrated and at Urfa, the ancient Edessa, . . . over two thousand people including women and children were burnt alive when an infuriated mob set fire to the cathedral where they had taken refuge.[43]

During this period the government controlled the press, and all papers were forced to publish every item the government desired, with penalties for noncompliance. Moreover, statements of any kind acknowledging the massacres were verboten until the massacres became impossible to deny. By controlling the press, the government issued utterly false statements about the Armenians—so ridiculous that not even the Turks would believe them.[44]

Lepsius states that there were many "Turkish fabrications" against the Armenians. In every single town and district community leaders and priests were imprisoned and forced by the authorities, under threat of death and renewal of massacres, to sign false declarations, lies, reports, and documents, claiming that the Armenians had engaged in "rebellious" uprisings. Failure to comply might mean death for many Armenians. For example, following the massacre at Diarbekir the authorities offered the 400-family Armenian community a small amount of assistance, provided that the bishop sign a telegram blaming the Armenians for the massacres. The bishop refused.

Three weeks after massacres at Erzingan, the local bishop was given a telegram to sign and send to the central authorities and the sultan claiming that the Armenians, by their own acts, had provoked the massacres. After refusing to sign, distinguished Armenian men in the community were arrested and tortured. At Sivas, Christians were subject to all types of atrocities to force them to denounce their fellow Armenians by signing declarations alleging they had provoked the Turks to massacre.[45]

One official in high standing declared that no one should be deceived by "silly government statements" attributing the massacres to Armenians. They had come about because of the sultan's anger at being forced by Europe to sign a scheme of reforms toward Christians. In a show of power, the sultan had 7,000 Armenians killed.[46]

At Seert as well, all types of tortures were used by authorities to force Armenians to sign declarations that they themselves had provoked the massacres. In the district of Agen, authorities required Armenians to sign certificates verifying their voluntary acceptance of Islam. In Urfa, Europeans as well as heads of different religious communities were molested by authorities with demands that they sign declarations charging the massacres were provoked by Armenians.[47]

In October 1895 hundreds of Armenians of Marash were killed, and a telegram begging the protection of the governor was sent by the heads of three Christian communities. Of course, protection was denied. An official declaration was sent out the next day by the Porte that no massacre had taken place and that the Protestant pastor and the bishops who had sent the telegram requesting protection had lied.[48]

During 1895 endless stories were relayed by the government via telegraph regarding Armenian secret societies; Armenian revolutionary committees; murder of Turkish pashas by Armenians; and Armenian agitators in Paris, London, Constantinople, Athens, and even Armenia. The Porte easily suggested that wherever three Armenians put heads together, there was a revolutionary committee. Proof of Armenian conspiracy could easily be verified, the government asserted, by the presence of dozens of Armenian bodies hanging in the streets of Constantinople.[49]

Abdul-Hamid II, fearing that one day there would be a mounting of popular wrath against Turkey by Europeans and Armenians, decided to solve the "Armenian problem." In October of 1895 the "Red Sultan" (Abdul-Hamid II) initiated a systematic extermination of Armenians at Trebizond. An irrelevant incident was used by a band of Kurds as sufficient reason to attack an Armenian village in the mountain region of Sassoun. When Armenians successfully defended themselves, the government sent regular troops to suppress the "revolution." Turkish troops massacred about 300 Armenians and burned down a number of villages. Europe intervened again, demanding reforms in the Armenian vilayets of Kharput, Diarbekir, Van, Bitlis, and Erzeroum. When Abdul-Hamid II was pressured by foreign powers to sign a draft of a reform project, he simultaneously gave orders to commence additional Armenian massacres.[50]

Yves Ternon indicates the massacres, with few exceptions, occurred in areas in which the European Powers had urged reform measures be implemented—Van, Erzeroum, Bitlis, Kharput, Diarbekir, and Sivas. As pressures upon Turkey from England, France, and Russia increased, tensions at Trebizond intensified and finally exploded. The simultaneous nature of attacks on various areas leaves no doubt they were planned. *No Christians would have been spared had the attacks simply been outbreaks of Moslem fanaticism. Yet non-Armenian Christians went unharmed.* Strict orders had been given that only Armenians should be exterminated. Exactly the same pattern was followed everywhere, down to the smallest details.

Yves Ternon gleans the following chronological pattern in the 1894–96 massacres:

1. *Before the massacres.* Reforms required by Europe over Turkey's treatment of Armenians were advertised among the Moslems to create unrest. Then rumors were circulated announcing an imminent Armenian attack. Moslems were armed, and posters were placed on mosques. *Muezzins* (criers at the mosques inviting Moslems to prayer) incited Moslems to murder. Kurds and other Moslems from neighboring towns were armed from the local military depot. Army personnel were alerted and their numbers were frequently augmented. A poster preserved from Arapkir illustrates an inflammatory intent:

All Mohammed's children must preform their duty and kill all the Armenians, plunder and burn their houses. No one should be spared by order of the sultan. All those who do not obey this manifesto will be considered like Armenians and killed. Every Muslim thus will prove his obedience to the government's orders by killing first the Christians with whom he has been a friend.[51]

The Reverend Edwin Bliss, in *Turkey and the Armenian Atrocities,* explains that when inflammatory placards were scattered throughout Asia Minor, the entire Turkish community became agitated. Soon Turks feared a European-supported Christian uprising. The absurdity of an Armenian revolt, Bliss claims, can be attested to by the comparatively few Turks remaining unarmed, while not one Christian in a hundred, scarcely one in a thousand, possessed a weapon. Yet the government's goal of instigating anti-Christian sentiment was attained by instilling fear in Moslems. Such a tense situation existed only in some parts of the country, but the largest segment of the Moslem population, namely, Circassians, Kurds, and Turks, was not fearful.[52]

2. *Massacres.* The massacres generally commenced at a fixed hour—about noon—at the sound of a bugle. They usually began in the bazaar, afterwards spreading into residential areas. Murder by burning to death was commonplace—probably because it is neat and leaves no traces.

3. *Authorities.* Strict orders were given by authorities that only Armenians be killed. Other Christians were not to be harmed. Authorities were almost always indifferent or complicitous. Both Turkish soldiers and officers engaged in plunderings and massacres.

4. *Technique.* After the massacres ended, torture of Armenians continued until "confessions" were obtained. Armenians could choose between abjuration and death. Confessions were used to lend credence to the government's Armenian "conspiracy" theory.[53]

To Turkish accusations of Armenian rebellion, Greene responds,

The very idea of such a thing is ridiculous; for, in the first place, the Armenians are only one-tenth of the Sultan's subjects, and nowhere constitute a majority of the population except in the city of Van, where, strange to say, there has been no outbreak at all. Secondly, they are exclusively a commercial and agricultural people, possessing neither arms, nor a knowledge of their use. Third, they are people of sense, and know that their only hope is through European intervention.[54]

In their book, *Letters from the Scenes of the Recent Massacres in Armenia,* James and Helen Harris, who journeyed through Turkey under the sponsorship of various British humanitarian organizations, recount some incidents that occurred in Malatia during the massacres. They report:

. . . most of the leading [Armenian] Protestants were slaughtered, and the flesh of their chief men carried round the market for sale at 20 paras (about 1 d.) the oke (2½ lbs.)! . . . In one of the churches . . . people were burned. . . . [55]

The estimate of losses sustained by the Armenians during the 1895–96 massacres varies. However, Ternon concludes that a minimum of two hundred thousand people were killed. To this figure, he adds one hundred thousand forced conversions, and a minimum of one hundred thousand kidnapped women and girls put into Turkish harems.[56] This suggests at least four hundred thousand losses.

Some of the areas experiencing massacre between 1894–96 were: Sassoun, Shenik, Gelieguzan, and Talori, Trebizond, Akhisar, Erzingan, Bitlis, Gumush-khana, Baiburt, Urfa, Erzeroum, Diarbekir,

Arabkir, Malatia, Kharput, Sassoun and Talori (a second time), Sivas, Aintab, Amasia, Marsovan, Gurun, Kaisarria (Turkish: Kayseri), Zeitun, Urfa (a second time), and Van. Armenians in these areas as well as surrounding cities and villages were hideously murdered.[57] In an interesting incident, forty-three survivors from Galata, thirty from Van, and thirteen from Erzeroum were picked up by the Wilson Liner *Douro* of Hull. When the Turkish government would not accept the ship's cargo of coal unless the Armenians were handed over, Captain Robert McCrum of the *Douro* made a courageous stand and refused. The Turks later accepted the coal unconditionally. Unfortunately, rescue of Armenians was rare.[58]

In 1896 Prime Minister Gladstone of England, Georges Clemenceau of France, and many other European dignitaries expressed their moral outrage at the handling of the "Armenian Question" in Turkey. Sultan Abdul-Hamid II and his ministers politely replied that Turkey's treatment of Armenians was an "internal problem."[59]

The Adana Massacres, 1909

The next large-scale massacre of Armenians occurred after the Young Turks, who had adopted the slogan "Liberty! Equality! Fraternity!" ascended to power in 1908. Armenian leaders had supported the new "constitutional" government when the Young Turks had assured equal citizenship rights to all inhabitants of the Empire.[60] In April 1909 the Armenians of Adana in Cilicia received a "reward" for loyalty rendered the Young Turks when the whole province of Cilicia was desolated, worldly possessions of Armenians looted, and sixty-three thousand Armenians massacred.[61] Thus within a year after the Young Turks held the reigns of power, the Adana massacres ensued.[62]

A Turkish statesman contends that even before the Young Turks assumed power, they had intended to exterminate Armenians. According to Mehmed Cherif Pasha, one-time Turkish ambassador to Sweden and a former Young Turk who later became an active member of the anti–Young Turk "Liberal Opposition Party," the massacres at Adana were provoked by orders emanating from the Young Turks who attempted to shift the blame for the killings to Sultan Abdul-Hamid II.[63]

The Young Turks were preparing to exterminate the Armenians of the Ottoman Empire once and for all. The new "constitutional" government of 1908 had proven itself to be reactionary by 1909.[64]

The Boycott of 1912

The boycott of Greek and Armenian stores in 1912 lasted for several months, spelling ruin for hundreds of tradesmen. The Young

Turk government created groups to intimidate Moslem peasants who made purchases from Christian businessmen. When they arrived at Christian stores, Turkish peasants were diverted to Turkish stores, where bad quality goods and higher prices soon broke the boycott. Turkish competitors resented Armenian popularity; and that Armenian importers were owed money by Moslem merchants merely fueled this explosive situation.[65]

Lepsius asserts that the massacres and boycott were organized by the government.

The opinion that the massacres of Christians in Turkey are explosions of popular passions . . . is in no way supported by the facts. The massacres in Turkey are organized by the government and by nobody else. But the idea that the ruin of Christian business may help the Turkish commerce, may have been a motive contributing to governmental measures.[66]

American Ambassador Morgenthau claims that the 1912 boycott was an "official boycott" and was directed against all Christians in Constantinople and Asia Minor.[67]

Dismissal from Army and Jobs

After the Young Turks established a "constitutional" government in Turkey, Christians as well as Moslems were mobilized for the army. Armenians from every part of Turkey were called upon for military service, but many paid exemption money to avoid conscription. Yet within a span of several weeks even holders of exemption certificates were enrolled.[68]

In accordance with a governmental decree, Armenian soldiers and gendarmes were disarmed by January 1915. Throughout the Empire Armenian soldiers were deprived of their arms and put into work battalions (*Inchaat Tabouri*) consisting of from fifty to one hundred men. They provided slave labor for Turkish troops, becoming beasts of burden carrying food and equipment during the Turkish retreat from the Caucasus. In various locations squads of disarmed Armenian men ranging in number from fifty to one hundred were chained in groups of four, taken to isolated areas beyond cities, and executed. Only some Armenians were aware of the killing of fellow Armenians near Erzeroum and the Persian border.[69]

The 1915 genocide was government policy and deliberate. This is evidenced by the action taken months before the genocide began. Armenian government officials and employees were dismissed from their posts, Armenian soldiers were taken from combat positions and put into labor battalions, and Armenian officers were put into prison.

American Ambassador Henry Morgenthau said of the Armenians:

> Up to that time most of them had been combatants, but now they were all stripped of their arms and transformed into workmen. Instead of serving their countrymen as artillerymen and cavalrymen, these former soldiers now discovered that they had been transformed into road labourers and pack animals. Army supplies of all kinds were loaded on their backs, and, stumbling under the burdens and driven by the whips and bayonets of the Turks, they were forced to drag their weary bodies into the mountains of the Caucasus. Sometimes they would have to plough their way, burdened in this fashion, almost waist-high through snow. They had to spend practically all their time in the open, sleeping on the bare ground—whenever the ceaseless prodding of their taskmasters gave them an occasional opportunity to sleep. They were given only scraps of food; if they fell sick they were left where they had dropped.[70]

Simultaneously, and for no valid reason whatsoever, Armenian civil servants were fired and their passports granting them freedom of movement within the Empire were cancelled. During the final ten days of February 1915 Armenian government officials and employees were relieved of their posts. By early June of 1915 Armenian officials in the whole of East Anatolia were deprived of their posts and arrested. Armenian physicians working in Turkish civil and military hospitals since the beginning of the war were subject to the same treatment.[71]

Finally, Armenian leaders were arrested and deported. The entire intelligentsia was eliminated—publicists, deputies, poets, notaries, advocates, doctors, jurists, writers, civil servants, bankers, merchants, and anyone of influence and means. Thus Armenians were left without leaders. And without leadership, they were defenseless and easy prey for deportation.[72]

Disarming of Armenians

At approximately the same time the Turks were conducting ruthless searches for arms among the Armenian population. In the years following the revolution of 1908, Armenians had been permitted to bear arms for self-defense against the Kurds, whom the Young Turks were unable to disarm. The same arms that Armenians had recently been granted the privilege to carry were now presented as evidence of Armenian plots for insurrection and treason.[73]

The massacres and atrocities that had become a regular part of Armenian life between 1895 and 1909 would soon burgeon into general and full-scale extermination.[74]

AS ABDUL HAMID . . . surveyed his shattered domain, he saw that its most dangerous spot was Armenia. He believed . . . that these Armenians, like the Rumanians, the Bulgarians, the Greeks, and the Serbians, aspired to restore their independent medieval nation, and he knew that Europe and America sympathized with this ambition. . . . How could the Sultan free himself permanently from this danger? . . . There was only one way of ridding Turkey of the Armenian problem—and that was to rid her of the Armenians.

. . . And now the Young Turks, who had adopted so many of Abdul Hamid's ideas, also made his Armenian policy their own.

—AMERICAN AMBASSADOR HENRY MORGENTHAU

2

INTERNAL STRIFE

ARMENIANS had been subjected to discrimination and treated as outsiders on their own ancestral lands since the Ottomans instituted the *millet* system in 1453. But their condition worsened as the empire began to crumble and one country after another gained its independence from Turkey. Both (1) a crumbling empire pressured by Europe for "reforms" toward her Christian minorities and (2) Armenian desires for autonomy created havoc for the Turkish government. The "Armenian Question" became an increasingly urgent matter. As the empire's territorial losses mounted, Turkey's government, rightly or wrongly, perceived that Armenia might soon be lost. In the minds of Ottoman rulers, Armenian Anatolia was the very heartland of Turkey.

At the same time as Turkey's control over her territories was diminishing, Armenian political parties created a "normative upheaval" within Turkish society by challenging the legitimacy of the traditional *millet* system. This state of affairs promoted strife (or strain) within the system and contributed to the value-added process leading to genocide.

21

REAL OR THREATENED DEPRIVATION:
DEFEAT IN WAR AND LOSS OF EMPIRE

The capitulations, one of the earliest Turkish reform measures improving the condition of some non-Moslems in the Ottoman Empire, were treaty rights regulating the position of foreigners in Turkey. Since Ottoman law was so radically different from European or American law, no non-Moslem government wished its citizens residing in Turkey to be subject to such law.[1] Thus the sultans had granted specific rights to Europeans and subject peoples of the empire, permitting non-Ottoman subjects in Turkey extraterritorial privileges during their travels or residence in Ottoman domains.

However, Viscount Bryce contends that the capitulations clearly reflected a contempt for non-Moslems, even though they granted foreigners in Turkey their own post offices, courts, and prisons. The sultan perceived Christians as unclean and used the capitulations to reduce Christian contact with the Ottoman judicial system and administration.[2] The practice of capitulations traces back to Roman law and came into existence in the Ottoman context in 1535 when a wide range of privileges was granted to Francois I of France by Suleiman I.

The capitulations had the following negative consequences: (1) when European powers gained a paralysing hold on the empire's political workings, the Turks began to develop a bitter and vengeful xenophobia, and (2) Armenians in Ottoman Turkey were insidiously endangered by the capitulations because they were given no assurance of security under Ottoman law. Consequently, Armenians who were astute and/or well-to-do sought protection from foreign powers to secure a somewhat safer and unmolested life. But as Armenians increasingly looked to foreign powers for resolution of their grievances, they became objects of suspicion by the Ottoman government, which suspected them of serving as foreign agents. Faith in European powers led Armenians to hold an extremely erroneous and dangerous belief: should the condition of Armenians in Turkey become unbearable, European governments would intervene on their behalf.[3] The inaccuracy of their optimism would became clear in the catastrophe beginning in 1915.

While Armenians placed their faith in foreign powers, the Ottoman Empire was beginning to crumble and dwindle in size. Actually, Turkey's influence and might had been waning for several centuries. The Turks had attempted to conquer Hungary for a century and a half but were thrust back from the gates of Vienna in 1683. They never penetrated so far into Europe again. Arnold J. Toynbee points out that the Allies had been laboring for a hundred years to liberate Turkey's subject peoples—beginning with national liberation struggles of the Serbs and Greeks.[4]

As foreign powers exerted pressure upon Turkey to adopt western, liberal institutions, the position of Armenians and other subject peoples in the Ottoman Empire deteriorated. In addition, successive Russian defeats ended with Turkey's loss of a portion of her sovereignty in the Treaty of Kutchuk Kainardji (July 1774).

Both European and Russian pressures contributed toward a westernizing movement begun by Selim III and Mahmud II. It was Mahmud II who in 1826 initiated an early and significant reform by effectively breaking the power of the janissaries, who had eventually attained the status of a type of praetorian guard that commanded, as much as it served, the government. The rule of Mahmud II was marked by administrative reforms and receptiveness to European influences; his breaking of the power of the janissaries, formed in 1430 and considered to constitute "the flower of the Ottoman troops," exemplifies this reformist bent.[5]

Simultaneously, the decline of the Ottoman Empire was accelerated in 1821 by the revolt of the Greeks against Turkey. In 1827 Britain, France, and Russia called for an armistice. The Turks refused, after which the Allies, with Russia attacking on land, completely destroyed the Turkish and Egyptian fleets at the Battle of Navarino. The Porte finally yielded, and Greece was declared an independent state in accordance with the London Protocol of February 1830.

In the Treaty of Turkmen Tchai (1828) the territories north of the Araxes River, which included Etchmiadzin, were ceded by Persia to Russia. This treaty was politically significant, since it severed Persia's political involvement in the Caucasus, forcing Armenia to rely increasingly upon Russia as Turkish abuses increased. Later, the Russians would fight to attain Armenia as their frontier in the Caucasus.[6]

With the signing of the Treaty of Adrianople (14 September 1829) ending the Russo-Turkish War of 1828-29, Turkey promised better treatment of Orthodox Christians in the empire and granted Russia the right to intervene on their behalf. According to the treaty, however, those territories occupied by Russia during the war, with few exceptions, were returned to Turkey. As Russia withdrew from Armenian lands, more than 90,000 Armenians migrated westward.[7]

The period of Turkish reform (*Tanzimat*) began in the 1830s in response to Europe's condemnation of previous Ottoman massacres of Greeks and European and Russian demands for better treatment of Christians. Sultan Abdul-Medjid in 1839 sought to avoid European intervention in Turkey by proclaiming the *Hatti-Sherif*.[8] This proclamation promised to protect the property, life, and honor of all Ottoman subjects, regardless of religion or race.[9] Christians were (theoretically at least) given absolute equality before the law. Tax farming (discussed in Chap. 1) was to be abolished.[10] Had this decree been adhered to, no further European intervention into Turkish affairs would have been necessary. But, as Burtt states, "unfortunately it [the decree] met with the usual fate of Turkish reforms and was not put into practice."[11]

In 1844 Sultan Abdul-Medjid pledged that no former Christian who turned Moslem and later became an apostate to the Moslem faith should be put to death. The ambassador of Great Britain, supported by other powers, extorted this pledge from the sultan after the public execution of a young Armenian in Constantinople who, after declaring himself a Moslem, reclaimed his Christian faith and was tortured and put to death. Despite this pledge, Moslems who embraced Christianity continued to be quietly eliminated.[12]

Frederick Greene, in *Armenian Crisis in Turkey*, points out that anyone who abandoned the Moslem faith would immediately forfeit all his special privileges and, in addition, incur punishment as a "criminal." Apostasy from Islam was viewed as a treasonous act by the sultan. Converts from Islam were arrested and imprisoned on grounds of "avoiding conscription" or any other convenient fictitious charge; they were assigned to distant military posts or unspecified dungeons.[13]

In 1850 Sultan Abdul-Medjid was forced by European powers to grant Protestants the same rights other Christian communities of the empire "enjoyed." The sultan consequently granted them a charter, assuring them the rights of a distinct civil community and liberty of conscience. But Greene points out, as of 1896 Protestants in Istanbul had never been permitted to erect a single church in spite of having sufficient funds, owning sufficient property, and having petitioned fifteen years for a *firman* to do so. Moreover, Ordoo's Greek Protestants who had a church were not even permitted to worship in it.[14]

Attempts to introduce reforms were hindered by a ploy developed by the Turkish government after the Crimean War (1853–55). Originally, the war between Russia and Turkey started over acquisition of land in the Caucasus. Britain and France, as usual, feared Russian expansion in Turkey, so they eventually entered the war and fought alongside Turkey.[15] The Turkish government, after defeating Russia with European aid, was alerted to a way to play Russia and European powers off against one another to her benefit. Burtt comments that in the Crimean War,

. . . England had checked the ambition of Russia, while the Turk laughed in his sleeve at the thought that he could play off the Western Powers one against another. There can be no doubt that the Sublime Porte rightly discerned the weakness of its opponents, for "a united Europe in which the Great Powers trusted each other and might be counted upon to act with pure disinterestedness, could always have brought the Turks to reason." To the persecuted Christians the war proved a miserable failure, and has long been regarded as a political blunder, aptly described by the late Lord Salisbury when he said, "We backed the wrong horse."[16]

The Treaty of Paris (March 1856), ending the Crimean War, admitted Turkey to the European Congress with France, Britain, and Austria supporting her integrity, promising not to interfere in Turkey's internal affairs. The treaty marked the growth of European responsibility for a just government in Turkey; this reduced the possibility of Russia's separate intervention into Turkish affairs. Thus Russia lost the right to protect Christians in Turkey, and the Danubian Principalities were placed under "the guarantee of the Great Powers." Although the Treaty of Paris provided no immediate relief for the sufferings of Armenians, it clearly indicated that European powers doubted Turkey's fitness to govern.[17]

This mistrust of Turkey can be seen in the European powers' awareness of discrimination against Christians in Turkey and their insistence that Article 9 of the treaty read:

His imperial majesty the sultan having, in his constant solicitude for the welfare of his subjects, issued a *firman*, which while ameliorating their condition without distinction of religion or of race, records his generous intentions toward the Christian population of his empire, and wishing to give further proof of his sentiments in that respect, has resolved to communicate to the contracting powers the said *firman*, emanating spontaneously from his sovereign will.[18]

European powers felt certain that Turkey would be a menace to peace in Europe if reforms were not initiated. Thus the Treaty of Paris forced Sultan Abdul-Medjid to grant the celebrated *Hatti-Houmayloun* ("Illustrious Rescript"), which reflected his "generous intentions" toward his Christian subjects. This *firman* granted equality to Christians, ensuring security of person, honor, goods, equality of taxation, and many other reforms. All subjects of the Porte were promised equal rights by the edict, which obstructed no one from professing his religion.[19]

Since the reforms assured in the *Hatti-Houmayloun*, just as those in the *Hatti Sherif*, were not implemented, the powers remonstrated with Turkey in 1859. In 1860 Russia requested an international inquiry regarding the position of the *rayahs* in Bosnia, Herzegovina, and Bulgaria. In 1867 a combined French, Austrian, Russian, and English inquiry concluded that "Christian equality did not exist in the eyes of Islam," since Christian testimony was invalid in a court of law; Christians could be cast into prison without official, written orders, and judges remained as venal as ever. In short, Christians were still unable to obtain justice.[20]

Meanwhile, Ottoman supremacy was again being challenged. For some time Egypt had been only nominally Turkish. Egypt, a Turkish vassal state, had almost outstripped Turkey in power but had been kept from taking over the empire by the intervention of Russia in 1833 and Great Britain in 1840. Led by France in 1860, the West was brought into action by a war between Maronites and Druses and a semiautonomous sanjak emerged in Lebanon under the protection of Europe.[21]

During the summer of 1875 Herzegovina responded to Turkish misrule and oppression with an insurrection against the Turkish government. Montenegro, Serbia, Bosnia, and Bulgaria were overtly sympathetic toward their Christian brethren who were at war. In October 1875 the sultan declared that high taxes, which were one reason for the revolt in Herzegovina, would be lowered from their exorbitant rates, taxes in arrears would be forgotten, and Christians would be represented on state councils. Meanwhile, Turks were massacring Christians from Dalmatia, increasing tensions even further. Bulgaria and Montenegro secretly began providing aid to Herzegovine rebels, and the Prince of Serbia publicly declared that Serbia could not remain indifferent to the fate of the Herzegovines. Meanwhile, Germany, Austria, and Russia made a concerted effort to secure peace.

As war raged, Bulgaria became involved. Early in May of 1876 the Turks, in an attempt to quell the Bulgarian movement, carried out a wholesale extermination of Bulgarian Christians. People of both sexes were killed, women were outraged, property was stolen or destroyed, and villages were burned.[22]

The Bulgarian massacres meant a brutal death for twenty thousand men and women villagers.[23] Reacting to these massacres, Bulgaria declared war upon Turkey in July 1876. Great Britain then intervened to propose that Bosnia and Bulgaria be permitted local self-government without becoming independent of the Porte. Prince Milan of Serbia refused this proposal and the war continued. Just as Turkish armies prepared to invade Serbia, Russian interposition checked the Turks.

Mean   ile, on 30 May 1876 during the Bulgarian massacres, Sultan Abdul-Aziz was confined to a palace in Constantinople, where he committed suicide on 4 June. The son of Abdul-Medjid, Murad (Amurath) V was proclaimed sultan in Abdul-Aziz's place. However, Murad V's rule was short, since he proved so imbecilic that he was deposed on 31 August 1876 and was succeeded by his brother, Abdul-Hamid II.[24]

Deterioration of the Ottoman Empire characterized Abdul-Hamid's reign. Abdul-Hamid, the "Red Sultan," ascended the throne at an admittedly critical period in the history of the Ottoman Empire. Turkey lost not only Bulgaria in the first two years of his reign, but also experienced the severance of important provinces in the Caucasus. Remaining vestiges of sovereignty in Serbia, Rumania, and Montenegro, and effective control of Herzegovina and Bosnia were lost. Greece had already attained independence and Egypt was beginning to free herself from Ottoman misrule.

The sultan, taking stock of his inheritance and seeing the empire crumbling before his eyes, blamed Europe for its disintegration. It was Europe that had attempted to bring relief to imprisoned nations, since only Serbians had proven capable of attaining their own independence. Great Britain, France, and Russia, Abdul-Hamid believed, were ready to set free other subjugated countries.[25]

In 1877 Russia and Turkey were again at war. The 1877–78 Russo-Turkish War was more of a bid for freedom by subject peoples of Turkey than a consequence of rivalries between the European powers. The Bulgarian atrocities of 1876 served as a catalyst for the war. The atrocities, combined with the Pan-Slavist ideology then pervading Russia, provided the impetus that led Russia into the war, even though neither the foreign minister nor the tsar were Pan-Slavists. Russia, after a discussion with the European Powers, declared:[26]

We made it pre-eminently our object to attain the amelioration of the condition of the Christians in the east by means of peaceful negotiations and concerted action with the great European powers, our allies and friends. During two years we have made incessant efforts to induce the Porte to adopt such reforms as would protect the Christians of Bosnia, Herzegovina and Bulgaria from the arbitrary rule of the local authorities. The execution of these reforms followed, as a direct obligation, from the anterior engagements solemnly contracted by the Porte in the sight of all Europe. Our efforts, although supported by the joint diplomatic representations of the other governments, have not attained the desired end. The Porte has remained immovable in its categorical refusal of every effectual guarantee for the security of its Christian subjects. . . . Having exhausted our peaceful efforts, . . . Turkey, by its refusal, places us under the necessity of having recourse to arms. . . . [27]

These words, uttered by Tsar Alexander II, the "tsar-liberator," on 24 April 1877 constituted a declaration of war on the Ottoman Empire. Slavic peoples now looked to Russia for protection from Turkey.

When Plevna (Bulgaria) fell on 11 December 1877, Russian troops advanced toward the Ottoman capital. They were halted at Adrianople (Edirne) only by the armistice of 31 January 1878, which established the "preliminary bases of peace" whereby Rumania, Montenegro, and

Serbia were to become independent; Bulgaria was to become autonomous; Herzegovina and Bosnia were permitted autonomous adminis-
trations. Armenia, having made no request for autonomy or independence before the war, was not even mentioned. One major reason why
Armenia had not opted for independence was her fear of Russian annexation and subsequent absorption into the Russian Orthodox faith.
In fact, the Armenian patriarch, Nerses Varzhabedian, through the is-
suance of a pastoral letter, requested that Armenians remain loyal to
the Ottoman state.

Yet after the Russo-Turkish War the Armenian leadership changed
their position to one favoring Armenian autonomy, since the Kurdish
irregular cavalry in the pay of Turkish regular forces had been engaging in the extermination of Armenians during the war. On 26 July
1877 an article by C. B. Norman, special correspondent of the *Times*,
related what he had witnessed between Sabatan and Koprukoy, near
Kars, an excerpt of which follows:

I have not seen one Christian [Armenian] village which has not been abandoned
in consequence of the cruelties committed on the inhabitants. All have been
ransacked, many burnt, upwards of 5,000 Christians in the Van district have
fled to Russian territory, and women and children are wandering about naked.[28]

When Armenians became convinced of these atrocities, the Armenian National Assembly sent a legation to Grand Duke Nicholas at his
Adrianople headquarters, whereupon Count Ignatyev, Russian ambassador to Constantinople, drew up the following clause to be included in
the upcoming peace treaty at San Stefano (the modern Yeshilkoy):

For the purpose of preventing oppressions and atrocities that have taken
place in Turkey's European and Asiatic provinces, the sultan guarantees, in
agreement with the tsar, to grant administrative local self-government to the
provinces inhabited by Armenians.[29]

Russian victory in the Russo-Turkish War resulted in a preliminary
treaty between the belligerents at San Stefano.[30] Ultimately, Turkey
and Russia signed a final peace treaty at San Stefano on 3 March 1878.
After some discussion the wording of Article 16, of particular rele-
vance to the Armenians, was agreed upon. It reads:

As the evacuation by the Russian troops of the territory which they occupy
in Armenia [note: Armenia in this treaty is still called "Armenia," not Turkey],
and which is to be restored to Turkey, might give rise to conflicts and complica-
tions detrimental to the maintenance of good relations between the two countries, the Sublime Porte engages to carry into effect, without further delay, the
improvements and reforms demanded by local requirements in the provinces

inhabited by Armenians, and to guarantee their security from Kurds and Circassians.[31]

The Treaty of San Stefano reduced the empire by stripping Turkey of a good deal of its Balkan territories. However, European powers feared Russian acquisition of land and began negotiations to curtail Russian expansion. Lord Salisbury of Britain demanded that a European congress address the issue even though the conditions set forth in the Treaty of San Stefano had proven to be less beneficial to Russia than England had anticipated. Lord Beaconsfield also rejected the treaty as a final settlement of the war, whereupon Russia consented to submit the San Stefano Treaty to a congress at Berlin. Britain, ironically, covertly began to support Turkey. British revulsion at Turkey's Bulgarian atrocities had subsided and was replaced by a strong anti-Russian feeling.[32] Thus European leaders showed little concern for the Armenians—even though they had remained conciliatory in the face of misgovernment.

All signatories to the San Stefano Treaty had agreed that they would negotiate no deals with Turkey between the San Stefano and Berlin conferences. Yet Britain, in a breach of promise, met secretly with Turkey on 4 June on the Island of Cyprus, only five days after Russia and Britain had settled their differences over the status of Turkey's Asiatic frontier. Britain proceeded to sign a secret agreement with the Ottomans in which she promised to defend Turkey's Asiatic frontier should there be a Russian attack. Britain, in return, was given lease of the island of Cyprus. Disclosure of this covert, forbidden agreement almost prevented the Berlin meeting.

The clandestine Cyprus Convention proved catastrophic for the Armenians because of the inclusion of the two following paragraphs:

If Batum, Ardahan, Kars or any of them shall be retained by Russia, and if any attempt shall be made at any future time by Russia to take possession of any further territories of his imperial majesty the sultan in Asia, as fixed by the definitive treaty of peace, England engages to join his imperial majesty the sultan in defending them by force of arms.

In return, his imperial majesty the sultan promises to England to introduce necessary reforms, *to be agreed upon later* [emphasis added] between the two powers, into the government, and for the protection of the Christian and other subjects of the Porte in these territories.[33]

In Article 16 of the Treaty of San Stefano, Russia had agreed to provide an army of occupation for protection of Armenians, *but neither the Cyprus convention nor the later Treaty of Berlin provided safeguards for Armenians.* In fact, while the British and Turks were negotiating at Cyprus, the Turks were capitalizing upon the opportunity provided by the withdrawal of Russian troops from Turkish Armenia to resume their pillaging.[34]

As European powers intervened to keep Russia out of Turkey, the Turks became angered at what they took to be Armenian partiality for Russians. They destroyed villages and brutally killed Armenians, especially in the vicinity of Bayazed and the Alashkerd plains. Understandably Armenians began to yearn for self-government.

As atrocities mounted and became more severe between the Crimean and Russo-Turkish Wars, Armenians, in hopes of gaining self-rule via a European protectorate, dispatched representatives to the Berlin Conference in 1878. Nothing was gained at Berlin. Consequently, some Armenians resolved to fight for justice. Henceforth, Armenian "revolutionary" societies began to appear.[35]

In addition to gaining nothing at Berlin, the Treaty of Berlin actually cancelled some of the benefits granted Armenians in the Treaty of San Stefano. Turkey's new role vis-a-vis the Armenians was clarified as follows in Article 61 of the Treaty of Berlin of 8 July 1878:

> The Sublime Porte undertakes to carry out, without further delay, the improvements and reforms demanded by local requirements in the provinces inhabited by Armenians, and to guarantee their security against the Circassians and Kurds.
>
> It will periodically make known the steps taken to this effect to the powers, who will superintend their application.[36]

Rivalries between European powers and Russia over which country could maintain a presence in Turkey were reaching their zenith, and the consequences of Britain's alteration of the Treaty of San Stefano would have devastating effects upon the Armenians in the future. Only Russian troops could have provided the Armenians in the provinces safety against Turkish lawlessness. However, Russia's access to such a privilege was an "object of obsessive imperial jealousy" to the British.

Walker comments on the consequences of Article 61 of the Treaty of Berlin in the following analysis:

> This article, together with the Cyprus Convention, brought the Armenians no security at all. The government of Turkish Armenia, if anything, deteriorated after their signature. In turn, Armenian self-defence groups and revolutionary societies grew up, provoking heavy retaliation. The most common British attitude was of studied ineffectualness; and Russia, partly for internal reasons and partly for the threats from Britain contained in the Cyprus Convention, refused to go to the aid of Turkish Armenians.[37]

The Treaty of Berlin freed Rumania, Montenegro, and Serbia;

made Bulgaria a principality under Turkey; and ceded Batum, Kars, and Ardahan to Russia. The European powers were granted the right to supervise Turkish reforms; in other words, they could intervene in Turkey to improve the condition of oppressed peoples of the empire. The treaty also guaranteed religious liberty and freedom to peoples of Rumania, Bulgaria, Montenegro, Eastern Roumelia, Serbia, and all Ottoman subjects throughout the empire to publicly practice one's faith. Furthermore, Armenians could use their language in courts and offices and were free to erect as many schools as they wished.[38]

Abdul-Hamid, while no doubt relieved that the treaty spared his empire Russian domination, was at the same time fearful and resentful of Europe, since Turkey was dependent upon foreign powers to help fight Russia. Furthermore, he detested having to pay for Europe's protection against Russia by initiating reforms for Christians. His real wish was to gain freedom from outside intervention and reconquer lost portions of his empire. To achieve these goals, he waged a battle against internal reformers from within and Christian peoples (whom he had never trusted) from without the empire.[39]

As the sultan surveyed the shattered remains of his domain, he considered Armenia to be a vulnerable spot. Rightly or wrongly, he believed the Armenians, like the Bulgarians, Greeks, Rumanians, and Serbians, aspired to the restoration of their medieval independent nation, and he knew that Europe and America supported Armenian independence. How could he rid himself of the Armenian threat? American Ambassador Henry Morgenthau comments that an enlightened administration could simply have resolved the problem by granting subject peoples civil rights such as security of property, life, and religious practice, thus transforming Armenians and others into free, loyal, and peaceful subjects.[40] Instead, the Turkish government incited minorities into mutual massacres.

The first large-scale massacres of 1895–96 occurred when armed Kurds, the Hamidians, were deployed against the unarmed Armenians. Greene, after the 1895–96 massacres asks, "Why . . . have they [Armenians] been massacred?" To his own question he replies:

Because Europe did intervene and compel the Sultan to accept a Scheme of Reforms which would give the Christians equality with Mohammedans before the law, and a proportionate share in the judicial, civil and police administration in the six eastern provinces.[41]

Though the sultan appeared to accept various types of reform schemes, he believed that to implement them would (1) endanger his authority and (2) threaten the supremacy of the Turks, the traditional ruling class. To him, the infidel had no right to live in a Moslem state, except in a state of subjugation. Abdul-Hamid wished to make the reforms inoperative.[42]

Turkey was humiliated by repeated military defeats suffered since the late seventeenth century, including rebellions of Moslem chieftains in Syria, Egypt, Barsa, and Baghdad, followed by the revolts of the Balkan peoples.[43]

In the 1912–13 Balkans Wars the Ottomans were expelled from the Balkan provinces they controlled, except Thrace and Constantinople. Turkey denounced all treaties and suspended all reforms at the outbreak of World War I. All attempts to provide Armenians even a modicum of security failed to materialize.[44]

The Young Turks who had assumed the reigns of power after Abdul-Hamid II were also unable to halt the decay of the empire. Austria soon annexed Bosnia and Herzegovina, while Bulgaria became completely independent, Italy conquered Tripoli, and Turkish rule was smashed in Albania. In all, *the empire's territorial losses would eventually mount to about 424,000 square miles.* Consequently Turkey would cling tenaciously to Armenian Anatolia.[45]

In spite of protests from European ambassadors in Turkey, capitulations were abrogated by a notice issued by the Turkish cabinet on 1 October 1914. Such an act was one aspect of the Young Turks' goal to rid the empire of foreign tutelage. They now focused upon creating a "Turkey for the Turks." This objective became the central point of Turkish policy in her relations vis-a-vis both foreign powers and her subject peoples.[46]

NORMATIVE UPHEAVAL

Armenian intellectuals in the nineteenth century and later other segments of Armenian society experienced a national awakening. This was partially spurred on by a European-induced cultural revival during the eighteenth century. Europeans had become somewhat familiar with Armenian culture through Catholic Mekhitarist fathers at Saint Lazarus Island in Venice and Mekhitarist priests in Vienna. The Orientalist School in France was translating major works of Armenian literature and history, and German linguists were arduously reclassifying Armenian into the Indo-European family of languages.

At the end of the eighteenth century Armenian schools were opened in the Ottoman Empire. Then, in the latter half of the nineteenth century, secondary schools sprang up in Constantinople, Scutari, Erzeroum, Van, and Ismit. The intellectual elite of the Turkish-Armenians were trained at these schools. French and American

Catholic and Protestant colleges were set up in Constantinople, Aintab, Marsovan, Tarsus, and Kharput. In spite of the policy of Russification adopted after 1884 in eastern Armenia, secondary and higher educational institutions were opened in Etchmiadzin, Moscow, and Tiflis in Russia. Armenians were educated in Russian universities in St. Petersburg and Moscow and at Dorpat in Estonia. In Western countries they attended universities in Italy, Switzerland, France, Germany, and the United States.

Armenian literature flourished during the latter half of the nineteenth century, dominated by the works of Abovian and Raffi. Both were romantic in nature, and their patriotic writings addressed the struggles and sufferings of the Armenian people. Simultaneously, an Armenian press was established, and at least fourteen Armenian papers came into existence (in Constantinople) between 1820 and 1866. In addition, monthly reviews surfaced in Moush and Van, and Armenian newspapers emerged in Georgia and Transcaucasia. The journals of Mekhitarist priests were published in Venice and Vienna.

In this fertile soil Armenian political consciousness and action were nourished. Armenian families of Anatolia sent their sons to study in Constantinople, and Constantinople families sent their children to London or Paris. The *amiras*, a wealthy class of Armenian traders in Constantinople, sent their children to be educated in Paris, where for the first time Armenian youth breathed free air. Having experienced this sensation, Armenian students became fully aware of the backward conditions and glaring injustices prevailing in Turkey. Disenchanted with the status quo, they drafted the Armenian National Constitution, which was proclaimed in 1863 after laborious negotiations with the Porte. This constitution expanded the rights of Armenians in the empire and made the Armenian patriarch their representative to the Porte.[47]

The constitution represented a success for the Armenian *Illuminati*—liberal Armenians who championed ideas of democracy and freedom. The traditional system had been one in which the affairs of the Armenian community were governed by the oligarchic rule of conservatives—*Non-Illuminati*. The constitution made provision for a general assembly that was vested with legislative powers for the Armenian community. Such power pertained to cultural and religious affairs, such as building new churches and opening schools. Constitutional powers did not encompass political rights and obligations; these remained under the jurisdiction of the Ottoman government. Abdul-Hamid realized that the constitution served to appease the desires of European diplomats for fair treatment of Armenians. Thus he soon moved to suspend the constitution and the parliament it had advocated. Afterward, the trials and tribulations of Armenians continued to escalate. With this action in 1876, the period of *Tanzimat* (1839-1876) was brought to a close.[48]

It is doubtful the Armenian National Constitution could have benefited the Armenians as a whole or saved them from future disasters, since there was no Turkish counterpart to the Armenian Constitution. Such a counterpart was impossible; the empire was an autocracy that lurched from reformist to reactionary periods at the whims of any new ruler. The effectiveness of the Armenian Constitution was dependent upon the continuation of *Tanzimat*, the Ottoman era of reform.[49]

As Ottoman oppression increased, some Armenians began to reject Turkey's theocratic system. Simultaneously, Armenian intellectuals were bombarded by nationalist ideas from three different sources: (1) fellow Armenians in Russian Transcaucasia, where radical, Populist ideas had been prevalent in recent decades, (2) American Protestant missionary schools located in Anatolia and Turkish Armenia, and (3) Armenians living in Constantinople who had attended European educational institutions.

Armenians had begun some rudimentary attempts at political organization, such as local groups and secret societies, in the early 1870s. In 1872 the Armenians of Van province organized for self-protection. They founded *Miuthiun I Perkuthiun*, the "Union of Salvation," which was the first organized revolutionary society of Turkish Armenians. On 3 March 1872 when forty-six persons from the city of Van pledged themselves to the society's platform in hopes of winning freedom for their people, they declared: " . . . gone is our honor; our churches have been violated; they have kidnapped our brides and our youth; they take away our rights and try to exterminate our nation . . . let us find a way of salvation . . . if not, we will soon lose everything." Other Armenian organizations, such as *Sev Khatch Kazmakerputhiun* ("Black Cross Society," 1878) and *Pashtpan Haireniats* ("Protectors of the Fatherland," 1881) later emerged.[50]

In 1882-83 members of "Protectors of the Fatherland" were caught by Ottoman police in Erzeroum. Seventy-six were tried and forty were found guilty. This constituted a political confrontation.[51]

Henceforth, Armenian political parties would provide Turkey with justification for the Armenian massacres. At the Berlin Congress in 1878, the Armenian delegation had requested no more than reform measures from the Porte. An Armenian movement espousing liberty and national consciousness was not even heard of in Europe until 1885.[52]

The Union of Salvation paved the way for the *Armenakan*, the first real Armenian political party, founded in 1885 in Van. One of the major concerns of the *Armenakans* was to protect their compatriots from Kurdish incursions against Armenians. To do this, they acquired arms and munitions from Persia and even from Turkish officials (by bribery). Some Armenian activities were interpreted by the Turkish government as representing a large revolutionary apparatus and were highly publicized in Turkish newspapers in Constantinople. Actually, some Armenians did engage in defensive actions against the Turks.[53]

As Gerard Chaliand and Yves Ternon comment,

... in spite of the divergence and hesitations that it had aroused, an Armenian national movement had been born, the result of suppression, and with no other goal than to make it possible for a people to survive. This movement did not seek to create a national state . . . but . . . could easily [be accused] . . . of trying to do so.[54]

British reports state that the general Armenian population possessed a "minimum capacity for causing any serious trouble to the Turkish Government." Yet the government's exaggerated notion of the strength and numbers of the "revolutionaries" created distorted Turkish perceptions of even such innocuous Armenian activities as those of a cultural, charitable, or religious nature. Individual Turks were rewarded with promotion and personal honors for presenting such inaccurate interpretations of Armenian activities. By and large, the Armenian revolutionary groups represented a small minority of young, romantic idealists who operated without cooperation from staid, more conservative-minded Armenian community leaders.[55]

In August of 1887 in Geneva, Switzerland, the *Hunchak* Revolutionary Party, theoretically Marxist, was formed by Armenians who had never lived under the Turkish flag. Its goal was to further revolutionary activity in Turkish Armenia. Whereas the *Armenakans* considered revolution to be a future phenomenon, the *Hunchaks* wanted political and national independence for Turkish Armenia. The party selected the name *Hunchak*, the Armenian word for bell, because *Hentchak* was reminiscent of Alexander Herzen's journal, *Kolokol* ("Bell"), which espoused Russian social revolutionary ideology. The *Hunchaks* proved to be the only nineteenth-century Armenian political party that unambiguously advocated an independent and unified Armenian Republic.[56]

Most Armenian parties did not opt for an independent state. Fa'iz El-Ghussein, a Bedouin eyewitness to the 1915 genocide, contends that Armenians wanted better treatment from the government—not an independent state. He explains:

I have enquired of many Armenians whom I have met, but I have not found one who said that he desired political independence, the reason being that in most of the Vilayets which they inhabit the Armenians are less numerous than the Kurds, and if they became independent the advantage to the Kurds would be greater than to themselves. . . . The Armenians, therefore, prefer to remain under Turkish rule, on condition that the administration is carried on under the supervision of the Great European Powers, as they place no confidence in the promises of the Turks, who take back to-day what they bestowed yesterday.[57]

The *Hunchaks* first political affray was the Kum Kapu Demonstration of 14 July 1894, intended to attract European attention to the plight of the Armenians in Turkey. The demonstration began at the Armenian Cathedral in the Armenian Quarter of Kum Kapu in Constantinople. Here, during Sunday mass, Harutuin Tjankulian read the *Hunchak* demand for Armenian reforms. Next, he smashed the Turkish coat of arms at the Armenian patriarchate, following which a procession of Armenians converged upon Yildiz Palace, the sultan's residence, to stage their protest and present their demands for just treatment. Their demands were ignored; instead, a number of *Hunchak* leaders and demonstrators were placed under arrest and killed. This was the first time that Armenians had dared such a protest since the Turkish conquest of Constantinople.[58]

Four months later, on 30 November 1894, the American Minister to Turkey, Alexander W. Terrell, sent word to Grover Cleveland about the massacres in the Sassoun district. The Americans suggested the presence of an American on the commission investigating the massacres. The request was denied by the Sublime Porte. Rather than comply with the Americans, *Turkey alleged that American missionaries were inspiring Armenian revolutionaries;* Turkey's bad image in the United States, the Porte contended, was created by American missionary supporters. Thomas Bryson, in *American Diplomatic Relations with the Middle East,* reports that by early 1896 the Ottoman Government issued a decree requiring all revolutionaries and American missionaries to leave the country—the missionaries because they were disbursing supplies to destitute Armenians.[59]

Meanwhile, between 18 and 30 September 1895 the *Hunchaks* staged the Demonstration of Bab Ali in Constantinople. The *Hunchaks* presented their list of demands, the so-called Protest Demand to the sultan. European ambassadors to Turkey had been invited in advance by the *Hunchaks* to witness the demonstration, again in hopes of eliciting European sympathy to the plight of Armenians in Turkey.

The *Hunchak* demand was simply that previous reform schemes agreed to by the Porte be upheld in Turkey. On 18 September 1895 the demonstration began. Government soldiers were posted near administrative buildings, and the police were placed on alert. Just before noon on Monday, *Hunchak* leaders entered the Armenian patriarchate, from whence thousands of demonstrators were to walk to the sultan's palace. Garo, leader of the demonstration, was to present the sultan a petition on behalf of the Armenians of the six provinces and Constantinople.

As Garo Sahakian and other demonstrators approached the Gates of Bab Ali, they were denied admittance by a Turkish officer, and *zaptiehs* (Turkish police) seized Garo. Fighting and violence ensued, and Garo was imprisoned. The next several days witnessed the arrest of hundreds of demonstrators, and prisons were soon loaded with wounded Armenian men, and the streets of Constantinople were littered with scores of dead Armenians.

Nalbandian lists the *Hunchaks* petition of grievances against the Porte (the "protest demand"):

(1) the systematic massacre of the Armenians by the Turkish government, (2) the unjust arrest and the cruel punishments of prisoners, (3) the Kurdish injustices, (4) the corruption of tax collectors, (5) the massacre at Sassun [1894]. It [the Hunchak Party] demanded: (1) equality before the law; freedom of the press; freedom of speech; and freedom of assembly; (2) that all persons under arrest be given the right of *habeas corpus*, and that the Armenians be granted permission to bear arms if the Kurds could not be disarmed; (3) a new political delineation of the six provinces; (4) a European governor for the six Armenian provinces; and (5) financial and land reforms.[60]

In the petition the *Hunchaks* expressed their belief in egalitarianism; they demanded rights not only for themselves but for other Ottoman subjects as well.

Following the bloodshed at Bab Ali, Europeans and Americans were distressed by violence toward Armenians. Consequently, England, Russia, and France, supported by Italy, Austria, and Germany, demanded the introduction of the Armenian Reform Program of 11 May 1895. Sultan Abdul-Hamid affixed his signature to the said program on 17 October 1895, but as usual no changes were forthcoming. By 1896 numerous bids for reform had failed, and *Hunchak* activity was on the decline. As Nalbandian points out,

The Hunchaks relied in vain on the European Powers to use coercive measures against the Sultan for the purpose of making him put into effect the Armenian Reform Program which he had signed in October, 1895. The activities of the Hunchaks had only helped to enrage Sultan Abdul Hamid II, who already hated the Armenians and feared that they, like the Balkan countries, would obtain their freedom.[61]

In their demands, the *Hunchaks* did not even mention that Armenians who had become American citizens after living in the United

States were treated as Ottoman subjects if they returned to Turkey. Bryson explains:

The United States had long been guided by the basic principle that people have the right to emigrate from their native lands and take up new citizenship by process of naturalization. . . . Under the imperial edict of 19 January 1869, the Sublime Porte refused to accord these peoples [the Armenians] their new legal status, claiming they were still Ottoman subjects. . . . in subsequent years the status of naturalized Americans caused considerable friction. The matter was *partially* [emphasis added] settled after the turn of the century, but in the decade of the 1890s it continued to cause bad feeling.[42]

The futility of *Hunchak* attempts to elicit foreign assistance can be gauged by a consideration of American responses to Armenian cries for help. American citizens favored intervention in Turkey to help the Armenians, but President Cleveland held that the European powers involved in the Berlin Treaty should deal with the Armenian Question, and America should maintain her policy of nonintervention. Yet many pro-Armenian groups, supported by Congregationalist, Presbyterian, and Episcopalian clergymen in America, as well as by business leaders from Chicago, Boston, and New York, favored Armenian-relief efforts. In addition, Senator Call of Florida submitted a Senate resolution urging the use of force to help establish an Armenian state and protect American interests in Turkey.[43] Obviously, these actions were to no avail.

The next Armenian political group to emerge was the Federation of Armenian Revolutionaries, frequently called *Dashnaktsuthiun* ("Federation"). This group was formed through unification of various Armenian groups. The Federation was founded in Tiflis, Georgia (in Russian Transcaucasia) in summer 1890. Before combining forces with the Federation, the *Hunchaks* required that their own socialist ideology, even though repugnant to many non-*Hunchaks*, be incorporated into the Federation's platform. The issue was, at least temporarily, resolved at a conference in Tiflis.[44] However, the union of the parties was short-lived, since the *Hunchaks* withdrew from the Federation decrying antisocialist leadership and inertia by the Federation. The split was finalized after the Central Committee of the *Hunchakian* Revolutionary Party published official notices (18 May 1891) declaring that they had no connection with *Dashnaksuthiun*. At its First General Congress in the summer of 1892 the Federation of Armenian Revolutionaries adopted a new name, *Hai Heghapokhakan Dashnaktsuthiun* ("Armenian Revolutionary Federation") or "*Dashnaks*" and dropped the name *Hai Heghapokhakanneri Dashnaktsuthiun* ("Federation of Armenian Revolutionaries").[45] To this day, the *Dashnak* Party is the most popular Armenian democratic political organization in the world.[46]

The *Dashnak* program incorporated socialistic principles and predicted the ultimate victory of the proletariat over the bourgeoisie. Consideration was also given to the problems of other peoples, namely, Turks, Kurds, Arabs, and Yezidis who wished to improve the Turkish government. The party's program advocated economic and political freedom in Turkish Armenia through rebellion and the following demands:

1. The future democratic government of free Armenia, serving the interests of the general public, shall of course be established by the vote of all adults, based on the principle of a free and nondiscriminated electorate. In order to truly protect these rights, the principle of free election must be extended more and more from the central government to the peasant of the remotest province.

2. The strictest provisions for the security of life and labor.

3. Equality of all nationalities and creeds before the law.

4. Freedom of speech, press, and assembly.

5. Give land to those who have none and guarantee the tiller the opportunity to benefit from the land.

6. The amount of all taxes should be decided according to the ability to pay and according to communal principles, which for centuries have been deeply rooted in our people.

7. Eliminate all forced and unpaid labor such as the *gor* and *begar, angaria, olam, etc.* [These terms describe various forms of forced labor and tribute to the government and powerful land owners.]

8. Eliminate the military exemption tax and establish conscription according to the locality and needs of the time.

9. Assist in every manner the intellectual progress of the people. Make education compulsory.

10. Assist the industrial progress of the people by giving them modern methods of production. . . .

11. Assist in strengthening the communal principles of the peasants and artisans, by advancing those communal establishments and methods which have appeared on the soil of Armenia as a result of local and historic influences. Broaden the area of such communal establishments, from the quarter to the village, to the province, and then to the whole country; in that way, at the same time, safeguard each member of society from the disasters of nature and the mishaps of everyday life.[47]

The *Dashnaks* desired a "nonterritorial cultural autonomy" that would guarantee every citizen national cultural rights, regardless of where he lived.[48] The 1892 program epitomizes a belief in democracy and the inalienable rights of the individual to life and property. They proposed " . . . equality of all races and creeds before the law, security of life, honor and property, freedom of speech and assembly, freedom of religion, universal suffrage, compulsory education for all, [and] free enterprise and fair distribution of land among the peasantry."[69]

Note that the *Dashnak* program of 1892 made no mention of the word "independence," much less of an independent Armenian state. The *Hunchaks*, on the other hand, had clearly stated that they wanted an independent Armenian state, encompassing Armenian lands in Turkey, Russia, and Persia. The earlier *Armenakan* program had supported Armenian self-rule but not a politically independent Armenian state. Yet all three parties felt that revolutionary methods were necessary to relieve the plight of Armenians in the Ottoman Empire.

In addition, the *Hunchaks* and *Dashnaks* clearly distinguished between "peaceful Moslem Turks" and the "corrupt Ottoman government" toward whom their revolutionary activities were directed. Turkish organizations advocating reforms in the country were actively supported by these Armenian parties. A prime example of Armenian attempts to reform the system, rather than acquire an independent Armenian state, are evidenced by the agreement in 1907 between the *Dashnaks* and the Committee of Union and Progress, the Young Turks. The *Dashnaks* hailed the Young Turks' Constitution of 1908. They also made attempts to improve the lot of the Kurds.[70]

Thus Djemal Pasha's statement in his *Memories of a Turkish Statesman* appears inaccurate indeed. He alleges:

> As the Armenians were bent on founding an independent State in which they could impose their will on the Kurds and Turks, who greatly outnumbered them, the latter [the Turks and Kurds] naturally tried to frustrate this plan.[71]

Frequently, in his *Memories of a Turkish Statesman,* Djemal speaks of Armenian desires for independence. Yet only the *Hunchaks* (certainly not a very popular Armenian party) proposed the independence of Turkish-Armenia. Djemal claims that Armenians were a pawn Russia played to acquire Turkish lands. Thus, he asserts, Turks and Kurds naturally regarded Armenians as a snake let loose against them by Russia "for snatching a very large part of Anatolia, which was inhabited exclusively by Turks and Kurds."[72] This latter notion, indicating that Armenians would help Russia acquire Armenian lands, certainly contradicts his previous statement of an Armenian desire for independent statehood.

Within a year after the Bab Ali incident, the *Dashnaks* staged another demonstration in Constantinople. On 24 August 1896 they took over the Imperial Ottoman Bank, simultaneously engaging in other acts of agitation in different sectors of the capital. Since Armenians were well aware that European nations had national interests in the bank, they staged the incident to attract European attention to the plight of Armenians in Turkey.

During the actual siege of the bank, Babken Suni, a seventeen-year-old youth, led twenty-six revolutionaries to take over the bank and its occupants and block the entrances. Foreign ambassadors were alerted that the bank and everyone inside, including the Armenians, would be blown up if demands were not granted within forty-eight hours. The ambassadors immediately supported the cause of the revolutionaries. However, by the time they conceded to the demands, four *Dashnaks* (including Suni) were dead, five were wounded, and the rest were in danger of being starved out.

In the days that followed the Imperial Ottoman Bank incident, the Turks retaliated by butchering six thousand innocent Armenian men, women, and children on the streets of Constantinople under the eyes of European ambassadors. The Europeans lodged protests but to no avail.[73]

The revolutionaries themselves were saved by M. Maximoff, First Dragoman of the Russian Embassy, who negotiated quite skillfully to have the building vacated. The revolutionaries were ushered away to a yacht belonging to the director of the bank. They complained that the Europeans had failed the Armenians who were incapable of single-handedly obtaining justice from the Turks. The *Dashnaks* demanded autonomy (self-rule) for Armenians within the empire.[74]

The *Supplement of the Graphic* of London describes the scene:

Amid the crowd in the streets . . . were seen groups of Mussulmans and Kurds, all armed with bludgeons, iron staves, or clubs, and acting under the directions of men in turbans, who were evidently Softas ["clerics"]. These gangs chiefly sought out Armenians, but often they struck down passers-by indiscriminately. . . . In all quarters of the city Armenians were brutally murdered.

Prime Minister Gladstone of England referred to Abdul-Hamid II, the sultan at that time, as "the assassin who sits on the throne of Constantinople."[75]

Some Turcophiles have argued that Armenian nationalism and revolutionary activity were the reasons for the Ottoman government massacres of Armenians. The Ottoman bank seizure is generally provided by them as supporting evidence. Many well informed Europeans, however, detect flaws in such ruses justifying the massacres. Ambassador Paul Cambon related in a report (1894) to French Premier and Foreign Minister Casimir Perier that in 1878, a strong Armenian nationalism did not even exist, "or, if it existed, it did so only in the minds of a few educated men, who had taken refuge in Europe." Armenian nationalism emerged at a later date as a response to tax-gouging, massacres, and Hamidian pillage and persecution.[76]

Facts did not really matter, however, since Abdul-Hamid II did not wish to have any non-Moslems in Turkey. Later, the Young Turks would desire that there be no non-Turks in Turkey.

I'LL TELL you something, my friend. . . . There are two sorts of men . . . the human animals [and] . . . the human angels. . . . Among the human animals also belong the world's great men—the kings, the politicians, the ministers, the generals, the pashas. . . .

—KRIKOR OF YOGHONOLUK

3

POWERFUL LEADERSHIP WITH TERRITORIAL AMBITIONS FORMING A MONOLITHIC AND EXCLUSIONARY PARTY

IN 1908, the *Ittihad ve Terraki Djemieti* (Committee for Union and Progress), frequently referred to as the Young Turks, ascended to power in Turkey in a bloodless revolution that deposed Sultan Abdul-Hamid II. When the Young Turks found they could not halt the decline of the Ottoman Empire, they began to espouse a Pan-Turanist philosophy advocating the expansion of the empire in an easterly direction to unite with other "Turkic" peoples.

Talaat, Enver, and Djemal Pashas formed the undisputed ruling triumvirate of the Young Turks. After a coup d'etat in 1913, they eliminated all opposition to their party and philosophy. Thus the *Ittihad ve Terraki Djemieti* became the political monolith of the empire. The powerful Young Turk party, which supported a philosophy of Pan-Turanism (a geographic and "racial" unity of Turkic peoples), exhibited a ferocious racism. "Turkey for the Turks" became their obsessive goal. Pan-Turkist desires for territorial expansion and the exclusionary nature of the party provided another determinant of the value-added process leading to the Armenian genocide.

POWERFUL LEADERSHIP WITH TERRITORIAL AMBITIONS

In 1908 the Young Turks overthrew Sultan Abdul-Hamid II in a bloodless revolution and began their ascent to a position of absolute power. By 1910 Young Turk politics was dominated by a triumvirate—Enver, Djemal, and Talaat. Enver was a member of the party's Central Committee (*Merkez-i-Umumi*) from 1908–10; Talaat from 1908–10 and 1911–16; and Djemal had become a member before 1908.[1] These three men were to provide the leadership of the Armenian genocide.

Before becoming minister of the interior in Turkey, Talaat (1874–1921) had been assistant director of postal offices in Salonika. He was said to be the brains behind the Committee for Union and Progress and was the main channel through which secret decisions of the party's Central Committee were translated into policy.[2]

Talaat's political orientation can be summed up in the following statement he made to Halide Edib, a prominent Pan-Turkic ideologist and poetess:

I have the conviction that as long as a nation does the best for its interest, and succeeds, the world admires it and thinks it moral.[3]

Talaat's hostility toward minorities in the Ottoman Empire can be gleaned from the following statement Talaat made to American Ambassador Henry Morgenthau just before World War I:

. . . these different *blocs* in the Turkish Empire, he [Talaat] said, had always conspired against Turkey; because of the hostility of these native populations, Turkey had lost province after province—Greece, Serbia, Rumania, Bulgaria, Bosnia, Herzegovina, Egypt, and Tripoli. In this way the Turkish Empire had dwindled almost to the vanishing point. If what was left of Turkey was to survive, added Talaat, he must get rid of these alien peoples. "Turkey for the Turks" was . . . Talaat's controlling idea.[4]

Ambassador Morgenthau discussed the Armenian Question at length with Talaat and concluded:

. . . Talaat was the most implacable enemy of this persecuted race. . . . He told me that the Union and Progress Committee had carefully considered the matter in all its details and that the policy which was being pursued was that which they officially adopted. He said that I must not get the idea that the deportations [of Armenians to the deserts of Arabia] had been decided upon hastily; in reality, they were the result of prolonged and careful deliberation.[5]

Halide Edib examined Talaat's extermination of the Armenians, explaining:

There are two reasons why people exterminate each other 1) the idealist principle and 2) the material interest principle. Tal'at (the Minister of the Interior of
the Ottoman Empire, and the chief organizer of the Armenian genocide) decided
the extermination of the Armenians on the idealistic principle.[6]

In a communication from Minister of the Interior Talaat to Delegate
Djemal Bey of Adana, issued on 15 March 1915, Talaat accepted full
responsibility on behalf of the *Ittihad ve Terraki Djemieti's* (hereafter
referred to as the *Ittihad*) Central Committee for the decision to annihilate the Armenians. He affirmed:

> It is the duty of all of us to realize . . . our intention to wipe out of existence
> the known elements who have obstructed the political progress of our State for
> centuries. . . . We must accept the full responsibility, and . . . we must strive to
> carry to success all the activities that have been undertaken.
>
> As was stated in our letter of February 28, 1915 the Jemiyet has decided
> to . . . annihilate various opposing forces that have obstructed our way for
> years, and for that purpose it is obliged, unfortunately, to resort to bloody
> means. . . .
>
> Until the successful completion of the activities undertaken for the Arme-
> nians, it would not be right to bother ourselves about the *others* (Greeks, Arabs,
> Syrians).[7]

Enver (1881–1922), the second member of the ruling triumvirate,
was a hero of the revolution of 1908. His photograph sold by the hundreds on the streets of Turkey. Enver had completed military college at
twenty-five and was catapulted to power at age twenty-six after his
successful revolt against Sultan Abdul-Hamid II. In 1914, at age thirty-
one, he was a brigadier general and also minister of war in Said Halim's cabinet. At the start of World War I he became vice generalis-
simo.[8]

Enver was an avid Pan-Turkist. Even before the war, his ideological orientation made him a patron of the *izji*, the Turanian youth movement modeled on the British Boy Scouts. The banner of the movement
showed a grey wolf (*boz kurt*) on a red background; the banner symbolized the legend of the grey wolf leading the Turks out of Central
Asia.[9] According to Turkish mythology, the Turks had been confined to
a valley for four centuries, whereupon a blacksmith melted iron rocks,
thus opening up a gate, after which the Turks were delivered "under
the leadership of a Grey Wolf." The grey wolf symbol of the *izji* implied
that the Turk's destiny was buried in his racial origins, rather than in
the multiracial nature of the Ottoman Empire. However, the *izji* banner was a deliberate affront to Islam, since the narrow racial intolerance it espoused excluded acceptance of other Moslems and also
presented a sinister threat to those defined as outside of the Turkic

racial category.[10] Enver's Pan-Turanism (or Pan-Turkism) would be evident throughout his entire career.

After being escalated to the position of minister of war, Enver thought that war with Russia would expedite his dream of a Pan-Turkic empire and retrieve territories ceded to Russia after Turkey's loss of the Russo-Turkish War.[11] To realize his expansionist ambitions, he ordered the creation of the *Teshkilat-i-Makhsusiye* (a paramilitary "Special Organization") on 5 May 1914; its primary purpose was to prepare territories beyond the borders of the Ottoman Empire, such as Iran and the Caucasus, for a Turkish conquest. Dr. Nazim of the Committee of Union and Progress headed the organization, while Behaeddin Shakir was responsible for carrying out decisions. The organization, though probably not originally established to exterminate Armenians, would later be used for that purpose.[12]

When Enver was in control of the Ottoman Third Army, Russia experienced military setbacks in Europe. Enver wished to capitalize upon Russian military defeats and advanced his army to Sarikamish, a Russian military post. He hoped to gain control of the fortress of Kars and forge eastward to Baku. Enver had previously told German Gen. Limon von Sanders of his great ambition to advance his army through Afghanistan to India. Enver's military offensive against Sarikamish was launched on 25 December 1914 but within two weeks 80 percent (75,000 men) of the Ottoman Third Army were dead. His "Pan-Turanian army" was shattered when his troops were overcome by winter; only Enver and a few others survived the elements. After the Sarikamish disaster, Enver never took personal command again. This Turkish defeat may have been the decisive factor precipitating the ensuing Armenian catastrophe, since Enver used the Armenians "as scapegoats for his folly."[13]

Morgenthau states that in a communication dated 15 April 1915 to mayors and governors, Enver Pasha, like Talaat, accepted responsibility for the Armenian genocide and admitted "deporting" Armenians to the deserts Arabia. On one occasion, when Ambassador Morgenthau told Enver that the situation with the Armenians had gone further than Talaat and Enver had probably anticipated and therefore their "underlings" must be responsible for the destruction of the Armenians, Enver, "greatly offended . . . that things could happen in Turkey for which he and his associates were not responsible," responded:

You are greatly mistaken. . . . We have this country absolutely under our control. I have no desire to shift the blame on to our underlings and I am entirely willing to accept the responsibility myself for everything that has taken place. The Cabinet itself has ordered the deportations. I am convinced that we are completely justified in doing this owing to the hostile attitude of the Armenians toward the Ottoman Government, but we are the real rulers of Turkey, and no underling would dare proceed in a matter of this kind without our orders.

We shall not permit them [Armenians] to cluster in places where they can plot mischief and help our enemies [the Allies]. So we are going to give them new quarters.[14]

The "new quarters" referred to by Enver were barren deserts where the Armenians would die. A German Catholic ecclesiastic said that Enver had declared in the presence of the papal envoy at Constantinople, Monsignor Dolci, that "he would not rest so long as a single Armenian remained alive."[15]

Djemal Bey, the third member of the ruling clique, had the reputation of having started his career as a "pasha's darling page boy." Ahmet Djemal (1872-1922) had completed military academy in 1895 and was later attached to the Third Army stationed at Salonika. In 1903 he was military governor at Constantinople and in 1906 he became a member of the Committee for Union and Progress. In 1909 he was made Vali of Adana and was appointed Vali in Baghdad in 1911. Djemal served as minister of the marine in 1914. During World War I he was dispatched to Syria as commander of the Fourth Ottoman Army.[16]

American Ambassador Morgenthau's conclusion about Djemal is revealed in the following statement:

. . . Djemal was a man with whom assassination and judicial murder were all part of the day's work. Like all the Young Turks his origin had been extremely humble. He had joined the Committee of Union and Progress in the early days, and his personal power, as well as his relentlessness, had rapidly made him one of the leaders. After the murder of Nazim [discussed later in this chapter], Djemal had become Military governor of Constantinople, his chief duty in this post being to remove from the scene the opponents of the ruling powers. This congenial task he performed with great skill, and the reign of terror that resulted was largely Djemal's handiwork. Subsequently Djemal became a member of the Cabinet, but he could not work harmoniously with his associates. . . .

Feroz Ahmad corroborates Morgenthau's view when stating that Djemal "was efficient and ruthless, and the Committee used him in situations requiring these qualities. . . . "[17]

As minister of marine, Djemal represented the rapidly ascending policy of the Turkish government—Pan-Turkism. He detested all subject Ottoman peoples, such as Greeks, Circassians, Arabs, Jews, and Armenians, and he was determined to Turkify the whole empire. Djemal considered that the land of the conquered countries making up the Ottoman Empire belonged to Turkey. He claims in his *Memories of a Turkish Statesman* that it is the Turks who are "the incontestable owner of Asia Minor," and the Armenians (who, by the way, were living on their *own* ancestral homeland) should "not throw covetous glances at what is its [Turkey's] property by undeniable rights."[18]

Djemal further claims that "until after the Crimean War of 1856 the Turks and Armenians lived together on the best of terms and the former were never guilty of any wrongs against their Armenian neighbors." Then Djemal points out that the janissaries were abolished at the beginning of the nineteenth century. Obviously, he did not consider the janissaries, made up of boys taken from Christian families, as a cruel or abusive institution. Nor does he consider institutionalized discrimination and the lack of legal status for Christians (inherent in the *millet* system) as unjust.[19]

Djemal claims in his *Memories of a Turkish Statesman* that he had nothing to do with the "deportations and massacres" of Armenians and that he knew nothing of such occurrences until they actually began, since he was in Syria commanding the Ottoman Fourth Army. He charges:

Public opinion will recognize that I had nothing to do with the deportations and Armenian massacres. . . . I am equally innocent of ordering any massacres; I have even prevented them and caused all possible help to be given to all emigrants at the time of the deportations.[20]

However, El-Ghussein, a Bedouin Moslem eyewitness to the genocide, contradicts Djemal's assertions of innocence when he reports:

The authorities of Urfa applied for a force from Aleppo, and *by order of Jemal Pasha—the executioner of Syria*—Fakhry Pasha came with cannon [emphasis added]. He turned the Armenian quarters into a waste place, killing the men and the children, and great numbers of the women, except such as yielded themselves to share the fate of their sisters—expulsion on foot to Deir-el-Zur [in the Syrian desert]. . . . [21]

Talaat, Enver, and Djemal were all aware of the decline of the Ottoman Empire. Turkey had once been master of millions in the Balkans and a threat to all southeastern Europe. In the years just before World War I, the empire had been undergoing an accelerated process of decline, and Turkey was reduced to a small part of its former size and experienced a gradual attrition of its hegemony. The loss of the 1912–13 Balkan Wars left Turks "shocked" by their many European defeats.[22]

Talaat and Enver's elevation to power, seemingly so full of promise to Turkey, had not reversed the loss of territories. Turkey was an "unnerved" nation from top to bottom. While Turkey was losing previously conquered lands, Germany's Ambassador to Turkey, Baron von Wangenheim, repeatedly bombarded the Turkish leadership with plans for regaining lost empire. Eventually, the Turks would believe him.[23]

Before proceeding further, it is essential to understand the concept of "Turan" and the imperialistic role it would play in Turkish ideology. Ternon points out:

> The word Turanian is a linguistic term; it is neither ethnic nor geographic. The ethnic and geographic interpretations it has accumulated have an irrational metaphysical meaning. Turan is the land of the Turanians, a land of desert mountains and vast steppes, dotted with lakes and great rivers. Beyond Anatolia, it extends south of the Caspian across the provinces of northern Iran and north of the Caspian as far as Afghanistan, Uzbekistan, Kazakhstan, Kirghizistan, and Sinkiang to the mountains of the Altai, cradle of the Turanian race. It was in Central Asia that the tribes had joined together during the great empires of Attila, Genghis Khan, and Tamerlane. Osmanli Turks, Azers, Tatars, Turcomans, Uzbeks, Kazaks, Kirghizes, Yakutes, Altais, and even Mongols all belong to the same race. All are conscious of being Turanian and have a single desire: to reunite in order to resume the ancestral fight for Tura against Arya, some fifty million Turanians against Aryan Europe.[24]

Turks had not really given much attention to their "racial" identity until European Turkologists, such as Max Muller, Radloff, Vambery, de Guignes, von Le Coq, and Russian and European Turkologists had conducted anthropological, historical, and linguistic research, making Turanian intellectuals aware of their racial and cultural ties to a "glorious history." The Turks learned that most "Turkic" peoples were living under foreign systems, namely, Chinese, Russian, Afghani, and Iranian, which were attempting to assimilate them.[25] These peoples lived in countries east of Ottoman Turkey.

Having been run out of Europe, the Turks turned east to Central Asia, the root of their racial origins to the then fifty-five million Turkic people who lived there. By their eastward movement the Turks would return via the path through which they had come into Europe, heading back to Anatolia and also Central Asia.[26]

That Pan-Turanists viewed Armenians as an obstacle to the expansion of their empire is evident in the charge made by Pan-Turkist writer Tekin Alp, who said:

> The Greek is pushing us back from the seaboard; the Armenian has cut off our line of retreat and is separating us from the Turanian steppes.

In fact, a *New York Times* article, dated 13 January 1915, revealed that Talaat had told the councillor of the Greek patriarchate that Turkey, henceforth, would only have room for the Turks.[27]

Turkey's Pan-Turanist dream of eastern conquests is a major reason for the Armenian genocide. Historian Richard Hovannisian explains:

... eradication of the Christian Armenian element from Anatolia and the eastern provinces would remove the major racial barrier between Turkic peoples of the Ottoman Empire, Transcaucasia, and Transcaspia. Enver's dream of a Pan-Turanic empire would be a step closer to realization.[28]

The Turks continually refused to acknowledge that Armenia was not their land, just as Bulgaria, Macedonia, Egypt, and other occupied countries had not been theirs. By clever maneuvers they attempted to make it theirs. One such maneuver involved renaming Armenia and calling it "Anatolia." Political expedience had prompted Turkey to use the designation "Anatoli" or "Eastern Anatolia" after the Russo-Turkish War of 1878. Prior to the war, Anatolia was officially referred to as "the Armenian Territory." That Armenians were in the majority in Anatolia was obfuscated by the Turkish government's redistricting ("revilayeting") of the eastern Vilayets of Ottoman Turkey after 1878. Frederick Greene stated in 1896 that " 'Armenia' is a name forbidden in Turkey."[29]

The tenacity with which Turkey would cling to Armenian Anatolia is revealed in a statement made by Djemal Pasha after Turkey's loss of World War I. Djemal remarked,

... Turkey is beginning afresh the struggle to prevent the loss of the sacred ground of Anatolia, which alone remains to the Turks.[30]

But Turkey's imperialism involved more than just Armenia. Arnold Toynbee asserts in *Turkey: A Past and a Future* that "the Turks have ... an irredenta to win." This contention is verified in the following statement by Tekin Alp, a Pan-Turkish ideologist:

Irredentism, which other nations may regard as a luxury—though often a very terrible and costly one—is a political necessity for the Turks. ... If all the Turks in the world were welded into one huge community, a strong nation would be formed, worthy to take an important place among the other nations.[31]

The Turkish attempt on Sarikamish had been irredentist. During Turkey's brief occupation of Northern Persia, Turkish forces began their extermination of the Syrian and Nestorian Christian peoples of

Urmia, viewing them as a barrier between the Turks of Anatolia and those of Baku and Azerbaijan. A few months later, irredentist policy would provide Turkey a reason for the Armenian deportations.[32]

Tekin Alp, in imperialist fashion, asserts that the Pan-Turanist dream could only be realized by crushing Russia, "because the very districts which are the object of Turkish Irredentism—Siberia, the Caucasus, the Crimea, Afghanistan, etc.—are still directly or indirectly under Russian rule." The "et cetera," Toynbee states, refers to "nothing less than the province of Kazan." This would include the alluvial plains of the Kama and the Volga in European Russia.[33]

The Turkish government's policy of territorial expansion is manifested by its handling of *muhajirs* ("refugees"). At the Young Turks 1911 Congress they resolved to promote immigration from the Caucasus and Turkistan to Turkey, find land for the immigrants, and hinder Christians from acquiring real estate. Christians were to be killed and Moslem families would be moved into their residences, assuring Turkey's expropriation of Christian land.[34]

Government resettlement of Circassians Kurds, and Turks on Armenian lands became a common practice. When the Ottomans lost the Balkan Wars, thousands of Turks were expelled from Macedonia and Thrace; and they were consumed with a hatred of Christians because of their expulsion. These *muhajirs* returned to Turkey and were settled in Anatolia, and approximately 750,000 of them were Turks from the western part of Thrace. All were settled into homes that had belonged to Armenians.[35]

After April 1913 the plunderings of Kurdish chiefs intensified as did their atrocities toward the Armenians, since the government encouraged them to seize Armenian lands. As Armenians fled to cities to avoid Kurdish abuses, the Turkish government continually settled *muhajirs* on abandoned Armenian land. This "vast robbery" was in force in "numbers" of villages.[36]

Resettlement of refugees is too complex a process to be accomplished without planning. The frequency of its occurrence in 1915 highlights the calculated planning indicated by the government's policy. For example, when Armenians were deported from the town of Zeitoun in 1915, Turkish *muhajirs* from Macedonia were present and took immediate occupancy of Armenian homes.[37]

At this juncture the Young Turks declared war and repudiated the capitulations, and the Ottoman Empire entered World War I on 30 October 1914. On the following day the Committee for Union and Progress issued a proclamation enunciating its expansionist war aims:

Our participation in the world war represents the vindication of our national ideal. The ideal of our nation and people leads us towards the destruction of our

Muscovite enemy, in order to obtain thereby a natural frontier to our empire, which should include and unite all branches of our race.[38]

Even the loss of the war did not stop the imperialistic Pan-Turanist dream. After World War I General Mehmed Vehib Pasha, representing Turkey in negotiations with the newly independent Republic of Armenia at the Batum Peace Conference in 1918, issued a statement elucidating the tenacity of Turkish expansionist sentiments regarding Armenia.

You see that destiny draws Turkey from the West to the East. We left the Balkans, we are also leaving Africa, but *we must extend toward the East.* Our blood, our religion, our language is there. And this has an irresistible magnetism. Our brothers are in Baku, Daghestan, Turkestan, and Azerbaijan. We must have a road toward those areas. *And you Armenians are standing in our way.* By demanding Van, you block our road to Persia. By demanding Nakhichevan and Zangezur, you obstruct our descent into the Kur Valley and our access to Baku. Kars and Akhalkalak seal our routes to Kazakh and Gandzak [Ganja]. *You must draw aside and give us room.* Our basic dispute rests on these grounds. We need two broad avenues which will allow us to advance our armies and to defend ourselves. One of these routes is Kars-Akhalkalak-Borchalu-Kazakh, leading to Gandzak; the other passes over Sharur-Nakhichevan-Zangezur to the Kur Valley [emphasis added].[39]

As Zarevand points out, "*in the eyes of the Turkish Nationalists, the guilt of the Armenians consisted in just being there, in their own ancient homeland.*"[40]

FORMATION OF A MONOLITHIC AND EXCLUSIONARY PARTY

During the latter part of the nineteenth century, Turks who desired radical social changes in the empire were strongly influenced by social and political movements sweeping across Europe. These provided the impetus for the first Turkish revolutionary groups that were small, lacked cohesion, and had no influence. Some Turkish secret societies were formed but for the most part were aimless, having in common nothing except a hatred of Europe.[41]

The Young Turkish movement arose when Ottoman might was weakened under Abdul-Hamid. The founders of the Young Turks believed that radical reconstruction of the Ottoman Empire would permit Turkey's independence from foreign intervention. Those imbued with these ideas were exiled by Abdul-Hamid II to Paris, where the ideological founders of the new movement congregated. In France the Young Turks became absorbed in the doctrines of the French Revolution—

constitutional government through a representative parliament, religious toleration, equality of all to serve in the military, abolition of caste privileges, and legal equality of all citizens.[42]

The Young Turks, at least in their early stages, were antiimperialistic.[43] However, by the early twentieth century, Enver and Talaat were enthusiastically supported by young army officers who despised European military superiority and dreamed of a new wave of Ottoman victories over the infidels.

In 1906 the Young Turks transferred their headquarters from Paris to Salonika where the Ottoman army was fighting a guerilla war against Greeks, Rumanians, and Bulgarians who were struggling to rid themselves of Ottoman domination.[44] The leadership of the army in Salonika felt encouraged to challenge the sultanate after the successful 1905 Russian Revolution. The Russian example provided the incentive that spurred nationalist Turkish officers to leap from critical theorizing to armed revolution.

At Salonika, where army officers had greater freedom than in Constantinople, a society for Ottoman freedom was formed in September 1906. The society merged with Ahmet Riza's organization (a splinter group of Ottomanist Young Turks) in September 1907.[45] The Committee of Union and Progress, *Ittihad ve Terraki Djemieti*, was the product of this union. Its Central Committee (*Merkez-i-Umumi*) was in Salonika, and local organizations of the committee quickly sprang up in principal cities of the province. However, to the young army officers at Salonika, ideologies were not the key concern. As Ternon indicates,

The only thing that mattered to them was the preservation of the Ottoman empire, which they and their forefathers had served for so many generations. Their actions as well as their discussions revolved around one central question: how could they save the state? The order of the day was quite simple: liberty and fatherland; constitution and fatherland. They had scarcely envisioned a plan for realizing their ideas when the power to do so fell into their hands.[46]

The Revolution of 1908

On 2 July 1908 Commander Niyazi Bey, an Albanian member of the Committee of Union and Progress, accompanied by a small group of partisans, took to the mountains of Macedonia. In late May Lieutenant Enver Pasha, accompanied by 150 men, joined Niyazi Bey, and the revolution began. Soon, 800 Turkish soldiers were sent by Abdul-Hamid to Monastir (now Bitola) to put down the insurgents; but rather than firing on their comrades, the soldiers killed their commander, Shevki Pasha. Then, shouting "Liberty, Equality, and Fraternity," they joined the revolutionaries. Even Abdul's bodyguard supported the revolutionaries. Commander Osman Pasha, who was dispatched to replace Shevki Pasha, was also murdered. Clearly, the Turkish army was uniting in Macedonia in support of the rebels. Next, Albanians from the countryside joined forces with the revolutionaries. Between 19 and 22 July telegrams constantly flowed from army chiefs in Macedonia to Yildiz Palace, where Abdul-Hamid had isolated himself. The telegrams demanded that the Constitution of 1876 be reinstated.[47]

On the night of 22-23 July the *Merkez-i-Umumi* located in Salonika seized the telegraph offices and invited delegates of Macedonian Young Turk local committees and village mayors to meet in Salonika the next morning. By 10:00 A.M. religious and civil authorities were present. Greeks, Bulgarians, and Turks embraced as different nationalities and religions experienced a sense of reconciliation.

The sultan was warned by the revolutionaries that if he did not accept an ultimatum of liberal demands being sent to him within twenty-four hours, the second and third battalions in Macedonia would march on Constantinople. The sultan charged the Grand Vizier Hilmi Pasha to imprison all rebels, but the vizier and Abdul-Hamid's other advisors convinced him that Enver's rebels represented a ground-swell movement. Twenty-four hours later, on 24 July, Abdul-Hamid succumbed to the threats of the Young Turks.

Niyazi and Enver came down from their mountain retreat with their troops, and the Hamidian regime was finished. On 17 December 1908, Sultan Abdul-Hamid formally abdicated. The result was a pseudoparliament with the Young Turks controlling all of the mandates.[48]

The Young Turks were surprised by their own victory. Having been nurtured in a Western European political environment, they were impregnated with ideas of both nationalism and democracy. They believed in "Ottomanism" for subject peoples and were spurred to revolutionary activity by their fervor and patriotism. Yet, as Ternon states, "they had no economic or political training, no experience, and no real ideology to help them, only a few stray western ideas and an unshakable faith, though in embryonic form, in the Turkish nation." Morgenthau presents the following speech delivered by Talaat in Liberty Square, Salonica, in July 1908:

To-day arbitrary government has disappeared. We are all brothers. There are no longer in Turkey Bulgarians, Greeks, Servians, Rumanians, Mussulmans, Jews. Under the same blue sky we are all proud to be Ottomans.[49]

Upon assuming the reigns of power in 1908, the *Ittihad ve Terraki Djemieti* was very unstructured, and its political stance was unclear. It was made up of young officers, lower-level functionaries, intellectuals (doctors, lawyers, teachers, and journalists)—mostly people of the middle class. A crucial question facing the party was: should they institute federalism with provincial autonomy or centralization with limited administrative reforms? That is, would all peoples in the empire be considered equal ("Ottomanist" orientation), or would only the Turks be granted full citizenship rights ("nationalist" orientation)? The "Ottomanists" wanted constitutional equality for all citizens, regardless of religion or ethnic background, but the Turkish "nationalists" (the Turanists) did not accept this concept of citizenship, favoring instead a homogeneous Turkish nation that would tolerate other nationalities but not grant equality to non-Turks.[50]

In their early days of power the Young Turks felt that Christians might be an asset to the empire and did not intend to destroy them. However, the Young Turks failed to understand that non-Turkish peoples of the empire would not consent to losing their identity in a "colorless Ottomanism" that denied each nationality the right to free development. The decentralized state in which minorities could realize their aspirations failed to materialize. As Ternon comments:

A political revolution would have brought about administrative decentralization. By opposing it the Young Turks supported the old regime. Any program of decentralization would no doubt have come head on into confrontation with the conservatism of the masses of Muslims who had remained politically unsophisticated; indeed the minorities themselves were not likely to collaborate with a real Ottomanization, which assumed the suppression of their separate identities. But the committee did not hesitate: it opted for the Turkish solution [nationalism], with all the consequences which that presupposed.
... Ottomanism was thus abandoned without ever having been put into practice.[51]

The Central Committee of the *Ittihad*

The *Ittihad* Party had a general assembly and was supervised by a vice-president and a Central Committee. As early as 1908, Central Committee members were the sole determiners of the party's political decisions. At that time the Central Committee, who were elected in an initial *secret* meeting, was composed of a mere eight members: Talaat, Enver, Midhat Shukru, Huseyin Kadri, Urguplu Mustafa Hayri, Habib Bey, Ahmet Riza, and Ipekli Hafiz Ibrahim.[52]

In 1909 there was a counterrevolutionary move by Abdul-Hamid II's supporters, but this was suppressed by the Young Turks. Sultan Abdul-Hamid was replaced by the servile, cooperative Mehmet V. *This move crushed any viable opposition to the Young Turks.*[53] From this point on, the Young Turks began to form the monolithic political structure of Turkey.

In 1910 the *Ittihad's* Second Congress took place in Salonika. Delegates worked hard to solidify the party, which was moving in the direction of nationalism. The 1909 period was one in which the Young Turks' policy of "Ottomanization" was manifesting itself as one of "pounding the non-Turkish elements in a Turkish mortar." The 1909 Adana massacres (discussed in Chapter 1) attest to the validity of this observation.

The membership of the Central Committee had changed almost completely by 1910. There were seven members, of whom only Hayri and Midhat Shukru were from the original clique. The new members were Ayub Sabri and Haci Adil. Also new to the committee were Dr. Nazim and Omer Naci—fanatic nationalists. Ziya Gokalp, from Diyarbekir, the major theorist of Pan-Turkism, was also a first-time member of the committee. Gokalp's Turkism sought " 'to uncover the Turkish national culture,' in order to realize the historical mission of the Turkish nation."[54]

In 1911 membership on the Central Committee rose to ten. Talaat was a member, and there were three newly elected members—Ali Fethi, Ahmet Nesimi, and Ali Huseyinzade. Huseyinzade's nomination marked the beginning of the Russian emigrant influence. Their arrival in Constantinople was in the following sequence: 1908—Agaev and Akcura; 1910—Mehmet Rasulzade then Huseyinzade, the Tatars of the Kazan and Crimea, the Uzbeks, the Azers, and students from Bukhara and Tashkent.[55]

That the *Ittihad* had dispensed with Ottomanism and embraced Pan-Turanism by 1911 is made clear by one fact. In that year all three of the founding fathers of Pan-Turanism—Ali Huseyinzade, Yusuf Akcura, and Ismail Gasprinsky—were elected to the *Ittihad's* Central Committee. Soon afterwards, the headquarters of the Pan-Turkists was moved to Istanbul.[56]

During the 1911 Congress, the government dropped the facade of "Ottomanism" with its "melting pot" ideology and eliminated any possibility for the development of a pluralistic society. The Young Turks saw that nationalism, if carried to a logical extreme, did not go along with their pretension about equality of peoples. However, they were "not so reckless as to break openly with Islam. . . . " Their program was very palatable to Moslems.[57]

Arnold Toynbee reports that in October 1911 the *Ittihad* Congress in Salonica passed the following resolutions:

The formation of new parties in the Chamber or in the country must be suppressed and the emergence of new liberal ideas prevented. Turkey must become a really Mohammedan country, and Moslem ideas and Moslem influence must be preponderant. Every other religious propaganda must be suppressed. The existence of the Empire depends on the strength of the Young Turkish Party and the suppression of all antagonistic ideas. . . .

Sooner or later the complete Ottomanisation of all Turkish subjects must be effected; it is clear, however that this can never be attained by persuasion, but that we must resort to armed force. The character of the Empire must be Mohammedan, and respect must be secured for Mohammedan institutions and traditions. Other nationalities must be denied the right of organization, for decentralization and autonomy are treason to the Turkish Empire. *The nationalities are a quantité negligeable* [sic]. *They can keep their religion but not their language. The propagation of the Turkish language is one of the sovereign means of confirming the Mohammedan supremacy and assimilating the other elements.*[58]

The 1911 Young Turk policy was not a threat to Moslem subject peoples, but even non-Turkish Moslem subjects, namely, twelve million Arabs, were viewed as negligible quantities. Turkization of them was a goal. The Arabs referred to this policy as "Pan-Islamism without Islam," since the spread of the Turkish language was used by the Turks to secure Turkish, not Moslem, supremacy and homogeneity.[59]

As we can clearly see, the party came to take a position diametrically opposed to that which had been toyed with during the "liberal" days in Paris when equal rights for all Ottoman subjects had been advocated. It was the 1911 Congress that resolved to promote immigration from the Caucasus and Turkistan, settle *muhajirs* on Armenian lands, and hinder Christians from acquiring real estate.[60]

By the 1911 Congress the party was overtly *exclusionary* toward other nationalities in the empire. They were not really viewed as "Turkish." As nationalist members of the party, such as Ziya Gokalp, Omer Naci, and Dr. Nazim increased their numbers, other members of a more liberal bent, such as Ahmet Riza and Habib, left the party. Yet there was some attempt on the part of the *Ittihad* to counterbalance the intransigent nationalism, since the number of Pan-Turkists on the Central Committee in 1912 decreased to five. However, Talaat and Shukru "carried the day."[61] As Morgenthau relates,

The political world at that time was not used to seeing the different organizational structures of a party control the actual functions of a state, and although analysts worried about the secret aspects of the Ittihad, they were mistaken in their understanding of the responsibilities of its members. All the European politicians agreed . . . that the key figure in the regime was Talaat, "the only one who had exceptional natural talents."[62]

The Fifth Congress of the *Ittihad's* Central Committee opened on 10 September 1913 and resolved to encourage "the progress and development of the various segments of the empire's population" and, to attain that end, decided to "adopt as a fundamental domestic policy the use of the area's predominant language." This could be interpreted as a recognition of separate national identities.[42]

Morgenthau asserts that such ideals could not be translated into reality; religious prejudices still divided Turkey. Above all, Morgenthau claims, the losses of large portions of the Turkish Empire through wars had by 1914 destroyed the prestige of the Young Turks' "new democracy." Ternon claims:

The nearly complete amputation of the empire's European territories and the development of a strong reactionary party led the Ittihad to adopt an intolerant attitude toward minorities, while at the same time insisting upon loyalty to Ottomanism. One must, however, look elsewhere for the primary cause for the ideological change [from its early liberal days] within the Ittihad. It came from a strong sentiment in Ottoman political life favoring Turkism, from a collective zealotry brought in first by the intellectuals but then spreading to all social levels. The nationalist wing of the party led the masses to Turkism. Thereafter it was the masses which pushed the entire party toward an explosion of racial fanaticism.

A ferocious, exclusionary race consciousness had emerged among the Turks.[44]

The 1913 Coup d'Etat and the Emergence of a Monolithic Party

By 1913 Talaat, Enver, and Djemal had totally abandoned their expectations of reforming the Turkish state and "had developed an insatiable lust for personal power." Turkey had not become a progressive nation. Ambassador Morgenthau concludes that by 1913,

I saw that Turkey consisted of merely so many inarticulate, ignorant, and poverty-ridden slaves, with a small, wicked oligarchy at the top, which was prepared to use them in the way that would best promote its private interests. And these men were practically the same who, a few years before had made Turkey a constitutional state. *A more bewildering fall from the highest idealism to the crassest materialism could not be imagined* [emphasis added].[45]

In 1913 Talaat, Enver, and Djemal, backed by forty members of the Central Committee, conducted secret meetings and manipulated elections, filling offices with its own henchmen. In Constantinople the supreme chief of the Central Committee ruled the country and party like a "boss" during America's most "unregenerate" days. The entire organization could be described as an "invisible government," and, according to Morgenthau, *"the Young Turks were not a government; they were really an irresponsible party, a kind of secret society, which, by intrigue, intimidation, and assassination, had obtained most of the offices of state"* [emphasis added].⁴⁶

In addition to the forty men in Constantinople, subcommittees were set up in all important cities throughout the empire. Only men who "took orders" were placed in power, and they, in turn, appointed only certain people for specific positions. Morgenthau contends that "no man could hold an office, high or low, who was not endorsed by this committee."⁴⁷

The Young Turks dominated Ottoman politics until a split occurred within the party ranks in 1911, and one faction of the Committee for Union and Progress formed a genuine party called the "Liberal Opposition Party," which posed an immediate threat to the Young Turks. Within one month from its inception, the opposition party won a by-election in Istanbul, whereupon the *Ittihad* dissolved parliament and procured an overwhelming majority in a corrupt general election in April 1912. Again, army officers took to the hills in Albania, but this time with the intention of crushing the illegal power of the *Ittihad*. Through military maneuvers and threats, the young soldiers, called the "Savior Officers," forced the Young Turks to relinquish power in July of 1912.

Meanwhile, the Italians had invaded Libya in 1911. In October 1912, a mere three months after the Savior Officers had expelled the Committee for Union and Progress from office, the Turks were driven from Macedonia. Except for Thrace, this spelled the end of "Turkey in Europe."

By an act of murder, Talaat, Enver, and Djemal wrested power from all other factions in a coup d'etat which took place on 26 January 1913. Kiamil Pasha, grand vizier, and Nazim Pasha, minister of war, headed the Liberal Opposition party, which was then in control of Ottoman Turkey. The opposition party, which was renowned for its enmity toward the Young Turks, intended to surrender Adrianople to Bulgaria after the Ottomans lost the Balkan Wars. The Young Turks had waited in the wings for six months to seize the first opportune moment to overthrow the liberals, and now was the time, because the Turkish population viewed the loss of Adrianople as "still another milestone toward their [own] national doom."

Talaat and Enver quickly gathered two hundred followers about them and marched to the Sublime Porte. Nazim was shot. Talaat and Enver, leaders of the mob, forcibly entered the council chamber. Kiamil, the grand vizier, was forced to resign immediately or be shot also. Morgenthau reports:

As assassination had been the means by which these chieftains had obtained the supreme power, so assassination continued to be the instrument upon which they depended for maintaining their control. Djemal, in addition to his other duties, became Military Governor of Constantinople, and in this capacity he had control of the police; in this office he developed all the talents of a Fouché, and did his work so successfully that any man who wished to conspire against the Young Turks usually retired for that purpose to Paris or Athens. . . . The Young Turks had destroyed Abdul Hamid's regime only to adopt that Sultan's favourite methods of quieting opposition. Instead of having one Abdul Hamid, Turkey now discovered that she had several. *Men were arrested and deported by the score, and hangings of political offenders—that is, of the ruling gang [Liberal Opposition Party]—were common occurrences* [emphasis added].

After the new grand vizier, Mahmud Shevket Pasha, was murdered in June 1913, a military dictatorship was imposed.⁶⁸

Feroz Ahmad, in his book *The Young Turks*, describes the Young Turks in the following terms:

The Unionists were men of a different stamp [than was Abdul-Hamid]. To them politics was much more than a game and having seized power they meant to hold on to it. To do so they were willing to use all possible means, so that repression and violence became the order of the day. Nothing was sacred in the pursuit of power and those guilty of dissent must be prepared to pay with their lives.⁶⁹

In addition to being a dictatorship, the *Ittihad* had long since operated clandestinely. The secrecy of the *Ittihad* had been developed in its earlier days when Sultan Abdul-Hamid had been replaced by Sultan Mohammed, a kindly elderly man who became a mere "rubber stamp" for the wishes of the committee. Morgenthau says of Sultan Mohammed:

His state duties consisted merely in performing certain ceremonies . . . and in affixing his signature to such papers as Talaat and his associates placed before him. This was a profound change in the Turkish system, since in that country for centuries the Sultan had been an unquestioned despot, whose will had been the only law, and who had centred in his own person all the power of sovereignty. Not only the Sultan, but the Parliament, had become the subservient creature of the Committee, which chose practically all the members, who voted only as the predominant bosses dictated.⁷⁰

As Ahmad concludes, "by 1914 the Unionists had assumed complete political control. . . . One tact for their survival was that they governed from behind the scenes, controlling the new regime without overtly appearing in the political arena."⁷¹

General Liman von Sanders, who had been sent by the Kaiser to

Turkey in 1913 to reorganize the Turkish Army before World War I, once said of the *Ittihad:*

This committee always possessed a certain mysterious something. I could never learn how many members it had, nor who they were, except for the most famous, who were known to everyone.[72]

Ahmad reports (in his 1969 book) that "the inner workings of the Committee remain a mystery because the records were lost during that chaotic decade, having been distributed to a number of scholars who were entrusted with the writing of a history of the CUP [Committee of Union and Progress]."[73]

Mevlanzade Rifat, a former director of the *Ittihad* Central Committee who had participated in its secret sessions, reports that it was in the Central Committee early in 1915 that the plan was first formulated to destroy the Armenian people. Talaat presided over the meeting. Those in attendance were Enver, Dr. Behaeddin Shakir, Dr. Nazim, Ghara Kemal, Hassan Fehmin, Cevad, and Oghlou Ahmed. Dr. Nazim presented the main report which took the following ruthless stand:

If we are going to be satisfied with the kind of local massacres that occurred in Adana and other places in 1909 . . . if this purge is not going to be universal and final, instead of good, it will inevitably result in harm. *It is imperative that the Armenian people be completely exterminated; that not even one single Armenian be left on our soil; that the name, Armenian, be obliterated.* We are now at war; there is no more auspicious occasion than this; the intervention of the great powers and the protests of newspapers will not even be considered; and even if they are, the matter will have become an accomplished fact, and thus closed forever. *The procedure this time will be one of total annihilation—it is necessary that not even one single Armenian survive this annihilation* [emphasis added].[74]

The genocide was decided upon, planned, and put into action under a total blanket of secrecy. Ida Alamuddin, in *Papa Kuenzler and the Armenians,* reports:

the Ittihad had met and decided in secret on the systematic extermination of all Armenians still in Turkey. The Turkish government took every precaution to prevent news . . . from leaking out. It was only after some months—and when it was too late for anything to be done—that the outside world first heard of this. Jehad, Holy War, had been declared.[75]

Marjorie Housepian describes the mysterious disappearance of Armenian leaders and men of the community. Inquiries into their whereabouts were met with vague and inaccurate information. She notes that European papers were not reporting such incidents. Naim Bey, a Turkish official who was ordered to kill Armenians and refused, reported that government messages sent to area governors with details of the deportations and massacres were always ciphered. Naim himself had been instructed to destroy all evidence of such messages after having deciphered and delivered them. Secrecy and deception were the standard operational procedure for the *Ittihad*.[76]

Evidence supporting the Young Turks' exclusionary position toward non-Turks and genocidal intentions toward the Armenians is revealed in a letter from Medmed Cherif Pasha to the editor of the *Journal de Geneve*. Cherif, one-time Turkish minister to Sweden, had for a time been active in the meetings of the Young Turks after they overthrew Abdul-Hamid. When Cherif realized that the *Ittihad* had abandoned the idea of democratic government in Turkey, he formed the Liberal Opposition Party. Cherif reports that the Young Turks had planned the Armenian genocide as early as six years before it began (which, incidentally, is 1909, the year of the Adana massacres). In 1915, in a letter to the *Journal de Geneve*, reproduced in the 15 October 1915 *New York Times*, Cherif comments,

To be sure, the state of mind of the Unionists was not revealed to the civilized world until they had openly taken sides with Germany; but for more than six years I have been exposing them in the *Mecheroutiette* [his newspaper, published first in Constantinople and then in Paris] and in different journals and reviews, warning France and England of the plot against them and against certain nationalities within the Ottoman borders, notably the Armenians, that was being hatched.[77]

The *Teshkilat-i-Makhsusiye* ("Special Organization")

The extent to which the party controlled the genocide is evident if we consider the functions of the *Teshkilat-i-Makhsusiye*, created for Enver's attack on Sarikamish but not originally organized to exterminate Armenians.[78] Like the Sultan's Hamidian Cavalry, the Special Organization provided an important vehicle for the destruction of Armenians. It was independent of and set apart from government services, free to act, and armed with full powers. In addition to directing the Kurds and peoples of Transcaucasia in subversive activities along the entire length of the Russo-Turkish border, the Special Organization was charged with "dealing brutally with the unresolved question."

Heading the Special Organization were Atif Riza, Dr. Nazim (both members of the Central Committee), and Aziz Bey, the head of the secret police. Cevad, military governor of Constantinople, automatically ratified the Special Organization's decisions. The positions occupied by Cevad and Aziz give evidence of the police and paramilitary nature of the organization which, incidentally, enjoyed total immunity. Dr. Bahaeddin Shakir became the driving force of the Special Organization and executed orders issued to him from Constantinople. He was the sole recipient of money and telegrams from the Central Committee. Soon, the empire's administration was controlled by the Special Organization, which saw to it that party decisions were enforced to the letter.[79]

Common criminals (*chetehs*) were recruited for membership into the Special Organization and convicts sentenced to death were freed from prisons throughout the empire. Upon being released, they were put on the organization's rolls, formed into bands, trained, and sent into action in the eastern vilayets. By the beginning of 1915 these "troops" joined with the regular police, the Kurdish tribes, and other Hamidians to persecute the Armenians in eastern Anatolia. The *Ittihad's* bribery funds allocated large sums of money for their equipment and training.

Party leaders, deputies, and provincial secretaries-general verbally transmitted instructions to the *chetehs*. Frequently, such directions arrived by telegram to various provincial administrators. Valis ("provincial governors") and other administrative officers could at any moment be required to give blind allegiance to members of the organization. These members were empowered to dismiss or punish those who failed to obey orders. The *teskaras* ("documents") revealed at the trial of the unionists after World War I specify the power and function of the Special Organization.[80]

In mid-February 1915 the Central Committee of the Committee for Union and Progress embarked upon its plan to exterminate the Armenians. Such a decision is a natural consequence of the racist, nationalist Pan-Turkic ideology combined with the Pan-Turanist irredentist policy of "Turkey faces East." World War I provided the Young Turks with the propitious moment to solve "the Armenian problem." As Christopher Walker states, "the war provided a thick black velvet arras, behind which the Young Turks could act with impunity."[81]

When the Turkish Cabinet, in spite of protests from all foreign ambassadors, issued a notice that there would be an abrogation of the capitulations on 1 October, Turkey became independent of foreign tutelage.[82] The now monolithic and exclusionary Committee of Union and Progress combined the Pan-Turanist dream of "Turkey for the Turks" with their control of state power necessary to make their dream a reality. Count Wolff-Metternick writes on 30 June 1916 that no power any longer existed that could control the fanaticism and chauvinism of the "many-headed hydra" of the committee. The committee's demands for the total elimination of the Armenian people could not be escaped. In the capital and vilayets, committee members were in place to insure that all officials, from Valis to Kaimakans, carry out the orders of the *Ittihad*.[83]

EVERYONE has realized today that the only ideal for the Turks is Turkism. . . . There is a growing tendency towards nationalism among the Turkish youth today. What we want is to transform this tendency into a great and sacred faith.

—ZIYA GOKALP

4

DESTRUCTIVE USES OF COMMUNICATION

A NATIONALIST and racist ideology, Pan-Turanism pervaded Turkey in the early twentieth century. This ideology, espoused by the government, was disseminated through papers, periodicals, poetry, novels, drama, history, and theology in an efflorescence of nationalist literature, all of which excluded Armenians from the great Turanist dream. Simultaneously, the government initiated a propaganda campaign aimed at arousing the masses to extirpate the Armenians through genocide. Propaganda promoted by the Young Turks labeled Armenians as treasonous, dangerous, and "enemies of the state." The Turkish government, armed with an aggressive ideology and a plethora of propaganda directed against the Armenians, soon drove the Turkish and Kurdish masses to frenzy, thus making them willing participants in genocide.

AGGRESSIVE IDEOLOGY

In the 1870s the area of real racial and national awakening of Pan-Turanism was Baku, Azerbaijan, the metropolis of the eastern Caucasus. Baku was the home of a prosperous and relatively enlightened,

Turkicized Azerbaijani population. The bulk of Azerbaijanis were Shiite Moslems, but they were linguistically related to the Sunni Turks. However, religious squabbles between Shiite and Sunni were irrelevant to Azerbaijanis in the face of Russian and Armenian political strength in Baku.[1]

By 1875 Baku's Moslem intellectuals displayed a pro-Turkish posture shaped by the Pan-Turkist, Tatar educator and publicist, Ismail Bey Gasprinsky, and the Azerbaijani playwright called the "Moliere of the Orient," Mirza Feth-'Ali Akhundzade, whose dominant ideological leanings were Pan-Turkist.[2]

Ismail Gasprinsky led the Pan-Turanist movement in Azerbaijan. In 1879 he founded the paper *Terjuman* ("The Interpreter")—a harbinger of a Tatar and Caucasian Turkic renaissance. Zarevand describes the role played by the Azerbaijani Pan-Turkists:

> On the one hand, these vanguards of the national movement fought against the danger of russification. On the other, they tried to reform the religious cultural life of the Tatar peoples, and to disseminate learning among the ignorant masses. For this reason they were persecuted as Kiafirs (infidels) by the conservatives. In spite of this, they were able to win over the enlightened element among the youth. Violent clashes took place. We may characterize this era as the *mektebji-medresseji* (public school versus theological seminary) struggle.[3]

At the beginning of the twentieth century, among the Turkish Azers at Baku, Pan-Turkism provided a revolutionary doctrine. The Moslem bourgeoisie of Baku were in the vanguard of the movement, which was financed by wealthy landowners and industrialists. Two men were in the forefront of Azerbaijani Pan-Turkism—Ali Huseyinzade and Ahmet Agaev; they would assume key roles in Turkish politics after 1908.[4]

The real progenitor of Pan-Turanism in 1895 was Tatar "Idil literature." Starting in 1895, many poets and writers aroused the racial and national consciousness of a new Turkic generation. The foundations of popular patriotic literature, which gained momentum after the 1905 Russian Revolution, were established during the Idil period. In every field—theology, drama, history, philosophy, poetry, and novels—there was a veritable blossoming of nationalist literature. Yusuf Akcura, a nationalist and Turkic racist, was inspired by Idil literature. It was Akcura who first distinctly conceptualized the political program and doctrine of Pan-Turanism. His article, *Uch Tarz-i Siyaset* ("Three Pathways of Policy"), published in 1904 in the Cairo paper *Turk*, is to the Pan-Turkist what the *Communist Manifesto* is to the Marxist.

It was from Azerbaijan, where the papers *Kaspii* and *Ekinji* ("The

Plowman") were published in 1881, that the message of Pan-Islamism issued forth. In Azerbaijan, Huseyinzade (Ali Merdan Bey), along with others, developed the ideological foundation that later gained popularity with the Young Turks. Ali Huseyinzade was born in Salyan, Russian Azerbaijan, and received a Ph.D. in 1888 at St. Petersburg (now Leningrad) University. From 1889–95 he studied medicine at Istanbul's medical school. In 1903, when the sultan's spies suspected him of liberal, nationalist ideas, he fled to Azerbaijan where he pursued publishing and teaching. After the Ottoman Constitution was declared in 1909, he went back to Istanbul and was elected to the Central Committee of the *Ittihad ve Terraki* in 1911. During World War I he and Akcura toured Central Europe as propagandists of Pan-Turanism for the political committee *Turan Khyeti*. Huseyinzade's poetry serves as a barometer of the ideological shifts of the Young Turks, which led them from Ottomanism to Turkism to racism. Huseyinzade exerted a strong influence on Turkish ideology, as he was the one to introduce Pan-Turanism into Turkey in 1889 when he wrote under the symbolic pen name A. Turani.[5]

As early as 1905 there were Azerbaijani massacres of Armenians who blocked the path uniting Azerbaijan and Turkey. The massacres, initiated by Huseyinzade and others, started in Baku and spread to Nakichevan, Shushy, Yerevan, Gandzak (Turkish: Ganja), and Tiflis. Azerbaijani assaults against Armenians persisted for an eighteen-month period preceding and subsequent to the 1905 Russian Revolution; the diversion caused by the turmoil in Russia provided the Azerbaijanis ample opportunity to destroy Armenians. Later, in 1915, World War I would provide their Turkic brothers a propitious occasion to exterminate the Armenians.[6]

During the 1890s, while the Azerbaijanis were experiencing a racial awakening, Turkish institutions were bombarded by three competing ideological currents. The first of these was Ottoman Union (*Osmanli Ittihadi*), a uniting of the various nationalities of the empire; second was Pan-Islamic Union (*Islam Ittihadi*); third was Pan-Turkish Union (*Turk Ittihadi*), the weakest of the three movements. Sultan Abdul-Hamid II believed in Islamic *Ittihad* and persecuted all nationalists who supported Pan-Turkish union. His actions, however, were no deterrent to the desire of Turkic peoples themselves for a Pan-Turkic union. In 1906 Arminius Vambery, a Turkologist and famous Orientalist, upon returning from Central Asia and other Turko-Tatar countries, reported:

The watchword of the Mohammedan subjects of the Tsar is "Unity." . . . The goal of the Tatars is close alliance of the branches and the clans of the Turkish nation.[7]

During this period Ziya Gokalp wrote his famous poem, *Turan*. Gokalp was a Turanist who dropped his Moslem name, Mohammed, and adopted the Turanian name Gokalp ("blue hero"), keeping his second name, Ziya, as his first name. His poem, which follows, became the basis of Pan-Turanist ideology:

In my feelings, which are the voices of thy past
The throb of my pulse, the sound of my heartbeat,
And not in the pages of History I read, comprehend and extoll
All the triumphs distant and near, of my noble chosen race.
Not in the pages of History, because there
In a dusty frame, in a slanderous ambit,
Attila and Jehghiz, the geniuses who have crowned
My race with conquests, appear smeared and shameful,
While Caesar and Alexander are displayed in glory.
In my pulse's throb! Because my heart does full well
Recognize Oghuz Khan, who though as yet unknown to science,
Lives nonetheless in my veins, with grandeur and majesty.
Oghuz Khan! It is he who inspires my elan not Turkestan:
The Turk's Homeland is a great and eternal land, *Turan*.

In this poem, "Turan" refers to a "pure" Turkish country. The youth of Turkey received this poem rapturously.[8]

Gokalp's writings shed light upon his mode of thought:

Patriotism assumes various forms with respect to religion, morality, law, and fine arts. A real patriot should be loyal in all these spheres of life.

Turkism is not a political party movement. It is a scientific, philosophical, and literary movement. In other words, it is a movement of cultural drive and regeneration. . . . Since this is so, however, Turkism cannot remain altogether indifferent to political ideals. . . .

We can find the right way if we leave the wrong road that we have been following since the *Tanzimat* era.[9]

Intellectuals like Gokalp crystallized Pan-Turanist thought and had two objectives—one internal and the other external. The internal objectives were to cleanse Turkish life of "adulterating and polluting foreign elements"; to nationalize Turkish literature, language, and religion; to revive earlier Turkish institutions, culture, and traditions; to make pre-Ottoman Turkish history popular; and to inspire a racial-national consciousness. The external objectives were to scientifically verify the cultural and ethnological bond uniting all the Turanian peoples, to create solidarity and unity among Turanians, and to build a common Turanian "soul."[10]

By 1908 Akcura and other Pan-Turanists had already foreseen the decline of Ottomanism and Pan-Islamism and were preaching their ideas. Having successfully taken over the Istanbul branch of the Committee for Union and Progress, they next infiltrated the Central Committee based in Salonika. Their immediate objective was *"to make Turkism and Pan-Turkism the guiding (though secret) principle of the ruling party."* Ahmed Emin, a Turkish political writer, describes the political expedience of the Young Turks in 1914:

The methods followed by the dethroned Sultan to gain power were still fresh . . . as tempting examples. . . . [Central] Committee leaders began to follow them more closely. . . . Full advantage was taken of the impressive effect of secrecy and mystery. Religion was used as a basic agitation to secure popularity. *Worst of all a blind and aggressive Turkish imperialism became the dominating motive of the Committee's policy. Phrases like "Ottomanism" and the "unity of all elements of the population in Turkey without distinction of creed and religion" were still used; but the meaning given to them was no longer the meeting of the different elements on a common and neutral ground, through mutual sacrifices as citizens of the Ottoman Empire possessing equal rights. These were simply assumed to mean assimilating the non-Turkish elements of the population, through coercive methods if necessary.* [11]

In the works of Pan-Turkist Tekin Alp, the Turanian race is glorified for creating soldiers, being heroic, and being brave. In addition to these attributes, Pan-Turkists contend that the *Turks are a master race who are born to rule* [emphasis added].[12] This belief is typified by a statement made in 1919 by a Magyar who considered himself Turkic. He related the following to author C. U. Clark:

All these subject nationalities, Serbs, Slovaks, Rumanians, whom the Supreme Council (of the Paris Peace Conference) is cutting off from our body politic, must inevitably return (to us), *for they are naturally subordinate, and we are naturally the masters.* But you can't be expected to understand that for you are Indo-European, Aryan, and we are Turanians.[13]

This powerful nationalist ideology made religion its tool, as is evidenced in a statement made by Enver Pasha: "Make Koran serve Turan." Enver wished to exploit religion for the state's own ends. However, not all Moslem clergy did at first accept Pan-Turanism, because the Moslem religion stipulates that Islam is a supranatural faith and, consequently, its power transcends that of the state. Since the *mollahs* ("priests") were loyally followed by the people, they waged war against Pan-Turanism by using the *Melami*, a widely circulated periodical of the powerful Moslem fraternity, to disseminate their views. Consequently, the government relented in its efforts to convert the older *softas* ("clerics") to Pan-Turanism and began directing its efforts toward young clerics.[14]

Zarevand states that in reality Pan-Turanist ideology was geared toward the destruction of the Moslem dogma—its authority, and moral constraint—since Pan-Turanism placed a priority on race rather than on religion.[15] However, the government was not adverse to declaring a Holy War to encourage the cooperation of the masses in the destruction of Armenians. Ida Alamuddin claims that "in this way emotions might be still further inflamed."[16]

PROPAGANDA WAR

The Young Turks had no official propaganda ministry. Yet the propaganda inundating the empire can be viewed as government sponsored, since many of those propagating it were on the Central Committee of the *Ittihad.*

As previously noted, it was beyond the Turkish borders among some Moslem peoples of Russia, namely the Kirghiz, Tatars, and Bashkirs, that Pan-Turanism experienced its real birth. In Ufa and Kazan, two northern Russian Tatar cities, two important Pan-Turanist publications, *Turk Yurdu* ("Turkish Fatherland") and *Turk Ojaghi* ("Turkish Hearth"), came into existence. The headquarters for both of these publications would, along with their founders, later relocate in Istanbul and Ankara, rendezvous points for Young Turks.[17]

Russian Turanists such as Azerbaijanis provided the financial backing for *Turk Yurdu* (Turkish Fatherland), which became the most famous of the periodicals, serving as a data source for Turanist studies. Yusuf Akcura directed the periodical and wrote most of it. The objectives of *Turk Yurdu* were to excite patriotism, to clearly establish the "racial identity" of Tatars and Turks, and to reestablish a Turanian community emulating that of the thirteenth century. The periodical was ideologically oriented, leaning heavily upon the terminology of Ziya Gokalp and Huseyinzade, that is, Turkization, Islamization, and modernization.[18]

From 1908 onward, Turanist ideology, inspired by the *Ittihad,* dominated both literary and political circles of the Ottoman Empire. During this time a plethora of Turkish associations and periodicals emerged, such as: *Turk Dernegi* and its accompanying journal of the same name (1909–1911); a review association called *Turk Yurdu* (1911); *Turk Ojaghi,* a three-thousand member club in the capital made up of officers, doctors, teachers, students, and lawyers (1912); and two periodicals—*Halka Dogru* ("Toward the People") (1913) and

Bilgi ("Knowledge") (1913). These supposedly apolitical organizations, journals, and magazines camouflaged a group of very determined militants—poet Mehmet Emin, Yusuf Akcura, Ahmed Agaev,
historian Fuat Koprulu, Ali Huseyinzade, writers Halide Edib and Ce-
lal Sahit, and Ismail Gasprinsky (collaborator on several journals).
Ziya Gokalp, Omer Seyfettin, and Ali Canip, founders of the Salonikan
publication *Genc Kalemler* ("Young Writers") joined the group in
1912.

In 1910 Halide Edib published her famous tendentious novel entitled *Yeni Turan, The Fate of a Turkish Woman*, which is still considered by some to be one of the "Gospels" of Pan-Turkism. In the novel
Edib depicts the ideals, struggles, and ultimate triumph of Pan-
Turanism.

The society *Yeni Hayat* ("New Life") and its organ *Yeni Felsefe*
("New Philosophy") soon combined with the society *Yeni Lissan*
("New Language") and its organ *Genc Kalemler* ("Young Writers").
These two associations merged into one great ideological movement.
In this way the Turkists launched a furious attack to win the minds of
Ottoman youth.[19]

During this period universities established chairs for Turkish studies, with emphasis upon Pan-Turkism and social sciences. Turkish
youth yearned to participate in the Turanian adventure. Turkism even
gained favor with the *softas* stimulated by the efforts of theology professors. The Pan-Turanist ideology conquered the proletariat, peasant
classes, workers, and merchants. People spoke of Turkish artisans and
laborers. Soon the country was overcome by a "vast surge of xenophobia."

In 1913 when Turkey suffered territorial loss after her defeat in the
Balkan Wars the popularity, control, and power of the Young Turks
were well-established.[20] Even before this time, almost all members of
the Young Turks had joined the *Turk Ojaghi*. Pan-Turkist university
professors were chosen by the minister of education, and all instruc-
tion in primary schools, universities, *medresses* ("theological
schools"), and military academies was Pan-Turanist. Agaev had been
appointed inspector in charge of Constantinople schools and had "re-
formed" the teaching of Turkish literature and history.

Not only did Pan-Turanist ideology overcome the Turkish masses,
but it dominated the government, since Talaat Pasha selected administrators on the basis of their adherence to the party line. Yves Ternon
notes:

Pan Turkish sentiment reached its peak at the outbreak of the First World
War. Patriotic journalists predicted the fall of the Russian empire and the rise of

the Turanian empire from its ashes. It was this huge tidal wave, issuing forth from the very depths of the people's collective consciousness, which then inundated all the levels of Turkish society.[21]

By this time the myth of a Turkish "race" had been popularized by the nationalist propaganda of the Young Turks. The Armenians would suffer the consequences of the new scientific racism. Ottomanism might have integrated them into Turkey, but Pan-Turanism could not. As Ternon observes:

It is indeed only via the myth of pan-Turkism that one can come to understand the mechanism of genocide. There was the intrusion of an undesirable element into what proved to be a delicate matter: the assimilation of the various racial groups in the empire destroyed the precarious balance. The need to remove the foreign Armenian element took precedence over more immediate preoccupations. Like all the great crimes of modern time, the Armenian genocide took place according to the logical processes of all obsessional neuroses.[22]

The Use of Rumors

Rumors may facilitate hostile outbursts toward target groups if they are transformed into actual beliefs. They may also provide immediate and future justification for acts of violence that could otherwise never be condoned. Israel Charney puts it thus:

Genociders rationalize and extenuate their actions so that, quite sincerely, they believe that they are acting in self-defense of one sort or another. There comes a point when people no longer recognize their bloodthirsty destruction for what it is. Before long, it is as if man's marvelous machinery for experiencing has itself been killed.[23]

Charney also argues that it is the combination of our readiness as human beings to be destructive with the readiness of social institutions to invoke and sponsor violence that trigger genocide.[24] In other words, it is individual as well as social corporate readiness to violence that is so very dangerous, and rumors often serve as the trigger to set off a violent outburst of man against man.

As early as 1896, rumors were circulated by the government of Abdul-Hamid II that directed hostility against Armenians. Frederick Greene explained:

Persistent efforts are made to obscure the situation and to alienate sympathy from the Armenians on the ground that they are rebels. Some color has been given to this idea by the wild talk of a few desperate Armenians outside of Turkey, but, . . . there never has been anything that can be called an Armenian insurrection. The very idea of such a thing is ridiculous; for, in the first place the Armenians are only one-tenth of the Sultan's subjects. . . . Secondly, they are exclusively a commercial and agricultural people, possessing neither arms, nor a knowledge of their use. Third, they are people of sense, and know that their only hope is through European intervention.[25]

The Young Turks would resort to the same tactics their predecessors had previously used against the Armenians in the 1894-96 massacres, namely, propagating rumor to mobilize the Turkish masses against the Armenians. Though European statesmen and missionaries proved these rumors false, the *Ittihadists* did not cease in their efforts to disseminate inflammatory information to create a volatile situation. In 1909 Mevlanzade Rifat, a Young Turk leader, asserted:

Spreading the word that the Armenians are planning a revolt and are seeking the establishment of an Armenian national home in Cilicia, *they [the Committee for Union and Progress] began the campaign to incite the common people against the Armenians* [emphasis added].[26]

Andre Mandelstam of the Russian Embassy in Constantinople said that the *Ittihad* manipulated rumor to convince Turks that Armenians were planning a revolt to establish a national home in Cilicia. The government was able, by using such tactics, to incite the Turks against the Armenians.[27]

The notion of a "general Armenian rebellion" was continually promoted and circulated by the Young Turks' ruling coteries. However, even Mevlanzade refutes such propaganda in his work *Dark Folds of the Turkish Revolution* in which he states unequivocally that the massacres had forced Armenians in some areas to resort to rebellion as a means of self-defense.[28]

The perpetual theme of rumors used by the Young Turks to justify the genocide of Armenians is summed up in a telegraph dated 15 April 1915 from the *Ittihadists* to Djemal Bey, government delegate at Adana:

. . . the government which represents Islam and the Turkish people, and the Committee of Union and Progress, intending to forestall the presentation of the Armenian question in any place and in any manner, taking advantage of the freedom which the war has granted us, has decided to end that question once and for all, by deporting the Armenians to the deserts of Arabia. . . . The following serve as a justification for that plan:
(a) The Armenian voluntary forces serving in the enemy armies;
(b) The Armenian parties in the interior of the country, which have been organized to give a body blow to our Army;
(c) The uncountable firearms and war material discovered and confiscated everywhere in the country.[29]

Herbert Adams Gibbons, a British student of Ottoman history and correspondent in Adana at the outbreak of the genocide, sheds some light on Turkey's claims that Armenians were serving in enemy armies. He comments:

> It is unfair for the Ottoman Government to cite, as basis for its charges against its Armenian subjects, the fact that Armenians in large numbers are fighting in the Russian army. As a result of the war of 1877, Turkey was compelled to cede a portion of Armenia to Russia. The Armenians of these territories have been for nearly forty years under Russian rule, and are naturally, as Russian subjects, fighting against Turkey. In giving the fact that there are Armenians in the Russian armies as a reason for doubting the loyalty of the Armenians in Turkey, the Turks and their German apologists have traded upon European and American imperfect knowledge of the history and geography of the regions beyond Van.[30]

Johannes Lepsius summarized the Ottoman charges of treason against the Armenians in the following six points:

1. Garegin Pasdermadjian (Armon Garo), member of the Ottoman parliament, had deserted to Russia and joined the volunteers.
2. English and French naval commanders had sent agitators into Cilicia where the population was engaged in shooting and espionage.
3. Armenians in Zeitun had resisted the commands of the military authorities.
4. The Armenians of Van had taken up arms against the government.
5. Turkish opponents of the Ittihadists had contrived against the government and used as accomplices several members of the Hnchakist [sic] party.
6. The combatants of Shbin Karahisar had barricaded themselves in the ancient citadel and fought against Turkish troops.

Lepsius claims that even if all of these things had been true, it would be "fantastic" to construe an Armenian revolution from only those factors listed above.[31] In a similar vein, Gibbons claims that Armenian revolutionaries were posing no threat which could not be averted by simply arresting a few agitators rather than resorting to wholesale destruction of Armenians.[32]

Ambassador Morgenthau says that in 1915 when placards were posted in cities and villages demanding that Christians take any arms in their possession to headquarters, Armenians were alarmed since they fully comprehended the consequences of being defenseless while their neighbors were armed. Yet many of them obeyed the command and turned in their rifles to Turkish officials. Immediately, they were thrown into prison on charges of treason, their weapons being used as "evidence" proving an imminent Armenian revolution.[33]

Charges of treason were leveled at the Armenians despite the fact that they had traditionally been referred to as "the loyal millet" (*millet-i-Sadika*) and had fought heroically for Turkey—even in a war against Russia with whom they were supposed to be engaging in treason.[34] As late as February 1915 Enver had said to the Armenian Bishop of Konya:

> I am giving you my thanks and using this opportunity to tell you that the Armenian soldiers of the Ottoman army are executing their duty in the theatre of war scrupulously, as witness my own experience. I wish you to communicate to the Armenian nation, known for its complete devotion to the imperial Ottoman government, the expression of my satisfaction and gratitude.[35]

Yet earlier in the summer of 1914, when Union and Progress agents attempted to enlist the aid of the Armenians of Erzeroum and Van to further a revolution behind the Russian front, the Armenians had refused. The Young Turks considered the refusal to be "treasonable behavior."[36] In addition, when Enver Pasha was defeated at Sarikamish in 1914, he blamed his failure on the Armenians, using them as scapegoats and "claiming that they acted as spies among the civilian population, and in the battle area."

None of this sufficiently explains the Armenian exterminations, since *prior* to the Battle of Sarikamish, Armenians were already being massacred. According to Aziz Samih, who served as chief of the Historical Department of the Ottoman War Ministry during the genocide, orders requiring attacks on Armenian villages had arrived in eastern Turkey between 29 October and 25 November of 1914, whereas the Sarikamish attack on Russia was in December 1914.[37] Therefore, we can only interpret the contradiction in Enver's praise of Armenians and his eventual deeds against them as an attempt to deceive Armenians and European statesmen into a sense of security so that no threat to Armenians might be perceived, and, consequently, no defensive measures would be considered necessary to safeguard them.

Enver and Talaat also used the "incident at Van" as justification for exterminating Armenians for revolution and treachery. According to Morgenthau, Turkish policy for years had been to claim an Armenian "revolution" after having provoked Armenians into overt acts of self-defense and violence. In Van, when the Turks demanded 4,000 Armenian soldiers, the people fought to protect the men, knowing that they would be murdered. Van was then attacked on the pretext of revolution. After the genocide had begun and Armenians had been deported from Van by the government, Ambassador Morgenthau discussed the treatment of Armenians with Halil Bey, then Turkey's minister of foreign affairs. Halil admitted that the Young Turks had made a serious mistake in trying to annihilate the Armenians, but, reports Morgenthau, "then, like all the others, he went back to the happenings at Van, the desire of the Armenians for independence, and the help which they had given the Russians. I had heard it all many times before."[38]

Perhaps by sheer repetition the Turks thought they could change such propaganda into fact. However, Stanley Kerr, in *The Lions of Marash*, proves that their claims are blatantly false, since Armenians were deported from Van before the Armenians resisted the Turks there on 20 April *after* the deportation from Zeitun and *after* Turkish soldiers had already destroyed over eighty Armenian villages in Van territory.[39]

Another "revolution" occurred in Zeitun. In *Papa Kuenzler and the Armenians*, Alamuddin points out that during the mobilization for war by Turkey in 1914, men from Zeitun in Cilicia went into the Turkish Army. In spite of the many atrocities against the people of Zeitun, they only resorted to self-defense in spring of 1915, when a number of Armenian women there had been raped, after which the Armenians attacked the Turkish gendarmes.[40]

Words from the diary of a Swiss eyewitness from Geneva corroborate Alamuddin's facts. The following entry was made in the diary of the eyewitness on 14 March 1915:

> . . . all direct communication with it [Zeitun] has been interrupted. Turkish troops have left Aleppo for Zeitoun— some say 4,000, some 6,000, others 8,000. With what intention, one wonders? . . . Armenians have no wish to revolt and are prepared to put up with anything the Government may do. Contrary to the old-established custom, a levy was made at Zeitoun at the time of the August mobilisation, and they did not offer the slightest resistance. None the less, the Government has played them false. In October, 1914, their leader, Nazaret Tchaoush, came to Marash with a "safe conduct" to arrange some special points with the officials. In spite of the "safe conduct" they imprisoned him, tortured him, and put him to death. Still the people of Zeitoun remained quiet. Bands of zaptiehs (Turkish gendarmes), quartered in the town, have been molesting the inhabitants, raiding shops, stealing, maltreating the people and dishonouring their women. *It is obvious that the Government are trying to get a case against the Zeitounlis, so as to be able to exterminate them at their pleasure and yet justify themselves in the eyes of the world* [emphasis added].[41]

This observation supports Morgenthau's assertion that the government provoked Armenians to self-defense and then made claims of Armenian "revolution." Andre Mandelstam comes to the same conclusion as Morgenthau and states:

Not withstanding the deceitful communications of the Turkish Government, there has been no Armenian revolution or revolt—not in the least. The Armenians took up arms only when they were threatened with massacre.[42]

Many Europeans who analyzed scores of documents and the testimony of European eyewitnesses to the genocide insist that the overwhelming majority of Armenians fulfilled every obligation of citizenship to the Ottoman government during the first months of the war. The Armenian Patriarchate, revolutionary organizations, and many other societies urged the Armenians to actively support the Ottoman cause.[43]

Turkish propaganda, however, continued unabated as the government accused Armenians of killing Turks and Kurds. An accurate account of what really happened may be gleaned from a statement made by El-Ghusein, a Moslem Bedouin, eyewitness to the genocide, who said that he saw Turks taking photographs of dead Armenians dressed in turbans. The photographs were to be dispatched to Constantinople. El-Ghusein comments:

The Turkish Government thought the European nations might get to hear of the destruction of the Armenians and publish the news abroad so as to excite prejudice against the Turks. So after the gendarmes had killed a number of Armenian men, they put on them turbans and brought Kurdish women to weep and lament over them, saying that the Armenians had killed their men. They also brought a photographer to photograph the bodies and the weeping women, so that at a future time they might be able to convince Europe that it was the Armenians who had attacked the Kurds and killed them, that the Kurdish tribes had risen against them in revenge, and that the Turkish Government had had no part in the matter.[44]

On 26 May 1915 Talaat presented the Grand Vizier Said Halim Pasha a document charging that Armenians were in league with the enemy, impeding movement of troops and provisions, plundering and killing the innocent population of Ottoman towns and cities, attacking military forces in the country, and so on. He claimed that for these reasons, *this kind of rebellious element should be removed from areas of military activity and "deported" to desert areas in the eastern part of the Syrian province.* Everyone was to be deported, with no distinction made between those innocent or guilty of "revolutionary" activity. Talaat insisted that any such distinction was "utterly impossible," because "those who were innocent today might be guilty tomorrow."[45]

The deportations were begun by Talaat without formal approval from the ministerial cabinet. However, Talaat, concerned with the international repercussions of such an act, presented the ministerial cabinet with a *fait accompli* and then demanded their approval. On 27 May a decree gave military authorization to eliminate civilians involved in treason or espionage and to collectively deport cities and towns that were "suspect." On 30 May a general decree for these deportations was published, creating special committees (to give a humanitarian appearance) to "protect" the lives and property of the deportees.[46]

The false impression given by the terms "resettlement" and "deportation," euphemisms for actual genocide, become clear if we consider the following abstract from the writings of a German nurse, published in October 1915 in *Sonnenaufgang*, an organ of the "German League for the Promotion of Christian Charitable Work in the East":

> They have marched them off in convoys into the desert on the pretext of settling them there. In the village of Tel-Armen (along the line of the Bagdad Railway, near Mosul) and in the neighbouring villages about 5,000 people were massacred, leaving only a few women and children. The people were thrown alive down wells or into the fire. *They pretend that the Armenians are to be employed in colonizing land* situated at a distance of from twenty-four to thirty kilometres from the Bagdad Railway. But as it is only the women and children who are sent into exile, since all the men, with the exception of the very old, are at the war, this means nothing less than the wholesale murder of the families, since they have neither the labour nor the capital for clearing the country [emphasis added].[47]

Thus "deportation" was just another name for mass murder, since there was no provision made for the "journey." Arnold Toynbee describes the pitiful condition of Armenians who were deported to Der-el-Zor in the Syrian desert:

> The malaria makes ravages among them, because of the complete lack of food and shelter. *How cruelly ironic to think that the Government pretends to be sending them there to found a colony: and they have no ploughs, no seeds to sow, no bread, no abodes; in fact they are sent with empty hands* [emphasis added].[48]

Gibbons observes that after Armenian men were murdered for "treachery," the government had to find a way to rid themselves of old people, women, and children. They could not claim treachery on the part of women and children, since that excuse would not be accepted abroad, so they came up with a plan which appeared to be a *military necessity*—"deportation."[49]

A German correspondent for the *Kolner Gazette*, Harry Stuermer, relates in his book, *Two War Years in Constantinople*, that the Turkish government welcomed any pretext for "falling like wild animals on the Armenians of the eastern *vilajets* [*sic*] . . . " on the grounds:

This was . . . "the restoration of order in the war zone by military measures, rendered necessary by the connivance of the inhabitants with the enemy, treachery and armed support. . . . "
    The Turkish. . . . aimed [to destroy] . . . the whole Armenian people, not only in Armenia itself, but also in the "Diaspora," in Anatolia Proper and in the capital. . . . In this case they could scarcely go on the principle of "evacuation of the war zone," for the inhabitants were hundreds of miles both from the Eastern front and from the Dardenelles, so they [the Turkish government] had to resort to other measures.
    They suddenly and miraculously discovered a universal conspiracy among the Armenians of the Empire. It was only by a trick of this kind that they could succeed in carrying out their system of exterminating the entire Armenian race. The Turkish Government skilfully influenced public opinion throughout the whole world, and then discovered, nay, arranged for, local conspiracies. They then falsified all the details so that they might go on for months in peace and quiet with their campaign of extermination.
    In a series of semi-official articles in the newspapers of the Committee of Young Turks it was made quite clear that *all* Armenians were dangerous conspirators who, in order to shake off the Ottoman yoke, had collected firearms and bombs and had arranged, with the help of English and Russian money, for a terrible slaughter of Turks on the day that the English fleet overcame the armies on the Dardenelles [emphasis added].[50]

It is important to note that the Turks to this day refer to the Armenian genocide as "deportation for military necessity." Had they really wished to relocate Armenians, the Young Turks would have welcomed help in expediting the matter, but Martin Niepage indicates in the following that deportation was not the true objective of the Young Turks:

The object of the deportations is the extermination of the whole Armenian nation. This purpose is . . . proved by the fact that the Turkish Government declines all assistance from Missionaries, Sisters of Mercy and European residents in the country, and systematically tries to stop their work. A Swiss engineer was to have been brought before a court-martial because he had distributed bread in Anatolia to the starving Armenian women and children in a convoy of exiles. The Government has not hesitated even to deport Armenian pupils and teachers from the German schools at Adana and Aleppo, and Armenian children from the German orphanages, without regard to all the efforts of the Consuls and the heads of the institutions involved. The *Government also rejected the American Government's offer to take the exiles to America on American ships and at America's expense* [emphasis added].[51]

At first, the Sublime Porte refuted allegations of atrocities against Armenians through official communiques, even going so far as to assert the loyalty of the empire's Armenians. But as public indignation rose abroad, the Porte blamed Armenian "treachery" for the state's measures against them. The government did not even note that the former declarations were glaringly contradicted by the latter.[52]

In Geneva during the height of the genocide the Turkish consul general made a declaration to the press on 27 August 1915. He claimed that Armenian men, women, and children were fully protected and secure in the hands of Turkish authorities. On 14 October 1915 Dr. Rifat, a member of the Young Turk Committee in an interview with a representative of the Danish newspaper *Extrabladet*, claimed that Turkish Armenians were involved in a *conspiracy* threatening Turkey's existence by plotting Constantinople's fall into the hands of the Allies.[53]

As repressive measures continued, Talaat received telegrams from his officials in the provinces claiming that Armenian uprisings had been put down everywhere. Such telegraph correspondence was conveyed to neutral diplomats and newspaper men at Constantinople as "proof" of the imminent Armenian danger. Talaat declared to neutrals that this was wartime and that the government was being severe but not cruel.[54]

To justify arrests of prominent Armenians in the country's capitol, the official organ of the *Ittihad*, the *Tanin*, prepared the vast Armenian plot story. It asserted that there was a conspiracy by liberal *Hunchaks*. Well before the war a number of Egyptian revolutionaries had been arrested at Constantinople and placed in prison. Afterwards they and Armenians thought to be *Hunchak* party members were publicly hanged in the square in Hayazet before the war minister. On 17 June there were seventeen hangings, twenty more on 18 June and more on 20 June. The Turks desperately wished to prove to the public that the Armenians were conspiring in very sinister events.[55]

A perfect example of the propaganda used by the Turkish government *before* the genocide to incite the masses to genocide is still used *today* by them to rationalize their actions. Yet the words of the Young Turks themselves convict them of their crime, and no amount of denial of the Armenian genocide can erase the truth presented by American Ambassador Morgenthau and many other statesmen and eyewitnesses. After the loss of the war, Talaat still promoted the same propaganda against the Armenians as he had in the past, claiming "deportation" of many Armenians for treason. Talaat explains in his *Memoirs*:

I admit that we deported many Armenians from our eastern provinces but we never acted in this matter upon a previously prepared scheme. The responsibility for these acts falls first of all upon the deported people themselves. Russia, in order to lay hand on our eastern provinces, had armed and equipped the

Armenian inhabitants of this district, and had organized strong Armenian bandit forces in the said area.[56]

Djemal himself verifies that *all* Armenians were deported, not just those who might pose a threat in military areas when saying that, "it was through the Government Proclamation to the vilayets that I first learned that *all* [emphasis added] Armenians were provisionally to be deported to Mesopotamia [barren deserts], where they were to remain until the end of the War."[57] Of course, they did not return.

Djemal Pasha, in the following statement from his *Memories of a Turkish Statesman* again states that *all* Armenians were deported:

I am certainly firmly convinced that the Armenians planned insurrections which endangered the rear of our Army in the Caucasus and which might under certain circumstances have completely destroyed it. *Consequently my friends held it more expedient to transfer the whole Armenian nation to another region where they could do no harm,* than to expose the whole Ottoman Empire to a catastrophe which would have involved Russian occupation of the whole of Asia Minor [emphasis added].[58]

This from a man who claimed to have no knowledge of the genocide.

Ambassador Morgenthau had frequently discussed the deportations with high ranking Turkish officials. He concludes:

. . . the Turks never had the slightest idea of reestablishing the Armenians in this new country [the Syrian deserts]. They knew that the great majority would never reach their destination and those that did would either die of thirst and starvation, or be murdered by the wild Mohammedan desert tribes. The real purpose of the deportation was robbery and destruction; it really represented a new method of massacre. *When the Turkish authorities gave the orders for these deportations, they were merely giving the death warrant to a whole race; they understood this well, and, in their conversations with me, they made no particular attempt to conceal the fact* [emphasis added].[59]

On 19 October 1918, after Turkey's loss of World War I, a speech was made by Turkey's new Prime Minister Damad Ferid Pasha in which he blamed the leaders of the Young Turks for the Armenian genocide. Damad Ferit's assertion that the government expelled Armenians into the deserts of Arabia on claims that it was necessary for military, strategic considerations could not be upheld under critical scrutiny.[60]

However, Turkey today denies the genocide of the Armenians, even though Damad Ferid Pasha, as Chaliand and Ternon indicate, "officially recognized" the atrocities against the Armenians and blamed the Committee of Union Progress for committing them. When presenting Turkey's case in Paris on 11 June 1919 at the Paris Peace Conference, Damad Ferid Pasha said:

... Turkey deplores the murder of a great number of her Christian co-nationals. . . .

Latterly, the truth has begun to filter through into European public opinion. The *great trial of the Unionists at Constantinople* has proved *the responsibility of the leaders of the Committee—who all of them occupy high positions in the State—for the war and the other tragic events* [emphasis added].[61]

AND I looked, and behold a pale horse: and his name was Death, and Hell followed with him. And Power was given unto them over the fourth part of the earth, to kill with sword, and with hunger, and with death, and with the beasts of the earth.

—REVELATION 6:8

5

ORGANIZATION OF DESTRUCTION

THE SYSTEM OF EXTERMINATION

IN HIS WORK, *Armenia: The Cradle of Civilization*, David Marshall Lang asserts the Young Turks had planned the Armenian genocide before the outbreak of World War I. He supports his contention with the fact that the deportation of Armenians in the spring of 1915 was *quickly* executed upon a signal from the government. Arnold Toynbee provides evidence indicating early planning of the genocide in testimonies from the American Committee Report confirming that in many areas of Turkey *muhajirs* took possession of Armenian homes as soon as they were evacuated. Moreover, the number of *muhajirs* replacing the Armenians in any area was the same as the number of Armenians being deported; the *muhajirs* were also in the right place at the right time and ready to move in on a moment's notice. Toynbee views such facts as "damning pieces of evidence" against the Young Turks, proving incontrovertibly that the genocide was deliberate and well organized.[1]

These *muhajirs* had been run out of Balkan countries after the Balkan War and wreaked their vengeance on the Armenians. Dr. Mabel Elliot, American Medical Director of Near East Relief during World War I, comments, " . . . all the passions and policies and hatreds of millions of human beings were turned loose, unrestrained."[2]

A decree dated 27 May 1915 authorized the military to dispose of civilians *suspected* of treason and espionage by collectively deporting them from cities and towns. A few days later on 31 May Enver told German Ambassador Wangenheim that the "counterrevolutionary" movement against Armenians would be intensified in the following ways: the Armenian press and Armenian schools would be closed; Armenians would get no mail delivery; and *suspicious* families would be sent to Mesopotamia—away from centers of insurrection.[3]

The deportations began in April 1915, although other sporadic massacres had taken place over the preceding months. The whole Armenian population of every Armenian village and town was systematically stripped of any weapons and possessions and driven into the streets.[4]

For some there was immediate death, for others the suffering was worse than death. Dr. Lepsius of the German Orient Mission described the deportations as brutal, orders for the evacuation frequently being given only an hour before its start, thus making it impossible for families to unite with their members, so that children had to be abandoned. Those children left behind were taken by Turks and converted to Islam by force.[5]

A unique feature of the Armenian genocide is that it was carried out not only by the central government, the military, the police, and hired criminals, but by "ordinary" men and women. Viscount Bryce indicates that ordinary peasants murdered Armenians with clubs, axes, hammers, saws, spades, and scythes.[6]

Arnold Toynbee claims "the crime was concerted very systematically, for there is evidence of identical procedure from over fifty places."[7] The following typifies the basic pattern:

1. *Killing of Able-bodied Men.* Initially, the public crier of a given locale or an official proclamation posted in public would order all Armenian able-bodied men to go to the government building ("*konak*"). The proclamation ordered deportations and provided justification for such, while assuring Armenians of government benevolence. Upon arrival at the *konak*, men were imprisoned for a few days without explanation, after which they were marched out of town and bayoneted or shot at the first secluded spot. All men old enough to father children were killed outright to eliminate the possibility of a new generation of Armenians.[8]

Occasionally there was a loophole of safety for Armenians—conversion. Most often, however, this was either not permitted or the conditions associated with it were intolerable. For example, in a town in Anatolia, conversion was permitted if one surrendered one's children under twelve to the government to be raised in unknown Moslem "orphanages," which were really *dervish* (nomadic Moslem devotees) convents.[9]

2. *Destruction of Women, Children, and Elderly.* Women, children, and old men, following the destruction of the young men, were granted a grace period of a few days and then notified by public crier or by official proclamation that they were to be deported immediately. The government's line of reasoning was as follows: men were a threat and should be killed immediately, since a leader might emerge from their ranks and defy the deportation order. But valuable lead need not be wasted on women, children, or old men who could simply languish and die of hunger, thirst, exhaustion, or exposure to the elements in the desert during forced deportation.[10]

Police and military guards accompanied convoys of Armenians exiled to the deserts. The guards were often brutal men released from prison (*"chetehs"*) for the express purpose of assisting with the deportations. Armenians were subject to beatings and cruel abuse. Some of the women were not killed, but seized by Turkish and civilian officials and consigned to harems. Some others chose to embrace the faith of Islam in order to avoid the fate of their fellow Armenians.[11]

Morgenthau relates how Turkish gendarmes would notify the Kurdish tribes that Armenian victims were approaching, telling Kurds that the opportunity to destroy the Armenians had finally arrived.

Detachments of gendarmes would go ahead, notifying the Kurdish tribes that their victims were approaching, and Turkish peasants were also informed that their long-waited opportunity had arrived. The Government even opened the prisons and set free the convicts. . . . Thus every caravan had a continuous battle for existence with several classes of enemies—their accompanying gendarmes, the Turkish peasants, and villagers, the Kurdish tribes and bands of *Chetes* or brigands. . . . The [Armenian] men who might have defended these wayfarers had nearly all been killed or forced into the army as workmen, and . . . the exiles themselves had been systematically deprived of all weapons before the journey began.[12]

Accompanied by gendarmes, convoy after convoy (of mostly women and children) was marched along without food or water. Soldiers, guards, and local populations (encouraged to take part in the genocide by the government) saw Armenians as serving two purposes—gold and rape. Money was generally stolen from Armenians at the very beginning of forced marches. Attractive females were either snatched away and forced into Turkish homes or were raped and beheaded on the spot.[13]

Dr. Mabel Elliot considers the following story to be typical of many of those relayed to her by young Armenian girls who had survived the genocide:

> I was twelve years old. I was with my mother. . . . It was very hot and many of us died because there was no water. They drove us with whips . . . to the Arabian desert. My sisters and the little baby died on the way. We went through a town. . . . The streets were full of dead—all cut to pieces. There were heads and arms and legs and blood. . . .
>
> . . . We came to a place on the desert, a hollow place in the sand, with hills all around it. There were thousands of us there, many, many thousands all women and girl-children. They herded us like sheep into the hollow. Then it was dark, and we heard firing all around us. . . . We thought they had got tired of driving us. All night we waited for them—my mother and I—we waited for them to reach us. But they did not come, and in the morning when we looked around, no one was killed. . . .
>
> They had not been killing us. They had been signalling to the wild tribes that we were there. The Kurds came later in the morning, . . . and many other kinds of men from the desert. They came over the hills and rode down and began killing us. All day long they were killing; you see there were so many of us. All that they did not think they could sell, they killed. They kept on killing all night, and in the morning—in the morning they killed my mother.

Mabel Elliot felt that the stories many severely mutilated Armenian women told her about the deportations " . . . were like revelations of the mind of a madman."[14]

Dr. Lepsius reports there was a regular trade all over Turkey in Armenian women, girls, and even children. Toynbee confirms Lepsius's contention and relates the following confirmation of that trade:

> One Moslem reported that a gendarme had offered to sell him two girls for a medjidieh (about three shillings and twopence). They sold the youngest and most handsome at every village where they passed the night; and these girls have been trafficked in hundreds through the brothels of the Ottoman Empire. Abundant news has come from Constantinople itself of their being sold for a few shillings in the open markets of the capital; and one piece of evidence in Lord Bryce's possession comes from a girl no more than ten years old, who was carried with this object from a town of North Eastern Anatolia to the shores of the Bosphorus.[15]

The Bryce report states that when women were carried away during the deportations, " . . . their babies were left on the ground or dashed against the stones."[16]

The *Ittihad* unrelentlessly pursued the destruction of the Armenian people. If they survived the death marches, they would most likely be killed at Aleppo. In the spring of 1915 Midhat Shukru, general director for deportations, departed Constantinople and went to Aleppo to organize the transportation of the remaining survivors of deportations to the barren deserts. The former vali of Bitlis, Mustafa Abdulhalik, now prefect of Aleppo, supported the deportations. Abdullahad Nuri, the assistant director of deportations, and Ayub Sabri, who was Abdulhalik's second in command, both assisted Abdulhalik.

The intentions of the *Ittihad* are clarified in the following official correspondence sent to functionaries at Aleppo by Talaat on 15 September 1915:

To the Police Headquarters at Aleppo: It has already been communicated on the orders of the Cemiet [*Djemieti*], that the government has decided to exterminate entirely all Armenians in Turkey. Those who would oppose this order and decision cannot be a part of the government. Without regard for women, children, and the infirm, however tragic may be the methods, without listening to conscience, one must put an end to their existence.[17]

Talaat assured civil servants who hesitated to murder Armenians because of their scruples or fear of punishment that they would be granted immunity:

For excesses committed along the way against the people in question by the population, which is serving to realize the government objectives, there will be no legal repercussions (3 October 1915).[18]

In November 1915 Talaat ordered that all Armenians in the eastern provinces be destroyed "by secret methods." In January 1916 he repeated that order.[19] Talaat Pasha ordered (1) that Armenian children be taken from the "Turkish orphanages" in which they had been placed and killed and (2) that Armenian women who had been forced into marriage with Turks be deported to the desert. Later, he was to order that Armenian children who were adopted and Turkified by Turkish families be killed also. By late 1915 Talaat wished to complete the extermination of many Armenian survivors at Aleppo. Consequently, he issued a series of directives for their destruction at concentration camps.[20]

Deportations

Zeitun

At Zeitun mass deportations began on 10 April 1915. Armenians were charged with treason or rebellion and exiled from every corner of Anatolia. This despite the comment of a Swiss eyewitness to the genocide in his diary on 14 March 1915 that, "the Armenians have no wish to revolt and are prepared to put up with anything the government may do." The eyewitness further states that the Turks committed innumerable atrocities against the people of Zeitun, and when Armenians fought to defend themselves, the Turks claimed that Armenians were aggressing against Turks. Thus, the government would be "able to exterminate them at their pleasure and yet justify themselves in the eyes of the world."[21]

The exile was carried out by Turkish General Fakhri Pasha who arrived in Zeitun with 3,000 soldiers and two officers in late March 1915. In Zeitun Armenians had paid taxes and claimed their legal right to military exemption. Nonetheless, Fakhri Pasha demanded immediate Armenian enrollment into the army. Some 40 or 50 men succumbed to coercion and enrolled, but they were soon jailed by the Turks. In retaliation, approximately 25 Armenian men launched an offensive against Turkish troops occupying their town, and a twenty-four hour battle ensued, resulting in 301 Turkish casualties. After this setback, the Turks captured an Armenian monastery and burned it to the ground. Then deportations began, and ·Zeitun was swiftly emptied of Armenians. Thereafter, the inhabitants of other Cilician towns, such as Furnus, Albistan, and Geben were also deported.[22] The Armenians were replaced by Turkish *muhajirs* by the latter part of May.

Between 6,000 and 8,000 of the exiled Armenians were first sent to the Konya district. Survivors of Konya were sent to Der-el-Zor in the Syrian desert. Between 15,000 and 16,000 people had been sent directly to Der-el-Zor,[23] the final destination for many exiled Armenians. Conditions at Der-el-Zor were so atrocious that Armenians beseeched the Turks to send them back to the swampy, uninhabited, malaria-laden areas of Konya, but they were denied this request. Toynbee charges there was "nothing but death in the swamps."[24]

Deportations from Marash, a large city in the valley below Zeitun were next. On 19 August after weapons searches a few days before, the death march began.[25]

Van and Djevdet Bey

Enver Pasha's brother-in-law, Djevdet Bey, assumed the governorship of Van in February 1915. He is described as "unpredictable," "barbarous," and given to extreme brutality.

Under the pretext of searching for weapons, Djevdet began a reign of terror in various villages of Van province. Armenian leaders in the city endured his abuses, but when Djevdet insisted that 4,000 Armenian recruits be made ready for the Ottoman army, his demand was refused, and he was offered 400 instead. Djevdet refused to recognize legal exemption and demanded more men.

During weapons searches in Van, gendarmes were uncontrolled in their abuse of Armenians, murdering whomever they chose. In self-defense and retaliation, the Armenians attacked a Turkish patrol at a nearby village; this drove Djevdet into a fury. The Armenians, though distraught, still refused to acquiesce to Djevdet's demand for 4,000 men, realizing that men taken into the military would most assuredly be murdered by the government.

Despite being poorly armed, the Armenians of Van attempted to protect their 30,000 population and quarters and, in the process, inflicted severe damage upon Turkish strongholds. Their weaponry consisted of 300 rifles and approximately 1,000 outdated weapons and pistols.

On 19 April all Armenian villages over which Djevdet had jurisdiction were attacked by Turkish soldiers. The total male population· of Akantz (northeast of Van), numbering 2,500, was murdered. Morgenthau states that in 80 villages in the environs north of Van, 24,000 Armenians were killed in only three days. At sunset all men in the villages were shot. Dr. Clarence Ussher, a missionary and representative of the United States in Van, said that there was absolute proof that 55,000 Armenians were killed at villages in close proximity to Van.[26]

On 20 April Turkish soldiers attacked some Armenian village women who were walking to Van, but one escaped. When two Armenian soldiers approached the Turks demanding an explanation, they were shot. Morgenthau says that the women were raped and killed in order to force the Armenians to action, thus providing the Turks with a legitimate justification to lay siege to Van. After five weeks of fighting, Russian soldiers appeared, and the Turks fled to nearby villages, "where they found appeasement for their anger by further massacres of unprotected Armenian villages."[27]

Christopher Walker states that the five-week-long battle of Armenians with the Turks was legitimate self-defense–not rebellion. It was a response to Djevdet Bey's terrorism of the entire Armenian community.

Because the advance guard of the Russian soldiers entering Van on 17 May 1915 were Armenian volunteers, Van temporarily came under Armenian control. However, six weeks after their arrival, the Russians retreated, accompanied by many Armenians who preferred to make the perilous and agonizing journey back to Transcaucasia with the Russians than stay in Van.[28]

Constantinople

The most tragic month in Armenian history was April 1915, when in almost one single blow the Young Turks eliminated the Armenian intellectuals and elite of Constantinople on charges of collaboration with Van "revolutionaries." Ternon states that the charges were false, since such a collaboration was geographically impossible.[29]

Constantinople, which had long been the Armenian cultural center, was the scene of the arrests of 235 leading Armenian writers, educators, politicians, lawyers, and other Armenian intelligentsia by Turkish police on the night and early morning of 23 and 24 April 1915.[30] For three days arrested men were kept at the central police station from whence they were later exiled to the Turkish interior—half to Chankiri, the remainder to Ayash. Renewed arrests raised the number of men deported to 600. Almost all were slaughtered in the wilds of Anatolia. Simultaneously, the police in Constantinople had arrested roughly 5,000 poor young Armenian men from the provinces who were employed in Constantinople as laborers, messengers, and doorkeepers. Like their predecessors, they were taken into the interior and killed.

Such treatment was totally unexpected by the Armenians of the capital, since they were loyal to the regime. Some like Krikor Zohrab (the Armenian Deputy for Rodosto) were actually personal friends of prominent Young Turk leaders. Zohrab had provided shelter for Talaat during the April 1909 counterrevolution against the Young Turks. In spite of this, Krikor, along with Vartkes, his fellow deputy, were forced into the interior where they were bludgeoned to death with other Armenians.[31]

Fa'iz El-Ghusein reports:

[The Union Party] . . . sent Zohrab and his colleague Vartakis [sic] away from Constantinople, with orders that they should be killed on the way, and it was announced that they had been murdered by a band of brigands. . . .

It is said that the Unionists ordered that all the Armenian Deputies should be put to death, and the greater number of them were thus dealt with. . . . Dikran Ghilighian, the well-known writer, who was an adherent of the Committee of Union and Progress, was killed in return for his learning, capacity, and devotion in their cause. Such was the recompense of his services to the Unionists.[32]

Talaat did not deny that he ordered the arrests and mass murders of prominent Armenian leaders of Constantinople on 23 and 24 April.

Djevdet in Bitlis

After Djevdet's lack of success at Van, he began calling his killing battalions *kesab taburi* ("butcher battalions"). The defeat at Van resulted in Djevdet's retreat west and south, followed by an attack on Sairt, where he murdered much of the Armenian and Assyrian populations. Next, he went to the town of Bitlis and was supplied with 10,000 reinforcements from Erzerum. By 25 June Bitlis was surrounded by Turkish troops, and nearly all Armenian men were arrested and killed. Women and children, following the usual pattern, were distributed to Turks and Kurds like chattel. Other "useless ones" who were still alive were deported south to their death. Djevdet had proven himself more brutal at Bitlis than he had been at Van. (Note the deployment of vast numbers of troops—in this case 10,000—by the Turkish government for extermination purposes, even though this necessitated the diverting of troops from the war effort.) Limon Von Sanders, German Commander in Syria said, "the collapse of the Turkish Palestinian front was due to the fact that the Turks, against my orders and advice sent all their valuable forces to the Caucasus and Azerbaijan where they fought the Armenians."[33]

El-Ghusein reports the following eyewitness account:

. . . in the Vilayet of Bitlis the authorities collected the Armenians in barns full of straw (or chaff), piling up straw in front of the door and setting it on fire, so that the Armenians inside perished in the smoke. He [the eyewitness] said that sometimes hundreds were put together in one barn. . . . He told me, to my deep sorrow, how he had seen a girl hold her lover in her embrace and so enter the barn to meet her death without a tremor.[34]

An estimated 15,000 were killed during the siege, massacres, and deportation at Bitlis. As in the Hamidian days, great care was taken to destroy not only the town dwellers but the Armenian peasantry as well. All picturesque villages surrounding Bitlis, such as Rahva and Khultig, were systematically destroyed.

Moush and Sassoun

The villages on the Moush plain were attacked and destroyed by Turks before the town of Moush itself was overrun. The villages on the Moush plains, the Bulanik district (northeast of Moush), and the town of Sassoun came under attack in late May. The Turks and Kurdish irregulars, however, proved to be no match for the Armenians in any of these areas. Thus a truce was affected by the end of May. A few weeks of calm ensued, but by the end of June a forceful Turkish assault overwhelmed the entire region—Moush, Sassoun, and Bitlis. Additional Turkish troops from Erzeroum came with mountain guns. Armenians of the villages and towns were subjected to frightful tortures—limbs twisted, noses beaten down, teeth knocked out, and finger nails pulled out. Daughters and wives were publicly raped before their fathers and husbands.

In July Turkish military efforts were directed against Moush. Guns and infantry were brought from the city of Moush, and the Kurds reorganized and invaded from the north, west, and south. Plains Armenians faced starvation, and thousands of them fled to Mount Andok, where they had found refuge during attacks in the past. Their ammunition was quickly depleted, but they continued to struggle with scythes, knives, and stones. On 5 August 1915 the Turks captured the mountain and exterminated almost all of the Armenians.

On 10 July Armenian men from the approximately 100 villages around Moush were rounded up for extermination by the *Teshkilat-i-Makhsusiye*, which included Turkish prisoners expressly released from jails to help expedite extermination. Though villagers offered resistance, they were eventually overcome by the *Teshkilat* forces who drove them into concentration camps and then bayoneted them to death.

The women and children of Moush were driven out of the city into large wooden sheds (constructed solely for extermination) at nearby Armenian villages and burned to death "amid scenes of horror, and the vilest, most sadistic brutality from the Turkish guards." Before the decimation of the Armenian people at Moush, 60,000 Armenians had inhabited the town and its surrounding villages. Very few survived.[35]

El-Ghusein reports:

At Moush, a part were killed in straw-barns, but the greater number by shooting or stabbing with knives, the Government hiring butchers, who received a Turkish pound each day as wages.[36]

Erzindjan

Armenians were deported from Erzindjan in April 1915, following a several-day grace period granted them to sell their property at ludicrously low prices. They were told by authorities that no one being deported would be harmed, and, to assure this, Armenians would be given safe escort to their new destination by the Turkish military. In early June the first convoy of forced exiles departed from Erzindjan. Wealthy people had retained carriages for their journey. Deportations continued for three full days. Many Armenian children were spared the death marches by being given to Moslem families. Later, however, authorities would decide to eliminate reprieves for children and exile them also.

On 11 June regular troops from the Eighty-sixth Cavalry Brigade had been sent out to meet the convoys on the pretext of keeping "the Kurds in order."[37] The deportees were attacked early in their journey, and their clothes were stripped from them. Upon their arrival at Kemakh Gorge, some Armenians were bayoneted to death. Most, however, had their hands tied behind them and were thrown into a ravine where the Euphrates flows between two rock walls. This method of extermination was quick and expedient, as large numbers of people—20,000 to 25,000—had to be eliminated. Roughly half of the Armenian population of Erzindjan were murdered at Kemakh Gorge by 14 June.[38]

Hassan Tahsin and Erzerum

In 1915 both Baiburt and the city of Erzeroum were in the province of Erzeroum. A young Pan-Turanist, Hassan Tahsin, was governor there. He had formerly been governor of Van previous to Djevdet's appointment.

In early spring Armenians of Erzeroum were victimized by the tortuous arms searches occurring elsewhere. At a public meeting on 18 April, Armenians were branded as enemies and "traitors" to the empire, and Moslems were ordered not to shield Armenian friends or be punished themselves.

Erzeroum was serving as a convergence point for various convoys of exiles from other regions. Armenian refugees deported from Melazker and Pasin arrived in Erzeroum in late May. Half-starved and totally exhausted, they were kept on the outskirts of the city for seven days in the rain, after which they were sent to Kemakh Gorge. Another convoy of peasant Armenians, primarily women and children, arrived in Erzeroum from the plains villages on 4 June and departed westward to Kemakh Gorge, where bands of irregulars shot the remnants of the convoy.

Forty families were deported from the city of Erzeroum on 16 June. Their destination was Diyarbekir, via Keghi and Palu. Almost all were killed between the two latter towns. On 19 June approximately 10,000 Armenians departed for Baiburt. The people of Baiburt, northeast of Erzindjan, were exiled from their homes in three convoys totaling 17,000 people. They were deported by forced marches to Erzindjan and Kemakh Gorge and exterminated. On their way to Erzindjan, Tahsin, the governor, "checked their security." They were then diverted to Kemakh Gorge, rather than being sent to Sivas, supposedly their ultimate destination. Men were killed. Women and children were sent to remote burning desert locations of the empire; some were sent east, some to Mosul, some south to Raqqa, and others went to Aintab and Aleppo.[39]

A *New York Times* article of 9 March 1916 reports that the Russians, upon entering Erzeroum, found sixteen Armenians alive. They were all that remained out of the "usual Armenian population of 40,000."[40]

Shabin Karahisar

June 1915 reflected another bleak month in the plight of Armenians in Turkey. In contrast to Zeitun and Sassoun, Armenians of Shabin Karahisar, the birthplace of the famous Armenian hero General Andranik, had not defied Ottoman misgovernment. However, in June 1915 Armenians took to nearby hills, since they knew the government's intention of exterminating them. From 2 to 30 June they fought in self-defense but were eventually overwhelmed and exterminated to the last man. Garo Pasdermadjian reports:

At Shabin-Karahissar, nearly 5,000 Armenians, for twenty-seven days without interruption, in the same month of July, kept busy another division of Turkish troops with their artillery. There took place one of the most tragic and heroic episodes of the present war. When the ammunition of the Armenians was almost gone, on the last day of the struggle, nearly 3,000 Armenian women and girls drank poison and died in order not to fall alive into the hands of the savage Turks. If the supply of poison had not given out, all the women would have done likewise. An eye-witness, . . . related how on that last day Armenian mothers and girls, with tears in their eyes and with hymns on their lips, received poison from the Armenian physicians and apothecaries for themselves and their little ones. When the supply of poison gave out, those who were unable to obtain any uttered terrible wailing, and many of the girls cast themselves down from the rocks of the Karahissar citadel and committed suicide.[41]

Trebizond

Early in June the province of Trebizond housed 53,000 Armenians. In late June a proclamation was posted on the streets ordering deportation of Armenians. Signor Gorrini, the Italian counsel in Trebizond, notes:

The official proclamation of internment came from Constantinople. It was the work of the central government and the "Committee of Union and Progress." The local authorities and indeed the Muslim population in general, tried to resist, to mitigate it, to make omissions, to hush it up. But the orders of the central government were categorically confirmed, and all were compelled to resign themselves and obey.

The consular body intervened, and attempted to save at least the women and children. We did, in fact, secure numerous exemptions, but these were not subsequently respected, owing to the interference of the local branch of the "Union and Progress Committee" and to fresh orders from Constantinople.[42]

Toynbee reports that "great crowds" from the city of Trebizond were driven to the edge of the Black Sea, put on boats, taken some distance from shore, and thrown overboard.[43] Other Armenians from Trebizond were killed during forced marches.

Deportations peaked during the last week of June and the first week of July. By 7 July Armenian homes were virtually empty. Everyone had been expelled, including the sick, old, and Catholic Armenians (constituting a substantial proportion of Trebizond's Armenians). Many were driven southward, along the Deyirmeni River of Trebizond toward Gumush-khana, but few made it beyond the village of Djvizlik, only six hours away. The Macedonian caretaker of the local branch of the Ottoman Bank reported that the Yel-Deyirmeni River swept a number of mutilated—the women with their breasts cut off—and absolutely naked corpses out to sea every day.[44]

Italian Consul Gorrini places the estimate of Armenians in the city of Trebizond at 17,000 before the genocide, but he reports that by 23 July 1915 there were barely 100 left. Gorrini states that for "one appalling month" he watched.

The passing of gangs of Armenian exiles beneath the windows and before the door of the consulate; their prayers for help, when neither I nor any other could do anything to answer them; the city in a state of siege, guarded at every point by 15,000 troops in complete war equipment, by thousands of police agents, by bands of volunteers and by members of the "Committee of Union and Progress"; the lamentations, the tears, the abandonments, the imprecations, the many suicides, the instantaneous deaths from sheer terror, the sudden unhingeing of men's reason, the conflagrations, the shooting of victims in the city, the ruthless searches through the houses and in the countryside; the hundreds of corpses found every day along the exile road; the young women converted by force to Islam or exiled like the rest; the children torn away from their families or from the Christian schools, and handed over by force to Muslim families, or else placed by hundreds on board ship in nothing but their shirts, and then capsized and drowned in the Black Sea and the river Deyirmen Dere—these are my last ineffaceable memories of Trebizond, memories which still, at a month's distance, torment my soul and almost drive me frantic.[45]

Kharput

By the time deportations began at Kharput on 1 July 1915 the city had already been converted into a center of genocidal activities, since it served as a point of aggregation for convoys of deportees from other provinces. American Consul, Leslie A. Davis, an eyewitness to the genocide, wrote from Kharput on 1 July 1915:

As one walks through the camp [of refugees from Erzeroum and Erzingan numbering several thousand], mothers offer their children and beg one to take them. In fact, the Turks have been taking their choice of these children and girls for slaves, or worse. . . . They have even had their doctors there to examine the more likely girls and thus secure the best ones.[46]

Kharput, an Armenian intellectual center—south of Trebizond, far from any border, and far inland—was home to Euphrates College, a progressive and distinguished educational institution started by American missionaries in the late nineteenth century. Nonetheless, Kharput experienced the common pattern of savage weapons searches, arbitrary arrests, brutalization, and photographing of confiscated weapons as proof of revolution. After 13,000 Armenian Ottoman soldiers stationed at Kharput were murdered, the deportations began.[47]

Morgenthau reports that the first 2,000 of these soldiers were deported on 1 July. Rumor had it that they were being sent to build roads, but less than a day's walk away from Kharput, almost all were killed in a mountain pass. The following day, 2,000 more were deported toward Diyarbekir. Morgenthau relates that "even the wives of the Kurds came with their knives and murdered the Armenians."[48] Morgenthau confirms the active role played by women in the genocidal effort through records of the American State Department from which he learned:

Early in July, 2,000 Armenian "ameles"—such is the Turkish word for soldiers who have been reduced to workmen—were sent from Harpoot to build roads. . . . practically every man of these 2,000 was massacred, and his body thrown into a cave. . . . A few days afterward another 2,000 soldiers were sent to Diarbekir. . . . Government agents went ahead on the road, notifying the Kurds that the caravan was approaching and ordering them to do their congenial duty. Not only did the Kurdish tribesmen pour down from the mountains upon this starved and weakened regiment, but the Kurdish women came with butcher's knives in order that they might gain that merit in Allah's eyes that comes from killing a Christian. . . . Throughout the Turkish Empire a systematic attempt was made to kill all able-bodied men, not only for the purpose of removing all males who might propagate a new generation of Armenians, but for the purpose of rendering the weaker part of the population an easy prey.[49]

The first convoy exiled from Kharput contained four Armenian professors from Euphrates College. Professor Ernest W. Riggs, principal of the college, reported on 19 July 1915 the fate of some of the Armenian faculty: (1) Professor Tenekedjian—thirty-five years at the college, professor of Turkish and History, arrested and murdered; (2) Professor Nahigian—thirty years at the college, studied at Ann Arbor, professor of Mathematics, murdered; (3) Professor Vorperian—exiled with his family and murdered; (4) Professor Boudjikanian—employed at the college for sixteen years, studied at Edinburgh, professor of Mental and Moral Science, murdered.[50]

A grim and vivid account of the expulsions of Armenians from Kharput was documented by an American consul to Ambassador Morgenthau in Constantinople. He saw a convoy of 3,000 leave Kharput; it consisted of women, young girls, and children, accompanied by seventy gendarmes. After three days, men from mountain tribes descended upon the Armenians, robbing, killing, and carrying off pretty women. The "protective" gendarmes actually encouraged the activities of the tribesmen and then deserted the deportees at Malatia after having stolen everyone's money. Next, the local Kurdish bey had possession of the convoy.

One hundred and fifty of the men between the ages of fifteen and ninety were rounded up and slaughtered two days later. Meanwhile, the new Kurdish "protectors" engaged in further robbery. This caravan was eventually joined by another convoy of sufferers from Sivas. Together they continued—18,000 people in all, subjected to girl-snatching, robbery, violence, and murder. At the Murad River (eastern Euphrates) forty days after their departure, the bodies of at least 200 men were seen floating in the river, their blood-drenched clothes still on the banks. Twelve days later, almost demented from suffering, the caravan of exiles reached another village,

and here the Kurds took from them everything they had, even their shirts and drawers, so that for five days the whole convoy marched completely naked under the scorching sun. For another five days they did not have a morsel of bread, nor even a drop of water. They were scorched to death by thirst. Hundreds upon hundreds fell dead on the way, their tongues were turned to charcoal, and when, at the end of the five days they reached a fountain, the whole convoy naturally rushed towards it. But here a policeman barred the way and forbade them to take a single drop of water. Their purpose was to sell it at from £T1 to £T3 [sic] the cup, and sometimes they actually withheld the water after getting the money. . . .

When they passed an Arab village in their naked condition, the Arabs pitied them and gave them pieces of old clothes to cover themselves with. Some of the exiles who still had money bought some clothes; but some still remained who travelled thus naked all the way to the city of Aleppo. The poor women could hardly walk for shame; they walked all bent double.[51]

When this convoy reached Viranshehir only twelve days later, a mere 300 of the 18,000 were still alive. All the men, children, and sick women were rounded up and burned to death four days later. Stragglers were ordered to continue. Ten days later at Aleppo, 150 women and children were all that remained of the two convoys.[52]

Kaisaria

In a letter dated 12 July 1915 from Aneurin Williams, published in the *New York Times* on 18 August 1915, it was revealed that court martials had taken place in Kaisaria (Turkish: Kayseri) during which 12 Armenians were hanged and many were clubbed to death. A letter in the *New York Times* to the American Armenia Relief Fund Committee describes how Armenians from Kaisaria were marched, along with Armenians from Erzerum, Trebizond, Sivas, Kharput, Bitlis, Van, Diyarbekir, Samsun, and Urfa, to their deaths. The letter reports:

> We now know with certainty . . . that the Armenians have been deported in a body from all the towns and villages in Cilicia to the desert regions south of Aleppo. The refugees will have to traverse on foot a distance, requiring marches of from one to two or even more months.
>
> We learn, besides, that the roads and the Euphrates are strewn with corpses of exiles, and those who survive are doomed to certain death, since they will find neither house, work, nor food in the desert. It is a plan to exterminate the whole Armenian people.[53]

Viscount Bryce reports that by the end of July, many Armenians from Kaisaria had been deported by government order. Regarding Armenians at Talas and Kaisaria, the order reads: " . . . All the Armenians are to leave in batches of 1,000—the men, separated from the women, in one direction and the women in another."[54]

Many doctors and notables of Kaisaria were hung before the deportations, and their relatives were compelled to take the corpses down from the gallows. The Turkish governor of Kaisaria had said: "I will not leave here so much as the odo   of the Armenians; go away into the deserts of Arabia and dump your Armenia there."[55]

Sivas

During the winter months of 1914–15, persecutions of Armenians at Sivas began. In this town the Armenians had armed in self-defense to fight brutal government attacks. Yet their extermination followed the usual pattern. Arms searches began in the entire province during April 1915, and the tortures accompanying them were unimaginable. For example, Lord Bryce relates:

> In Khourakhon, a village near Sivas, one man . . . was actually shod like a horse, one . . . was castrated, and another . . . was done to death by putting a red-hot iron crown on his head. Under threats of such tortures many Armenians were compelled to buy arms and give them up to the authorities. The tragicomical part of the whole business was that the Turkish officials entrusted with

the mission of collecting arms were themselves selling them to Armenians at a good profit. The object of these infamous proceedings seems to have been the wish of the Turkish Government to place the Armenians in the category of rebels, and accuse them of having hidden arms in spite of official warnings.[56]

By the end of June, massacre and deportation of Armenians had begun. Men were separated from the women and killed. In Samsun, near the town of Sivas, most men were killed with axes, as the Turks did not want to "waste" their shot and powder.[57] The women and children were driven southeast. The Armenians from the town of Sivas had numbered 25,000 before the deportations, but only a few hundred were to survive. Of the total 160,000 Armenians from the entire province of Sivas, a mere 10,000 were to survive to the end of 1915.

Ankara

All villages and towns in eastern or central Anatolia experienced similar types of persecutions. In Ankara (Turkish: Enguru), the Armenian Catholic population numbered 15,000–20,000 and exhibited no nationalist aspirations. They were even Turkish speaking. Nonetheless, forced marches began only a few weeks after the Apostolic Armenians had been exiled. Count Pallavicini, the Austrian ambassador in Constantinople, attempted to use his influence to protect them, but this only postponed their death sentence temporarily.[58]

Ambassador Morgenthau tells of the following occurrences at Ankara:

At Angora all Armenian men from fifteen to seventy were arrested, bound together in groups of four, and sent on the road in the direction of Caesarea [Kaisaria]. When they had travelled five or six hours and had reached a secluded valley, a mob of Turkish peasants fell upon them with clubs, hammers, axes, scythes, spades, and saws. Such instruments not only caused more agonizing deaths than guns and pistols, but, as the Turks themselves boasted, they were more economical, since they did not involve the waste of powder and shell. In this way they exterminated the whole male population of Angora, including all its men of wealth and breeding, and their bodies, horribly mutilated, were left in the valley, where they were devoured by wild beasts. After completing this destruction, the peasants and gendarmes gathered in the local tavern, comparing notes and boasting of the number of "giaours" [infidels] that each had slain.[59]

Marsovan

Marsovan was an intellectual center for Armenians and was home to Anatolia College, an American Protestant institution housing 425 male and 276 female students. More than half of the faculty of Anatolia College were Armenian, as was nearly half of Marsovan's population (12,000 Armenians) before the deportations. Only 100 to 200 Armenians were to survive. The principal of Anatolia College, Theodore Elmer, indicates that Anatolia College, considered American property, attempted to provide refuge for as many Armenians as possible. U.S. Ambassador Morgenthau had received assurances from both Talaat and Enver that Armenians on the school's grounds would be safe. Yet the Turkish governor of Marsovan alleged that he had never received such information. Thus the few Armenians seeking sanctuary at Anatolia College were murdered. Seventy-one men and boys, along with 62 girls spared earlier deportation, were exiled in early August of 1915 and died in the desert.[60]

Diyarbekir

The large city of Diyarbekir, "inferno of torture," was a point of convergence for Armenian caravans of deportees from various parts of Anatolia. Reshid Bey was sent by the *Ittihad* to the vilayet of Diyarbekir with his gang of notorious murderers (Rushdi Bey, Khalil Bey, Ahmed Bey El-Serzi) to carry out the extermination directives.[61]

A soldier at Diyarbekir by the name of Shahin Bey had assisted in the slaughter of a number of Armenian women and men and told the following story to Fa'iz El-Ghusein:

... I saw an Armenian girl whom I knew, and who was very beautiful. I called her by name, and said "Come, I will save you, and you shall marry a young man of your country, a Turk or a Kurd." She refused, and said: "If you wish to do me a kindness I will ask one thing which you may do for me." I told her I would do whatever she wished, and she said: "I have a brother, younger than myself, here amongst these people. I pray you to kill him before you kill me, so that in dying I may not be anxious in mind about him." She pointed him out and I called him. When he came, she said to him, "My brother, farewell. I kiss you for the last time, but we shall meet, if it be God's will, in the next world, and He will soon avenge us for what we have suffered." They kissed each other, and the boy delivered himself to me. I must needs obey my orders, so I struck him one blow with an axe, split his skull, and he fell dead. Then she said: "I thank you with all my heart, and shall ask you one more favour"; she put her hands over her eyes and said: "Strike as you have struck my brother, one blow, and do not torture me." So I struck one blow and killed her, and to this day I grieve over her beauty and youth, and her wonderful courage.[62]

By the end of August 1915 a staggering 570,000 Armenians had been killed in Diyarbekir, including those from Diyarbekir proper and those exiled there from other vilayets.[63]

Musa Dagh

A dramatic rescue occurred in September 1915 at Musa Dagh, "the mountain of Moses" (today Hatay). Here the tough Armenian mountaineers of the six villages comprising Musa Dagh were ordered to prepare themselves for deportation in eight days. This order came on 13 July 1915. Franz Werfel, in his epic book *The Forty Days of Musa Dagh*, describes the siege that began with each Armenian household receiving the following verbal orders:

As an Ottoman subject you are liable to the decrees and enactments of the Kaimakam of Antioch. You, together with the rest of the population of this nahiyeh, from Suedia to Musa Dage [*sic*], are ordered to set out eastwards, on a day shortly to be specified. Your entire family to go with you. You have no right to raise objections of any kind against the general order of migration—neither as concerns your own person, nor those of your wife and children, nor for any other member of your establishment. . . . **⁶⁴**

There was resistance to the deportation order, and a mere sixty families followed the government's directive. None of those who departed was ever heard from again. The people remaining in the six villages ascended the mountain of Musa Dagh, taking their farm implements, their flocks, and food. They gathered every weapon possible—350 horse pistols, some old flintlocks, 120 modern rifles, and shotguns.

On 21 July the eight days' grace given them before deportation expired. The Turks launched an attack on the mountain with an advance guard numbering 200 regulars ("*nizams*"). The Turkish commander had previously boasted that he could eliminate the Armenians in one day. He failed, and 3,000 Turkish regulars and many "irregulars" were called to lend their assistance. Every mountain pass was eventually guarded by Turks with sophisticated weapons. Yet in the dead of night the Armenians encircled the Turkish force, and the Turks retreated.

Fighting resumed, and the food supply of the Armenians was finally depleted, whereupon they made two flags, one bearing the English words, "**CHRISTIANS IN DISTRESS: RESCUE**," and the other simply displaying a large red cross. Both flags were fastened to tall trees along the coastal region, and despite heavy fogs and rains, on a Sunday in September 1915, fifty-three days into the siege, a French battleship, the *Guichen*, was heading straight for Musa Dagh. Another flagship, the *St. Jeanne d'Arc*, soon arrived, accompanied by one English and four French vessels. The Armenian community was transferred to Port Said. The number of Armenian men, women, and children rescued during the episode is estimated to be 4,200.**⁶⁵**

Urfa

In March 1915 eighteen prominent families of Urfa were deported to Raqqa. Afterward, the town's menfolk wanted to retaliate but were dissuaded from doing so by their elders on the grounds that their arms and ammunition were too meager for an effective defense. The following day over 200 Armenians were taken prisoner.

From the summer of 1915 until the end of 1916, Urfa was full of deportees—primarily naked women and children—from Kharput and Erzeroum en route to the deserts of Mesopotamia. Thousands of Armenians were driven through the town, and the roadsides were littered with bodies.[66]

On 19 August 1915, 250 Armenians in Urfa were killed, and on 23 September, after 300 more were killed, community leaders opted to resist rather than be murdered. On 30 September a self-defense movement began. Soon Fakhri Bey, a Turkish general, arrived in Urfa accompanied by several hundred soldiers, his German adjutant, and heavy artillery. The Armenian revolt was quickly put down. Urfa was landlocked and received no relief from anywhere and by 23 October 1915, "the silence of death reigned over the Armenian quarter of Urfa."[67]

Christopher Walker comments:

All throughout the empire Armenians—disarmed, defenseless and terrorized—were being driven to their deaths, men mostly killed locally, women and children struggling over steep mountain paths to the parched deserts beyond, robbed of all they had, raped if attractive, and killed—thrown away like refuse, to be devoured by the scavengers of the desert. Those who survived were driven onwards in two directions—either towards Damascus, or along the Euphrates to Deir ez-Zor. The Damascus deportees escaped relatively lightly, many of them finding shelter in Arab villages between Aleppo and Homs; but an incomprehensibly frightful fate awaited those driven along the Euphrates, who were deposited in concentration camps which were little more than heaps of human wreckage. Only on a few occasions can the world have witnessed such a dense mass of suffering victims and such sadistic guards.[68]

CONCENTRATION CAMPS IN THE DESERT

During World War I the term "concentration camp" was being used to refer to places where people would be concentrated to await death.[69] As will be seen, the "camps" to which Armenians would be deported were the barren deserts. Here, there would be no shelter from the elements, no food and no water. Many atrocities would be perpetrated against them en route to their final destination—death.

In a letter to President Woodrow Wilson, Armin T. Wegner, a German eyewitness to the Armenian massacres, wrote the following in January 1919:

Parties which on their departure from the homeland of High Armenia consisted of thousands, numbered on their arrival in the outskirts of Aleppo only a few hundreds, while the fields were strewed with swollen, blackened corpses, infecting the air with their odor, lying about desecrated, naked, having been robbed of their clothes, or driven, bound back to back, to the Euphrates to provide food for the fishes. Sometimes gendarmes in derision threw into the emaciated hands of starving people a little meal which they greedily licked off, merely with the result of prolonging their death-agony. Even before the gates of Aleppo they were allowed no rest. For incomprehensible and utterly unjustifiable reasons of war, the shrunken parties were ceaselessly driven bare footed, hundreds of miles under the burning sun, through stony defiles, over pathless steppes, enfeebled into the wilderness of desolation. Here they died—slain by Kurds, robbed by gendarmes, shot, hanged, poisoned, stabbed, strangled, mown down by epidemics, drowned, frozen, parched with thirst, starved—their bodies left to putrify or to be devoured by jackals.[70]

A German eyewitness to the genocide, Dr. Martin Niepage, higher grade teacher at the German Technical School in Aleppo in 1915, asks,

. . . what becomes of these poor people who have been driven in thousands through Aleppo and the neighborhood into the deserts, reduced almost entirely by this time, to women and children? They are driven on and on from one place to another. The thousands shrink to hundreds and the hundreds to tiny remnants, and even these remnants are driven on till the last is dead. Then at last they have reached the goal of their wandering, the "New Homes assigned to the Armenians."

Niepage contends that what he saw in Aleppo with his own eyes was "the last scene in the great tragedy of the extermination of the Armenians . . . a minute fraction of the horrible drama that was being played out simultaneously in all the other provinces of Turkey."[71]

The *Ittihad* chose Aleppo as a convergence point for every convoy of refugees, even though the city itself had only a small Armenian community. In the beginning of May 1915 the first convoys from Zeitun reached Aleppo, and during the next three months a flood of deportees poured in from the mountains of Cilicia. By 30 July, 13,155 Armenians (or 2,165 families) had reached Aleppo, and 3,270 had been sent beyond. On their heels came convoys from the northeast—the first from Diyarbekir, consisting of 800 women with their children ten years of age and younger. They reached Aleppo on 2 August, after travelling forty-eight hours. The survivors of deportations from the vilayets of Erzeroum, Kharput, Sivas, and Trebizond were the next to arrive. Even though they had been exiled from their homes months earlier, they arrived in Aleppo at the same time as those refugees who were exiled from the eastern vilayets by train. They were not permitted to stay in the city and were forced into camps located in the outlying areas, later to be sent either southward toward Damascus or eastward toward the deserts of Mesopotamia. From May 1915 until the end of 1916 Armenians in the process of being transferred from camp to camp filled both Aleppo and Damascus.[72]

Reports of foreign witnesses, mostly German, serve to retrace the route of the exiles to their death. Between August and December of 1915, approximately 130,000 refugees set out for Damascus, the first arriving there on 12 August. Groups ranging in size from 200 to 2,000 arrived there two or three times a week. Some caravans of refugees were driven further toward Mala'an. Caravans awaiting deportation to new destinations were retained at Qadem, a suburb of Damascus, in forty tents. A concentration camp consisting of 20,000 exiles was located at Homs, further north. In another camp at Hama, between 10,000 and 12,000 Armenian refugees were dying.[73]

At camps between Meskene and Der-el-Zor along the Euphrates, Auguste Bernau, a representative of Socony Vacuum Oil Company of New York, saw thousands of scantily clothed Armenians without any type of shelter or food. Along the roads were mounds of anonymous graves. Again, the survivors were pushed further—toward Der-el-Zor. About 60,000 Armenians at Meskene were suffering the agonies of dysentery. Headed south, in the open desert areas at Abu-Herrera and Aqraqol Hamman, Bernau saw several hundred dying people who had had neither food nor water for a week. Five or six thousand Armenians had found shelter in houses at Raqqa. At Semga and Ziarat, along the banks of a river, hundreds of unfortunates could be seen huddled together. However, at the end of the road, Der-el-Zor, no more Armenians could be found. All had been killed.

Every day, more than a hundred Armenian refugees died at Aleppo, in full view of foreign witnesses. Decaying corpses, with the living buried among them, were piled in heaps all around the city. The refugees sought shelter in abandoned inns. The bulk of them, however, were beyond help—victims of dysentery and typhus.[74]

In November a doctor visited various camps. At Jerablus he witnessed *chetehs* selling as slaves 300 Armenian girls who had survived the deportations from Mardin, Diyarbekir, and Kharput.

By September 1916 not more than 15,000 refugees were dispersed between Meskene and Der-el-Zor along the Euphrates. With the arrival of winter, they were doomed. The 350,000 persons transported from Aleppo to the desert camps had perished. The convoys that had bypassed Aleppo heading for Ras ul-Ain no longer existed. All had been murdered.[75]

In February of 1916 Djevdet, who had been involved in the massacres at Van, Bitlis, and Moush, assumed his new post at Adana. Upon passing Ras ul-Ain, he saw 50,000 refugees, whom he immediately ordered killed. This was done by sending small groups of them into the deserts and butchering them there. This took until July 1916 to complete.

Ras ul-Ain was one of the major concentration camps. Two Ottoman army officers—one a Moslem Arab from Damascus and the other from Acre—had deserted their posts in August 1916. They described what they had seen at Ras ul-Ain to Sir Mark Sykes, who relates their account:

> The Armenians were dying of typhus and dysentery, and the roads were littered with their decomposing bodies. The empty desert cisterns were also filled with corpses. . . . The Turkish officers of the battalion were horrified at the sights they saw, and the regimental chaplain [a Muslim divine], on coming across a number of bodies, dismounted his horse and publicly prayed that the divine punishment of these crimes should be averted from Muslims, and, by way of expiation, himself worked at digging graves for the dead bodies. When marching from Ras ul-Ain to er-Radi the soldiers of the battalion often put up their hands to avert the sight of the numerous bloated naked corpses of murdered women who lay by the roadside. Two sayings were common among the common soldiers: "Ras ul-Ain is a shambles" and "No man can ever think of a woman's body except as a matter of horror, instead of attraction, after Ras ul-Ain". Ras ul-Ain was used as a place of concentration for Armenians, and 12,000 was the number usually there. The average number of the incoming parties and outgoing parties (viz., those go   g to be murdered) cannot be estimated accurately.[76]

Ras ul-Ain also served as a major stop for the Berlin-Bagdad Railroad. The railroad played an important role in the genocidal process.

The Berlin-Bagdad Railroad

Major routes of Asian Turkey linked at Aleppo, a convergence point for the Berlin-Bagdad railway. Eastward, the train traveled to Ras ul-Ain; southward, it traveled to the holy spots of Islam by way of the cities of Damascus, Beirut, and Medina.[77]

The railway served to expedite the work of exterminating Armenians. A German employee of the Bagdad railroad saw women and children stuffed into trams while men and boys were taken away on foot. The railway vans also carried Armenian orphaned children from

Anatolia to the interior of Turkey for distribution among Moslem families. At every station along the line, exiles were crowded and detained, awaiting their turn to be transported for interminable periods.[78]

A foreign physician who had resided in Turkey for ten years and was an eyewitness to the genocide recalls his experience as a passenger on the railway:

> Our train sped away, taking with us as many cattle-trucks packed with men, women and children, as the locomotive could pull. In these trucks one could see improvised hammocks swung above the crowd squatting upon the floor, and in these hammocks the tiny babies—the only individuals in all that crowd oblivious to the horrors of the situation, but doomed nevertheless, in all their innocence. . . .[79]

Ironically, the deportees were required to *pay* for the privilege of riding in a cattle truck, since those who could not pay were forced to walk. As the train passed over rivers, mothers, who could not bear to see their babies starving to death threw them into the river, quickly jumping in themselves afterwards.[80]

The Berlin-Bagdad railroad going through Aleppo was considered essential to Germany in its quest for eastward expansion. The military hoped to profit from the deportation of Armenians by putting them to work on building construction and roads.[81]

Between Ayran and to the north of Intilli, the military administration was using Armenians—mostly women and children—for breaking stones and digging. Niepage, a German eyewitness to the genocide, reports in 1915:

> There are 1,500 Armenians in good health—men, women and children, including grandmothers sixty years old and many children of six and seven—who are still at work on a section of the Bagdad Railway. . . . For the moment they are being looked after by Herr Morf, Superintendent Engineer of the Bagdad Railway; but the Turkish Government has registered their names too. As soon as their work is finished, . . . they are no longer wanted, "new homes will be assigned to them,"—that is, the men will be taken off and slaughtered, the pretty women and girls will find their way into harems, the remainder will be driven hither and thither without food through the desert until all is over. . . .
>
> One of them, Herr Greif, of Aleppo, reported corpses of violated women lying about naked in heaps on the railway embankment at Tell-Abiad and Ras-el-Ain. Another, Herr Spiecker, of Aleppo, had seen Turks tie Armenian men together, fire several volleys of small shot with fowling-pieces into the human mass, and go off laughing while their victims slowly perished in frightful convulsions. Other men had their hands tied behind their back and were rolled down steep cliffs. [Turkish] women were standing below, who slashed those who had rolled down with knives until they were dead. A Protestant pastor . . . had his finger nails torn out.

The German Consul from Mosul related . . . that, in many places on the road from Mosul to Aleppo, he had seen children's hands lying hacked off in such numbers that one could have paved the road with them.[52]

When Talaat Bey learned that German engineers had employed thousands of Armenian deportees to work on the construction of the railway beds and to dig tunnels through the Taurus Mountains, he insisted, despite German protests, that they be sent to Der-el-Zor.[53]

Talaat opposed keeping Armenians alive to perform labor and ordered dispensing with such "special privileges." However, a compromise was reached by the railroad company's engineers in January according to which Armenian laborers would not be killed until the work was completed, since the railroad provided a strategic communication route for the Turkish army. Most families of forced laborers were permitted to remain in the vicinity until March 1916, when Djevdet passed through Intilli and had the refugees massacred between Aintab and Marash.[54]

According to Walker, from the beginning of World War I until 1922 (at which time Armenian survivors who returned to their Turkish Armenian homeland were killed), 1,500,000 to 1,550,000 were murdered and another 200,000 forcibly Islamized.[55]

The figures to be presented assessing the numbers of victims of genocide are certainly underestimates, as they do not include Armenians killed at such places as Urmia, Salmas, and Dilman in Persia.[56] Missionaries reported that in Urmia not a single woman between ages seven to seventy was spared being raped, in spite of American attempts to provide relief to the Armenians of Urmia.[57] Nonetheless, we will consider only the extermination of the Turkish-Armenians.

In March 1916 Abdullahad Nuri sent a telegram, listing his operations to the office for deportations in Constantinople: in the area of Mesken and El Bab—35,000 dead; at the Karlik camp situated above Aleppo—10,000 dead; near Abu-Herrera, Dibse, and Qaraqol Hamman—20,000 dead; Ras ul-Ain—35,000 dead; refugees from Damascus and Der-el-Zor—200,000 (American Consul Jackson reports 300,000) dead. More were pushed toward Meskene, then Der-el-Zor. Aleppo and environs were emptied of Armenians, and exiles also arrived from eastern vilayets. They were also ordered killed by Abdullahad Nuri. Thousands of Armenians were murdered and dumped into the Euphrates. From Meskene to Der-el-Zor, the road was a veritable charnel house. The stragglers who remained at Der-el-Zor were ordered killed by Zeki Bey. In August 1916 they were led across the desert toward Mosul in separate groups. In the deserts of Suwar and Marata, all vanished.[58]

Anti-Armenian measures were virtually completed by the end of

1916. Figures of casualties produced by Lord Bryce and Dr. Lepsius as published in *Bericht* and later confirmed in Lepsius's *Deutschland und Armenien, 1914-1918* are essentially the same. Before the war, Armenians in the Ottoman Empire had numbered between 1,500,000 and 2,000,000. About 250,000 of these managed to escape into Russia, traveling either by sea or land. Of the 1,600,000 left, 1,000,000 were murdered, half of them women and children. Of the 600,000 who still remained, about 200,000 were forcibly converted to Islam. A wretched 400,000 survivors in rags and starving were found at the close of the war by the Allies. In May through September of 1918, 50,000 to 100,000 of these were eliminated during a Turkish invasion in the Caucasus. An estimated 250,000 or more were killed during 1919-1922 as Armenian survivors returned to their homes in Turkish Armenia and faced more organized murders. In 1915, when Joseph Burtt interviewed surviving Armenian children at an Athens orphanage, he found the average number of people killed in each family of the surviving children to be 26.[89]

By the close of the year 1916, the genocide of Turkey's Armenians was almost complete. In the following story of a little Armenian boy, Ternon depicts the struggle of a people for survival against all odds:

Is there any more moving symbol of the agony and courage of this people than the story of a ten-year-old child who had hidden by burying himself in the sands on the road to Deir es Zor? He could not speak; they had cut out his tongue. Whenever a convoy went by, he came out from under the sand and warned his people that they would be massacred farther along the road. He did not stop gesturing until the convoy had turned back. He then reburied himself until the next refugees came by.[90]

THE WHOLE Armenian nation is steeped in blood. It is impossible to grasp the fact that six great Christian Powers of Europe could look at these terrible massacres with folded arms.

—ARMENIAN PATRIARCH M. IZMIRLIAN

6

FAILURE OF MULTIDIMENSIONAL LEVELS OF SOCIAL CONTROL

WE HAVE now reached the final factor involved in the value-added process of genocide—the failure of social controls. Smelser contends that aggression can only occur on a large scale if sanctioned by the wielders of force in a society. He further asserts that overt displays of hostility might be halted at any time since agencies of the state, namely, the military and the police, have superior power and organization when compared to collectivities engaged in violence and can, therefore, put down disturbances.

How is it possible, then, that many societies with numerous powerful, institutionalized levels of social control (such as the military, police, and religious institutions) cannot curb genocide?

We will now direct our attention to some institutionalized levels at which destructive aggression may feasibly be hindered or stopped. These are grouped into two major categories. First, there are levels of social control that are outside of, or external to, the direct control of the victim group ("external controls") and, second, there are controls internal to, or within the domain of, the victim group, providing it with the capacity to defend itself against annihilation ("internal controls"). External controls consist primarily of: (1) the aggressor state and its citizenry, (2) other nations, and (3) religious institutions. These are possibly the most powerful mechanisms for the control of genocide, although they are not the only ones. Internal controls consist of the following: (1) interference by the victim group's ethnic state (political self-defense), (2) mobilization of the victim group's agencies of defense (sociocultural self-defense), (3) realization of impending group annihilation (psychological self-defense), and (4) physical ability to retaliate (biological self-defense). Thus internal control deals with social control through self-defense. (These categories will be further elaborated upon in Chap. 13.)

A failure at any one of these levels of control could result in an added cost in lives. But should most or all levels of social control prove ineffective, the consequences for the victim group would be devastating.

EXTERNAL CONTROLS

The Aggressor State and Its Citizenry

There is most certainly evidence of a lack of impartial enforcement of justice in Turkey during the late 1800s. The existence of separate court systems for Christians and Moslems plus the refusal of Moslem courts to accept the testimony of Christians left the Armenians without legal recourse. The following incident, Walker indicates, exemplifies Turkish justice in the 1880s:

The Ottoman system of law was a denial of law itself. It was symbolized at this time by the Kurdish brigand-chief Musa Bey, whose villainy and violence were so great that foreign representatives demanded his arrest. He was taken to the capitol, and, after a trial that was a mockery of justice, set free. An outcry resulted in the European press, and the Sultan thought it prudent to banish him to Arabia, whence he quietly returned to his former activities.[1]

Though the Turkish state was responsible for the deplorable condition of the Armenians, the government blamed the massacres of Armenians in the mid-1890s upon the Kurds. (Recall that the sultan created the Hamidian cavalry.) Walker contends that the Ottoman government not only failed to control the massacres but actually participated in them. He points to overwhelming evidence of governmental planning and forethought in the 1895 killings, asserting that "the government itself was guilty, and . . . the outbreaks were part of a premeditated Ottoman policy."[2]

The description of the deportations and massacres of 1915 in Chapter 5 provides sufficient evidence of governmental sponsorship of and participation in the genocide of the Armenians during World War I as well. There was direct involvement by government officials, police, and military personnel, as well as enthusiastic support and participation by the general populace.

The surest damning evidence against Turkey is the government's rejection of bids by the American government to take Armenians to America at America's expense on American ships. The Turkish government declined assistance from the Sisters of Mercy, European residents in Turkey, and from missionaries whose work they made systematic attempts to stop.[3] Obviously, had the government not wished to exterminate Armenians, they would simply have accepted such assistance rather than claiming they were helping the Armenians by deporting them out of war zones and into barren deserts supposedly for their own safety.

The Young Turks promoted the genocide under a shroud of secrecy. Ambassador Morgenthau reports that while in Constantinople he was deprived of the privilege of using cipher to communicate with American consuls and the letters were vigorously censored. He notes that Turkish authorities were determined to hide events occurring in Asia Minor so as to be able to continue the genocide.[4] In addition, the government ordered the burial of Armenian corpses when they became an object of attention and concern in European newspapers.[5] The Young Turks desired secrecy so as to pursue their goals unimpeded.

Turks not only controlled their own people through propaganda (discussed previously), but they also influenced Europe by manipulating the truth so that European publications presented Armenians in a negative light. The information gathered by El-Ghusein (see Chap. 5) describing how the Turks killed Armenians, dressing them in Kurdish clothes, photographing their bodies, claiming Armenians were murdering Kurds and keeping these pictures for release abroad, provides but one example of how the Young Turks controlled the mass media.[6]

Efforts to justify the extermination of Armenians by the sultan and next the Young Turks were made during World War I in various publications. For example, in Switzerland in 1918 Ahmed Rustem Bey, onetime Turkish ambassador to the United States, published *The World War and the Turkish-Armenian Question*. From beginning to end, the author justifies his government's genocidal policy toward the Armenians.[7]

The opportunity for liquidating the Armenians arose during a world war, just as the propitious moment for exterminating the Jews would arise during another world war twenty-five years later. The war freed the Turkish government from the control of world public opinion. The powerful countries of Austria and Germany, then Turkey's allies, did not officially protest the genocide. The Turkish government was fully aware that a German victory in the war would mean Turkey would escape any repercussions for committing genocide.[8]

Other Nations

As early as 1896 Frederick Greene wrote that the Turk's government "of oppression" was a "curse" to the Christian. He further states that "Europe, in permitting and well-nigh supporting the oppression, has been as great a criminal against the Turk as against the Christian."[9]

The American Committee for the Independence of Armenia made the following charge condemning the lack of control exerted upon Turkey by other nations of the world:

... the Armenian horrors of 1915, the direct responsibility for them belongs to the Turks, who perpetuated them; to the Germans, who possessed absolute power to prevent them, and did not, and to the neutral world, which did not make an earnest and timely effort to mitigate, if it could not prevent, this most ghastly and colossal crime in recorded history.[10]

In the same vein, El-Ghusein concludes:

... I would address myself to the Powers of Europe, and say that it is they themselves who have encouraged the Turkish Government to this deed, for they were aware of the evil administration of that Government, and its barbarous proceedings on many occasions in the past, but did not check it.[11]

The repercussions of Europe's apathy toward the Armenians were recognized immediately after the Sassoun massacres of 1895. At that time Greene observed that "the laxity of Europe has afforded opportunity for the merciless working of this system in all its vigor. It is born of religious and race hatred, and has in mind the crushing of Christianity and Christians."[12]

During the genocide, one European government *may* have influenced Turkey's atrocities against the Armenians— Germany. Arnold Toynbee explains:

It is, on the whole, unlikely that the German authorities initiated the crime. The Turks do not need tempters. But when that has been said, all that can be submitted in their defence has been exhausted; and if faint praise is damning, they assuredly stand condemned. For it is clear that, whoever commanded the atrocities, the Germans never made a motion to countermand them, when they could have been stopped at the start by a single word. It is no exaggeration to say that they could have been stopped absolutely, for it is obvious that, by entering the war, Turkey placed herself entirely in Germany's power. She is dependent on Germany. . . . *In every administrative centre throughout those districts where massacres and deportations have occurred—in Anatolia, Cilicia, and Armenia proper—there is a German consul. . . .*[13]

Ambassador Morgenthau likewise concludes: "*Let me say most emphatically, the German Government could have prevented it [the deportations and murder].*" Morgenthau points to the many times he attempted to enlist the efforts of Baron von Wangenheim, the German Ambassador to Turkey, on behalf of the Armenians, but to no avail. Morgenthau finally had the American government bring pressure to bear on the Foreign Office in Berlin, insisting upon cessation of atrocities. Morgenthau comments that "this resulted merely in a Note from the German Embassy to the Sublime Porte protesting against the horrors perpetrated by the Turks. The purpose of this Note was merely to absolve the German Government from all responsibility. It had no practical effect whatsoever."[14]

Niepage, in a similar vein, concludes that "the educated Moslems are convinced that, even though the German nation discountenances such horrors, the German government is taking no steps to put a stop to them, out of consideration for its Turkish Ally." Niepage further indicates that " *'Ta'alim el aleman' "* ('the teaching of the Germans') is the simple Turk's explanation to everyone who asks him about the originators of these measures."[15]

Gibbons, in *The Blackest Page of Modern History,* asserts that Russia's Transcaucasian policy and the Balkan policy supported by the Great Powers caused Turkey's fanaticism against the Armenians. Were there great Armenian massacres before there was an acute "Question of the Orient"? Yet Christian Europe, Gibbons contends, never exerted a concerted effort to control the scope of Turkish actions against the Armenians.[16]

To get a clear picture of the concern the Entente powers had for the Armenians, one should realize that in March 1915, before the genocide was fully operationalized by the Young Turks, the Entente powers were negotiating the partitioning of the Ottoman Empire. On 1 February 1916 Sir Mark Sykes, a Near East expert of the British Foreign Office, met in Paris with former Beirut Consul-General Francois George-Picot to delineate the British and French positions regarding the "Ottoman inheritance." They discussed two zones of interest: (1) the white zone—of importance to France, consisting of Cilicia, Lebanon, the Gulf of Alexandretta, and territories on the Taurus as far as the Persian border and (2) the red zone—of interest to the British, consisting of those Ottoman possessions south of the aforementioned area, especially Arab regions, where Britain reserved a right to form independent Arab states under her control. Sykes and Picot next went to Petrograd to discuss terms with the Russians, who also had vested interests in the Armenian vilayets.[17]

After various secret agreements negotiating the conflicting interests of the Entente powers over distribution of Armenian lands, the Sykes-Picot form was signed during 9 to 16 May 1916. Ternon perceptively asserts:

These secret agreements confirm the fact that the Entente powers had abandoned the Armenians to their assassins and that no one intended to grant them any territorial autonomy. . . . The deaths in Armenia merely changed the particulars of the problem. It carried no moral weight with the diplomats. Offered by the Turks, the solution to the Armenian problem was accepted without question by the Powers. . . .

By the beginning of 1917, the Armenian question as it had been introduced to the great powers in 1878, that is, respect for the fundamental political rights of the Armenian people in Turkey, was resolved for all the governments who had taken part in the original Berlin congress. The Turks had virtually destroyed the entire Armenian population. . . . The Central Powers had been more weak-kneed than actual accomplices. The Entente, confident in its military victory, had settled the future partitioning of the Ottoman empire and had wiped Armenia off the map.[18]

Attempts by international powers, namely Great Britain, France, Russia, and the United States, to exercise control over violent acts committed against Armenians have been historically complicated and, for the most part, unsuccessful. Russia, before the 1917 revolution, sought to protect the Christian population of the neighboring Ottoman Empire. Requests were made, reforms were suggested, and occasionally military force was used. At times, these efforts were somewhat unsuccessful, such as the rescue of the Van "revolutionaries."[19]

After the War the new Turkish government concluded that the Young Turks had committed criminal acts against Christians and Moslems and military court-martial proceedings found the perpetrators of the Armenian genocide guilty in absentia. Verdicts of guilty and death sentences were handed down for Talaat, Enver, Djemal, and Dr. Nazim, who had fled Turkey and were fugitives. The logical consequence of such a trial—punishment—never occurred. Hovannisian contends:

Throughout 1919 and 1920 the Western powers remained publicly committed to the establishment of a united Armenian state combining the Russian Armenian and the Turkish Armenian provinces, with an outlet on the Black Sea. The Allied leaders hoped that the United States would accept a League of

Nations mandate over the projected state, just as Britain and France were to assume supervisory control over several Arab provinces to be severed from the Ottoman Empire. Yet, wishes alone were not enough to organize an autonomous Armenian state, repatriate several hundred thousand refugees, and provide the resources for the defense and development of the state. While all the Allies advocated a free Armenia, none was willing to commit the requisite resources to make that goal a reality. The United States, under domestic pressure for rapid demobilization and recoiling into "splendid isolation," declined the Armenian mandate, while Great Britain and France, trying to preserve the rights acquired in their secret wartime pacts relating to the Near East, concentrated their energies on the Arab provinces, where they intended to impose a long-range presence. Rivalries flared repeatedly among the Allies over the spoils of war and zones of influence, thereby contributing to the long delay in drafting the Turkish peace settlement.

Meanwhile, a Turkish Nationalist movement aimed at preserving the territorial integrity of Anatolia by checking the Allies was formed. Headed by Mustafa Kemal ("Kemal Attaturk," the father of modern Turkey), the Nationalists won over much of the remnants of the Turkish army by 1919 and formed a countergovernment at Ankara by spring of 1920. By attacking the French garrison stationed at Marash in January and killing and driving out Armenians who had repatriated to the area under British and French auspices, the nationalists made their intentions known.[20]

Both the British and French, who had supposedly been in Turkey to protect the Armenians, withdrew at the expedient moment, leaving the Armenians facing further death and disaster. In *The Lions of Marash*, Stanley Kerr contends:

On 10 February 1920, the French garrison at Marash withdrew abruptly under cover of darkness, thus abandoning more than twenty thousand Armenians to the tender mercies of the Turkish Nationalist forces. The tactic of swift evacuation is not novel in military history, but in the case of Marash the retreat occurred even after it was known that the Turkish insurgents, who had besieged the city and devastated the Armenian quarters for three weeks, were themselves taking flight. The French maneuver caused considerable embarrassment in Paris and roused a storm of angry protests in England and the United States, but for the natives of Marash, the spirited mountaineers of nearby Zeitun and Hadjin, indeed for the Armenian inhabitants of all Cilicia, it led to renewed massacre and to final exodus.[21]

While besieging other towns and cities in Cilicia, the Turkish government sent out emissaries made up of some former Young Turk leaders who sought and received the assistance of Soviet Russia. The first Soviet gold shipment arrived in Anatolia during the summer of 1920.[22]

Following the Marash massacres, the Armenians appealed for other international protection. There were many cases of indifference and callousness by the French, and even some concerted French efforts to prevent measures for Armenian self-defense. The Armenians believed that they had been shamefully betrayed by the very powers who pledged to protect them.[23]

The Armenians were not only denied military support but were also neglected in negotiations enacting the peace treaties. Even though the United States had offered assistance to Armenian refugees during the war, they failed to support Armenians following the war. The United States was expected and encouraged to accept a mandate for Armenia. None of the other Allies would do anything until the United States took a position, and the United States, rather sadly, did nothing.[24] As indicated previously, the Armenians had lived with dreams of autonomy, and the British, French, and Russians had encouraged such visions through international treaties (such as San Stefano and the Treaty of Berlin). Sir William Wiseman of the British Intelligence Service commented (3 March 1919) regarding the failure of various countries to uphold their previous promises to the Armenians:

Among the things that the deplorable treatment of the Armenians reveals is the skill of the Powers with whom we are associated in "passing the buck." Both England and France before we entered the war officially announced that they would re-establish the Armenian people in their ancient rights and within their traditional boundaries, but as the extreme difficulty of their task becomes more and more apparent, they have earmarked the ugly job for Simple Simon, that is, for Uncle Sam.[25]

America had made generous offers of assistance to Armenians, but Johannes Lepsius, after analyzing many documents following World War I, concludes:

It must be acknowledged that the generosity and self-sacrifice of the Americans in humanitarian matters were almost boundless and incomparable. In the name of his Government Morgenthau submitted to the leading men of the Porte the proposal of settling the entire Armenian population of the Ottoman Empire numbering about 2 million people, including the 180,000 Armenians of Constantinople, in the United States of America.[26]

America had offered to take all refugees, but after Talaat refused, America still provided relief for Armenians. It must be recognized that without America's all-out effort, there would be no Armenians today. Work such as that done by Mabel Elliot, medical director of Near East Relief, was generously provided by Americans.[27]

After the War every Allied power pledged that the Armenians

would be given autonomy or an independent nation on their historic lands. When the Paris Peace Conference convened in January 1919, one of the first items on its agenda was the Armenians. A decision was made that "because of the historical mis-government by the Turks of subject peoples and the terrible massacres of Armenians and others in recent years, the Allied and Associated Powers are agreed that Armenia, Syria, Mesopotamia, Palestine and Arabia must be completely severed from the Turkish Empire."[28]

In August 1920, approximately two years after the war's end, the Treaty of Sevres was imposed on Turkey and was signed by the sultan's representatives. It was modest regarding the Armenian question, recognizing the freedom and independence of an Armenian republic and renouncing Turkish rights to portions of Erzeroum, Van, Bitlis, and Trebizond, which were to be included in the new Armenian state. The treaty nullified all religious conversion since the onset of the war, and families of Armenians or the religious community of kidnapped or lost persons could reclaim and search for such people through a mixed commission. The Turkish government was to assist in recovering women and children who were sequestered in Moslem households, supply information and seek extradition of persons found guilty of massacres of Armenians and war crimes, and allow nullification of the "notorious abandoned properties law, which had made the Ottoman state the beneficiary of all Armenian goods and properties having no living owners or legal heirs." Since thousands of Armenian families had been completely exterminated, the law had rewarded the Turkish government with tremendous wealth for having perpetrated the genocide. Hovannisian points out that "no power was willing to shoulder the moral and material responsibilities. Allied armies did occupy Egypt, Palestine, Syria, Mesopotamia and parts of Anatolia, but no troops could be spared for the Armenians who were to be left to their own devices."[29]

Soon, Mustafa Kemal ordered Turkish armies to breach the border and crush the Armenian republic, thus breaking the Treaty of Sevres. In December the Armenians were forced by the Turkish armies to repudiate the Treaty of Sevres and renounce claims to Turkish Armenia; in addition, they had to cede the former Russian Armenian districts of Surmalu, Kars, and Ardahan, as well as Mount Ararat, the symbol of Armenia. Hovannisian points out that "one of the ironies of the postwar era was that of all the defeated powers Turkey alone expanded its boundary, and this only on the Caucasus front at the expense of the Armenians [emphasis added]."[30]

The Allied governments now responded by seeking to normalize relations with Mustafa Kemal. He, too, was ready to make peace. Kemal sent envoys to Moscow and London and gained leverage in the next set of negotiations. The Treaty of Sevres was drastically revised at the Lausanne conferences in 1923. Western diplomats acceded to most Turkish Nationalist demands, "despite their sundry protests and face-saving gestures." Britain tried to salvage a national home or foyer for the Armenians under the confines and suzerainty of Turkey, but Turkey realized that no country was prepared to give more than lip service to protect Armenians and refused to yield. The absolute Turkish triumph was effected when the final versions of the Lausanne treaty mentioned neither the word "Armenia" nor "Armenian," as if Armenia or Armenians had never existed. With this treaty, the "Armenian Question" was abandoned internationally. Hovannisian claims that "if in 1878 they were deprived of fundamental rights and the security of life and property, in 1923 they no longer even existed in their ancestral lands."[31]

The Treaty of Lausanne, signed on 24 July 1923, did not contain a word about a homeland for the Armenians. This treaty was made, according to Nansen, "just as though they [the Armenians] had never existed." Despite universal demands for an Armenian homeland, despite its recognition in the Paris Peace Conference, despite President Wilson's planned Armenian boundaries, and despite the terms of the Treaty of Sevres, the Allies succumbed with weakness and callousness when they signed the Treaty of Lausanne.[32]

The Armenian homeland was lost. The failure of other nations was summed up by Stanley Baldwin and Herbert A. Asquith, 26 September 1924:

On September 26, 1924, former Prime Minister Stanley Baldwin and Herbert A. Asquith, the leader of the Liberal Party, presented a memorial to Ramsay MacDonald, the head of the Government, to grant an aid for the resettlement of the Armenian refugees, such grant to be administered by the Lord Mayor's Fund, giving the following principal reasons:
1. Because the Armenians were encouraged by promises of freedom to support the Allied cause during the War, and suffered for this cause so tragically . . .
2. Because during the War and since the Armistice statesmen of the Allies and Associated Powers have given repeated pledges to secure the liberation and independence of the Armenian nation . . .
3. Because in part Great Britain is responsible for the final dispersion of the Ottoman Armenians after the sack of Smyrna in 1922 . . .
4. Because the sum of 15,000,000 (Turkish gold) deposited by the Turkish government in Berlin in 1916, and taken over by the Allies after the Armistice, was in large part (perhaps wholly) Armenian money;
5. Because the present conditions of the refugees are unstable and demoralizing, and constitute a reproach to the Western Powers. . . .
We recognize, the document went on, with deep regret that it is impossible

now to fulfill our pledge to the Armenians. . . . But there is open to us another method of expressing our sense of responsibility and of relieving the desperate plight of the scattered remnants of the Turkish Armenians. The most appropriate territory for their settlement would surely be in Russian Armenia. Facilities are offered by the local Government."

It is in our opinion the duty of Great Britain to give substantial support to this scheme. We desire to express our view that, as some compensation for unfulfilled pledges is morally due to the Armenians, the British Government should forthwith make an important grant. . . .

(Signed) H. A. ASQUITH
STANLEY BALDWIN[33]

Religious Institutions

Henry Morgenthau, in *The Tragedy of Armenia*, charges the Young Turks,

. . . criticized their ancestors for neglecting to destroy or convert the Christian races to Mohammedanism at the time when they first subjugated them. Now, as four of the Great Powers were at war with them and the two others were their allies, they thought the time opportune to make good the oversight of their ancestors in the fifteenth century.[34]

Religion was used by the Young Turks:

when the Armenians were gone the Turkish populace was encouraged to plunder their goods and houses, and as the convoys of exiles passed through the villages the best-looking women and children were sold cheap or given away for nothing to the Turkish peasantry. Naturally the Turkish people accepted the good things the Government offered them, and naturally this reconciled them momentarily to the War.

Thus in the Armenian atrocities the Young Turks made Panislamism and Turkish Nationalism work together for their ends, but the development of their policy shows the Islamic element receding and the Nationalist gaining ground.[35]

Religion would soon become a tool in the service of the Young Turks.

Holy War—*Jihad*

The notion of a Holy War was hatched by German Ambassador to Turkey, Baron von Wangenheim.[36] Germany's plan was to set the Moslems against the Christians as a way to destroy the strength of the French and English in World War I. If both of these countries were preoccupied with Moslem uprisings, they would be forced to make peace with Germany. On 13 November 1914 the sultan of Turkey officially issued an appeal for *Jihad* ("Holy War") against "infidel" Christians. Afterward, a proclamation of the Sheik-el-Islam summoned all of the Moslem world to massacre its Christian oppressors.

Whereas the sultan's proclamation was official and public, a pamphlet explaining the *Jihad* was circulated in secret, elaborating upon details about how the extermination of all Christians, *except Germans* (and Austrians), was to be achieved. The secret pamphlet, printed in Arabic, was distributed in Egypt, Morocco, Syria, and India, as well as other countries having large Moslem populations. Morgenthau notes that the style of the pamphlet "was frenzied in its appeal to racial and religious hatred." The pamphlet branded the English, Russians, and French as oppressors of Islam. It depicted Moslems working while "infidels" lived luxuriously; Moslems suffering hunger as infidels ate; Moslems serving as slaves while infidels ruled. The pamphlet depicted the killing of Christians as a "sacred duty." The following section from the pamphlet reveals its fanatical intent:

> This holy war has now become a sacred duty. . . . Know ye that the blood of infidels in the Islamic lands may be shed with impunity. . . . The killing of infidels who rule over Islam has become a sacred duty. . . . as the Koran has decreed: "Take them and kill them whenever you find them." . . . He who kills even one unbeliever . . . shall be rewarded by God. . . . and let every Moslem, in whatever part of the world he may be, swear a solemn oath to kill at least three or four of the infidels who rule over him, for they are the enemies of God and of the faith. Let every Moslem know that his reward for doing so shall be doubled by the God who created heaven and earth. A Moslem who does this shall be saved from the terrors of the day of Judgment. . . . We shall lift up our voices saying. . . . Caucasus for the Caucasian Moslems, and the Ottoman Empire for the Ottoman Turks and Arabs. . . ."[37]

There were several levels of this "holy purpose." The "heart war," which urged the Prophet's followers to nourish a spirit of hatred for the infidel; the "speech war," which prompted every Moslem to war through the use of tongue and pen; and the "true war," which promoted "fighting and killing the infidel wherever he shows his head." Moslems were urged to wage war in their own countries and worldwide.[38]

The Holy War proved a failure from the first. Turks could not understand why Germany and Austria should be their partners in a holy war and, in addition, be exempt from victimization, since Germans and Austrians were themselves Christians. Though the Koran, Morgenthau claims, commands the slaughter of Christians, no exception in favor of Germans is made in the sacred volume.[39]

Although the Holy War did not materialize, there were some demonstrations that resulted in violence, namely, in Constantinople. The literature proved destructive to the Armenians, as Morgenthau indicates:

> Only one definite result did the Kaiser accomplish by spreading this inciting literature. It aroused in the Mohammedan soul all that intense animosity toward the Christian . . . and thus started passions aflame that afterward spent themselves in the massacres of the Armenians and other subject peoples.[40]

El-Ghusein contends that the Ottoman government continually inflamed Turks and Kurds to violent acts against the Armenians by corrupting the Moslem faith to attain their own ends. El-Ghusein, himself a Moslem, condemns the Young Turks' manipulation of the faith as a weapon against the Armenians. He expressed his dismay by questioning:

> Is it right that these impostors [Young Turks], who pretend to be the supports of Islam and the *Khilafat*, the protectors of the Moslems, should transgress the command of God, transgress the Koran, the Traditions of the Prophet, and humanity? Truly, they have committed an act at which Islam is revolted, as well as all Moslems and all the peoples of the earth, be they Moslems, Christians, Jews, or idolaters. As God lives, it is a shameful deed, the like of which has not been done by any people counting themselves as civilized.[41]

INTERNAL CONTROL

Interference by the Victim Group's Ethnic State: Political Self-defense

I believe the major factor preventing the Armenians from any effective defense was the absence of a state of their own. Many benefits concomitant with having a national state did not exist for them. Primary among these was a lack of allies committed to the Armenians. Regardless of whether allies are committed because of "natural" or expedient reasons, they would provide a defense in time of need. If a people are without a state through which they develop interactions with other governments, then there are no states motivated to come to their defense. In other words, in case of attack, no state has sufficient reason to utilize its military or declare war. After all, should people be killed, another state would suffer no detrimental effects. However, should an ally or economic partner be decimated, an adverse effect on other states could be expected. A people without a state offer neither favor nor benefits to other governments and, consequently, are viewed with indifference. This certainly gives genocidal governments a free hand in their persecution of stateless peoples. Note that neither the .

Armenians nor the Jewish people had independent states when their populations were being exterminated.

Armenia was divided between Russia and Ottoman Turkey. The repercussions of this are severe when a group is under military attack. The Russian Armenians had no army of their own to come to the aid of their fellow Armenians in Turkey and, of course, the Ottoman Armenians were also without an army. At the time of the genocide the Armenians possessed a meager supply of weapons, and even those were confiscated during weapons searches by the government.

The Armenian population might possibly have resisted the Turkish onslaught more readily had they a closer geographical unity. But over the years physical relocations and boundary changes, as well as diminution of the population through recurrent massacres, reduced the Armenian population to a minority in almost every area of Turkey. According to the statistics of the Armenian patriarchate for 1912, Kurds composed 16 percent of the population of the six Armenian vilayets, Turks constituted 25 percent, and Armenians made up 39 percent.[42]

Mobilization of the Victim Group's Agencies of Self-defense: Sociocultural Self-defense

Under the *millet* system, Armenians had suffered discrimination for approximately 450 years. In the late 1800s, Armenians had been brutally massacred by the hundreds of thousands. Finally, they optimistically believed they would find a period of respite under the Young Turk regime, which the *Dashnak* party had supported.

As previously discussed, the *Dashnak* party was the largest of all Armenian political parties by 1908. Unfortunately, the party placed its hopes in the Young Turks and supported them in their quest for power, believing the false promises of equality given the Armenians. Thus many Armenians claimed allegiance to the party destined to destroy them. At a time when Armenians might have been developing self-defense movements and warning other Armenians of impending danger, they were placing their trust in the Young Turks. In this way Armenian leaders and political agencies were coopted—that is, until it was too late.

El-Ghusein points out that the policy of the *Dashnaks* and the *Hunchaks* was loyalty to Turkey, since Armenians were more concerned with reforms than independence. He explains:

The programme of these two Societies is to make every effort and adopt every means to attain that end from which no Armenian ever swerves, namely, administrative independence under the supervision of the Great Powers of

Europe. . . . The Armenians, therefore, prefer to remain under Turkish rule, on condition that the administration is carried on under the supervision of the Great European Powers, as they place no confidence in the promises of the Turks, who take back to-day what they bestowed yesterday.[43]

The Armenians made numerous attempts at self-defense as evidenced by the resistance and fighting at Van and at Zeitun. There were innumerable acts of self-sacrifice and heroism by Armenians, but the effects of these were minor in comparison to the efforts exerted against them. Deportation efforts were often preceded by a search and seizure of illegal weapons. It is impossible to fight against armed soldiers with only bare hands. Those who had the strength to resist, even with bare hands, were killed first. All intellectuals and people with leadership abilities as well as strong young men were arrested and usually killed before the deportations began. "When the signal was given for the caravans to move, therefore, they almost invariably consisted of women, children, and old men. Anyone who could possibly have protected them from the fate that awaited them had been destroyed."[44] The Armenians themselves could in no way have exercised any control over Turkish aggression.

Realization of Impending Group Annihilation: Psychological Self-defense

An environment pregnant with promises of equality from the Young Turks, such as Enver's speech in praise of Armenian soldiers as late as February 1915, raised the hopes of Armenians for a just government. In reality, the genocide was about to begin.

Because of subterfuge practiced by the Young Turks, the Armenians were generally pacified. They were not aware of all that was happening, since the government made concerted efforts to muffle news of deportations. Later, as information leaked out, they were still not sure about what was actually occurring. Ida Alamuddin says that "at first the people who were living under the threat of deportation had no idea what was going to happen or whether all Armenian communities were affected or only those in the border towns."[45]

One method of insuring secrecy was "the sale of letters," an example of which is described by El-Ghusein. When the deportation of 700 men began, Turkish officials prepared letters with the signatures of the deportees and sent them to Armenian families so as to mislead them into thinking that the men were alive, thus keeping the murders of these men a secret. Individual families paid large sums of money for the letters. The government ordered a Kurd to kill the men who had written the letters and then deliver the letters to their families. Next, the government dispatched a man to kill the Kurd.[46]

By the time Armenians realized the government's intentions toward them, it was too late to launch a united, effective defense. Even had they known what awaited them in the future, their geographic dispersion and minority numbers in many provinces would probably have prevented them from launching an effective defense.

During the early phases of the genocide, Armenians truly believed the government's claims of deporting them to a place of safety. In some areas they were even told to leave the house key, so that the Turks could take good care of their belongings until their return.[47]

As at Adana in 1909, Armenians with arms fought to protect their loved ones and homes when they realized the impending danger. They resisted only when they were convinced that the Ottoman Government had failed them and that they were marked for extermination. At Adana, when they received assurances from the government at Constantinople that they would be protected against the local population, they believed and trusted the government once more. They continually accepted the government's lies. According to authentic, eyewitness testimony, in every instance of this kind there was a betrayal of their faith. Ottoman officials would promise they would not be harmed, the Armenians would lay down their weapons, and the government would butcher them.[48]

Physical Ability to Retaliate: Biological Self-defense

Gibbons assesses the effects of grueling agony that saps the desire to live.

Death became the one thing to be longed for: for how can hope live, how can strength remain, even to the fittest, in a journey that has no end: And if they turned to right or left from that road to hell, they were shot or speared. . . . Oh! if they would only massacre them, and be done with it, as in the Hamidian days! . . . the women would hold up their children, and cry for water. They had got beyond a desire for bread.[49]

El-Ghusein, based on information told him by a Turkish provincial governor, described the behavior of Armenian women as they were turned over to local butchers for assassination. El-Ghusein recalled the governor told him "he had seen one of these women eating a piece of bread as she went up to the butcher, another smoking a cigarette, and that it was as though they cared nothing for death."[50] Such behavior is reflective of a total block between oneself and one's environment, the only means of psychological self-defense available to people in a hopeless situation.

At Moush the government had hired butchers who were paid a Turkish pound each day for killing people. A Turkish doctor, Aziz Bey, who witnessed many murders, confided to El-Ghusein what he saw:

... four butchers, each with a long knife; the gendarmes divided the Armenians into parties of ten, and sent them up to the butchers one by one. The butcher told the Armenian to stretch out his neck; he did so, and was slaughtered like a sheep. The doctor was amazed at their steadfastness in presence of death, not saying a word, or showing any sign of fear.[51]

Again, we see that any hope for survival had long since ceased and psychological defense processes had taken over.

Ecological conditions, of course, contributed in a major way to the deaths of Armenians. Along with battling the elements of the weather—severe heat and severe cold without proper clothing or shelter—starvation and disease took a great toll. Dysentery and typhus were fatal to the undernourished.

Niepage points out that there was "a campaign of starvation" against the exiles aimed at the extermination of the whole nation. Hunger and thirst, he attests, destroyed the convoys, since even when approaching rivers, those dying of thirst were not permitted to drink. The only nourishment given was a daily ration of meal sprinkled on their hands, which they licked off. Niepage, a German eyewitness, describes the scenes opposite the German Technical School in Aleppo where remnants of convoys were dying:

Most of them are suffering from typhoid and dysentery. When one enters the yard, one has the impression of entering a mad-house. If one brings them food, one notices that they have forgotten how to eat. Their stomach, weakened by months of starvation, can no longer assimilate nourishment. If one gives them bread, they put it aside indifferently. They just lie there quietly, waiting for death.[52]

The words of a survivor, Armenian Protestant pastor and community leader, the Reverend Abraham Hartunian, summarize, in effect, the abandonment of the Armenians by many nations, thus giving the Turks a free hand to do as they chose. The Reverend Hartunian with the aid of Near East Relief, left Turkey and came to America. He had experienced the genocide from beginning to end and bemoans the fate of his people in the following lament:

Oh that we had realized from the start that all the European powers were thinking only of their own gain and were ready to sacrifice the Armenians!

Oh that we had known they were not our saviors, but murderers, more cruel than the Turks! They had not declared war to save enslaved and powerless nations but to buy oil, mines, and land by giving these same nations in exchange!

Oh that we had understood they were deceivers! They had not prepared to preserve the peace of the world but to preserve their own imperialism at the price of the peace of the world!

Oh that instead of relying on them and respecting them we had relied on and respected the Turk! The Turk openly declared himself our enemy and destroyed us. The Europeans, Judas-like, kissing us, betrayed us. The Britisher, the Frenchman, the German, the Italian, the Russian—all the Christian powers of the world are our murderers. . . . [53]

II

THEORETICAL INQUIRY
INTO THE JEWISH HOLOCAUST

THE MORE narrowly the membership of the in-group is defined, the greater is the range of permissible license of behavior towards those who are excluded from it. This range will be roughly correlated with the degree of exclusion; that is, it will be highest in regard to those who, by definition, are permanently and forever denied admission to the in-group. . . . at the extreme limit of social distance from possible inclusion in the in-group, human beings might be regarded as belonging to a different species toward whom, then, no humane principles need function as guides to conduct. . . .

—THEODORE ABEL

7

CREATION OF "OUTSIDERS"

A NECESSARY requirement for genocide is dehumanization of the victim group. This can be accomplished by two steps—the first is the creation of an out-group, or "outsiders," and the second is the directing of intense aggression against this target group. Both of these steps will be examined.

HISTORY OF INTERGROUP TENSIONS

Previously existing social cleavages within a society, such as religion, race, or class, provide a basis according to which a superordinate group may assign blame or responsibility for undesirable social conditions to a subordinate social group. Blaming specific groups for social ills is not an accidental or chance event but, rather, has its basis in a history of social divisions. Blaming Jews for all of Germany's social problems was based on a long history of social cleavages severing Jews from the social body and resulting in the German perception of

Jews as outsiders. To many Germans, Jews provided a socially acceptable, legitimate scapegoat. In his article "Sociology of Concentration Camps," Theodore Abel reflects upon the social cleavages that result in defining people as the "out-group." He indicates that

> human beings might be regarded as belonging to a different species toward whom, then, no humane principles need function as guides to conduct. . . . modes of conduct, once established and having become habitual, function as means of status distinctions and of the distribution of rewards and punishments and thus tend to be perpetuated by those who can benefit from them.[1]

Social divisions indicating that Jews did not belong to the "in-group" were clearly evident in Germany as early as 1781. In that year Christian Wilhelm von Dohm (1751–1820), political writer, historian, Prussian diplomat, and "liberal" German, expounded in his book, *Uber die burgerliche Verbesserung der Juden (On the Civic Betterment of the Jews)*, upon the need to change the contemporary Jew and his religion, thus removing the Jews' "disabilities" and paving the way for his emancipation. After 1781 the extent to which Jews must surrender their Jewishness to be granted full citizenship became the crux of an endless debate.[2] Even such "liberal" ideas as converting Jews to make them "acceptable" were anathema to some who charged that, "Christian persecution during the Middle Ages had not formed the debased character of contemporary Jews, for Jews had already displayed the same deficiencies in the Biblical period. . . . "[3]

The pressure to assimilate and convert Jews was unrelenting. In the 1840s Frederick William IV concluded that Jews constituted an unassimilable minority group in a Christian state. Yet even those Jews who assimilated were still viewed as different. Ludwig Borne, a Jew who converted to Christianity in 1818 to evade the effects of revoked emancipation in Frankfurt, concluded:

> It is like a miracle! I have experienced it a thousand times and still it remains ever new. Some accuse me of being a Jew, others forgive me for being a Jew, still others praise me for it, but all of them reflect upon it.[4]

Lucy Dawidowicz in her monumental work, *The War Against the Jews*, describes the thread of German anti-Semitism from Martin Luther to Adolf Hitler, both of whom were obsessed with notions of a "demonologized universe inhabited by Jews." Luther had written, "Know, Christian, that next to the devil thou hast no enemy more cruel, more venomous and violent than a true Jew."[5] Luther's work, nurtured by the foundation of anti-Semitism previously laid by the Catholic Church, was revived when the Nazis rose to power.

According to Dawidowicz, modern German anti-Semitism was the "bastard child" of a marriage between German nationalism and Christian anti-Semitism. Christian anti-Semitism was old and deep rooted, and during the Enlightenment German nationalism flourished as notions of Jewish emancipation gained momentum. Germany, confronted with the problems of adapting to liberal ideas, resolved the conflict by choosing "culture over civilization." Culture was viewed as "innate" and as a part of a specific people, whereas civilization was conceived to be external, not associated with the essence of a specific culture, people, or race. "Innateness" required that one be biologically German to be a part of the German culture. During the Enlightenment von Dohm wrote in favor of granting the Jews political equality, but Germany rejected such a radical idea. This intolerance was a clear intimation of the future.[6]

German nationalism intensified on the heels of Germany's defeat in the Napoleonic wars and inspired a backward-looking attitude to the remote days of German power and glory. A sense of nostalgia for bygone days of glory became pervasive.

Between 1789 and 1815 the ethos of Nazi Germany began taking shape. For a period of time the Napoleonic Wars favored France. The Germans detested the French and their dreams of emancipation—which, of course, would benefit the Jews. As German states were confederated under a French protectorate, a new nationalism grew transcending the boundaries of German states and the contemporary political situation. Dawidowicz claims this was the formative period that shaped the German national character, and it was at this time the Germans embarked upon defining and thus separating themselves from the French and the Jews. The philosopher associated with this movement was Johann Gottlieb Fichte (1762-1814). In his *Reden an die deutsche Nation,* published in 1808, he bade Germans to "have character and be German," proclaiming a messianic future for the Germans, since, " . . . among all modern peoples it is you in whom the seed of human perfection most decidedly lies, and you who are charged with progress in human development. . . . "[7] Fichte is referred to as the "Father of German Nationalism." He detested and denigrated Jews, calling them "a state within a state." The idea of emancipating Jews absolutely galled him.

Later, Ernest Moritz Arndt (1769-1860) and Frederich Ludwig Jahn (1778-1852) developed a concept of German nationalism linked with the word "*Volk,*" which purportedly represented the nature, depth of feeling, and essence of the German people. According to Jahn, the state was the house which preserved this *Volk.* Thus, the state came to be identified with a national spirit.[8]

At about the same time Christian Friedrich Ruhs (1781-1820) of the University of Berlin held that Jews should not be awarded rights of German citizenship, since they were a foreign people in a Christian state. He advocated converting Jews to Christianity so that they could acquire "true" German ethnic characteristics. The conversion, he claimed, would also serve the purpose of destroying the Jewish people. Since Jews, Ruhs posited, were a "state within a state," they could be permitted to be subjects, but not citizens, of Germany (a distinction later to be made by Hitler as well). He held that this "alien" group should be excluded from the army, guilds and corporations, and public office. Ruhs even suggested renewing the medieval yellow patch. The "wandering Jew," condemned to eternal homelessness by his rejection of the Messiah, could not be a part of the *Volk*, since its defining characteristic was rootedness.

German nationalism gained ground after Napoleon's defeat as Germans sought revenge toward their enemies—the French and Jews. Rights of Jews were quickly rescinded nearly everywhere in Germany. In addition, violent pogroms and attacks began against Jews, the most violent of which was the "Hep! Hep!" movement erupting in Wurzburg in 1819 and quickly engulfing Germany. The likes of this movement, with its battle cry "Hep! Hep! Hep! Death and destruction to all of the Jews!" had not been witnessed since the Middle Ages. This was the first time that German nationalism marked the Jew as its enemy.

Meanwhile, Bruno Bauer (1809–1882), reflecting the anti-Semitism of the newly emerging German socialist movement, wrote an article against political equality for the Jews, contending that they had never contributed to world civilization. Ironically, these ideas would later become the stock-in-trade for proclamations of the anti-Semitic right.

In this atmosphere of antipathy toward Jews, the Revolution of 1848 heralded a liberalization of public opinion, and the National Assembly convening in Frankfurt declared that the enjoyment of political rights was not dependent upon religious creed. Within a year, however, a reaction set in against Jewish emancipation. As news of liberalization hit the Rhineland, pogroms began and Jewish rights were either not granted or restricted.

Ideas of race were coming more and more into the limelight. A Conservative party was founded in Germany in 1848 advocating racism and anti-Semitism. Paul de Lagarde (1827–1891), who later became the *Volkish* patron saint of anti-Semitism, eventually called for an expurgation of any Jewish elements from Christianity and preached a Christian-German faith. De Lagarde wrote that the Jews were vermin—trichinae and bacilli—and should be thoroughly and quickly exterminated. (This theme of Jews as vermin was to continue into the Third Reich where it would be taken literally.) At the University of Bonn, a "science" of race was surfacing. A professor of ancient civilization, Christian Lassen (1802–1871), promoted the idea that Semites were "selfish and exclusive." Count Joseph Arthur de Gobineau (1816–1882), in his *Essai sur l'inegalite des races humaines*, insisted that social degeneration was caused by race mixing, which would dissipate pure racial blood and eventually destroy the Aryan race.

By 1873 Germany suffered a financial collapse brought on by worldwide depression. And the Jews were blamed for Germany's woes. Anti-Semites adduced that this collapse was conclusive evidence that Jews were engaging in financial manipulations and were, consequently, undermining the country. The latent anticapitalist sentiments of the peasants and lower-middle classes were reawakened and revitalized by the depression. These groups, extremely vulnerable to economic change, were easily prejudiced against the Jews, and spokesmen of anti-Semitism easily exploited the limited role of Jews in some branches of the "modern" economy.[9]

From the 1880s on there was a torrent of anti-Semitism that did not abate for almost twenty years. University professors and political parties espoused anti-Semitism. The phrase "the Jews are our misfortune" was popularized in the writings of Heinrich von Treitchke, a professor of history at the University of Berlin. In the fall of 1880 two schoolteachers, Bernard Forster (Friedrich Nietzsche's brother-in-law) and Ernst Henrici, assisted by a minor aristocrat, Max Liebermann von Sonnenberg, initiated an "Anti-Semites Petition"; it was publicly distributed by students. By the 1890s a dangerous form of anti-Semitism had moved quietly and insidiously through academic circles.[10]

Following the depression-ridden economy of the 1870s up to the 1890s, traditional life-styles underwent marked changes as a consequence of industrialism. Peasants and farmers feared for their way of life and their land. Charging a "Jewish conspiracy" against the traditional German life-style, peasants, farmers, and others feeling that German social and economic patterns were being disrupted formed the *Mittelstand*, a group which would later emerge as a political force. The group reflected the views of some discontented small farmers, peasants, small businessmen, artisans, lower-level professionals, and officialdom, who were hostile toward the rapidly burgeoning urban, industrial society and its politics. In the next forty years this group would become increasingly rightist.[11]

Anti-Semitism abounded and numerous anti-Semitic parties were formed. Anti-Semitic presses arose, such as Theodor Fritsch's (1844–

1933) publishing house, which began to issue *Antisemitische Corre-spondenz* in 1882. Fritsch's primary concern was to infuse all political parties with a fiery anti-Semitism.

In the 1890s the *Mittelstand*, viewing society through *Volkish* eyes, gave support only to conservative centrist parties, to German imperialism, and to anti-Semitism. In 1893, at the organizational zenith of the *Mittelstand*, the *Alldeutscher Verband* (Pan-German League) was formed. It provided a vehicle for the expression of German imperialism, nationalism, and overt anti-Semitism. By 1900 its membership reached 20,000. The occupational groups most highly represented in the *Verband* were university professors and lecturers (5,000); small businessmen (4,900); and civil servants and teachers (3,760). The *Deutschnationaler Handlungsgehilfenverband* (National Germanic League of Clerks) was also founded in 1893. "Jews or persons whose character is not blameless" were excluded from membership. Both the League of Clerks and the Pan-German League were political pressure groups.

A third *Mittelstand* parapolitical organization, also founded in 1893 and the most influential of the three, was the *Bund der Landwirte* (Agrarian League) that by the end of the decade had 250,000 members. This group consisted of large-scale and small-scale farmers held together by an anti-Semitic form of German nationalism. They proclaimed that agriculture and Jewry were in a struggle to the death. The *Bund* promoted expulsion of Jews from Germany, prohibited social relations between Jews and Germans, and boycotted Jewish stores. By this time anti-Semitic and *Volkish* student gymnastic and sports organizations were formed. Racist works were becoming required reading for right-wing students, and free anti-Semitic pamphlets were being sent to all German state officials.[12]

It is interesting at this point to note how German Jews were responding to the wave of *Volkish* anti-Semitism. The following is from a publication of the first organization within the German-Jewish establishment to emphasize the integrity and respectability of the Jew as a human being and his honorable, equal status as a German citizen. The organization, founded in 1893, the *Centralverein fur deutsche Staatsburger judischen Glaubens* (Central Union of German Citizens of the Jewish Faith) proclaimed in 1912:

Loyalty to Judaism serves the cause of the fatherland [Germany]; when we work together to uplift our moral and ethical community, we are in fact working in the interest of the fatherland. The great forces in Judaism—the ideas of unity, tradition, and optimism serve us well. . . . Because we are loyal [to Judaism] we are also loyal to the fatherland.

This proclamation reflected the feelings of the majority of Germany's Jews, and it is amazing that such strong feelings of belonging could exist in the historically hostile atmosphere we have just presented. It helps to bear in mind that Germany's Jews were by far the most socially assimilated of all European Jewry.[13]

By the late 1800s it was clear that the idealistic myth of the German Volk was to play a crucial role in the fate of the Jews. George Mosse, in Nazi Culture, explains that "a myth is the strongest belief held by a group, and its adherents feel themselves to be an army of truth fighting an army of evil."[14] We might say that the German myth was the Volk. The land of Germany and the bloodline of Germans were epitomized as all that was good and worthy of sacrifice and loyalty. There was an emphasis on the past, respect for all that was traditional, conservative, and tied to the roots of the country. It was almost as though a fusion took place that resulted in something mystical and unreal which was sought after at almost any cost.

Joseph Tenenbaum, in Race and Reich, asserts that the extent of Germany's absorption in the spirit of Volk is typified by the dialectic of George Wilhelm Friedrich Hegel, the nineteenth-century German philosopher who profoundly influenced German thought. Tenenbaum notes that concepts like patriotism, race, and nationalism were put on a pedestal of human, even divine, ideals; but Hegel added yet another divinity to this pedestal—the state. In Hegel's Philosophy of Right, the state is conceived to be the instrument through which human freedom and will manifest themselves—the "Divine Idea." Hegel states: "it is the moral whole, the State, which is the form of reality in which the individual has and enjoys freedom. . . . Law, Morality, and Government . . . alone [are] the positive reality and completion of Freedom." In discussing the practical aspects of Hegel's philosophy of the state, John Herman Randall asserts: "The outcome of all such notions is clear; rational criticism of such a living organism, such a mystical embodiment of the Will and Purpose of God on earth, is entirely aside from the point. Accept the State God has given you, live in it, die for it; but do not presume to question its wisdom or alter its form." We might say that the German state was now viewed as the "embodiment of the will and purpose of God on earth." Could this "embodiment of God" possibly do anything wrong or evil?[15]

Dawidowicz concludes that the generations upon generations Jews had spent on German soil assimilating into German culture stood for naught. Modern German anti-Semitism abounded in platforms, declarations, and credos revolving around the central thesis that Jews were aliens in the German nation—alien to its people, culture, and land.[16] By idealizing all that was traditionally German, all that was *not* of German blood and German soil, of course, represented the outsider, the enemy, standing in the way of total national unity and harmony. In Germany the word "enemy" became synonymous with "Jew."

Anti-Semitism was now different in nature. Traditional anti-Semitism centered on religion as the definitive point, but when Social Darwinism surfaced in the late nineteenth century, differences in religion gave way to differences in race. Accepting the idea that human society was a biological organism, the Darwinists contended that the biological factor was the most important one in all spheres of life. German exponents of Social Darwinism thus elevated Darwin's theory to the level of a world philosophy.[17]

Social Darwinism and the *Volk* ideal, both growing out of the nineteenth century, became intertwined. Previously, Count de Gobineau's *Essai sur l'inegalite des races humaines*, a book sponsored by Richard Wagner, claimed that blood purity was essential, since a mixture, or contamination, resulted in the degeneration of a people. "But," says Tenenbaum, "the most pleasing conclusion, as far as the Germans were concerned, was the 'discovery' that the Aryans were the cream of mankind and the Germans the cream of the cream, 'a race of princes.' "[18]

We can say that "outsiders" had now been created. Jews had been outsiders first to the Christian community, then to the social and national community, and finally to the "Aryan" racial community. Social divisions had become more and more dramatic. The new form of Jew hatred was fraught with a new form of danger. After all, a man can change his religion; it is a matter of personal freedom and personal choice. Race, on the other hand, is not a matter of choice, nor is it changeable. Yehuda Bauer concludes:

Until about the middle of the 19th century, anti-Semitism had been based mainly on religion; Jews were objectionable because, and only as long as, they refused to embrace Christianity. But now there arose a new, pseudoscientific racist theory, which held that Jews were a separate race—intrinsically inferior and evil—and a foreign body in any host nation. Nothing could curb the Jews' pernicious influence, the racists argued, except eliminating them from society altogether.[19]

There is a logical progression from religious anti-Semitism to racism to physical elimination of the out-group. To the Germans the "Jewish problem" begged a resolution—if not in one way, then in another. Anti-Semitism was not new to the world, and Germany was not alone in its desire to be *Judenrein* (free of Jews).

In retrospect it appears that many forces were at work in Germany to help bring the genocide to fruition. The Germans who had exhibited an affinity for general theories with a worldview (*Weltanschaung*) welcomed Darwinian theories espousing natural selection and survival of the most fit in a struggle for existence. Darwinism created fantasies of national superiority in many thinkers. According to Nora Levin, moreover, Germans possessed a deep-rooted need for transcendence and mission in conjunction with enough daring to carry through ideas to their ultimate. These tendencies added an appeal to the idea of genocide. Levin explains:

Faust with his overreaching will, Wotan willing his own destruction and Tristan and Isolde, dying in an ecstasy of love, are significantly German. This piercing of the ultimate has been described by Thomas Mann: "If Faust is to be the representative of the German soul, he would have to be musical, for the relation of the German to the world is abstract and mystical, that is, musical—the relation of a professor with a touch of demonism, awkward at the same time filled with arrogant knowledge that he surpasses the world in 'depth.' "

Levin goes on to say:

This "depth" has frequently resulted in a complete divorce of the ideological from social and political realities, a divorce which achieved its extreme expression in the extermination of almost six million Jews, a national deed which achieved no meaningful purpose, but was the expression of an "ideal."[20]

The logical conclusion of this type of *Weltanschaung* finally emerged in German thought and deed. Social Darwinist theories stressed that one's usefulness to society and also to the state should serve as a yardstick in measuring human worth. People should then serve the state, which would be accorded full powers of control.[21]

Pushing anti-Semitism to a zenith was Germany's loss of World War I (to be discussed under "Internal Strife"). Afterwards, the Weimar Republic, rising out of despair and hope, finally gave the Jews complete equality. But on 24 February 1920, only six months after the enacting of the Weimar Constitution, the German Workers' Party, later to become the *Nationalsozialistische Deutsche Arbeiter Partei* (National Socialist German Workers' Party, the Nazi party), issued a twenty-five point program, asserting that Jews were not members of the German *Volk* and that only persons of German blood were to be regarded as citizens of the German state.

National Socialism was to consummate the goal toward which omnifarious anti-Semitic groups had been striving for 150 years.[22]

INTENSIFICATION OF AGGRESSION AGAINST "OUTSIDERS"

Ideas such as those just discussed, in conjunction with conditions in Germany after World War I (though the Weimar period was one of relative security for Jewish people), resulted in increased levels of hatred against the Jews, and ideas became translated into actions. Response to this hatred was stimulated as well by propaganda. It must be pointed out that all factors in the theory of genocide work simultaneously together at all times; to isolate them conceptually simplifies analysis but should not mislead us into thinking that they occur in an isolated fashion. Genocide is the culmination of many factors coalescing at a particular point in history and in a certain way. Next, consideration of a series of events beginning in pre-World War II Germany and culminating in the Holocaust will be analyzed. Placed in a time sequence, these factors began with Hitler's ascension to power in 1933.

Boycott

Part of the general propaganda against the Jews concerned their supposed "control" of world financial affairs. The paranoia resulting from this idea was translated from the abstractness of world finance to attacks upon specific individual Jewish businessman, shops, and stores. Germany had recently suffered economic hardship, unemployment, and inflation (discussed in the next section). The Jews were mostly businessmen, serving as a "middleman minority" in Germany, performing economic functions, specializing in commerce, finance, and the professions.[23] They were vulnerable in that significant role as a target for hostility.

On 1 April 1933 the Nazi government directed its first official act against the Jews—the boycott of Jewish enterprises. This was supposedly a retaliation against a boycott initiated by *both* Jews and non-Jews against German products. Paul Joseph Goebbels (Reich Minister of Public Enlightenment and Propaganda) encouraged and rationalized the attack saying unfavorable foreign reports about the Nazis were "atrocity tales" spread by Jews that were negatively affecting German business. Julius Streicher (publisher of *"Der Stuermer"*) organized the boycott in retaliation against the Jews, but news of it produced panic in non-Jewish industrial circles, and Hitler was inveighed upon to abandon it. He refused to abandon it totally; instead, he limited it to a single day—Saturday, 1 April. A few days preceding 1 April, Nazi rowdies had driven Jewish physicians from hospitals and Jewish judges and lawyers from the courts.[24]

On 1 April the boycott was activated, and pickets were organized in front of all Jewish factories, stores, shops, and professional offices to deter anyone from entering. This campaign was flawlessly arranged, revealing the thoroughness and efficiency of Nazi espionage. It was easy to identify businesses owned by Jews, since lists of Jews and lists of Christians married to Jews, along with information regarding their financial assets had already been processed by the Nazis. To insure the completeness of these lists, they were rechecked on 7 June 1933. Propagandaleiter Bang sent the orders regarding "List M18, Jew Baiting," to all district directorates, stating,

You will receive in the next few days a list of the communities of your districts in which you will find the Jewish firms and businesses of your district. You will immediately check in your whole district whether the addresses given are correct or whether some have been forgotten. The highest importance is to be placed on accuracy since the list is to be printed.[25]

Then the order discusses ways to shame "miscreant" Germans from doing business with Jews by exposing their purchases in anonymous newspaper articles. The order also instructs female clerks working in Jewish shops to expose Germans shopping at Jewish shops.

The Nazis were perfecting methods of outlawing Jews, and the boycott (even though unsuccessful) had instilled in Germans the notion that destruction of the economic life of Jews was permissible, acceptable, and even desirable. Later acts of Germans would be based upon free license to act against the Jews. As Levin points out, this boycott precipitated other measures taken against the Jews that were more damaging to property, possessions, and later to life itself.[26]

The Legal Attack against the Jews

According to Dawidowicz, the Enabling Act (discussed in Chapter 9) bestowed upon Hitler the legal power by which he could later carry out a war against the Jews. In 1933 the Third Reich's first law against the Jews was promulgated—the "Law for the Restoration of the Professional Civil Service."

The following anti-Jewish legislation began almost immediately upon Hitler's ascension to power: the law for the restoration of the professional civil service (7 April 1933); the law regarding admission to the bar (7 April 1933); the law against the overcrowding of German schools and institutions of higher learning (25 April 1933); the Reich citizenship law (15 September 1935); the law for the protection of German blood and German honor (15 September 1935); the law regarding the legal status of the Jewish religious communities (28 March 1938); the decree regarding the reporting of Jewish property (26 April 1938);

and the decree on a penalty payment by Jews who are German subjects (12 November 1938). The phraseology of these laws and decrees
was deceptive, but the target was the Jew. Eventually some four hundred decrees and laws were to be enacted, their sole purpose being the
destruction of European Jewry.[27]

As levels of violence escalated, the legal battle against the Jews
increased also. Definition of the victim, a prerequisite for large-scale
persecution, was supplied. This definition was posited in 1933, being
further refined and clarified in the Nuremberg laws of 1935.

The Nuremberg Laws

On 7 April 1933 a definition of "non-Aryan" was drawn up. A non-
Aryan was a person with one Jewish parent or grandparent. This definition, the "Aryan paragraph," was soon applied to government agencies, organizations, and private individuals. Proving descent became
imperative for Aryans and non-Aryans alike. To be employed by the
Reich or party necessitated obtaining the records of your ancestors—
sometimes as many as seven documents. You needed your own birth
certificate, both parents' certificates, and those of all four grand-
parents. Putting "Aryan" clauses into effect by barring Jews from certain jobs and professions became a point of honor to many Germans.
The Jews, "the enemies of the State," soon began to reel under the
stigmata of isolation.[28]

The Nuremberg laws (1935) were another step toward genocide.
On 15 September 1935 two new laws were enacted—the Reich citizenship Law and the Law for the Protection of German Blood and German
Honor. Jews were separated not just socially but legally. Hitler moved
rapidly after assuming power to provide "legal" grounds for his war
against Jews, such as the Nuremberg laws of September 1935. These
laws launched a frontal attack upon all Jewish individuals living in
Germany. Up to 1935 Jews were hounded, beaten up, and persecuted.
These actions were officially deprecated or excused as an "irrepress-
ible" reaction by Germans to years of alien, that is Jewish, domination. The Nazis said that there would no longer be any need for Germans to act "illegally." People's natural feelings would be provided a
legal expression through the Nuremberg laws. By 1935 the Nazis were
bold, convinced that no international reaction could threaten them,
and the laws were enacted.[29]

A crude, brutal, daily anti-Semitism now emerged. In many villages and towns public slogans rang: "The Jew is our misfortune,"
"Let Judah Perish!" and "Jews not wanted here."[30]

Hans Pfundter, Wilhelm Stuckart, and Bernhard Losener, experts
on "racial law," drafted the 1935 "Law for the Protection of German

Blood and German Honor," which forbade Jews from marrying Ger-. man nationals and those of kindred blood; having extramarital relations with Germans; employing female domestics of German or kindred blood under the age of forty-five; and flying the German national colors.[31]

Dr. Kurt Blome, secretary of the Medical Association (later deputy director of the Reich Health Office) suggested that half-Jews be defined as Jews since, "among the half-Jews the Jewish genes are notoriously dominant."[32] The 1935 definition of Jew replaced that of 1933 and was published 11 April 1935. Lucy Dawidowicz summarizes it as follows:

> Briefly, the categories were: (1) Jew, (2) Mischling, first degree, and (3) Mischling, second degree. A Jew was anyone with at least three full Jewish grandparents. Also legally to be regarded as a Jew was someone who had two full Jewish grandparents and who belonged to the Jewish religious community when the law was promulgated September 15, 1935, or who joined later, or who was married to a Jew then or later or (looking to the future) who was the offspring of a marriage contracted with a Jew after September 15, 1935, or who was born out of wedlock after July 31, 1936, the offspring of extramarital relations with a Jew. Anyone who was one-eighth or one-sixteenth Jewish—with one Jewish great grandparent or great-great-grandparent—would be considered as of German blood.
>
> More complicated was the status of the "part-Jews." A person with two Jewish grandparents, who did not otherwise fit into the group defined as Jews, that is, who was not affiliated with the Jewish religious community, who was not married to a Jew, etc., was designated as "Mischling, first degree." A person with only one Jewish grandparent was designated as "Mischling, second degree." For the time being, these distinctions affected marriage and offspring of that marriage. Within a few short years they were to decide between life or death.[33]

This definition itself, though appearing harmless, signaled the beginning of the annihilation of German Jewry, since the Jew was now officially an enemy of the state. In addition, once Jews were defined and described, they could be isolated, expropriated, ghettoized, and exterminated.[34]

Raul Hilberg indicates that the most dangerous aspect of laws creating a "definition" of Jews was their administrative continuity—a factor distinguishing a destruction process from a pogrom. A pogrom results in a measure of damage to property and injury to people, but necessitates no further action. A destruction process, however, is aimed at the total destruction of a people and has continuity. Some steps may not inflict damage, yet they lead to further consequences. A dialectic occurs wherein each step provides the basis for the next stage.[35]

Legislative action against the Jews was renewed in May 1935 with the proclamation of a new Military Service Law, requiring Aryan ancestry as a prerequisite for admittance to the armed services; this excluded German Jewry who had always exhibited great pride about their defense of the fatherland. The elimination of Jews from military service, in effect, lowered their status as citizens. The hand of the SS (*Schutzstaffel*—to be discussed in Chap. 9) was evident in this action, for it was their established voice, *Das Schwarze Korps*, which published an editorial entitled "No Room for Jews in the Military" a few days before the official law was pronounced.[36]

No substantial anti-Jewish legislation was enacted for the next few years—until 1938. During this time the SS, the most prestigious and feared branch of the National Socialist movement, began asserting its hegemony in matters regarding Jews in all party and state institutions.[37]

Expropriation (The Laws of 1938)

The level of aggression moved ever upward through the decade of the 1930s, and more laws were enacted in 1938 that were to usher in doom for the Jews. These were the laws of 1938, with their concomitant economic persecution. Apart from their obvious economic destruction of the Jew, they also served to isolate him even further than did the racial laws, removing him from his place in the social world and paving his way to the concentration camps.

By 1938 Hermann Goering, the Nazi's "chief Aryanizer" (Reich marshal, air minister, Reich counselor for defense, and commissioner of the Four Year Plan), concentrated his efforts upon the expropriation of the Jews. In Jewish policy, centralization of agencies of control reflected the newfound powers of Reinhard Heydrich (former general in the SS, eventually chief of Security Police and Security Service), Goering, and Adolf Eichmann (Lt. Col. in the SS; chief of Amt IVB4 or Office for Jewish Affairs of Secret State Police; Reich Security Main Office). A more *effective, bureaucratic solution* to the "Jewish problem" was being sought.[38]

Between July and December of 1938 the ministerial bureaucracy destroyed the remaining vestiges of Jewish self-employed and business activity. Termination dates were set for the operation of commercial services, lawyers' offices, doctors' offices, and retail establishments. Trustee administration was imposed by appointees of the Economy Ministry upon retail establishments, real estate, industrial enterprises, and agricultural properties. Hilberg enumerates six decrees providing economic solutions to the "Jewish problem"; these were implemented in 1938, a year of onslaught against the Jews. The first decree, 6 July 1938—dealing with commercial services—provided for termination of Jewish business activities in guard services, real estate agencies, credit information bureaus, marriage agencies catering to non-Jews, visitors' guides, brokerage agencies, and peddling. The second decree, enacted on 25 July 1938, withdrew licenses from Jewish physicians. A third decree, dated 27 September 1938, prevented Jewish lawyers from practicing. A 12 November 1938 decree ordered Jewish retail establishments to cease all business activities by 31 December. In November 1938 Hitler and Goering decided to Aryanize all remaining Jewish enterprises. On 3 December 1938 the final decree was enacted requiring the forced sale of Jewish industrial firms, securities, land, forest, real estate, with all stocks, bonds, and securities required to be deposited with the Finance Committee.[39]

The first target in this pauperization of the Jews was the Jewish intelligentsia. Lawyers were forbidden to appear in court; doctors could have no non-Jewish patients; writers, journalists, artists, teachers, and musicians had become superfluous since it was illegal for them to practice their professions. As Ronald Donat claims, "their very existence was an anachronism."[40]

The Nuremberg laws of 1935 clearly placed Jews outside the protection of governmental authority. The escalation of legal, economic, and cultural persecution continued through the expropriation of all property, the inability to practice a profession or even operate a business. Also the government imposed restrictions upon emigration into or out of Germany. Eventually, Jews were required to wear armbands as public identification, even further segregating them from German society. Germany was saturated with anti-Semitic propaganda in the form of books, pamphlets, newspapers, radio broadcasts, and speeches at political gatherings. In November 1938 the German public participated in a violent display against the Jews known as the *Kristallnacht* pogrom.

Kristallnacht

The following incident, *Kristallnacht* ("Night of Glass"), served as a precipitating factor to genocide by lending government legitimacy and support to acts of anti-Semitic violence.

The incident occurred on 7 November 1938 when a Polish Jewish boy named Hershel Grynszpan shot Ernst von Rath, a member of the German legation to Paris. Von Rath died of his wounds a few days later. His death occurred on the anniversary of the Munich Putsch, and this served as a pretext for a large-scale pogrom against Jews throughout Germany. Enormous amounts of Jewish property were destroyed. The word *Kristallnacht* signifies the enormous amounts of glass spattered about as display windows were broken at Jewish-owned stores. During this episode synagogues were razed, property was destroyed and stolen, and tens of thousands of Jews were attacked, humiliated, and tortured. Almost one hundred Jews were killed in an outpouring of vicious anti-Semitism and hatred. *Kristallnacht* clearly defined to Germans the acceptable target, "the enemy of the state," and encouraged attacks upon that enemy.[41]

This violent pogrom had the approval of the authorities, and even those Germans later accused of committing crimes were only mildly reprimanded. In addition, the occasion was exploited by the government to accelerate the expropriation of Jews and to liquidate their community. On 12 November 1938, with Goering acting as plenipotentiary of the Four Year Plan, a one billion mark penalty payment was imposed on the Jews.[42]

Since *Kristallnacht* was destructive to Jewish property and lives, German insurance companies also suffered large financial losses. Pogroms such as this came to be viewed by the Nazis as costly and inefficient. Therefore it became necessary to devise more "efficient" means of dealing with the "Jewish problem."

Hilberg's analysis of the process of destruction of the Jews from their "definition" in 1933 to their mass murder in the early 1940s indicates that each step precipitated the next in a dialectic of death and destruction. Hilberg outlines the steps in the destruction process:

At first the concept of the "Jew" was defined; then the expropriatory operations were inaugurated; then, the Jews were concentrated in ghettos; finally, the decision was made to annihilate European Jewry. Mobile killing units were sent to Russia, while in the rest of Europe the victims were deported to killing centers.[43]

The next chapter will look at the condition of Germany after World War I and some of the societal and normative strains that served to intensify hostilities against the Jews.

WITH the key of Aryanism he [Hitler] opened the hearts of the average German. Race was his steed, anti-Semitism his whip, and the depression of the 1930s put him in the saddle.

—JOSEPH TENENBAUM

8

INTERNAL STRIFE

IF a society designates a particular group as "outsiders," then stressful social conditions may contribute to the value-added process by heightening social cleavages such as ethnic, political, class, and religious divisions. Frequently, several social "strains" that we refer to as "internal strife," become assimilated with one another and combine to ignite outbursts of hostility. Conditions fostering internal strife within a society include: real or threatened deprivations, economic competition, abrupt food shortages, unemployment, rising prices, falling wages, unpopular political measures, or any frustration—real, imagined, or anticipated. Some of these societal strains will be discussed in this chapter under "Real or Threatened Deprivation: Defeat in War and Loss of Empire." Strain in norms in relation to war, postwar demobilization, and rapid institutional change will be considered here under "Normative Upheaval."

Internal strife in pre-World War II Germany cannot be discussed without referring to the institutionalized anti-Semitism long rampant in Germany. Certain major catastrophic occurrences elevated this phenomena to dangerous levels. The consequences of Germany's defeat in World War I as well as the concomitant loss of empire created a good deal of internal strife, to be discussed in the following sections.

REAL OR THREATENED DEPRIVATION: DEFEAT IN WAR AND LOSS OF EMPIRE

According to George Kren and Leon Rappoport, many historians conclude that the peace terms dictated to Germany after World War I were so unreasonably punitive and impractical as to virtually guarantee World War II. Some scholars, they assert, view the two world wars as separate episodes of the same war, halted by a twenty-year armistice. During this period Germany faced many deprivations, material and nonmaterial. The general conditions prevailing in this state of affairs and lasting from 1919 to 1933 had a direct bearing upon the rise of Naziism and created a situation which, in conjunction with many other factors, increased the likelihood of a Holocaust.[1]

Joseph Tenenbaum proposes that "A lost war is a national disaster." For Germans, the loss of World War I was a double catastrophe—humiliation and poverty. After having nurtured themselves with notions of race superiority, Germans were now groveling in defeat. Other peoples were conditioned to react differently, namely, the French after the defeat of 1871. "The penalty for race superiority in prosperity," says Tenenbaum, "is a morbid drop of self-esteem in adversity, and the inferiority complex is never too far away from the superiority claim."[2]

To assuage their national conscience, the Germans transferred their feelings of failure and guilt to others. Guilt could not be transferred to anyone powerful who might retaliate. So, who could be a better, more powerless scapegoat than the ever-present Jew? By placing responsibility for a lost war upon the Jews, German racial consciousness was deepened, rather than crushed, by defeat. It was not the "celestial Teutons" who had lost the war but, rather, the Jews and the Marxists. *They* had surreptitiously and slyly administered the fatal stab in the back to Germany. *They* had caused Germany to reel and falter.[3] Hostility against the Jews was reaching high levels.

Passage of unpopular political measures, according to Smelser, may also be a form of strain that contributes to hostile outbursts against groups. The Treaty of Versailles (1919) was extremely unpopular in Germany, since it limited the military force to a mere 100,000 people. Obviously many professional military men were displaced in German society. This treaty was something concrete the Germans could focus upon and attack. Peter Merkl indicates the intense displeasure of an SS soldier with the treaty. The soldier's story is typical of those who turned to Hitler because of the poverty forcing them to give up their hopes, dreams, and education. As a young man this soldier was obliged to drop out of school and become a lumberjack, even though he had been a bright student. By age eleven he was reading socialist and anti-Semitic literature. After serving as a soldier in World War I, he said:

The signing of the shameful Treaty of Versailles and especially the recognition of the lying clause about our war guilt triggered great bitterness in me against the government we had then. I decided to become politically active. My struggle was directed first of all against the reactionaries. . . . I was convinced it was they whose hostility to the workers gave the Jews the weapons to stir up the workers against everything German. I had felt on my own body how the worker was treated like a second-class human being.[4]

The treaty also restricted Germany's military rearmament or actions to acquire *Lebensraum* ("living space") at the expense of neighboring and other countries. The Nazis later abrogated the Versailles Treaty, for Hitler would never permit Germany's loss of "honor" by conceding her "right " to acquire more territory. He considered *Lebensraum* to be the foundation of a people's life.[5] The sources of strain related to the treaty were capitalized upon repeatedly by Hitler and served to create greater dissatisfaction within Germany about the "unjust" way in which the country was dealt with after losing the War.

Under the declared Peace of Versailles, the political situation in Germany changed rapidly. Political change, unemployment, and inflation combined and added to the nation's woes. Problems accumulated, producing severe economic strain. The German middle class was suffering severe deprivation. One thousand million marks were required for war reparation, yet important industrial areas of Germany had been lopped off: Upper Silesia, the Saar territory, Alsace-Lorraine, Posen and West Prussia ("the Polish Corridor"), Danzig, and Eupen-Malmedy. Further restrictions of the German market came from the loss of a considerable portion of her overseas and European connections.[6] The cost of putting the wartime industries on a peacetime basis and demobilizing after losing the war placed terrific burdens on the small taxpayer. Those dominating German monopoly capital circles continually devised new methods for transferring reparations and other payments from World War I to the struggling workers and middle class.

The height of the inflationary development, begun during the war, was reached during 1921 and 1922; understandably, its effects were widely felt by the German population. By autumn of 1923 inflation reached catastrophic levels, creating even further impoverishment of workers and transforming a considerable portion of the middle classes to the level of proletarians. Millions in the lower middle class lost everything during this inflationary period. Yet the state paid heavy industry and the banks 600,000,000 gold marks, attempting to compensate for French occupation of the Ruhr; enormous profits were made by these concerns.[7]

Joachim Fest contends that the growing misery in Germany fostered the rise of Hitler, who by 1923 was already a leading figure in Bavarian politics. By this time Germany was overwhelmed by one crisis after another: a quickly repressed military putsch in Northern Germany, a fresh impetus to a separatist movement in the Rhineland, a struggle for the Ruhr provoked by France's narrow-minded policy there, increased influence by the radical left in Saxony and Thuringia, and hunger riots everywhere as the mark plunged. A revolutionary situation existed, charged with the expectations and mood of civil war.[8]

Strains usually overlap, as can be evidenced by what was transpiring in Germany before the Holocaust. Smelser asserts that perception of a real or threatened deprivation intensifies people's frustrations and increases the level of strain in society. The World Committee for Victims (1933) points to some very *real* economic deprivations in prewar Germany.

Preceding World War II, the first European country affected by the developing world economic crisis was Germany. Production dropped and unemployment rose; by the winter of 1930 over three million people were unemployed and employers began to lower wages. The Berlin *Finanzpolitische Korrespondenz* presented estimates of the average weekly decline in the wages of industrial workers. In summer 1929 wages were 44.60 reichsmarks; in March 1930, 39.05 reichsmarks. The yearly averaged weekly rate in 1928 and 1929 was calculated to be 42 and 45 marks, dropping to 37 marks by 1930 and 30 marks by 1931. By August of 1932, it fell to 20.8 marks and dropped even further thereafter. Estimates by *Finanzpolitische Korrespondenz* of total wage reductions of German workers and employees from July 1929 to July 1932 were approximately 38,000,000,000 marks.[9]

Accompanying wage and salary reductions were tremendous rises in unemployment. Official figures from the Reich minister of labor showed unemployment at over six million. These figures were considered to be an underreporting by the *Trade Research Institute* since they did not consider invisible unemployment—those who did not report their unemployment at the labor exchanges. According to health insurance statistics, this category would probably have added another two million to the ranks of the unemployed. The German Ministry of Labor figures showed approximately six million unemployed during the winter of 1931–1932 and about five million in the summer of 1932. These figures did not include: hundreds of thousands of people who had been unemployed for a number of years who were wandering the streets of Germany as tramps and beggars; destitute children and young unemployed people who found no work after leaving school; hundreds of thousands of merchants and tradespeople; and former "independent" and professional people now living on the verge of starvation. The actual number of people unemployed in Germany at the end of 1932 was approximately nine million. For those who were working, salaries fell.

Adding to this situation of internal strife was the declining position of the middle class, an influential sector of German society, which was getting increasingly worse. A statistical inquiry made by Theodor Geiger, *Die soziale Schichtung des deutschen Volkes* (1933), indicated that "the percentage proportion of the various classes in the total number of occupied persons" was: proletariat, 51.03; proletariods (such as small retailers, workers on own account), 13.76; new middle class (employees, officials), 16.04; old middle class (small proprietors), 18.33; and capitalists, 0.84. Geiger feels that the proportion of people in the proletariat may be overestimated; otherwise, the general distribution is probably accurate.[10]

As stated, the economic crisis reduced wide sections of the middle class to the level of the proletariat. Bankruptcies increased in number, and small tradespeople in towns and simple peasants were particularly severely affected. Segments of the population who had hitherto not known deprivation were hit by the crisis. Unemployment crept into the privileged sections of intellectual workers—teachers, engineers, doctors, lawyers, writers, and artists—and their standard of living fell lower and lower. One-fourth of university lecturers found no posts. Eight thousand graduated from technical colleges and universities in 1931–32, yet a mere 1,000 found employment in their professions; 1,500 returned to their studies "provisionally" and suffered great privation; 1,500 found temporary jobs such as waiters or street-hawkers; but only 4,000 remained totally employed.

Hartmannbund, the officially recognized doctors' association, found that 70 percent of German doctors were receiving less than 170 marks a month. The German legal association found its members to be in much the same situation. A statement issued by the Prussian minister of education showed that out of 22,000 teachers completing their training in the previous year, about 990 found posts—only temporary and auxiliary posts at that. These figures reflect Prussia only! Unemployment among chemists and engineers increased five times between April 1930 and April 1932, while unemployment in technical staffs doubled. The position of employed university lecturers grew worse every year. Hours were lengthened, and salaries were severely cut. Moreover, short-time working schedules increased: many industries worked a mere three to five days a week.[11]

All of this political dissatisfaction (Treaty of Versailles) and economic chaos produced widespread political disturbances. Merkl indicates that one response of Germans to this internal strife was an intensified hated of the Jews. He points out that *Judenkoller* ("a sudden outbreak of anti-Semitic mania in response to personal trauma such as the cultural shock experienced in 1918, unemployment, or divorce—of course with no objective connection to 'the Jews' except in the eye of the beholder")[12] among military civil servants increases under conditions of defeat and revolution; *Judenkoller* even occurs among businessmen in times of economic crisis. It was the rare person who proved so mentally stable that he would not say, " . . . my hatred against the Jews grew by leaps and bounds, and I became certain the Jews are Germany's misfortune."[13]

The dissatisfaction of Germans with the loss of World War I, the Treaty of Versailles, and postwar economic devastation contributed to German vulnerability to the claims of National Socialism. The worldwide depression of the 1930s greatly increased that vulnerability. These dissatisfactions combined with fertile anti-Semitism and provided Hitler with what he needed.

NORMATIVE UPHEAVAL

When viewing internal strife as one aspect of the value-added process contributing to the Holocaust, we considered the national humiliation, economic crisis, and unpopular political situation in Germany. Another aspect of internal strife is normative upheaval; this occurred in Germany after World War I as vast armies of people were uprooted and threatened by the social aftermath of war. As the whole social order was collapsing, a person who had been a "failure" was provided a chance for a fresh start. "When society was thrown back to zero, those whose own lives were at zero had their historic opportunity. This was Adolf Hitler's hour."[14]

Consider some of the normative upheavals in Germany. Hitler was assisted in his ascent to power by these upheavals and, also, because he shared many "pathological factors" with the post–World War I society that would escalate him to the top. Tenenbaum reports that the post-War era witnessed

. . . the overvaluation of the individual and of society that had met with such sudden disillusionment, the seething desires of restless millions and their inability to meet the demands of responsible and independent existence, the embittering experience of proletarianisation that went hand in hand with a search for objects of blame and hate, the erroneous attitudes and maniac emotions which made any realistic approach to life impossible and created that distorted image of man in which both Hitler and his age saw themselves.[15]

The disillusionment and social estrangement, the culture shock, the anger over ceded territories, and the generational pressures experienced by many in German society between the two world wars were sources of internal strife Hitler used to serve his own ends. A discussion of these social conditions is now in order.

Social Estrangement

As unemployment reached massive proportions, many unemployed, socially displaced World War I soldiers found their way into the ranks of Hitler's SS. In 1934 Theodore Abel, a Columbia University sociology professor, conducted an essay contest for the best life history of a follower of the Hitler movement. His request was honored by over 600 men and women who found themselves in the service of Adolf Hitler and mailed in their life histories to Abel. In 1981 Merkl published his insightful book, *Political Violence under the Swastika*, in which he analyzes the life stories from Abel's collection. Merkl comments:

The Nazi movement appears to have recruited itself from a variety of groups motivated by the social dynamics of prewar or postwar society. Their social crisis either stemmed from their unhappy in-between state between the major class communities, such as in the case of the white-collar or the old handicraft groups who had not found their way into the bourgeoisie or the working-classes. Or the crisis was the result of the impact of the German defeat in World War One on military men, civil servants, and countless others affected by foreign occupation or the cession of their homeland to other countries. In the former case, such processes of change as rural-urban migration or upward social mobility or decline, as dimensions of social experience, become very important, in as much as they often involve being caught between antagonistic major social classes. The non-commissioned professional military man whose career leaves him stranded between the classes; the rural-urban migrant or upwardly mobile person who never really arrived and cannot go back again either; the person uprooted by expulsion from occupied or ceded territory; the middle-class daughter who takes employment and finds herself ostracized by the traditional prejudices of the bourgeoisie—these are typical examples of victims of the social dynamics which tended to drive many of the Abel respondents into the Nazi movement and may have motivated millions of others to vote for it in the landslide years 1930 to 1932.[16]

In addition, returning soldiers and officers, already deeply disillusioned, came home to a world into which they no longer fit. A number of their former professions no longer existed ("real deprivation"), such as professional soldier, military cadet, and some categories of officials. Members of the uprooted nobility, students-become-soldiers, and radicalized and declassed members of the middle classes now felt the ground giving way beneath them. Those who had flocked into various military bodies at the time—the *Einwohnerwehr* (Citizens Defense Force of the early post-1918 period), the Ehrhardt Brigade, and the *Stahlhelm*—"steel helmets," Nationalist Ex-servicemen's Organization founded in 1918 and compulsorily absorbed by the SA (*Sturmabteilungen*, the Storm Troopers or "Brownshirts," the original NSDAP shock troops founded in 1921 and eclipsed politically by the SS in 1934) in 1933—provided the cornerstone of the young National Socialist German Labour Association, later to become the Nazi Party.[17]

Culture Shock

Merkl identifies the nature and extent of what we may regard as a type of strain in norms—culture shock. A prevailing attitude reflecting culture shock is represented by the statement of a soldier upon his return to Germany after World War I who simply said, "everything had changed. I simply could not adjust to the new relationships." This respondent had already turned anti-Semitic. Even among the respondents with a lot of military service, roughly half displayed culture shock. The remainder of Abel's respondents refer to shock regarding the moral disintegration of society, the new leaders of Weimar society, and a number of institutional changes. Others complained about the absence of discipline and order, a reaction of those who were disaffected and disillusioned.[18]

After analyzing Abel's life stories, Merkl concludes that soldiers having experienced *Fronterlebnis* ("the egalitarianism of the trenches and their common hostility to the enemy") suffered the most severe culture shock.

The bitter-enders and those stressing *Fronterlebnis* ["front-line experience" during World War I] have the highest number (88–90%) reporting culture shock. They stress such things as (1) the moral and social disintegration in postwar Germany, dissolute women, and immoral Communists, (2) the new Weimar leaders in government, business, and in the press, especially the real or alleged Jews among them, and (3) the disparagement of military honor, insignia, and symbols; internationalism and pacifism; and the shocking fall of the monarchy and its replacement by the multi-party state.[19]

Changes in norms also signified changes in what had heretofore been considered sacrosanct. Military defeat and minor revolutionary changes in Germany brought harassment and humiliation for returning soldiers by mobs and organized leftist groups. Merkl analyzes one of Abel's life histories of a returning officer who reported, "everything sacrosanct to a German soldier was stepped upon. I still remember painfully the day when they took away my sabre and insignia. . . . I was amazed at how the leading circles allowed themselves without a fight to be thrown out of the saddle. . . . Everything in the fatherland had begun to stagger. I was particularly demoralized when General Groener told the Kaiser that the oath of loyalty sworn by all the soldiers and civil servants was a mere idea. This cost me my innermost countenance." This respondent quickly joined the Free Corps going to fight in Upper Silesia.[20]

Normative conflict and upheaval were reflected in many areas of German life. Not even those who returned home permanently injured or marred felt that they were accorded enough respect. The sense of outrage experienced by the war invalid who was in conflict with the Weimar leadership soon brought him into the *Stahlhelm*. Since left-wing parties failed to accord respect and honor to the frontline soldier, the war invalid, the first citizen of the state, felt an intense dislike for Socialists. One returning invalid said, "the Socialists even gave me dirty looks because I always wore the ribbons of my Iron Cross in the lapel. . . ."[21]

Ceded Territory

Many Germans were uprooted and driven away from their homes after World War I because their towns or cities had been ceded to another country. Some of these persons became outraged superpatriots and eventually joined the Nazi party. This situation may have contributed to Nazi landslides in certain border areas north of Breslau (Wroclaw), East Prussia, and east of Frankfurt an der Oder. Non-German occupation of these areas spurred patriotic feelings and political interest. Merkl concludes:

In an age characterized by intense nationalistic passions and prejudices throughout the Western world, the momentous emotions aroused by the first World War and its aftermath often produced strong yearnings for national solidarity against the outside world. It did so with particular intensity among Germans born or residing abroad, German colonists in the colonies abroad or settlers among Poles or Alsations, residents of the ceded or embattled ethnic border areas of pre-war Prussia or Austria, and respondents in conflict with the Franco-Belgian occupation.[22]

Generational Pressures

The normative strains in German society, generational and political, were often juxtaposed. After analyzing the motivations of those who became SS officers, Merkl makes the following assessment of the strains in the German social structure:

There were obviously highly differentiated motive forces at work which had few common denominators except for frustrated upward mobility and an in-between or misfit status between the two powerful camps of the liberal bourgeoisie and the organized working class. The class resentments of the imperial sergeant who could never become an officer, the primary-school teacher who was held in contempt by the academically trained professions, or the half-proletarian by birth are examples as typical as were the upwardly mobile from the farm or from the urban working-class whose future was jeopardized by the economic consequences of a lost war. The patterns of social and spatial mobility, furthermore, clearly relate the age groups of the sample to German social and economic history: The older but upwardly mobile rural-urban migrants, the younger socially and spatially immobile residents of small towns and countryside, and the young, highly mobile drifters who were in social decline or stagnant. The relation of the three generations (prewar, war, and postwar) to the economic crises of the Weimar Republic also shows the highly mobile to have been far more often victimized by the Depression than were any of the other groups, and the war generation beset with economic troubles mostly in the decade of 1918–1919. Nevertheless, it was not the highly mobile "outside agitators" but rather the spatially immobile who were the most involved in the political violence of the NSDAP.[23]

Merkl notes the effects of these social conflicts and divisions, or normative strains, experienced by those who later became SS supporters. The results of these generational, social, and political conflicts created tensions providing a fertile ground for a genocidal mentality and attitude.

Another source of normative strain often came from cross-pressures within families themselves that created irreconcilable differences between spouses or between a couple and their social environment. These pressures separated people from both major social classes and also played a critical role in the social dynamics of the Nazi movement. Parents were adamantly split between anticlericalism and religious devotion or between a conservative party and the prewar Social Democrats. Class consciousness and a resentment of upper-class snobbery were a part the dynamic forces at work. In addition, there existed social splits between parents, such as a proletarian father and a bourgeois mother. This created class-identity problems in children. Caught in this dilemma, a man might desire to emigrate; his hopes for a military career might provide an avenue of escape from cross-pressures. Such a condition entailed additional pressures, since motives of achievement and merit conflicted with the ascriptive nature of bourgeois and aristocratic privilege that might block a man from attaining his goals.[24]

The Nazi movement fed on such conflicts and divisions, capitalizing on the differences between generations. The old and young were pitted against each other, fostering a division between age groups. This distinction operated within the *Volk* itself. The old were viewed as concerned with money and class (the two ideas linked by Naziism) and were considered to be cautious, whereas the young were supposedly romantic and idealistic, unconcerned with money and class but, rather, with serving the fatherland. "When Hitler damned the bourgeoisie, he was inveighing against the older generation, brought up under the Empire."[25]

The role of internal strife as a contributing force to the value-added process of genocide should never be underestimated, since the pressures it created catapulted Hitler to power. The social conditions in Germany during the 1920s and early 1930s created the necessary social strife to assist the Nazis in their ascension to power.

YES, we are barbarians! We want to be barbarians! It is an honorable title.

—ADOLPH HITLER

THE right to soil and territory can become a duty if a decline seems to loom for a great nation unless it extends its territory. . . . Germany either will be a world power or will not be at all.

—ADOLPH HITLER

9

POWERFUL LEADERSHIP WITH TERRITORIAL AMBITIONS FORMING A MONOLITHIC AND EXCLUSIONARY PARTY

POWERFUL LEADERSHIP WITH TERRITORIAL AMBITIONS

A LEADER who is highly motivated, psychopathic, and daring, with a propensity for inciting people to action is an important factor in the value-added process leading to genocide. Hitler was just such a leader with two goals uppermost in his mind—the acquisition of more land for Germany and the destruction of the Jews.

Hitler was outraged by the Treaty of Versailles, which restricted the military armament and activity of Germany to acquire *Lebensraum* ("living space") at the expense of neighboring and other countries. The Nazis later abrogated this treaty about which Hitler spoke while discussing the theme of German honor. "Germany was prepared for any concession save one; she would never sacrifice her honour, and part of this honour was a people's right to be able to determine and decide upon its own living space (*Lebensraum*)." Likewise, in a speech delivered on May Day 1939 he said, "the foundation of a people's life does not lie in doctrines or theories but in its own

Lebensraum, i.e., in what the earth gives it for its living." In *Mein Kampf*, Hitler stated that "the right to soil and territory can become a duty if a decline seems to loom for a great nation unless it extends its territory. . . . Germany either will be a world power or will not be at all." The sources of strain related to the treaty were capitalized on repeatedly by Hitler and would serve to deliver him many votes in future elections.[1]

Hitler's intense level of hatred is unquestionable. It is reflected in the following statement that reveals Hitler's mentality:

. . . I shall judge the depth of people's love for their country by the degree of hatred which they show to this rabble [the Jews].[2]

Hermann Rauschning was appointed president of the Danzig Senate by Hitler in the early days of Nazi power and resigned when he came to comprehend the evil of the Nazis. He later became their most bitter opponent.[3] After personally interviewing Hitler, Rauschning concluded that Hitler's leadership, the goal of which was a Germany and world which were *Judenfrei*, was responsible for the Jewish Holocaust. In a 1940 interview with Rauschning, Hitler stated,

. . . Living beings not merely conquer their enemies but also destroy them.

Brutality is respected. Brutality and physical strength and ruthlessness. . . . The masses want that. They need something that will give them a thrill of horror.

The world can only be ruled by fear.

I will tell you a secret. I have seen the vision of the new man [Hitler's "superman"]—fearless and formidable. I shrank from him.[4]

Hitler, the creator and very being of Naziism, was at the center of the war against Jewry. Levin comments that his death would have meant the end of the regime and the death camps. Hitler and Naziism were one and the same thing. He was the embodiment of National Socialism, the National Socialist par excellence. Not only was he the fuhrer, but also the protagonist of the whole Nazi movement.[5] The extent of the monumental power appropriated to him by the party was made clear at the NSDAP's (National Socialist German Workers' Party) first assembly, convening on 22 January 1921. Eisenberg's analysis of the party's platform clarifies the powers granted Hitler:

1. The political state is supreme. The individual's thoughts, feelings, ambitions, desires, and happiness are not important. He exists to serve the state.

2. The state is ruled by a Fuhrer. In a democracy the mass overwhelms the elite. Not so in a Fuhrer-State, where the leader is absolute and infallible. Only he is endowed with "mystic" qualities: only he knows what is best and how to achieve the ultimate good for "his" people.

3. The Fuhrer's subordinates are the instruments of his will. Their authority is derived from him. They are the elite selected by him as extensions of his "genius" to fulfill the special destiny of the Fuhrer-State. There is to be no free exchange of thought between the leader and the masses. The "flow" is in a downward direction only, from the topmost authority to all who are below him. . . .

4. Germany must have *Lebensraum*, ample living space for its people, its civilization, and its revolutionary philosophy.[6]

This was the primary organizational foundation of Hitler's power. The ideas and ideology of this party provided the basic organizational embryo that would grow into one of the most frightening institutions known to the world.

Leadership of the Holocaust machinery, of course, centered on Hitler, and his power was staggering. There was a fundamental law at work in Nazi Germany, the *Fuhrerprinzip* ("leadership principle"), which was the governing principle in the NSDAP since its inception. "According to the principle, each Fuhrer has the right to govern, administer, or decree, subject to no control of any kind and at his complete discretion, subject only to the orders he received from above."[7]

Thus all law and authority came from the fuhrer, the supreme being. An example of the strength of this indoctrination is the oath sworn by German soldiers from 2 August 1934 onward:

I swear by Almighty God this sacred oath: I will render unconditional obedience to Adolf Hitler, the Fuhrer of the German Reich and people, Supreme Commander of the Wehrmacht; as a brave soldier I will at all times be ready to sacrifice my life for this oath.[8]

Note that the oath was not sworn to the laws of the state or the constitution as under the Weimar Republic; it was pledged to the person of Adolf Hitler, by name. This was an oath to the "Fuhrer." Hitler's authority had come to incorporate the official and legitimate authority of the state office. His power resided not only in this oath but also in the magnetism and power he exuded. Even such world leaders as Lloyd George and Winston Churchill at times fell prey to Hitler's "charms."[9]

Hitler exerted a strong influence upon some of his not too weak-willed contemporaries. If these minds could succumb to his magnetism, then surely the masses would follow. Many people in positions of power and influence in Germany admired him, such as, Stewart Chamberlain, an English born, German national "intellectual," married to Wagner's daughter. He was thrilled by the young Hitler and envisioned a great future for Germany. In the following statement, we get an inkling of Hitler's effect and influence upon Chamberlain:

You have mighty things to do! My faith in Germanism had not wavered an instant, though my hope . . . was at a low ebb. With one stroke you have transformed the state of my soul. That in the hour of her deepest need Germany gives birth to a Hitler proves her vitality. . . . May God protect you![10]

Dr. G. M. Gilbert, former prison psychologist at the Nuremberg trials, interviewed prisoner Joachim von Ribbentrop, foreign minster under Hitler, who was sentenced at the Nuremberg trials to death by hanging. Von Ribbentrop gave a good description of Hitler's magnetism:

Of course, I was one of his most faithful followers. This is something that it is hard for you to understand. The Fuhrer had a terrifically magnetic personality. You can't understand it unless you've experienced it. Do you know, even now, six months after his death, I can't completely shake off his influence? Everybody was fascinated by him. Even if great intellects came together for a discussion . . . they ceased to exist and the brilliance of Hitler's personality shone over all. . . . Even at the discussions on the Munich Pact, Daladier and Chamberlain were simply overwhelmed by his charm. . . . I experienced it myself.[11]

Hitler's magnetism and dynamic appeal attracted all segments of the society, even the intellectuals. It was not just nationalists who admired Hitler, but also industrialists and Nobel prize winners. There were those who were somewhat squeamish about his violent methods, but they soon welcomed "real" authority and traditional German *Volkstum*, having grown tired of "weak" and "cosmopolitan" parliamentary democracy. The German intellectual, Werner Sombart (a notorious anti-Semite), hailed the end of free discussion. He proclaimed:

This art of discussion is gone. Not discussion but decision now dominates the scene. The creation of a political will comes about today by quite another way. It is no longer the indirect way of influencing public opinion but the direct way by the Fuhrer principle. . . . I, for my part, say Thank God that this is so![12]

Those who held high rank in the Nazi Party followed the fuhrer in both spirit and practice. The leaders who were on trial at Nuremberg following the war were not average men. On the contrary, Dr. Gilbert, after administering intelligence tests and studying the personalities of these criminals for many months, concluded that all of these party leaders (with the exception of Julius Streicher) were exceptional men, exhibiting above-average intelligence. In Gilbert's estimation, their rise to power, as well as their ruthlessness, were based not on their intelligence but, rather, on other personality characteristics—primarily a lust for authority and power, which they pursued with a "singleness of outlook and purpose, which comes about when a man loses his rational critical faculties under the sway of an all-pervading fanaticism. . . . It produced a singleness of mind directed to ruthlessness and evil. . . ."[13]

Hitler's dynamic appeal, combined with the creation of "outsiders" and the internal strife long rampant in Germany, escalated him to the top. He was obsessed with the attainment of his goals as early as two months after the conclusion of the armistice ending World War I. On 5 January 1919 the German Labor Party was formed. On 12 September 1919 Hitler joined the German Labor Party. At their first public meeting on 24 February 1920 Hitler announced the party's platform, "Point 4" of which relates to the Jewish Holocaust. It states:

Only a member of the race can be a citizen. A member of the race can only be one who is of German blood, without consideration of creed. Consequently no Jew can be a member of the race. . . .[14]

This party was the predecessor of the Nazi party. On 29 July 1921 the party changed its name to the *National Socialistische Deutsche Arbeiter Partei* (NSDAP) and was reorganized. Hitler became the first "chairman." In the same year the *Sturmabteilung* ("storm troopers" or SA) was founded with Hitler at its head. The SA was supposedly a private paramilitary force established to protect the NSDAP leadership from rival political parties. In actuality, the SA attacked political opponents on the streets. Goering was appointed head of the SA in March 1923.[15] On 16 September 1919 Hitler had written that *emotional anti-Semitism* leads only to pogroms, but the objective of *rational anti-Semitism* " . . . must unswervingly be the removal of the Jews altogether. Only a government of national vitality is . . . capable" of this goal.[16] The force with which Hitler pursued his "goal" leaves little to the imagination. Hitler explained:

We are obliged to depopulate as part of our mission of preserving the German population. If you ask me what I mean by depopulation, I mean the removal of entire racial units. And that is what I intend to carry out—that, roughly, is my task. Nature is cruel, therefore, we too may be cruel. If I can send the flower of the German nation into the hell of war without the smallest pity for the spilling of precious German blood, then surely I have the right to remove millions of an inferior race that breeds like vermin! . . . I shall simply take systematic measures. . . . There are many ways, systematical and comparatively painless, or at any rate bloodless, of causing undesirable races to die out. . . .[17]

By 1930 Hitler was establishing the machinery to accomplish his "task." He skillfully manipulated sophisticated segments of society. This was evident in a 1930 trial in Leipzig, which foreshadowed things to come. Three young officers were arraigned on charges of treason for admitting that they would never fire on Nazi infiltrators in the military. Hitler, during an appearance as a witness in court, succeeded in spellbinding and fooling Army officers into thinking that the notion of an imminent Nazi revolt was ridiculous. He declared Nazis would use only constitutional means to attain power, raving about a glorious, powerful future for Germany, and the generals succumbed to his antics. They even began to ponder the merits of National Socialism as a way to create a united Germany with a reborn, powerful German army. Hitler had succeeded in persuading military leaders that National Socialism could restore Germany to its former glory and greatness by throwing off the shackles of the Treaty of Versailles that limited the power of the German army. He further charged the Jews were responsible for this treaty and that the "Bolshevik-Jewish Conspiracy" could be eliminated by the Nazis. Hitler's impression upon the military was obvious when the three arraigned officers received only a mild sentence—eighteen months of fortress detention. Hitler was fortifying his power.[18]

Soon Hitler was able to bring together the idea of destroying the Jews with the actual power to do it. He turned the fantasy of the anti-Semitic dream of destruction into a reality by achieving the political power, commanding the technological and economic resources, and amassing sufficient military might to carry out the destruction process. His life was an obsession with the idea of a holy war against the Jew, the "Host of the Devil and the Children of Darkness." He was never to stray from his single-minded dedication to this goal—even at the end of the war.[19]

Hitler's National Socialism could only take root in a society ready to receive it. Creation of "outsiders," internal strife, and the rise of Naziism combined to create such a milieux. During the Great Depression Germany's main support for economic prosperity—world trade and foreign loans—collapsed. Dire want and unemployment prevailed for millions. The Nazis now became a serious political force, holding some sixty meetings a day in Germany. Hitler shrewdly convinced Germans that he could rescue them from the disgrace of the peace treaty. His pleas for a *Volksgemeinschaft* ("people's community") had a strong appeal. This comical yet sinister figure with a moustache had become the epitome of the Saviour and Prophet. Had he not always claimed that the Treaty of Versailles, the brainchild of the Jews, would destroy Germany?[20]

In his rise to power it was imperative that large segments of the society be won over. Hitler attracted some segments of the military, the financial leaders (industrialists and bankers), and the masses suffering from economic strain. In 1933 the Nazis polled only 44 percent of the popular electoral vote, but Hitler had not yet reached his full stride. When he did, he satisfied the deepest desires of most Germans who imagined him to be a mirror of themselves; he was the "seismograph of the people's soul."[21]

He won over the unemployed, those fearing the "Bolshevik-Jewish Conspiracy," the lower classes, the youth searching for a cause, and those who felt alienated after serving on the front lines during World War I. All of these groups had unexpressed needs, jealousies, and hatreds. All were ready to follow this man, Hitler, who had come from nothing. Wanting prestige and recognition, they were captivated by uniforms, thrilling slogans, titles, and the renewed feelings of German solidarity Hitler inspired. Hitler exploited these feelings, creating a frantically enthusiastic and later a terrorized mass, which would do his bidding and support his "insatiable appetite for power."[22]

When Hitler decided to physically exterminate the Jews, all followed his leadership without question. The *Fuhrerprinzip* would attain his goals; opposition had been removed. Simultaneously he had worked at all levels of society, from his closest associates to the lowest ranking soldier. When Hitler spoke, even Heinrich Himmler (chief of the German police in the Reich Ministry of the Interior; later reich minister of the interior) laid aside his own convictions. The phrase, "The Fuhrer is always right," invariably held a mystical significance for Himmler.[23]

Even when Hitler's world began crumbling, he demanded total loyalty and devotion to the cause of destroying the Jews of Europe. The war effort against the Allies even became secondary to the business of mass murder. Trains that could carry soldiers and supplies were, instead, directed by Hitler to carry Jews across Europe to the death camps. Lucy Dawidowicz indicates Hitler's overwhelming, obsessive hatred for the Jews in a statement from Hitler's last political testament, made on 29 April 1945:

I demand of all Germans, all National Socialists, men, women, and all the men of the Armed Forces, that they be faithful and obedient unto death to the new government and its President. Above all, I charge the leaders of the nation and those under them to scrupulous observance of the laws of race and to merciless opposition to the universal poisoner of all peoples, international Jewry.[24]

FORMATION OF A MONOLITHIC AND EXCLUSIONARY PARTY

To Smelser, "channels for expressing grievances" refer to structural components of a situation, such as agencies (military and/or police) that are willing and able to act to prevent a hostile outburst. The issue addressed here is this: Did the growth of the Nazi party lead to the formation of a monolithic party in Germany that excluded any thought deviating from its own? The formation of a monolithic and exclusionary party that would ultimately control all state agencies could encourage and contribute to the value-added process leading to the Holocaust.

In Nazi Germany all channels for expressing frustration about the economic situation, unemployment, loss of the war, and alienation were closed off to the populace. All political parties that could even suggest criticism of Germany or its government were destroyed. There existed no safety valve to allow people to channel their frustration and aggression into positive, constructive directions. Only one target was eventually created for all frustrations and aggressions—the Jews. All that was needed was a catalyst to trigger aggression, a legitimizing of that aggression, a government policy of channeling that aggression, and the government machinery to carry out the Holocaust. All of this was seen to by Hitler.

Note first that Hitler removed any possible elements that might resist his will during his rise to power. After he gained political control in Germany, he did a thorough and terrifying job of closing off all channels by which a frustrated Germany could reduce tension.

Hitler came to power on January 30, 1933, in a time of political paralysis. Within a few months, through terror, violence, and the innovation of concentration camps, he suppressed all political parties, the trade-union movement, the free press, and the political institutions of the Weimar Republic.[15]

The real power belonging to Hitler was concentrated into three organizations. All of the structures of the state he controlled could be used for his purposes, but he needed some very specialized organizational structures to carry out his horrible bidding. Azriel Eisenberg refers to the NSDAP, the SS, and the Gestapo as a "state within a state." These three organizations were the primary agencies that would implement the destruction of Jewry, and they also provided the nucleus of the bureaucratic terror machine in Germany. Each one will be briefly discussed.

1. The NSDAP. Hitler organized the National Socialist German

Workers' Party, later to become the NSDAP, as a state within a state. It was a conglomeration of people with a distinct way of life, festivals, rules, and norms. When the first assembly convened in Munich on 22 January 1921, its membership was already three thousand.[26] By 1928 the party had received less than one million votes. However, by 1930 it polled over six million, becoming the largest party in the country.[27]

2. The SS. Hitler's next organizational ace in the whole was the SS. Wearing black uniforms and a death's head badge of skull and bones, the *Schutzstaffel* ("SS"— Hitler's protective guard) was a law and power unto itself. Those who belonged to this powerful elite were bound by eternal allegiance to Hitler. In recognition of its meritorious service in the Rohm purge (to be discussed in this chapter), the SS was made an autonomous body in 1934. This group, which served under the leadership of Himmler, was the true ruler of Hitler's empire. Its members infiltrated the secret service and the police force. They also manned strategic positions in health services, agriculture, racial policies, scientific affairs, and the diplomatic corps.[28]

The SS was the most important and powerful Nazi organization for attaining Hitler's *Lebensraum* during World War II in Eastern Europe, and it was given independent status and a wide scope of activity on 13 July 1934. Its main role was that of a select protective guard of the ideology and leaders of National Socialism, and it embarked upon various programs implementing Nazi ideology. Candidates for this organization were forced to abandon their church affiliations and were trained in blind obedience to authority and intense hatred of Jews. They were also indoctrinated with the idea of German *Lebensraum*, accepting the notion that groups unable to be integrated into Germandom because of cultural or racial "defects" were to be removed from *Lebensraum* areas in one way or another.

In 1935 SS leader Heinrich Himmler created *Lebensborn* ("Well of Life"), a private SS organization, the express purpose of which was to educate and raise illegitimate children of SS men. Children deemed "racially valuable" were given to childless SS families, or they were cared for in Nazi-spirited institutions. The Nazis' objective was to promote a maximum number of "good racial births." This necessitated extending the boundaries of *Lebensborn* beyond the Reich proper. Kidnapping of children possessing "perfect racial qualities" from occupied countries served the goals of the Nazi SS.[29]

3. The Gestapo. Immediately after Hitler assumed the reigns of power, approximately two-thirds of the Berlin police force was purged. They were replaced by Nazis who were selected on the basis of their brutality. From this group sprang the *Geheime Staatspolizeiamt*, "Gestapo," the secret state police, a part of the SS. The overall chief of

this group of plainclothesmen was Heinrich Himmler, while their immediate head was Reinhard Heydrich. Their major tasks were to eliminate all Nazi opposition and all Nazi critics; all action against Nazi Party forces was forbidden. The Gestapo, unlike ordinary police, did not concentrate on the prevention and detection of crime; instead it was concerned with suppression of diverse types of independent political thought and the elimination of all opponents to the Hitler regime. "At first it was Goering's instrument of terror—itself a world of double cross, blackmail and murder. Members of the Gestapo arrested each other and intrigued in a welter of violent power struggles. . . . the Gestapo began to expand as an arm of the SS. . . ." Agency after agency was absorbed into the labyrinth of SS holding companies and their interlocking directorates; so devious and intricate was the structure that it could never fully be clarified, even by experts at the Nuremberg trials.[30]

Nora Levin points to another instrument of terror in the Hitler regime—the Sicherheitsdienst (SD), a section of the SS. With fewer than three thousand members, its intelligence and counterintelligence apparatus (using 100,000 informers) pried into the personal lives of all Germans. The diabolical genius Heydrich headed the SD; he pushed security to the zenith of efficiency by interlocking the work of the Gestapo and the SD. Soon the prisons would overflow with critics of the regime, and the first concentration camp—Dachau—would come into existence.[31]

Hitler utilized terror not only against his opponents and not solely as a deterrent, but also as a convenient instrument by which to educate the German people. With this instrument he extirpated inconvenient values. Concentration camps could be used not simply to break down prisoners and spread terror among the entire population, but, indeed, they could be used as a training ground in which to immunize Gestapo members against human emotions and attitudes.[32]

Within a short time after assuming power, a rapid series of events conferred absolute power upon Hitler. When on 30 January 1933 he took the oath of office as chancellor of Germany, one of his first acts was to prohibit public meetings and suppress publications believed to endanger public security. This was accomplished by 4 February. On 27 February 1930 the Reichstag building was set ablaze, and a Dutch Communist, Marinus van der Lubbe, was found on the spot. Levin indicates that this fire was Nazi instigated, but Hitler convinced the deteriorating and confused Hindenburg (the Reich president) that the fire signaled a Communist revolt, and the Reich president signed an emergency decree prepared by Hitler ("For the Protection of People and State"). Hitler seized this opportunity to rescind basic civil liberties, thus "protecting" the state from Communists.

. . . [Hitler's] decrees suspended all fundamental freedoms of speech, press, assembly, freedom from invasion of privacy (mail, telephone, telegram) and from house search without warrant. They gave the federal government the power to take over the state governments as needed to restore public security, and they imposed the death penalty . . . for treason, arson, railroad sabotage, and the like. Another set of decrees dealt with high treason, in a manner so deliberately ill-defined as to cover every possible form of dissidence, including the publication and dissemination of certain forms of printed matter.[33]

However, the Enabling Act was to provide the final consolidation of Hitler's power and would promote his leap to dictator. After this rescinding of liberties, the Nazis diligently pursued a two-pronged assault of pseudolegality and terror against their rivals. The SA, the private army of the NSDAP, had increased to 400,000—four times the size permitted for the German Army according to the Treaty of Versailles—and now accelerated its terror campaign against Socialists, Communists, trade unionists, and Jews. Simultaneously, Hitler was seeking a two-thirds vote during the first session of the recently elected Reichstag to pass the Enabling Act. This measure allowed the government, without any recourse to the Reichstag, the awesome power to promulgate emergency legislation for a specified period of time.[34]

Both Hitler and Hindenburg gave the various parties in Germany lavish promises that Hitler would not govern under the Enabling Act without consulting them. Unfortunately, they believed him. The centrist parties naively supported the Enabling Act, giving Hitler the required two-thirds majority. By a vote of 441 to 84, parliamentary democracy was interred in Germany. The Reichstag by this vote had literally committed suicide. The Enabling Act provided the power behind Hitler's rule. Under Hitler, the Reich cabinet was dutifully prolonged every four years thereafter by a rubber-stamp Reichstag, which met only a dozen times up to the war. Debating and voting no longer occurred in the Reichstag, and no speeches were heard except those of Hitler.[35]

The Enabling Act provided Hitler with the legal authority for dictatorship. It gave the government power for four years to promulgate legislation, even if it deviated from the Constitution. (Under this authority, Hitler himself renewed the act in later years.) In less than eight weeks, Hitler had accomplished his "legal" revolution, having terrorized the Communists, as he soon would also the Socialists, and with cynical deceit, having promised the rightists and Centrists that he would restore legality and share power with them. But by early July the NSDAP alone remained in existence. The Communists and Social Democrats had been suppressed. Under Hitler's prodding, the DNVP [the *Deutschnationale Volkspartei*, "German National People's Party"], followed by the smaller parties and the Catholic Center, proclaimed their own suicide by self-dissolution. "The party has now become the state," Hitler declared on July

8, 1933. *On July 14, a government decree legally solemnized the fait accompli and declared the NSDAP to be the only political party in Germany* [emphasis added]. Any attempt to maintain another party or form a new one would be punishable by three years of imprisonment, "if the action is not subject to a greater penalty according to other regulations,"—those dealing with high treason, unmistakably.[36]

A monolithic and exclusionary party now existed. By the end of 1933 the only bulwark of resistance to Hitler that still remained came from the SA, a behemoth of four million. Hitler came to regard the SA as a threat to his authority. Even though Ernest Rohm, its leader, had been an old comrade from the *Reichswehr* days of 1919 in Munich, Hitler was ready to eliminate him. The army and the SS were prepared for some months to destroy the SA. On 30 June 1934 Rohm himself and about two hundred of his SA men were murdered with horrible brutality. The SA was finished and would henceforth be merely a shadow of itself under the SS. The SS now emerged as the elite party that would eventually dominate all of Europe.[37]

The Rohm purge crushed all anti-Nazi activity. Nazi opponents had been effectively crushed in the streets, in Nazi controlled courts, and in the SS torture barracks. The random arrest and incarceration of victims was cloaked by the legal-sounding term *Schutzhaft*, "protective custody."[38] Violence and terror were on the upswing. Now total control of the military fell to Hitler, who reigned supreme.

Hitler's ascent to power permitted him to control the power of the federal states and for the first time in history, Germany was a totally centralized state. Separate powers were removed from individual states, and they fell under the authority of the national government. Even Bismarck had proven unable to accomplish this objective. Diets of the various states were dissolved and Nazi Reich governors were legally appointed to carry out Hitler's policies. Goering, in the key position of minister of interior in Prussia (which constituted over two-thirds of Germany at this time), was able to remove hundreds of republican officials, filling their positions with Nazis. Brutality, cruelty, trickery, lightening speed, and terror were his trademark. Later, Hitler never ceased to boast that he and National Socialism had attained power "legally."[39]

The first of the concentration camps sprang up very quickly during the first year of Hitler's reign; by late 1933 there were many in operation. The camps had been established by the SA to beat or murder victims (sometimes through pure sadism) and to blackmail victims' families for ransom. Following the Rohm purge, many Germans optimistically thought that the Nazis would consider their opposition to have been obliterated; therefore, the necessity for concentration camps would no longer exist. On Christmas Eve 1933 amnesty for 27,000 prisoners was announced by Hitler; unfortunately, Goering and Himmler ignored the order and released very few people. Himmler by now clearly realized the value of the concentration camps as a method of terrorizing the populace and eliminating resistance to the regime.

Following the Rohm purge, the concentration camps were controlled by the SS, with guard duty being given to the *Totenkopfvergaende*, the "Death's Head Units." Its numbers were recruited from the most hardened and ruthless Nazis, wearing on their black tunics the sinister skull-and-bone insignia. Millions of men, women, and children suffered unimaginable torture, debasement, and death at the more notorious prewar camps—Dachau, Buchenwald, Sachsenhausen, and Ravensbruck. But horror upon horror was to occur as the war progressed and the Nazis devised extermination centers, labor camps, and camps for so-called medical research.[40] (Theodore Eicke was now inspector of concentration camps.)

Meanwhile complaints were stilled outside of Germany as well as inside.

The friends of the Hitler Government are always ready to repeat the government's declaration that peace and order reign in Germany. *Dementis* are issued to calm feeling outside of Germany and festivals and parades are staged to distract attention from what is actually taking place. The few foreign tourists who still care to visit Germany under the present tyranny are not taken into storm troop barracks or into concentration camps. It is only by chance that the foreign visitor may be an eye-witness of the nightly tortures, shootings "while trying to escape" and secretly organized murders. Every message from foreign journalists to their newspapers, every telephone conversation, every visit they make is carefully noted, and they are threatened with immediate expulsion.[41]

Hitler's ascension to power was followed by terror as well as confusion. Even if one could find the proper agency of responsibility, it was foolish to complain or express opposition. The giant monolith, the Nazi Party, suppressed and removed all who dared to dissent. Levin describes the position of an individual who attempted to exercise his conscience in Nazi Germany. She points out:

The defenselessness of the individual in a totalitarian society has sometimes been described as slavery, a condition in which the individual has no independent existence but must obey blindly and do the tasks set for him to perform. . . . The individual German was free to make many decisions without grave risk, but he had to be careful of a supreme, if remote and invisible, power. This was much worse than an immediate master, because the power which a citizen in a totalitarian Germany had to obey and propitiate was inscrutable. A man could never be sure if he was obeying.[42]

A person who went against the Nazi regime was labeled an "enemy of the state" or a "public enemy," and as Levin contends,

... once declared a public enemy, he was treated as such by everyone and was outlawed from the human community. There was no appeal to ordinary justice, reason or decency or any hope of being restored to civil existence once outlawed. This was the Kafkalike world in which opponents of the Hitler regime found themselves. Liberals, Socialists, Communists, militant Catholics, protesting Protestants and anti-Nazi intellectuals were declared public enemies. Above all others, Jews were outlawed and labeled as people who had no right to exist, no matter how they behaved. The force of the inscrutable power in Nazi Germany was felt through systems of authority which overlapped each other. The function of one often vaguely merged into the functions of another, resulting in a deliberately contrived confusion and evasion of responsibility. The power of the state became faceless.[41]

Hitler had instilled terror into the population, especially when he demonstrated that even those in positions of power, such as Ernest Rohm, could be easily eliminated if they posed a threat to him. All viable opposition to the Nazi Party had been removed. Hitler, the SS, and the Gestapo were free to do as they chose. The Enabling Act had handed Hitler the ability to consolidate his power and eventually exert the ultimate of control over all government agencies.

THE worst set of crimes in the history of mankind were designed by professors, engineered by Ph.D.'s, and operated by baptized Christians who had turned their faith into a speculative ideology of genocidal potential.

—RANDOLPH L. BRAHAM

10

DESTRUCTIVE USES OF COMMUNICATION

AGGRESSIVE IDEOLOGY

IDEOLOGICAL MOVEMENTS, either religious, charismatic, or nationalistic, are potential methods of accentuating social cleavages. Dangerous value conflicts, which might serve as catalysts to violence, become manifest via such movements. In pre-World War II Germany, ideological factors combined to create an unimaginable force. The historic strain between Christianity and Judaism was accentuated and magnified by a conceptual linking together of Christianity and Nazism.

Azriel Eisenberg examines the 1921 platform of the National Socialist German Workers' Party. His analysis of the points of the platform relevant to our discussion of an aggressive ideology are the following:

1. None but persons of pure German blood may be members of the German nation.

171

2. The ideas of German superiority and the Fuhrer principle are the "religion" of Nazidom, replacing the "weak and obsolete" Christian faith and doctrines.
3. As a consequence, Nazism and its revolutionary teachings provide a new code of morality that negates the ethics and morals of Christianity and the Western world. Nothing is wrong or immoral if it advances the Nazi cause.
4. Germany must have *Lebensraum*, ample living space for its people, its civilization, and its revolutionary philosophy.
5. Nazism is destined to conquer the world.[1]

To achieve the above-stated goals, the Nazi party found it imperative that ideology be emphasized, and the Nazi movement took on the form of a charismatic religious movement. Thus the Nazis deliberately incorporated the language, ideology, and symbolism of religion. National Socialism assumed the character of a new faith, with its own liturgy, ideology, and element of hope. The terminology used by Goebbels, the Reich minister of public enlightenment and propaganda, in many of his speeches was intentionally religious. Naziism had evolved into a total worldview that excluded all others. Consequently, traditional Christianity became a rival, not a friend, of Naziism. Yet Hitler received the support of the Christian churches by combining the *Volk* ideal with Christianity, thus incorporating more traditional and religious Germans into the *Volk* idea. Then the *Volk* was linked with Naziism.[2]

This Nazi opposition to Christianity was served by elevating the worldview of Naziism into direct religious expression. But the Nazis were very careful to keep traditional Christianity intact while infiltrating it with their own meaning. Consequently, even the language used by Hitler and Goebbels in their speeches employed familiar Christian imagery. They discussed "the miracle of belief," made appeals to "Providence," and referred to *Mein Kampf* as the "sacred book of National Socialism." Even Hitler's closest associates were called his "apostles," and he himself was frequently viewed as the "savior."[3]

By filling the traditional framework of Christianity with new content, Christianity was bent into conformity with Nazi culture and ideology. In discussing Nazi ideology, Yehuda Bauer explains:

Jew-hatred was the central pillar of a pseudo-religion that transformed accepted moral values into their opposite, but within a framework of accepted and traditional ideas. The pseudo-religion was clearly inspired by Christian symbols, but subverted and changed them completely. Using these Christian symbols in a sacrilegious way, modern antisemitism, and especially Nazism of course, could use terms, quotations, and associations that were familiar to the Christian-educated mind. The unity of God the Father, God the Son, and the Holy Ghost became the Nazi "Father of the State, the Son of the Race and the Spirit of the Volk."[4]

Bauer continues in the same vein, concluding:

The image of the Jew as the symbol of the Devil in some of the premodern traditions made it easy to transform the Jew into the Devil himself, the content of the symbol, and thus to lead to the obvious conclusion that he had to be destroyed. When the Fuhrer became the substitute for the Savior, the former symbol of the anti-Christ became the target of an absolute hatred. The modern imagery fitted old concepts. The Jews were depicted as always being enemies of order and revolutionaries, while at the same time being capitalist. The Jews were not really nomads, but really parasites, "battening on the substance of others."[5]

Hitler, the Savior! The Jews, the enemy! The theme emerged clearly as a part of the Nazi ideology, as depicted in the *Guidelines for the Movement of German Christians (National Church Movement) in Thuringia (1933)*, which follows:

As with every people, the eternal God also created a Law for our people especially suited in to its racial character. It acquired form in the Fuhrer Adolf Hitler and in the National Socialist state which he formed.
This law speaks to us in the history of our people, born of our blood and soil. Loyalty to this Law demands from us the struggle for honor and freedom. . . .
. . . The way to the fulfillment of this German Law is through the German community of the faithful. In it Christ, the Lord, rules as grace and forgiveness. Here burns the fire of the holy willingness to sacrifice. In it alone does the Saviour meet the German people and bequeath to it the gift of a strong faith. It is from these communities of German Christians that the "German Christian National Church" must rise in the National Socialist state of Adolph Hitler, embracing the whole people.

One People!—One God!—One Reich!—One Church![6]

In fact, the war against the Jews became a "holy struggle."

William Shirer, a foreign correspondent in Berlin from 1934 to 1941, entered some of the news media propaganda prevalent at the time into his diary. One entry follows:

Berlin, January 9, 1940. . . . army is protesting to Hitler about the senseless brutality of the Gestapo in Poland, but I doubt if that will change matters. . . . Must note a new propaganda campaign to convince the German people that this is not only a war against the "plutocratic" British and French, but a holy struggle against the Jews. Says Dr. Ley in the *Angriff* tonight: "We know that this war is an ideological struggle against world Jewry. England is allied with the Jews against Germany. . . . England is spiritually, politically, and economically at one with the Jews. . . . For us England and the Jews remain the common foe. . . .[7]

Bauer makes a very perceptive point about the racist Nazi ideology, fathoming its true purpose, commenting:

Transcending German nationalism, though basing itself on it, Nazi ideology derived all positive qualities from a supposed Aryan background, but this only served as a cover-up for the claim of Germanic (German, Nordic, Scandinavian, etc.) blood to rule the world by conquering the land mass of Eastern Europe and utilizing its tremendous natural resources. "Aryan" actually had only the quality of distinguishing it from "non-Aryan"; the only non-Aryan was the Jew. Antisemitism was therefore not a result of Nazi racism, but the obverse was true: racism was a rationalization of Jew-hatred.[8]

Nora Levin also makes a similar point, claiming that at the center of Nazi ideology was the war against Jewry. Anti-Jewish ideology *was* Nazi ideology. All of the sociological, historical, and pseudoscientific books used in Nazi institutes and schools had no other central theme. Without this demonic, destructive core, the Nazi *Weltanschauung* had no substance. Levin points out that the essential emptiness of Nazi ideology became apparent after Hitler's fantastic conquests. The Nazis had no political, economic, or social program for the occupied territories. The only motive power operative at both the beginning and end of conquest was sheer exploitation by naked power. Europe was destroyed rather than remade. Neither was the German social order remade. Programs, administrative reorganization, and policy were subject to Hitler's whims, orders, or intuitions. His vagueness allowed others to improvise. The avowed promise and goal of Naziism—to regenerate Germany— was not the final result of his rule.[9]

George Mosse contends that the ideology of the Nazi revolution was presumed to be based upon Germanic traditions; while looking to the future, the revolution attempted to recapture a mythical past, and with that, the older traditions that many perceived to be Germany's only hope. The desire to recapture a morality associated with the *Volk's* past was combined with an omnipresent nationalism. The Nazis encouraged the belief that their ideology did recapture a true, historical *Volk*. In reality, the morality offered by National Socialists as typically Germanic was bourgeois, representing nineteenth-century values espousing an unostentatious dedicated life and the sanctity of the family and of marriage. Dedication was to be given to the *Volk* rather than to money making, and the modern bourgeoisie was condemned, since it had become "Judaized."[10]

PROPAGANDA WAR

Smelser believes communication, for example, organized propaganda and agitation, plays a key role in the value-added process leading to a hostile outburst, since people need to communicate with each other to spread negative, hostile beliefs and also to mobilize for attack against a particular group. Communication and consensus of opinion are prerequisites for molding individuals into crowds and hostile groups. Newspapers and other media may function to communicate hostile attitudes by disseminating the types of information that escalate hostile beliefs to the point of violent action. The author contends that a propaganda war must be stepped up before the actual occurrence of genocide. The mass media may, in a very organized fashion, spread rumors and interesting stories that attach hostility to a specific group, adding fuel to the genocidal process.

By the 1940s the Nazis eschewed disorganized efforts at dealing with the Jews, preferring to do their work in a methodical, bureaucratic fashion. Joachim Fest points out that after the Nazis ascended to power, they successfully dominated the mass media; this gave them the technical preconditions for imposing a program of thought and feeling capable of disciplining the entire nation as a single unit.[11]

Hitler grasped the role of the mass media, propaganda, and rumor; he would later make use of these tools to aid in the destruction of the Jews. In his discussion of the psychology of propaganda in *Mein Kampf*, Hitler claimed:

The function of propaganda [lies in] . . . calling the masses' attention to certain facts. . . . The whole art consists in doing this so skillfully that everyone will be convinced that the fact is real. . . . its effect . . . must be aimed at the emotions and only to a very limited degree at the so-called intellect.

. . . the first axiom of all propagandist activity [is] . . . the basically subjective and one-sided attitude it must take toward every question it deals with. . . . Its task is to serve our own right always and unflinchingly.

It [propaganda] must confine itself to a few points and repeat them over and over.

The art of propaganda lies in understanding the emotional ideas of the great masses and finding . . . psychologically . . . the way to the attention and thence to the heart of the broad masses.[12]

Hitler's ideas about the method and uses of propaganda coincided with those of Goebbels. The use of propaganda became the art of deception—an art at which Reich Minister of Propaganda Goebbels excelled. Some aspects of propaganda employed by the Nazis—*Nazi-Deutsche*, the Ministry of Propaganda, and the use of myth—follow.

Nazi-Deutsche

In *A Holocaust Reader* Lucy Dawidowicz analyzes the role of the German language itself as a propagandistic tool in the destruction of the Jews. *Nazi-Deutsche*, or "National Socialist German," has been dubbed by Victor Klemperer, one of its analysts, as *Lingua Tertii Imperii (LTI)*, "the language of the Third Reich."[13] The language developed during the infancy of the movement, flowering when the German National Socialists ruled Europe. *Nazi-Deutsche* typified what George Orwell (in *1984*) described as Newspeak, "a medium of expression for the world view and mental habits proper to the devotees" of existing, powerful ideological movements. Dawidowicz says that *Nazi-Deutsche*, like Newspeak, was designed to reduce, not to expand, the range of thought; it was intended to create a desired mental attitude by using words constructed for ideological and political purposes. In addition, it developed into a language that graphically illustrated witticism in the vein of Talleyrand and Voltaire; man was given words so that he might use them to conceal his thoughts. Such a language concealed far more than it communicated, since its very structure and vocabulary buffered both speaker and listener from reality.

The National Socialists incorporated into *Nazi-Deutsche* several unattractive and familiar characteristics of the German language. For instance, *Nazi-Deutsche* favors intransitive verbs and passive constructions, abounds in verbally weak sentences, and is plagued by vague, indeterminate meanings.[14]

Dawidowicz points out that it is very atypical of *Nazi-Deutsche* to use active sentences depicting active agents. The substance of sentences is generally lodged in verbal nouns. For example:

" . . . prompt Aryanization is to be sought. . . ."
" . . . the planned measures demand the most thorough preparation. . . ."
" . . . the handling of the problem will meet with certain difficulties. . . ."[15]

By using *Nazi-Deutsche*, individual and personal responsibility are disclaimed. Rather, the very sentence structure and its syntax convey a sense of things happening as a consequence of impersonal, overpowering forces of cosmic or natural character; processes occur and worlds are moved without any indication of a visible agent, as though destined by the progressive march of history or commanded by a power on high.

The German language is fraught with nouns with multiple meanings, one as unspecific as the next. These nouns were disproportionately used in *Nazi-Deutsche*, either alone or in combination with other nouns. The emergence of a new vocabulary ensued, composed of abstract nouns with vague, bland meanings intended to obfuscate reality, concealing it from outsiders and disengaging participants. *Aktion,* which means process, treatment, came to designate mass killing. *Behandlung,* meaning management, treatment, referred to killing. Reports make reference to "appropriate treatment" of Jews, and frequently to *Sonderbehandlung,* "special treatment." *Einsatz,* originally carrying a passive meaning, signifying that which is staked or risked, became commonly used in *Nazi-Deutsche* in military terminology, being used to denote diverse sorts of action implying dedication, risk, and commitment. The *Einsatzgruppen,* security police task forces, were assigned special duties involving mass murdering of Jews.

Code words and euphemisms, like *Aktion* or *Sonderbehandlung,* were intended to enshroud systematic programs of secrecy and murder, as well as making participation in murder palatable to executioners. This is clearly exemplified by the use of the words "mercy killing" and "euthanasia" to designate the killing of insane, deformed, or incurably sick "Aryan" Germans. Later, code names gave way to code numbers, which further served to depersonalize murders and dehumanize the murderers. The term "Final Solution" eventually became the code word for the destruction of European Jewry; the noun imparted a sense of purpose and idealism to participating killers, the adjective lending "an aura of apocalyptic conclusiveness" to their killing.[16]

The Ministry of Propaganda

The Ministry of Propaganda provided a vehicle for propagandizing against Jewry. Nazi Minister of Propaganda Goebbels had "distinguished" himself by writing a novel called *Michael: A German Destiny.* Michael represented the yearning German soul, full of visions. Evil is revealed to him in the form of Ivan, attempting to entice him into Bolshevism. The soul of Michael struggles with the tempter, saying,

But I am stronger than he.
Now I have him by the throat.
Now I hurl him to the ground.
There he lies.
The death rattle in his throat, and bloodshot eyes.
Perish, carrion! I trample on his brains.
And now I am free.

This spirit made Goebbels worthy of membership in the prestigious Hitlerized Academy of Poets.[17]

According to Hugh Trevor-Roper, Goebbels was "shamelessly brilliant," transforming Hitler's image into one of a charismatic leader and establishing Nazi myth. Goebbels began as a demagogue speaker at party functions; he later organized and manipulated censorship and propaganda and masterfully controlled the mass media throughout the Reich. Nothing was seen or heard on radio, cinema, the press, or party platforms except that which Goebbels judged politically expedient. Though the propaganda put out was uniform, it was not dull or predictable; however crude, violent, or unscrupulous, it was managed with the agility and sophistication of a master. Goebbels controlled the power of a deadly instrument and was quick to recognize the full potential of the political uses of the mass media in a dynamic totalitarian state.[18]

Trevor-Roper contends that Goebbels was always able to distinguish objective truth from this propaganda and could easily attach politically calculated fanaticism to his propaganda, making him extremely effective. Goebbels hated Jews, believing that his failure in a literary career was due to a Jewish monopoly. In 1925 he joined the Nazi Party.[19]

Jews were epitomized in the press as all that was evil and harmful. The publication most vehement in its attack on Jews was *Der Stuermer* (published from 1923–45), a tabloid owned and operated by Julius Streicher. His attack on the Jews between 1923 and 1945 was so destructive that during the Nuremberg trials he earned the unusual distinction of being guilty of "rhetorical crimes against humanity." He was sentenced to death and executed.

Streicher persistently presented Jews as loathsome and inhuman creatures, depicting them as bacilli, spiders, parasites, poisonous mushrooms, toads, vampires, rats, centipedes, vultures, and monsters. A children's book put out by his publishing house compared Jews to mongrel dogs, tapeworms, poisonous snakes, and bacteria. These images, along with similar rhetoric flowing from other major communication channels and agencies of the Third Reich, convinced some readers of the Jews' "inferiority."[20]

Publications such as Streicher's *Der Stuermer* reached as many as two million people. Streicher devoted a tremendous amount of newspaper space to alleged Jewish acts aimed at destroying Gentile society through murder and sexual corruption. Streicher counteracted the possibility that even a single Jew could be good and decent by presenting "evidence" that every Jew was dangerous and depraved. By 1936 *Der Stuermer* welcomed a worldwide "cleansing" program, claiming that "those who vanquish the world-Jew will save the earth from the Devil."[21]

To intensify Jew hatred, Nazi censorship was imposed upon periodicals, newspapers, and foreign books. In addition, all domestic artistic and literary output was rigidly controlled. "A wall was built around the nation. . . . Within this wall, Nazi culture had a free hand to determine, if it could, every man's attitude toward life." Along with literary censorship, the Jews were persecuted in the press. They were depicted as vermin, bacilli, and forms of inhuman creatures that should, quite logically, be exterminated for "hygienic" reasons.[22]

Anti-Semitism proved a functional method of increasing tension within a collective group (the Germans) against a substitute target, thus increasing the likelihood of combat with the target. It also served as a trigger to mobilize Germans against the target group after German dissidents had been suppressed by the Nazis.[23]

The mass media was manipulated to increase anti-Semitism. Generalized aggression based upon ethnic, religious, economic, or political cleavages is, according to Smelser, free-floating and makes prejudicial reference to a specific broad group of people; it is always present and available for expression on any convenient pretext. In Nazi Germany, no matter what a person's beliefs, affiliations, or political stance, it was not difficult to manipulate the hostility of the society as a whole against the Jews as a whole. Channeling of free-floating aggression to a broad class—the Jews—was an important function of the propagandistic mass media in Germany as well as an essential aspect of the Nazi movement.

The Ministry of Propaganda never slackened its reigns of control. Continual demonstrations were organized, accompanied by ceremonial violence. The *Kristallnacht,* an allegedly "spontaneous" anti-Semitic outburst, was but one of Goebbels's many "accomplishments." By autumn 1939, as Hitler prepared to launch his war, he himself decided that the Propaganda Ministry should be kept in the background. Goebbels still retained control over radio programs, victory films, his own paper (*Der Angriff*), and the party organ (*Das Reich*).[24]

In 1941–43 the course of the war changed when, among other things, Germany was defeated in Africa, was halted by Russia, and feared invasion from the West. With this change of events, the Propaganda Ministry reasserted itself to the German people. Goebbels aroused audiences by saying the Jews were behind all of Germany's enemies. He consciously used religious terminology in most of his speeches.[25]

The Use of Myth

In addition to propaganda, the use of myth served a function in arousing the masses against the Jews. Myths are extremely powerful in predisposing people to certain types of behavior. Nora Levin contends:

All nations develop myths out of their history. Often these are not only more potent than the facts of history but express a nation's way of interacting with the facts. In Germany, the myth-forming process has tended to repress national responsibility for wrong turns and errors. The mistakes have been converted into projections of another's guilt. The myths of the "stab in the back," the "encirclement" of Germany, the "contamination" of cosmopolitanism have displaced German responsibility and created external scapegoats. In the process leading to the exterminations, the myth of the Jew as "race poisoner" and the "enemy of the nation," and its inverse—the myth of Aryan race supremacy—have had a fatal power in German thought.[16]

Note Levin's emphasis on dehumanizing the Jews, thereby placing them in a group not worthy of humane treatment. By bombarding the German public with inadequate and untruthful information, responsibility for Germany's losses could be heaped upon the Jews. According to the author's theory, the bases for aggression were already present, and the mass media could be utilized to intensify and deepen hatred against the Jews. The Nazis used heightened levels of prejudice to their advantage by channeling more and more attention and publicity toward the Jews.

In discussing myth, Bruno Bettelheim states that to the uneducated person, the concept "race" is fraught with a wealth of emotional connotations that relate it more to mythical (magical) thought than to reason. People who are "different" produce such feelings of foreignness that even real contacts don't seem to counteract myths. Thus German propagandists could employ the concept of "racial difference" in their effort to make the Germans accept the idea of genocide. The idea of the inferiority of the Jewish "race" and concomitant dangers of race contamination were exploited by the media on a massive scale.[17]

An unchanging motif in pre-Nazi and Nazi policy was to blame the Jew for all of Germany's woes and problems. Nora Levin in her analysis of this approach concludes:

The Jew objectified and embodied all of the specific, intense hatreds of the Nazi era: he was the . . . traitor who gave Germany "the stab in the back" in World War I; he was both Marxist and international capitalist; he was both pacifist and instigator of World War II; he was the devil as well as the ally of the clericals. Above all, he was the debaser of the German race. Anti-Semitism, an old and deeply rooted phenomenon of Europe, and most especially of Germany, proved to be the single most important instrument used by the Nazis to consolidate their power at home and abroad. Vague and diffused anti-Semitism, always close to the surface of European life, was cleverly exploited by Hitler; again and again, Jew-baiting excited masses of people and raised them to frenzied, barbaric acts of destruction. In the end, millions were involved in the extermination of Jews in one way or another.[28]

Rumors were also important for the instigation and continuation of pogroms. In Poland, where according to Ronald Donat in *The Holocaust Kingdom*, anti-Semitism had slackened just prior to the War because both Poles and Jews perceived the threat of a common enemy, native anti-Semitism was reawakened by poisonous Nazi propaganda claiming that, "It was the Jews who started the war that destroyed Poland." "On the far side of the Bug River the Jews are living like kings and helping the Soviets to persecute the Poles." "Jews are typhus carriers." Even more important, Jews were considered outlaws and were deprived of legal protection, hence becoming fair game for any malicious German or Pole. The lowest elements in society very quickly grasped the implications of this—easy victimization.[29]

The Nazis used the book *Protocols of the Elders of Zion* (a notorious forgery) to add support to the myth of a Jewish world conspiracy. This work was a modern adaptation of the old notion of the Jews' conspiracy with the Devil, the Anti-Christ. Jews, it was asserted, served as agents of Satan, intent upon the goal of destroying Christians and Christianity.[30] The *Protocols* were fabricated in 1895 by a group of Russian emigres residing in France and were smuggled into the Czar's court. They had little impact in Russia. However, during the Bolshevik Revolution and later the civil war in Russia in 1919–1920, the monarchists who fled the country carried copies of the *Protocols* with them to the west. Their version claimed that the Russian Revolution was the result of a Jewish plot.

In spite of being a forgery, the *Protocols* were immensely popular. After World War I, large sales of the book were reported in Germany; high sales continued into the 1930s. The *Protocols* was translated into many European languages and sold many copies in England, Europe, America, and the Arab lands. During the decades between world wars, it served to rationalize Germany's many disasters—defeat in the war, hunger, and destructive inflation.[31]

By 1942 Goebbels, the minister of propaganda in Nazi Germany, capitalized on the perverted image of the Jew presented in the *Protocols*. The book elaborated upon the structure of a "secret Jewish government" with worldwide agencies striving to control all political parties, the press and public opinion, world governments, and banks. This clandestine "government" supposedly advocated Jewish domination of the world.[32]

According to Smelser, rumors grow in intensity, becoming increasingly inflammatory and fueling generalized aggression into hostility.

They become directed toward a specific group. Rumors attempting to degrade Jews and heighten fear existed for generations preceding Hitler. They usually centered on some purported ritual killings of people in observance of a Jewish religious holiday. In pre-Holocaust Germany, these old themes of ritual murder were revived and given new credence.

However, the destructive fantasy gripping the popular imagination in the twentieth century proved more powerful than the ritual murder charge—the myth of a Jewish world conspiracy. The "conspiracy" myth, like the earlier rumors of Jews poisoning wells and killing Christian children for their blood, lacked any semblance of reality, but this fact did not reduce its power. The "big lie"—the myth of Jewish world conspiracy—gained credence and grew. The modern myth was even more elaborate than the demonological, medieval notion asserting that Jews had conspired with the devil to destroy Christendom. Many aspects of modern world capitalism, revolution, labor movements, depressions, wars, and booms were interpreted as a Jewish plot for world domination. Just as the Jew was viewed as mysterious and sinister in the Middle Ages, so he was now symbolic of everything frightening in the modern world. The notorious forgery, the *Protocols of the Elders of Zion*, was substantiating "evidence" against the Jews.

The role the *Protocols* played in myth, rumour, and propaganda cannot be overestimated. When Goebbels became the party's propaganda chief (1928), he used the *Protocols* to accumulate votes for the party. As soon as Hitler assumed the chancellorship in 1933, the one-day Jewish boycott of 1 April took place, spurred by the *Protocols*, sections of which Julius Streicher had published in the *Volkischer Beobachter*.

Each time anti-Semitic legislation was enacted, it was preceded by a campaign of nonstop propaganda. The *Volkischer Beobachter* invoked the *Protocols* constantly, and Streicher's weekly, *Der Steurmer*, simultaneously alternated between lurid stories of German maidens being raped by Jews and the ritual murder of German children by Jews. The vile accounts presented in the newspaper *Der Steurmer* were particularly important, since it was one of the largest-selling periodicals in Germany. The paper was displayed on notice boards in villages and towns. Even more sinister, under Hitler the minister of education prescribed the *Protocols* as required reading in schools.[33]

By 1941 Goebbels claimed that all Jews, by virtue of their "race" and birth, were enemies of the state and must, consequently, be eliminated. By 1943 even some of those Germans holding university doctorates published solemn tomes indicating that the hypothesized Jewish ritual murder of Christian children was but a prelude to the Jews' ultimate plans—the destruction of all Christians.

Heinrich Himmler jumped on the propaganda bandwagon by dispatching investigators to England for the express purpose of acquiring British police announcements of missing Christian children. This information was used to validate and increase claims of Jewish ritual murders, thereby lending incredible virulence to anti-Semitism. In 1943 Goebbels devoted 70–80 percent of his foreign broadcasts to anti-Semitic propaganda, hoping to convince Britain, America, and France of the "Jewish Conspiracy." Specialization in the *Protocols* even became the forte of some German university professors.[34]

The myth of Jewish world conspiracy was the means by which the Nazi government attempted to make its foreign policy palatable to the German people. The policy was aimed at war, but even Hitler dared not admit this openly. Instead, from 1933 onward foreign policy was explained primarily as a defense against deadly encirclement by the Jews. Specifically, the Soviet Union was portrayed, as Hitler had always believed, as a country of subhumans ruled by the Jews. Goebbels frequently distinguished himself by outbursts on this subject at party rallies. In 1935 he declared Bolshevism to be a Satanic plot hatched in the Jewish nomadic brain. Goebbels asserted that the Asiatic-Jewish flood would not deluge the German bulwark. One year later he announced Bolshevism to be criminal and pathological nonsense concocted by Jews for the purpose of destroying European nations and then establishing world dominion on their ruins. At the same time, diligent researchers were producing books showing that all people of importance in the Soviet Union were Jews.[35]

By 1943 the winds of war had turned against Germany, but still the rationalization of a Jewish world conspiracy provided Germans with the will to fight on. Goebbels ordered propaganda stressing that Jews would gladly annihilate the Germans if the war were lost. The murder of Jews was escalated at this time. By 1944, as the Holocaust was approaching its conclusion, Nazi propaganda continued unabated. Now the mass media presented the Jews as the sole instigators and primary propagators of the war. Even as the Third Reich was crumbling and Berlin was about to be overrun, the Ministry of Propaganda continued to harp on the theme of Jewish world domination. It would be impossible for the world to have peace, the ministry claimed, if a subversive force of three hundred underground Jewish kings ruling the world could not be checkmated.[36] The myth lingered until the fall of the Third Reich.

The role of propaganda is clear in the following confession of a young, dying German solider to a Jew who was with a work crew at a hospital:

I need not tell you what the newspapers said about the Jews. Later in Poland I saw Jews who were quite different from ours in Stuttgart. At the army base at Debicka some Jews were still working and I often gave them something to eat. But I stopped when the platoon leader caught me doing it. The Jews had to clean out our quarters and I often deliberately left behind on the table some food which I knew they would find.

Otherwise all I knew about the Jews was what came out of the loudspeaker or what was given us to read. We were told they were the cause of all our misfortunes. . . . They were trying to get on top of us, they were the cause of war, poverty, hunger, unemployment. . . .[37]

WHILE the ancient Pharaohs constructed pyramids triangulating to the heavens to symbolize their union with the immortals, Hitler's gas chambers produced pyramids of corpses whose ashes descended to the netherworld of Hell, symbolizing his kingdom over the dead.

—HELEN FEIN

11

ORGANIZATION OF DESTRUCTION

A FREQUENTLY raised question regarding the Jews of the Holocaust is: "Why didn't they fight back?" The question implies that people allow themselves to be victims of genocide. Here we will see that a minority group cannot fight the entire machinery of a bureaucratically organized, powerful state. It is foolish to think that the Jews could defend themselves against the Nazis when much of Europe could not.

The organization of genocide is overwhelming. Smelser indicates that in a hostile outburst, aggression may be highly organized and integrated, with the military playing a specialized role. He explains that the level of organization of a hostile outburst will directly correspond to the degree of formal organization of a group. Thus we might say that if a state is bureaucratically structured, systematic aggression rather than unorganized, sporadic violence will occur.

Formally organized, systematic aggression was the method by which Hitler destroyed the Jews. The high level of organization of the Holocaust was certainly enhanced by the already existing high level of bureaucratization and rational organization of the German state.[1] The

185

Reich leadership of the Nazi party provided the chain of command through which Hitler's plan of conquest, conspiracy, and killing was channeled. Its members were sworn in annually and took an oath to Hitler, pledging unconditional obedience to him. Directly below Hitler were all the Reich leaders, all of whom reported directly to Hitler about specific facets of Nazi policy. Administrators carried out directives of their superiors.[2]

Hitler had said, "the solution of this problem [the Jews] will be carried out legally, and not by capricious acts."[3] Sporadic violence against the Jews was discouraged because it was neither sufficient nor thorough enough to accomplish Nazi goals. Since pogroms accomplished nothing lasting, actions against Jews became more systematic, and unauthorized killings came to be viewed as a problem affecting overall efficiency. Eventually, the "ideal" soldier was an efficient, dispassionate killer, engaged in systematic slaughter for a "higher cause."[4] Nazi work had to be implemented in an "orderly" fashion, allowing for proper and thorough planning of each action through memoranda, conferences, and correspondence. Anti-Semitism became a professional institution and mass murder an administrative process.[5]

Making murder a professional, bureaucratic business controls certain human factors. After all, mobs such as those involved in the *Kristallnacht* might become unreliable, for they could unexpectedly be moved to sympathy, perhaps by a child. To exterminate a "race," killing children is imperative. Thus replacement of a raging mob by a bureaucracy, inherent in which is obedience to authority, is required for thorough, comprehensive, and exhaustive murder. In a professional bureaucracy, with responsiveness to the will of an ultimate authority via a hierarchy of responsibility, emotions of actors are governed not by unpredictable passions but by organized routines of behavior.[6]

Concentration on the basic organizational structure in Germany that made the Holocaust possible and, simultaneously, a discussion of the destruction of the European Jews is our next concern.

DESTRUCTIVE ORGANIZATION OF THE STATE

As was discussed in the "Formation of a Monolithic and Exclusionary Party," (Chap 10) the real power of Hitler was concentrated in three organizations—the NSDAP, the SS, and the Gestapo. There is no need to elaborate upon them here again. Rather, the reader will remember they were an integral part of the Nazi organizational structure of destruction.

Raul Hilberg, in *The Destruction of the European Jews*, states that when we discuss the "machinery of destruction," we must note that no single agency handled the entire genocidal operation and no office coordinated and directed the whole process. Further, he explains that if we enumerate the private and public agencies that might be referred to as the "German government" and those referred to as the "machinery of destruction," we would conclude that they were identical offices. However, the term "government" is more inclusive, implying the totality of the administrative functions of a society. "Destruction" was only one very specialized activity of the government.

Hilberg indicates that the German administrative apparatus included the fuhrer, as well as four separate hierarchical groups—a ministerial bureaucracy, the armed forces, German industry, and the Nazi party. Despite their different historical origins and interests, all four groups agreed upon the destruction of the Jews. They became so totally fused they may truly be referred to as "machinery of destruction," each making its own contribution to the destruction process in the following way:

1. The Ministerial Bureaucracy. Staffed with civil servants, the ministerial bureaucracy implemented anti-Jewish decrees in the early stages of the destruction process. Writing the regulations and decrees defining the concept "Jew," which led to the expropriation of Jewish property and ghettoization of the German Jewish community, was the contribution of this agency to the genocidal effort.

2. The Armed Forces. By virtue of its control over huge territories in Western and Eastern Europe, the army entered the destruction process after the war began. Military units and offices participated in exterminating Jews via mobile killing units and the transporting of Jews to death camps.

3. Industry and Finance. Industry and finance played a major role in expropriating Jews—in the system of forced labor and also in the gassing of Jews.

4. The Nazi party. The party contributed a sense of "idealism" and "mission" to the "history-making" process, uniting the efforts of the four bureaucracies in action and in thinking.

With the bureaucratic machinery in place, Hilberg points out, the steps of the destruction process materialized in the following order: first, the concept of "Jew" was defined; second, expropriatory measures were enacted; third, Jews were concentrated into ghettos; and fourth, a decision was made to exterminate European Jewry. Consequently, as mobile killing units were operating in Russia and Poland, Jews in the rest of Europe were being deported to killing centers.

Hilberg summarizes the chronological development of this process as follows:[7]

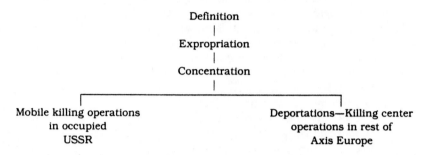

In spite of changes of policy (emigration [1933-40] and annihilation [1941-45]), the Nazis exhibited an administrative continuity in the destruction process that remained unbroken: the three steps introduced previous to 1940—definition, expropriation, and concentration—served as steppingstones to the killing operations. Hilberg contends that, "the path to annihilation leads directly through these age-old steps."[8]

We have already discussed Hilberg's first two steps, definition and expropriation, in "The Creation of Outsiders" (Chap. 7). The third step of the destruction process he analyzes is concentration. Thus a discussion of the ghettoization of the Jewish community is now in order.

GHETTOIZATION

Ghettoization concentrated multitudes of victims into small geographic areas, requiring Jews to be uprooted from their homes and moved. These steps were very important and should not be underrated. Helen Fein, in *Accounting for Genocide*, contends "successful segregation of the Jews is the most important proximate cause or intervening condition producing high victimization."[9]

Ghettoization, according to Hilberg, entailed the following five steps: (1) severing social contacts between Germans and Jews, (2) restricting housing, (3) imposing movement regulations, (4) creating identification measures, and (5) instituting a Jewish administrative machinery.

In Germany the process of ghettoization was directed at each step by the bureaucracy. Ghettoization does not necessarily mean that walled-in Jewish districts were established in cities composing the Reich and the Bohemian-Moravian Protektorat. (This was later done in Poland and Russia farther east.) Rather, the Jews in Germany were subjected to conditions exhibiting many characteristics of a ghetto which, as Hilberg explains, can be evidenced by these five conditions: (1) laws severing German and Jewish social contacts, such as race laws forbidding interaction between Germans and Jews; (2) housing restrictions, serving to evict Jews from their homes and crowd them into *Judenhauser;* (3) movement regulations, or rules restricting the mobility of Jews, such as no use of city transportation and withdrawal of communications (creating a ghetto); and (4) identification measures, requiring Jews to apply for identification cards stating that they were Jews in accordance with a decree of 23 July 1938.[10] Jews who wanted to emigrate had to obtain passports, which by a decree of 5 October 1938 required stamping with a large red "J." The easily identifiable passports were later to prove fatal to thousands of Jews who had moved to countries soon to be occupied by the Germans. On 5 January 1938 a proposal was put into effect requiring that Jews be assigned "Jewish" names, that is, names "created" by Ministerialrat Hans Globke, expert on names for the Interior Ministry. In a decree dated 1 September 1941 Jews over six years of age were required to wear a Jewish star when appearing in public. The Security Police extended marking procedures to apartments, and in 1942 Jews were required to paste a star of David on their doors—black print on white paper.

In these consecutive steps the Jewish community was socially isolated, crowded into special housing, restricted in its social movements, and made vulnerable by a system of identification. Yet there remained one more important element for complete ghettoization of the German-Jewish community, finalizing the stranglehold the Nazis could exercise on their future victims—a (5) Jewish administrative machinery. A German takeover of credible Jewish leaders and, hence, of the legitimate social institutions of the Jewish people occurred.[11]

The *Reichsvereinigung* and the *Judenrat*

The Jewish community organization was still decentralized in early 1933, each city having its own administrative organization that controlled hospitals, kept up synagogues, and ran Jewish schools. This administration functioned like a business, with each community having a *Vorstand,* a Jewish leadership group composed of prominent businessmen. In March of 1933 prominent Jewish leaders were called together by Direktor Heinrich Stahl, chairman of the *Vorstand* of the Jewish community in Berlin; he suggested forming a new national organization, the *Reichsvertretung der Juden in Deutschland,* "Reich Representation of the Jews in Germany," for political purposes of engaging in an open dialogue with the Nazis regarding the future of Jews in Germany as well as the issue of anti-Semitism. By the end of

1933 the organization was operative. However, the *Reichsvertretung* had little opportunity for dignified controversy; rather, it was increasingly occupied by education, emigration work, training, relief, and care of the sick.

On 4 July 1939—in accordance with a decree drafted by Ministerialrat Bernhard Losener and Rolf Schiedermair and signed by Interior Minister Wilhelm Frick, Minister of Education Bernard Rust, Deputy of the Fuhrer Rudolf Hess, and Minister of Church Affairs Hanns Kerrl—the *Reichsvertretung* was totally taken over by the Security Police. The decree changed the name of the organization to *Reichsvereinigung*, "Reich Association." The most important provision in this decree was the empowering of the Interior Ministry (the Security Police) to assign additional tasks to the Jewish *Reichsvereinigung*. With this provision, the Jewish administrative machine was transformed into a tool for the destruction of the Jewish people. As Hilberg states, "it [the *Reichsvertretung*] was converted into something that its founders had not imagined in their wildest dreams."[12]

Some of the additional tasks involved the use by Nazis of Jewish community publications to inform Jews of German orders and decrees. Jewish statistical experts kept the Gestapo posted regarding deaths, births, and all sorts of demographic changes, and Jewish apartments experts served the function of concentrating Jews in the special *Judenhauser*. Another hideous task was imposed upon the *Reichsvereinigung* at the end of 1941, when they were required to prepare lists of Jews to be deported to death camps in Eastern Europe, to notify their families of this, and to employ Jewish police, the *Ordnungsdienst*, to round up the deportees.

Remember that the Nazis did not create the *Reichsvereinigung* but, rather, took it over. The leaders of the Jews were Jewish leaders. Hilberg concludes: "the Germans controlled the Jewish leadership, and that leadership, in turn, controlled the Jewish community. The system was foolproof."[13]

In some occupied territories where organizations the equivalent of the *Reichsvertretung* existed, the Nazis coopted and subverted them. If such social organizations did not exist, Isaiah Trunk indicates, the Nazis established the *Judenrat*. These ramified Jewish organizations were originally created by occupation authorities to efficiently carry out all directives and regulations. According to the original plan (Heydrich's "urgent letter" of 21 September 1939), a "Council" composed of prominent, active Jewish leaders was established in each city of concentration and, in effect, served only one purpose—the execution of Nazi orders against the Jewish population.[14]

Thus the structure of the genocide was thoroughly organized and very efficient. No potential for destruction was overlooked. Even Jews inadvertently participated in the administration of their own destruction through the *Reichsvereinigung* and the *Judenrat*, established as intermediate levels of authority between the Nazi party and the Jewish population. The *Judenrat* (Jewish councils composed of Jewish leaders) conducted such business as taking of census, municipal services, management of dwellings, police services, and the like. One of their more painful duties was registration and selection of candidates for the work camps and deportations. The councils were limited to distributing meager supplies and maintaining low standards of sanitation; this was done only because the Nazis feared that they themselves were threatened by outbreaks of epidemics. Councils preserved order and peace, according to the standards of the Nazis.[15]

The councils tried to view themselves as a positive force at work on behalf of the Jews. However, Trunk describes them quite differently, indicating that they provided even a higher level of structure and organization for the Nazis to mobilize in the perpetration of the Holocaust, since the Nazis used them not to organize Jewish life or strengthen the structure of the ghetto, but as an instrument to realize their extermination plans for Jews in the occupied territories.[16]

Hannah Arendt believes that the councils did more harm than good but points out that one cannot generalize, since some councils were corrupt while others worked diligently to circumvent Nazi plans. Had the councils blatantly refused to function, chaos would have reigned supreme in the ghettos, forcing Jews to escape or rebel rather than try to exist under ghetto conditions. Arendt knows that most would have died anyway, but perhaps more European Jews could have survived.[17]

Concentration in Poland

In September 1939, when the German Army entered Poland, the concentration stage of the destruction process was well under way. The concentration was carried out more quickly here than in the Reich-Protektorat region. One reason for the drastic haste in Poland was that the German administration of Poland was in the hands of a large number of Nazi party men, who were less thorough, less careful, and less "bureaucratic" than the administrators in the Reich. A second reason for quick action in the East was that Germans had more disdain for Polish Jews than they had for German Jews, referring to eastern Jews as *Untermenschtum*, "subhumanity." However, the third and primary reason for rapid extermination of the Polish-Jewish population was its size—10 percent of the Polish population; out of a Polish population of 33,000,000, there were 3,300,00 Jews. After the division of Poland in September 1939 between Germany and Russia,

2,000,000 of these Jews were under Nazi domination. In Warsaw alone, there were almost 400,000 Jews. The bureaucratic structure in Poland shut off the Jews entirely from the rest of the world, in effect resurrecting the medieval ghetto.[18]

On 21 September 1939 a detailed concentration plan was sent by Heydrich to his *Einsatzgruppen*, the mobile killing units, who were then roaming Poland. According to Hilberg,

> Part I of the concentration order provided that the Jews were to be ejected from the territories of Danzig, West Prussia, Poznan, and Eastern Upper Silesia. These areas later became incorporated territory, that is, territory integrated into the administration of the Reich. The Jews from these areas were to be shoved into the interior of Poland, a territory later known as the "General Government." The Jews in the General Government were to be concentrated in cities. Only such cities were to be chosen as concentration points which were located at railroad junctions or at least along a railroad. On principle, all Jewish communities of less than five hundred were to be dissolved and transferred to the nearest concentration center.
>
> In Part II of the order Heydrich directed that a council of Jewish elders (*Altestenrat*, also *Judenrat*) composed of influential persons and rabbis was to be set up in each Jewish community. The councils were to be made fully responsible (in the literal sense of the word) for the exact execution of all instructions. They were to take an improvised census of the Jews in their area; they were to be made personally responsible for the evacuation of the Jews from the countryside to the concentration points, for the maintenance of the Jews during transport, and for housing upon arrival. There was no objection against Jews taking with them their movable possessions. The reason to be given for the concentration was that the Jews had participated decisively in sniper attacks and plundering.[19]

According to Part I of Heydrich's plan, a new type of territorial administration, first called the "General Government in Poland" and later simply referred to as the "General Government" (*Generalgouvernement*) was created south and east of the incorporated territories. This region contained approximately 1,400,000 Jews in 1939.

In accordance with the first phase of Heydrich's expulsion plan, approximately 600,000 Jews were to be transferred to the *Generalgouvernement* from the incorporated territories, raising the Jewish population of the *Generalgouvernement* from 1,400,000 to 2,000,000. The second part of Heydrich's directive required crowding these 2,000,000 Jews into closed quarters—ghettos. After 15 November 1939 the *Ostbahn* (the railway network of the *Generalgouvernement*) was set aside for the express purpose of "resettling" the Jews. Shortly before beginning this mass "resettlement," Higher SS and Police Leader of the *Generalgouvernement* Friedrich-Wilhelm Kruger, met with main division chiefs and *Gouverneure* and decided that Poles in the incorporated territories were to be sent to the *Generalgouverne-ment* along with the Jews. A total of 1,000,000 Jews and Poles were to be resettled by spring, at a rate of 10,000 per day.

By 1 December the trains began to roll into the *Generalgouverne-ment*. The movements had hardly begun when it was decided that the Reich and its incorporated areas were to be cleared of Gypsies, Jews, and also Poles. Depopulated regions were to be settled by ethnic Germans from Russia returning by "special arrangements" from Baltic states and other areas allocated to the Soviet sphere. Simultaneously, transports were being settled farther and farther east, until it was decided that Lublin district would be turned into a *Judenreservat*, a Jewish reserve.[20]

Part II of Heydrich's plan, ghettoization, was seen by him as a temporary solution to the "Jewish problem." Ghettos began appearing in the incorporated territories during the winter of 1939–40. The first of these major ghettos was created at Lodz in April 1940, and the giant walls surrounding the Warsaw ghetto were completed in October 1940. Many smaller ghettos were formed in the Warsaw district early in 1941. A ghetto was established at Krakow in March 1941, and the Lublin ghetto was created in April 1941, the same month in which the ghetto at Radom was finished. Simultaneously, the ghetto of Kielce, also in the Radom district, came into existence. Poland's third largest ghetto, Lemberg (the capital of Galacia), was established in December 1941. As 1941 drew to a close, the ghetto-formation process in the *Generalgouvernement* was ending, leaving only a few ghettos to be set up during 1942.

Lodz became the prototype for the ghetto-formation process, and the Jewish machinery there reflected, by its very organization, the dual role the ghetto was to play in the destruction process: (1) it served a survival function through its health, welfare, and supply functions, and (2) it served a destructive function through its Central Bureau, the Registration and Records Office, and especially, through its police, organized according to a German model.[21]

The ghettos accounted for the murder of one-fifth of the total Polish Jewish population. Soon, the speed of the extermination process would be escalated.

The *Einsatzgruppen* in Russia

One organized method of killing Jews was the *Einsatzgruppen*, the movement of killers to victims. Another such method was the death camps, involving the movement of victims to the killer. Both were highly organized and efficient means of destruction.

While planning the invasion of Russia in the spring of 1941, Hitler made a decision stipulating that small mobile units of the police and SS should be dispatched to Soviet territory to roam from town to town, killing Jews on the spot. Soon after the operations began in occupied Soviet areas, a second order was handed down by Hitler dooming Central, Western, and Southeastern European Jewry. In Russia, the killers were to be dispatched to seek out victims, while in other areas the victims were to be transported to the killers—to killing centers. Those who could not be destroyed by one method surely would be exterminated by the other. The sending of killers to their victims will be considered first.

When the German Wehrmacht attacked Russia on 22 June 1941, it was accompanied by the police and mechanized killing units of the SS, both of which were tactically subordinated to field commanders but could, otherwise, pursue their own special business. The mobile killing units, under an arrangement with the German Army, were operating on the frontline areas.

The Reich Security Main Office, the RSHA, was the sole agency permitted in forward areas during the destruction of the Russian Jews. This agency was Heydrich's creation, and his machinery became a part of the destruction process in 1941. It was during this year that Heydrich laid the foundation for the mobile killing units and the deportations to killing centers. He put this organization together piece by piece over a period of years, and it reflected a characteristic trait of the German government apparatus as a whole, namely, the RSHA along with its regional machinery was a fusion of civil servants and party men.[22]

The first known reference to the operations of the *Einsatzgruppen* appears in the "Barbarossa" directive, signed by Field Marshal Wilhelm Keitel. The code word "Barbarossa" was used for the invasion of the USSR. In this directive, the *Einsatzgruppen* was not mentioned by name, but it was stated in the directive that the *Reichsfuhrer-SS* would be assigned special duties in Russia by the fuhrer. It was further stated that the border of the USSR would be closed off at the beginning of the operations except to units carrying out special duties.[23]

On 4 April 1941 a draft proposing an Army-RSHA agreement was sent from General Quartermaster of the Army Wagner to Heydrich outlining the terms for the deployment of the *Einsatzgruppen* in Russia: killing measures could be carried out against the *civilian* population and mobile units would operate in army group rear areas and army rear areas. It was made very clear that the *Einsatzgruppen* were to be subordinated to the military but that the RSHA would give them functional directives from Heydrich, Chief of the Security Police and SD.

In May 1941 the final draft of negotiations between the RSHA and the army were completed. This draft differed from a previous draft in one important respect: the *Einsatzgruppen* could operate in corps areas located on the front lines in addition to army group rear areas and army rear areas. This important difference meant that Jews would be cut down extremely quickly, with no forewarning or chance for escape. This version of the agreement enacted between the army and the RSHA partners was endorsed by Heydrich and Wagner at the end of May.[24]

On 31 July 1941, six weeks following the invasion of Russia and the concomitant first full death sweep of the *Einsatzgruppen*, Goering gave Heydrich absolute power to organize the "Final Solution." Previously (1939), Goering had chosen to evacuate the Jews from the Reich. Goering ordered, "I hereby charge you with making all necessary preparation with regard to organizational and financial matters for bringing about a complete solution of the Jewish question in the German sphere of influence in Europe."[25]

A total of four *Einsatzgruppen*, each of battalion size, were operative in the Holocaust. Two of the leaders, Chief of SD-Inland Otto Ohlendorf and Criminal Police Chief Artur Nebe, came straight from the RSHA. However, most *Einsatzgruppen* officers were professional men, such as a physician, lawyers, and even an accomplished opera singer. They were not chosen from hoodlums or common criminals. Most were in their thirties, and it appears that none of them sought this assignment, but they all became "efficient killers."

The *Einsatzgruppen* totaled about 3,000 men drawn from the Security Police, the SD, and a battalion of Order Police from Berlin; there were also some *Waffen-SS* men. The group of murderers was completed with the addition of indigenous units of Ukrainians, Latvians, Estonians, and Lithuanians serving as auxiliary police.[26]

The *Einsatzgruppen* followed upon the heels of the German armed forces and invaded Soviet-held territory. Their instructions were to destroy the Jews. From the Baltic to the Crimea, the *Einsatzgruppen* adhered to a basic strategy. First they instigated indigenous anti-Semites to riot against the Jews, photographing and filming pogroms in order to demonstrate that all people, not just Germans, regarded Jews as enemies against whom it was necessary to protect oneself. During these pogroms, German Security Police stayed in the background, far from the limelight.

Second, after the initial outburst, the *Einsatzgruppen* chiefs organized a systematic annihilation of the Jews. Afterwards units of the *Einsatzgruppen* (Security Police Commandos or *Einsatzkommandos*) were reinforced by indigenous collaborating auxiliary battalions. By alternately applying chicanery and terror, Security Police rounded up

Jews at specified places and times for "resettlement." Those Jews who did not report were to be shot.[27] Hannah Arendt states:

the extermination program that was started in the autumn of 1941 ran, as it were, on two altogether different tracks. One track led to the gas factories, and the other to the *Einsatzgruppen*, whose operations in the rear of the Army, especially in Russia, were justified by the pretext of partisan warfare. . . .[28]

When the *Einsatzgruppen* first entered the USSR, there were about five million Jews living under the Soviet flag, four million of whom lived in territories later overrun by the Nazis. Many Jews lived in cities, and the *Einsatzgruppen*, by moving quickly upon the heels of the army, trapped Jews in large population centers before they could realize what was happening. This, as explained previously, was the reason that the RSHA insisted upon sending its mobile units to frontline areas. Units of *Einsatzgruppe A* quickly entered the cities of Lepaya, Kaunas, Riga, Yelgava, Tallin, Tartu, and other large suburbs of Leningrad, accompanying advance units of the army. The first tanks to enter Zhitomir were accompanied by three cars of *Einsatzgruppe C*. *Kommando 4a* of *Einsatzgruppe C* was in Kiev when it fell on 19 September. *Einsatzgruppe D* was moving into Hotin while it was still being defended by the Russians. Incidents of this type are too numerous to list, but we must remember that the *Einsatzgruppen* moved so rapidly that Jews were killed, as Hilberg puts it, like "sleeping flies."[29]

The speed of killing began to increase as the Germans organized and standardized the killing operations. Generally, a site located outside of a town was selected for the executions. The Jews were marched off or trucked to outlying areas and forced to dig pits or trenches. Men were taken first. The site of killing was supposed to be closed off to outsiders. *Einsatzkommandos* then stripped the victims of their clothing and possessions, lined them up, and machine-gunned them into trenches.

Of course, a little variety occurred in the procedures for murder. Some commanders preferred the method of machine-gunning victims en masse, letting them topple into the ditches as they were shot. Some used the "sardine method," having a group of people lie down at the bottom of a ditch, and cross firing the victims from above. Then, the next batch of victims laid down, with their heads at the feet of the dead. After several layers, the graves were closed.[30]

An example of the work of the *Einsatzgruppen*, a matter for boasting in some Nazi reports, froze the Nuremberg Court when read to them by Sir Hartley Shawcross on 27 July 1946, who quoted an affidavit from Hermann Grabe, a German civilian works engineer who was on the disused Dubno Airport of the former Polish Volhynian province on 5 October 1942, and described the mass murders he witnessed with his own eyes:

. . . An old woman with snow-white hair was holding this one year-old child in her arms and singing and tickling it. The child was cooing with delight. The parents were looking on with tears in their eyes. The father was holding the hand of a boy about ten years old and speaking to him softly; the boy was fighting his tears. The father pointed towards the sky, stroked the boy's head, and seemed to explain something to him. At that moment the SS man at the pit shouted something to his comrade. The latter counted off about twenty persons and instructed them to go behind the earth mound. The family I have described was among them. I well remember a girl, slim and with black hair, who, as she passed me, pointed to herself and said: "Twenty-three years old."

I then walked round the mound and found myself confronted by a tremendous grave. People were closely wedged together and lying on top of each other so that only their heads were visible. Nearly all had blood running over their shoulders from their heads. Some of the shot people were still moving. Some lifted their arms and turned their heads to show that they were alive. . . . The pit was already three-quarters full. I estimated that it held a thousand people. I looked for the man who did the shooting. He was an SS man who sat at the edge of the narrow end of the pit, his feet dangling into it. He had an automatic pistol on his knees and was smoking a cigarette. The people—they were completely naked—went down some steps which were cut in the clay wall of the pit and clambered over the heads of those who were lying there to the place to which the SS had directed them. They lay down in front of the dead and wounded. Some caressed the living and spoke to them in a low voice. Then I heard a series of shots. I looked into the pit and saw that their bodies still twitched or that their heads lay motionless on top of the other bodies before them. Blood ran from their necks.

I was surprised that I was not ordered off, but I saw that there were two or three postmen in uniform near by. Already the next batch was approaching. They went down in the pit, lined themselves up against the previous victims and were shot. When I walked back round the mound, I noticed that another truckload of people had arrived. This time it included sick and feeble people. An old, terribly thin woman was undressed by others, who were already naked, while two people held her up. The woman appeared to be paralysed. The naked people carried her round the mound. I left with my foreman and drove in my car back to Dubno.

On the morning of the next day, when I visited the site, I saw about thirty naked people lying near the pit—about thirty to fifty metres away from it. Some of them were still alive; they looked straight in front of them with a fixed stare and seemed to notice neither the chilliness of the morning nor the workers of my firm who stood around. A girl of about twenty spoke to me and asked me to give her clothes and help her escape. At that moment we heard a fast car approach and I noticed that it was an SS detail. I moved away to my site. Ten minutes later we heard shots from the vicinity of the pit. Those Jews who were still alive had been ordered to throw the corpses into the pit, then they themselves had to lie down in the pit to be shot in the neck.[31]

The Operations Situation Report of *Einsatzgruppe C*, dated 7 October 1941, indicates that 33,771 Jews were executed in Kiev on 29 and 30 September, exceeding the maximum daily capacity of the Auschwitz gas chambers. Most Jews from Kiev were murdered at a desolate ravine on the city's outskirts, Babi Yar.[32] Here the Germans carried out the largest, single massacre of Jews, with the news reaching the outside world even while the war was still in progress.[33] The destruction there was so intense that Elie Wiesel poignantly proclaims, "Kiev brings to mind Babi Yar. Kiev *is* Babi Yar."[34] Units of *Einsatzgruppen* in the Baltic were equally diligent. A report of 15 October 1941 stated that they had exterminated approximately 120,000 Jews in Latvia, Lithuania, White Russia, and Estonia. In total, the *Einsatzgruppen*, supported by collaborators and the German armed forces, butchered about two million Jews.[35]

DEPORTATIONS TO GHETTOS AND CAMPS

Extermination of Jews required a massive deportation of Jews from countries in which they were living to labor camps, to camps for old or infirm people, to "medical research" centers, to ghettos, and the like. Country by country the Nazi machinery picked up its victims, beginning the agonizing, inhumane trail to death.

We will briefly view the fate of the Jewish community country by country in an effort to depict the enormous scale of activity of the organized Nazi machinery of destruction. The statistics we present stating the Jewish presence in countries before and after the Holocaust are staggering and almost incomprehensible.

Central and Eastern Europe

Mass deportations began in the Reich in September 1941, and they were not terminated until the destruction process ended. The objective of these movements was now annihilation of Jews, not emigration. Until death camps were constructed, however, Jews were being dumped into ghettos in incorporated areas and occupied Soviet areas farther east. In the incorporated territories, the target city was the ghetto of Lodz.[36]

Germany

In Germany, at the beginning of the Hitler regime, there were 499,682 Jews. The plebiscite in the Saar in 1935 added another 3,117 Jews to the Reich, bringing the new total to 502,799. The 1939 census indicated that less than half of that number—213,930—remained in

Germany, many having fled because of Nazi rule. By September of 1944, the count of Jews in Germany was 14,575. After the armistice was concluded, there were 20,000 Jews in Germany; this figure included concentration camp survivors returning to Germany as well as those who passed the war in hiding.[37]

Previous to November 1941, Jews had emigrated from Germany, but following this date, Himmler refused to allow Jews to emigrate. Deportation replaced immigration. The first deportations of Jews numbered 1,000 Jews from Stettin and 160 Jews from Schneidemuehl; both occurred in the spring of 1940, when the Jews were sent to Piaski (Lublin Reservation). Very large-scale deportations started on 16 October 1941 to Lodz, Lublin, Warsaw, and Minsk.[38] The last of the deportations from Germany were on 25 March 1945.[39]

Austria

In Austria the suddenness of the Anschluss caught the Jewish population totally unprepared for Nazi annexation, and deportation steps occurred quickly.[40]

. . . From October 20, 1939, to September 1, 1944, 15,344 males and 28,077 females were deported in 71 convoys to camps at Nisko, Opole, Kielce, Modliborzyce, Lagow-Opatow, Lodz, Riga, Minsk, Izbica, Wlodawa, Theresienstadt, Auschwitz. On a territorial basis, they were divided as follows: 11,200 in the Government General; 5,460 in Lodz; 13,150 in Minsk and Riga; and 13,611 in Theresienstadt. . . . The first deportations from Vienna began in mid-December and January, 1939. The last Jews to be evacuated left in the spring of 1942. Of the 190,000 Jews in Austria, who at the end of 1939 amounted to barely 60,000, there remained only 7,000 in 1946.[41]

Bohemia and Moravia

Czechoslovakia, which lost the Sudetenland in the Munich Pact (29 September 1938), was deprived of its independence on 14 March 1939. By a special Hitler decree (16 March 1939), Czechoslovakia became the Protectorate of Bohemia and Moravia, thus becoming a territorial part of the Greater Reich. The country was subject to complete military occupation, and the Jews suffered the same deplorable fate as other Jews in the Reich and its conquered territories. All "niceties" were dispensed with if a country had the status of a Protectorate, where undisguised brutality reigned—just as it did in the Reich proper. A directive dated 24 October 1941 reveals the following orders:

During the period of November 1 to December 4, 1941, the Security Police has been ordered to evacuate 50,000 Jews from the Old Reich, the Ostmark [Austria], and the Protectorate of Bohemia and Moravia. Their destination, the area of Riga and Minsk. The evacuation [deportation] will take place in the freight trains of the Reichsbahn, a thousand persons to each train. . . . On the basis of agreements concluded between the Chief of Security Police and SD, the Ordinary Police takes charge of the convoys of the transport and will form escort commandos in the proportion of one guard for each 12 Jews. . . . The commandos will be released from their task, as soon as the [Security] Police take over.[42]

There was a total of 350,000 Jews in former Czechoslovakia; those killed are estimated at 300,000.[43] The final estimate of the death toll in the Bohemia-Moravia Protectorate is 71,000.[44]

Poland

Even though the fate of Polish Jews was discussed when treating the *Einsatzgruppen*, the statistical consequences of the Holocaust in Poland are recorded here. It is clear that the devastation in Poland was beyond belief. There were 3,300,000 Jews in prewar Poland. After the liberation, there remained a mere 100,000. Adding the 200,000 refugees who survived in the USSR to this list brings the number of survivors to 300,000.[45]

Western Europe: France

France was a new experience to the Nazis who had not encountered difficulties in carrying out their scheme of destruction in the Protektorat or in Poland. When the Nazis dynamited seven synagogues on 2 October 1940, the French reacted with shock and indignation. But on 27 September 1940 a decree requiring compulsory Jewish registration was promulgated in the occupied zone; the decree required marking Jewish stores with the Star of David. On 2 June 1941 compulsory Jewish registration became a fact in the nonoccupied zones. As in many other countries, the Jewish *Judenrat* was utilized to make the Jews their own executioners. However, in France neither the Jews nor the French proved ready puppets.

Yet in May 1941 a mass raid on "Polish" Jews in France netted some 3,600 men and women, including the president of the Federation of Polish Jews in France. These people were interned in concentration camps and were later the first to be deported.[46]

On 28 June 1942 the following statement was issued by the Chief of SD and Security Police:

Provisions have been made to run daily special trains with a capacity of 1,000 persons each, from the middle of July and the beginning of August, respectively, by which at first 40,000 Jews from occupied France, 40,000 from the Netherlands, and 10,000 from Belgium will be carried out.[47]

Many of the arrested Jews were assembled in the Velodrome d'Hiver stadium and then transported to the following camps: Compiegne, Pithiviers, Drancy, and Beaune-la-Rolande. From there, these wretched people were shipped eastward—destination Auschwitz.

French-Jewish deaths resulting from the deportations amounted to 35 percent of a prewar population of 350,000. Out of 100,000 deported, only 3,000 returned.[48]

The Benelux Countries

Holland

Of all the Western countries, Holland's Jews received the harshest treatment. On 21 May 1940 Holland was invaded and conquered in a time span of five days. Arthur Seyss-Inquart became Reich commissioner of the Netherlands on 21 May 1940 and Lt. General Hans Rauter was chief of police and security. Seyss-Inquart was an old hand at Jewish liquidation as he had already served in Poland. The Nazis were quick to enact anti-Jewish legislation—forced registration of Jews, expropriation and Aryanization of Jewish property, the discharge of Jews from public posts, and the formation of Jewish councils on the model of the *Judenrat*. Additional anti-Jewish legislation to hasten the "final solution" was quickly laid down.

On 9 February 1941 the Nazis, in a burst of vandalism and cruelty, raided the Jewish quarters in Amsterdam. Later, the Nazis attempted an encore of the same performance, but Dutch workers came to the assistance of the Jews. During the riots which followed, however, German police arrested four hundred Jews, later shipping them to Buchenwald and Mauthausen. The Dutch countered this outrage by declaring a general strike, which held the Nazis in abeyance until 1942, at which time deportations were resumed.

As elsewhere in Europe, 1942 marked the point at which previous economic and civic devastation wrought upon the Jews changed into physical devastation—deportation and annihilation. In March 1942 Jews from the northern and southern provinces of the Netherlands were sent to the ghettos of Amsterdam. An actual deportation schedule became operative in June 1942, provisions already having been made for special trains to transport the Jews to Auschwitz. The deportation goal for Holland was 40,000. Trains departed from Westerbork to Auschwitz once or twice a week, each carrying its doomed "cargo" of from 1,000 to 2,000 Jews.[49]

The statistics for Holland are grim. There were 110,000 people deported, only 6,000 of whom were ever to return. Almost the entire Jewish population of Holland was destroyed.[50] Of those deported, 60 percent were sent to Auschwitz; most of the others were killed in Sobibor, and some were sent to Theresienstadt.[51]

Belgium

The Jewish experience in Belgium ran a different course from that of Holland, at least for the first two years after the Nazi invasion. Because Belgium had a king who did not flee the country after the invasion and was still accorded a certain amount of recognition helped to account for the better condition of Jews. Also, the Jewish "problem" was less acute in Belgium and was considered a matter of internal policy for two years after invasion.

However, the early, initial phase of moderation was marked by Jewish disenfranchisement. In October 1940 a Nazi decree was enacted requiring registration of Jews as well as Jewish firms, exclusion of Jews from Belgium's economic life, and removal of Jews from their public offices. The population, being fair-minded, ignored or foiled the implementation of most decrees. The situation in Belgium was displeasing to the Nazis. On 25 November 1941 a form of Western *Judenrat* was organized to be used against the Jews.

Measures against the Jews became increasingly severe until two decrees (11 March and 8 May 1942) imposed forced labor upon "idlers"—the entire Jewish people. Under this convenient pretext, able-bodied Jews were forced out of Belgium and deported to labor camps at Pas-de-Calais and Northern France to build fortifications along the Atlantic coast. After this, there were numerous middle-of-the-night raids upon Jewish districts in Brussels and Antwerp, during which Nazi commandos verified identification papers with their own lists, then dragged the frightened victims to a temporary assembly place, from whence they would be sent to Malines.

The mass deportations from Belgium began the same day as the start of the depopulation of the Warsaw Ghetto—22 July 1942. Out of the original 90,000 Jews in Belgium, 45,000 who left Belgium were apprehended by means of Nazi dragnets in France and deported by way of Drancy. Of those remaining in Belgium, 27,000 were removed to Malines. The Belgian Resistance Movement in concert with the Jewish underground organization, *le Comite de Defense des Juifs*, forewarned the Jewish population, provided shelter for fugitives, and bravely attacked trains and infiltrated camps to liberate as many victims as humanly possible. The Belgian queen and Cardinal Van Roey also helped to alleviate the situation as much as possible. Twenty-seven thousand Belgian Jews, foreigners and citizens alike, were deported and presumed dead.[52]

Luxembourg

Luxembourg was also a Benelux country, and when annexed to the Reich, the Jewish population numbered 3,500. The goal of making

Luxembourg *Judenrein* was tackled early, and only a small number of Jews were granted permission to leave. Approximately 600 to 700 victims were deported to the East—Theresienstadt and Auschwitz— and only 30 of these survived. Out of a total of 3,500 Jews, 500 survived.[53]

The Scandinavian Countries

Even though the Scandinavian countries had a small Jewish population, they did not escape the Nazi wrath. The Danes, who were guaranteed political sovereignty by the Nazis at the time of their occupation (9 April 1940), did not put up a fight. Even after Denmark was compelled to join the anti-Comintern Pact in November 1941, there were many instances of Danish recalcitrance to Nazi attempts to enforce decrees against Jews.

When Himmler pressed for deportation, the Danes heroically offered sanctuary and help to whomever they could. Groups and individuals came to the rescue of Jews, forewarning them of Nazi intentions and hiding them in private homes, shelters, and hospitals. When the Gestapo conducted raids on Jewish houses, they were already empty, with the exception of 470 old people who were captured and transported to Theresienstadt. Simultaneously, operation "little Dunkirk" was implemented, and a flotilla of fishing boats gathered at Oresund harbour, where Jews were directed by scouts, students, or whoever could help. From there, they were boarded on all available vessels and taken to Swedish waters. Thus, more than 6,000 Jews and 1,376 half-Jews—men, women, and children—reached Sweden within three weeks.[54] Of those sent to Theresienstadt, all but 45 returned. This was truly a miracle of survival.[55]

Both Norway and Finland offered assistance to the Jews, though they met with less success than had the Danes. Norway's Jewish population was 1,700, and in October of 1940, they were barred from some professions; by June 1942 registration and confiscation of Jewish property were decreed. Arrests followed, and the Norwegian Resistance movement aided Jews in their flight over almost impassable terrain. On 25 October 1942 all Jewish males over sixteen were arrested, and in November women and children suffered the same fate. The Norwegian public and church condemned the Jewish persecution, but this did not prevent the deportation of 750 Jews to Stettin by boat and finally to Auschwitz. Approximately 1,000 reached Sweden safely; of these 531 were gassed at Auschwitz.[56] A mere 12 of the 750 Jews ever returned.[57]

Finland managed to resist German demands for a period of time, and in a 1942 interview, Foreign Minister Witting said, "Finland is a decent nation." He added, "We would rather perish with the Jews than

hand over the Jews to them [the Nazis]."[58] In spite of this valiant attempt by the Fins, only a small number of Jewish pregnant women,
children, and 160 stateless refugees were taken from Finland to Sweden; other Jews fell into the Nazi dragnet.[59]

Italy

Italy had become a Fascist country more than a decade before
Germany had. But Italy was not as anti-Semitic, even though an Aryan
manifesto was decreed on 14 July 1938, resulting in an elimination of
Jews from positions of responsibility. Yet the Germans were irked by
Italian failures to live up to the racial laws. Even worse to the Nazi
mind, Italy interfered in countries such as Yugoslavia, Greece, and
France. The Italian-occupied South of France, the Cote d'Azur, was a
veritable haven for Jews with means. Jewish cultural life was permit-
ted to thrive, with the synagogue on the Boulevard Dubouchage in
Nice becoming a symbol of Jewish survival. Many dislocated refu-
gees—writers, rabbis, and journalists—lived unmolested under the
Italian flag.

On 10 July 1943, when British and American troops invaded Si-
cily, Mussolini lost the reigns of power. Jews, anticipating an evacuation to Italy, were concentrated in Nice. Due to political bungling, this
mission failed, and those Jews who could not escape to villages and
mountains were sent to Auschwitz.

Following the Italian-Allied Armistice, Italy was divided—with a
Fascist Verona government in its north and a Badoglio government in
its south. On 10 September the Nazis took Rome, corralling 8,000
Jews. There was no strong Papal protest. The number of Jews sent
from Rome to Auschwitz was 1,127, and the number deported from
Verona was 10,271, with 2,824 of these doomed to Auschwitz. Between 20,000 and 22,000 Jews from Italy are estimated to have been
exterminated, and of the 10,000 Jews deported, only 605 ever returned.

The Balkans

The Nazi military campaign against Yugoslavia and Yugoslavian
Jews was punitive and harsh in reaction to the Yugoslav government's
conclusion of a treaty of friendship with the Russians on 5 April 1941.
Preceding the war, Yugoslavia had harbored approximately 70,000
Jews, and those living in the Italian zone had always had some degree
of protection from Nazi-inspired persecution.

Serbia

In Serbia Jews were corralled in the Belgrade ghetto in the most disreputable section of the town, where misery, overcrowding, and disease were prevalent; the Nazi solution to such congestion was shooting ghetto dwellers. The murders were "justified" on the grounds that Jews were accomplices in revolt and sabotage.[60] The "problem" was dealt with on the spot when Franz Rademacher and SS colonels Weimann and Fuchs decreed:

... The males would be shot by the end of the week, which would solve that problem, and ... the rest of about 20,000 Jews, women, children, and old people, as well as 1,500 Gypsies, except the males, who were to be shot, would be concentrated in a ghetto in the Gypsy sector of Belgrade. A minimum of food would be provided for the winter, and as soon as the question of the final solution of the Jewish question was reached and the technical means were available, the Jews would be deported by water to the reception camps in the East.[61]

Einsatzkommandos were detailed to execute the Jews. In February 1942, 6,000 Jews resided in the Semlin camp, but by May of the same year the "Jewish problem" in Serbia had been solved.[62] The entire 6,000 were put to death in mobile gas vans. At least 50,000 Yugoslavian Jews lost their lives in the "final solution."[63]

Croatia

On 10 April 1941 Croatia was granted independence by Nazi Germany. Tenenbaum reports there was an "orgy of destruction" perpetrated against Jews by the Croatians themselves who were so cruel to the Jews that even the German plenipotentiary in Zagreb voiced some condemnation. Only those Jews who were in the Italian occupied zones—Dalmatia and Montenegro—were relatively safe and stood a chance of surviving the Holocaust. At the labor-extermination camps at Laborgrad, Jasenovac, and also on Pago Island, 8,000 Jews were tortured to death.[64]

Contrary to the condition of Jews in Italian-occupied zones, Jews in German zones of occupation were in desperate straits, especially in Bosnia-Herzegovina where the local Moslems totally destroyed the Jews. Also hard hit were the Jews in Sarajevo, where a pre-War population of 8,000 Jews dwindled to a mere 1,140 found there in 1946. Deportations and massacres continued. Zagreb is typical of the destruction wrought upon the Jews in Croatia: before the war, the Jewish population was 12,000; afterwards, it was 1,647.[65]

Greece

Greece was overrun by the Germans on 6 April 1941, after which time a combined German, Italian, and Bulgarian force reigned. Greece contained approximately 75,000 Jews, of whom 50,000 lived in German-occupied Salonika. The patriotic Greeks, who displayed little anti-Semitism, did not harm the Jews. About 900 Jewish families resided in the Italian-occupied zone and were afforded Italian protection for as long as was possible. After 6 February 1943, the brutal Major Anton Brunner arrived in Greece from Vienna to inaugurate a deportation-ghettoization plan. Between April and May of 1943, 50,000 Jews were deported to Auschwitz in twenty to twenty-five transport trains; there were from 2,000 to 2,500 Jews on each train. Another 3,000 to 4,000 provided forced labor for railroad construction projects and were later deported.[66]

After 10 September 1943 Athens was a German-occupied city, and the Italian armistice of 25 September 1943 gave the Germans administration over other parts of southern Greece. On 27 April 1943 the "Conqueror of the Warsaw Ghetto," General Juergen Stroop, took over the function of higher SS leader. Now Germany had all of Greece in its grasp. The cruel and resolute Stroop rapidly carried out annihilation plans, as the death penalty was extended to any non-Jews attempting to aid Jews. Yet, the Greek underground persisted in assisting Jews. The Orthodox Church is credited with having saved more than 10,000 Jews by issuing a circular for all parishes, priests, and convents, exhorting them to offer safety and succor to the victims of the Nazis.[67] Of the 65,000 Jews taken to Auschwitz, only 1,475 returned.[68]

Bulgaria

Bulgaria, another Balkan country, was home to 28,000 Jews before the war. After becoming aligned with the Axis in March 1941 Germany soon requested that Bulgaria eliminate its Jewish population, but the Bulgarian people resisted this demand. Yet on 22 March 1943 the first convoy set out to the East, with a second on 25 March and a third on 29 March. The Bulgarian people continued in their assistance to the Jews, often delaying Nazi plans.[69] Lt. Colonel Otto Hoffmann, suggested that because Bulgarians were raised among Greeks, Armenians, and Gypsies, they simply could not comprehend the faults of the Jewish character and, consequently, did not wish to destroy the Jews.[70] In all, 15,000 Jews were deported to Lublin, Auschwitz, and labor camps in the Warsaw district.[71]

Rumania

On 5 September 1940 German troops reached Rumania. The Rumanians however, did not even wait for the Germans to take the initiative in solving the "Jewish question," being old hands at anti-Semitic practices themselves. They had in their grasp a prewar population of approximately 800,000 victims. The Rumanians could not rid themselves of the Jews fast enough, turning them over to the Germans so quickly that the Germans were forced to return some. Jews were massacred and deported constantly. Out of 850,000 Rumanian Jews, 425,000 perished.[72]

Slovakia and Hungary

Slovakia

Slovakia was the first satellite country to fall in with Germany's scheme of deportation. On 2 November 1938 there were 90,000 Jews in Slovakia. On 25 March 1942 the first deportation train carrying 20,000 Jews undertook its journey, and other trains, marked TD (Transport David) departed Slovakia three or four times a week. Victims from Slovakia were directed to Lublin, Auschwitz, Poniatow, Warsaw, Lubartow, Sobibor,and Treblinka. In 1942, 60,000 Jews suffered deportation; only 284 returned to Slovakia. A total of 13,000 more of the remaining 20,000 Jews were deported in the fall of 1944.[73]

Hungary

Hungary had an enlarged territory—incorporating Northern Transylvania, some previously Magyar-governed territory, a small section of Subcarpathian Ruthenia, and some Slovakian districts—and housed a Jewish population of about 800,000. In much of Hungary there was little resistance to Nazi plans for the Jews, even though occasionally, for example, under Premier Nicholas Kallay, there was an attempt to protect some Jews.[74]

During a six or seven month period, over half a million Jews in Hungary's enlarged territory were lost. The ashes of about 400,000 of them were left in the Auschwitz crematoria and improvised incinerators operative in ditches. Jewish losses in Hungary proper (preceding awards and annexations to Hungary by the Nazis) numbered 240,000 out of a Jewish population estimated to be 481,000 in 1941. By 1946 Hungary's Jewish population was only 240,000.[75]

By 1945 the effort to eliminate the Jews of Europe had almost succeeded. Approximately 6 million were dead, and the cultural and religious life of the East European Jew was extinguished forever.[76] These figures present the facts, but they can never convey the human agony experienced by these people to the death.

DEATH CAMPS: METHODICAL MADNESS

The killing operation depicted the final phase of Nazi organization. In the early phases of the killing operations, the selection process followed a strict organizational plan. Hitler's personal chancellery created an appropriate department to handle the process in the Reich Ministry of Interior. This, in turn, resulted in the creation of three innocuous-sounding organizations: the Reich Association Hospital and Nursing Establishment, which located the victims; the Charitable Foundation for Institutional Care, which financed the killings; and the nonprofit Patient Transport Corporation, which shipped death candidates to murder plants.[77]

Concealment of Nazi goals was essential to the success of the killing operations. Steps were taken to mislead and fool the victims. Euphemisms were a primary tool in deluding the Jews. For example, the killing centers were collectively referred to as "the East." Specific camps might be designated as "labor" and "concentration" camps. Sites of mass killings would be referred to as PW camps (as at Auschwitz) and transit camps (as at Sobibor). At Auschwitz, gas chamber and crematorium units were referred to as "special installations, bath houses, and corpse cellars." The killing itself was called "special treatment."

Those who comprised the inner circle of the Nazi hierarchy were sworn to secrecy. Even though "leaks" occasionally occurred, no one helped the Jews. One such instance occurred in 1942, after a gas expert toured the camps and communicated what he had seen to a fellow passenger, a Swedish diplomat, traveling on the Warsaw-Berlin Express. The diplomat, in turn, related the incident to Stockholm, but the Swedish government never released the information.[78] Precautions to insure secrecy were also practiced through visitor control. Visitors were never shown the brothels or crematoriums. Should they note the smoking chimneys, they were told that corpses of victims of epidemics were being incinerated.

From the outset, difficulties in dealing with the Jewish problem were organizational and administrative. Hitler's chain of command thought in terms of "solutions," ranging from technical and administrative talents, to transport, to the final gassing.[79] Millions of Jews perished as a consequence of medical experiments, death marches, gas chambers, and gas vans.[80]

Shipments of people to camps were determined on the basis of the "absorptive capacity" of the killing installations and upon the need for slave workers at the numerous industrial enterprises profiting from establishing branches in the vicinity of some death camps. Industrial enterprises of the SS, as well as famous German firms, namely, the Krupp Werke, I. G. Farben, and Siemens-Schuckert Werke, established plants at Auschwitz and near the Lublin death camp. Cooperation between businessmen and the SS was excellent. Approximately 25,000 of the 35,000 Jews working in one I. G. Farben plant died. Killing through labor was the objective.[81]

The business of the destruction of Jews in the camps had become exactly that—a business. The killing centers were, upon close examination, like modern mass-production plants. The quick, efficient procedures meant that a person could get off a train in the morning, and by evening his corpse would already be burned and his clothes packed for shipment to Germany. Those who were not immediately killed were not "wasted," since they might prove useful for medical experiments or diversion for the guard troops.

The organization responsible for the extermination plan being instituted was set up as follows. The Security Police and Security Service were under the overall command of Heydrich. Their task was to round up all the Jews. Adolf Eichmann, as link between the RSHA and the WVHA (the SS—Wirtschafts-Verwaltungshauptamt, Head Office for Administration and Economy), under Oswald Pohl detailed the transportation to the death camps. Himmler, as Reich leader of the SS, provided the means of liquidation once the Jews were in the camps. As chief of the Death's Head Units of the SS, Lt. Gerald Theodor Eicke was appointed inspector of the concentration camps. Later, Eicke and his staff were assigned the task of running and controlling all of the death camps.

The camps themselves were divided on the basis of the purpose which they served—labor or extermination. "Grade 1" camps, such as Dauchau, exhibited the least intolerable conditions. Those categorized as "Grade 2," such as Flossenburg, were much worse. Finally, those ranked as "Grade 3" exhibited extremely horrible conditions and resulted in the loss of many lives. The actual extermination camps were also divided. One type (such as Auschwitz and Maidanek) provided for the liquidation of prisoners almost immediately upon their arrival or as soon as their working capabilities had been depleted. Others (such as Chelmno, Sobibor, Belzec, and Treblinka) gassed all new arrivals except those used for burial details.[82]

In the camps proper, a discernible hierarchy existed. At the top was the commander who assumed overall responsibility for the camp. Next was the Schutzhaftlagerfuhrer who was in charge of inmate con-

trol. The chief of administration handled financial matters and pro-
curement. Below this level were the deputy-*Schutzhaftlagerfuhrer*,
the adjutant, the camp engineer, and the camp doctor. In addition,
there was a scattering of minor officials—a few hundred officers and
men who served in camps before the war. Many of these were SS men
renown for their ability to carry out any order.[83] The various camps
served as basic training for SS who were taught to be emotionally
unresponsive to victims' sufferings.[84] Some of the second-rate SS
troops made up the guard forces; others held the posts of block leader
or detail leader. These "brutes and bullies," sometimes holding the
very lives of the prisoners in their hands, were encouraged to treat
prisoners in as severe a fashion as possible.[85]

There was some attempt to set up self-government in prison
ranks, but it should be kept in mind that when such positions were
offered to inmates, they served Nazi goals: the SS wanted to use the
inmates against each other. Some of the positions were: senior camp
inmate, appointed by the SS for the purpose of spying against other
prisoners; orderly room officer, responsible for the camp administra-
tions's files, barracks assignments, roll call preparation, and the distribution of rations; labor records officer, assigned to keeping card in-
dexes for the camp and, early on, able to help some inmates by
altering records; senior block inmate, selected to maintain order with
chosen barracks orderlies and to dole out rations; prisoner foreman,
charged with labor details and responsible directly to the detail leader
in the Nazi hierarchy.[86] The need for this inmate organization explained why some Jews were left alive; the "chosen" came from the
temporary congestion of the gas chambers and crematoriums.

Like everything else in the camps, the confiscation of property was
highly organized; it entailed an assembly-line method. Inmate groups
picked up baggage left in transport freight cars or on platforms. Other
inmates collected clothes and valuables from dressing rooms, which
were antechambers to gassing rooms. Women's hair was cut off in
barber shops near the gas chambers. Gold teeth were extracted from
corpses. Human fat from burning bodies was poured back into the
flames to speed up the cremation process.[87] Articles of clothing were
sorted, packed, and shipped off to Germany. The gold was melted
down and sent to the German Reich Bank. Ashes from corpses were
used as fertilizer, and bones were made into superphosphate. There
was some attempt to make soap from the fatty parts of bodies.[88]

Everything was run as if on a tight timetable. If Jewish convoys
did not undress fast enough, they were assisted by having the clothing
torn from their bodies.[89] Before the numbers became overwhelming,
the stripping for the "showers" was itself well organized, especially at
Treblinka. The men's line had several steps. In the first step of the

process, coats and hats were surrendered. Next, the jackets were taken. Afterwards, shoes were removed and tied together with a piece of string. Following this, the victims were divested of their trousers, and, finally, their shirts and underwear were taken.

An SS guard had shrewdly observed that victims who were winded died more rapidly in the gas chambers. Therefore, a cordon of guards with whips forced the victims to run to the gas chambers in search of refuge. A record was set at Treblinka where the destruction procedure from time of arrival of cattle cars to the moment bodies were removed from the gas chambers took a mere forty-five minutes.[90]

Some guards manifested sadistic tendencies through perverted excesses which, at times, took the form of massive orgies or sexual aberrations. A woman guard at Auschwitz, Irma Grese, used a whip to cut open breasts of well-formed Jewish women. The victims were then taken to a doctor who performed a painful operation while Grese watched, obviously aroused. There was one *Oberchasfuhrer* in charge of crematoriums who selected a group of beautiful women, lined them up naked, and practiced shooting at them. Several were hit repeatedly before dying.[91]

An example of sadistic behavior can be evidenced in a practice of the SS in which they picked two young men from the barracks to fight each other. The youngsters, having previously practiced methods of causing blood to flow from their nose or cheek without inflicting much harm upon one another, would perform their ritual bloodletting, knowing that once the SS saw them bleeding, they would be satisfied and leave.[92]

The Nazi hierarchy provided some minor, ineffective solutions to these problems. They established brothels, with Polish women as prostitutes; they used inmates rather than guards to be in charge of disciplinary action; they got rid of personnel who overdid things. This last, however, was a rarely applied measure.[93]

While processing prisoners toward their final destruction, no opportunity to use and abuse victims was overlooked by the Nazis. This can be seen by the medical experimentation performed in the death camps. Experiments were initiated for almost any reason; perhaps someone might want to test a hypothesis or test a serum. Frequently, doctors requested the use of habitual criminals who would serve as their guinea pigs. "Criminals" included the "race-defiling Jewish habitual criminals." Medical experimentation was particularly fascinating to Himmler and he figured prominently in this area.[94]

The acme of experimentation was reached by doctors who strongly identified with Nazi aims. Their activities expanded the scope of the destruction process. One method used was nonsurgical sterilization of "inferior" women.[95] One form of this involved injection of a plant extract; another was the introduction of an irritant into the uterus by means of a syringe. A different procedure, imposed upon men, was the use of x-ray. Three years of such testing indicated the x-rays were less likely to produce sterilization than was operative castration. In 1942 Dr. Ernst Grawitz performed experiments on women at Ravensbruck to determine the healing effect of sulfa drugs. The first step involved infecting women with various germ cultures, leaving them untreated so as to be able to observe the course of the infection.[96] At Dachau, subjects were malaria infected and, afterwards, treated with various drugs. In both instances, many deaths resulted from the administration of large doses of drugs.[97]

Dr. Sigmund Rascher, an Air Force physician, tried to ascertain human reactions to high altitude and also capacity to sustain life at high altitudes. Conditions of ascent and descent from various altitudes were tested in equipment constructed for the purpose of simulating such conditions. Since heart action was involved in this testing, a whole new series of killings was initiated, due to the stress placed upon this organ. One victim's heart was still beating during an autopsy, so the doctors began experiments testing for the length of time which the heart remained active after death.[98] Rascher also sought to determine the effect of rapid depressurization in the production of a gas embolism. After being forced to participate in parachute-descent tests, some people were afterwards kept under water until they died. Autopsies revealed that air embolisms did not prove fatal.[99]

Other subjects were immersed in water ranging from 35 to 40° F until they grew stiff. Experimenters then measured the time taken to die. This supposedly aided the Nazis in determining the plight of fliers who crashed into icy seas. Prisoners were also exposed to cold winter air, and, when their screams presented a disturbance, Dr. Rascher anesthetized them.[100] In other experiments, Rascher observed that no purpose was to be served by rewarming severely chilled people. However, such experiments continued to be pursued by Rascher at Himmler's behest.[101] Apart from imposing gruesome deaths upon human beings, these experiments produced no "practical results." They contributed absolutely nothing that proved helpful to German fliers.[102]

It should be noted that whenever experimentation was performed and whatever its nature, the supply of guinea pigs was filled by requests through appropriate channels. All things were done in an orderly fashion. The SS Main Economic and Administrative Office instructed various camps as to the number of inmates required for experimentation and also transported them. After some victims were gassed in cyanide experiments and after some men had one testicle removed in sterilization experiments, the bodies were shipped to Strasbourg University where they were preserved for later study, the results being published in journals. Later, upon the advance of the Allied front, the bodies were dismembered and burned.[103] Thus the advancing Allies were indirectly responsible for some deaths. When forced to retreat, the SS evacuated camps and took prisoners with them. Many, of course, did not survive the ordeal of death marches. Anyone who could not continue walking was beaten to death or shot.[104]

Gassing, or course, took a heavy toll in human lives. A variety of methods existed by which gassing operations were performed in the camps. In some instances, small groups of Jews were taken to awaiting gas vans, their clothes were collected, and then they were gassed. Others undressed at train platforms, then were marched to inhalation chambers, being assured that if they inhaled deeply, they would strengthen their lungs. Still others were marched in naked columns to the gas chamber/bath houses.

The gas van was produced by the RSHA. Though primarily used to exterminate women and children, this first killing center in the woods at Chelmno was responsible for the deaths of 100,000 Jews.[105] Afterwards, two provisional, crudely built gas chambers located at two farmhouses, with the capacity to destroy 400 to 500 people per day, served the Nazi goals. The bodies were burned in a large trench.[106]

A widely used method of gassing, resulting in very rapid processing of victims, was devised at Auschwitz. Here, *Badeanstalten* (bath houses) were attached to crematoriums. In these "showers," solidified hydrogen cyanide (Zyklon) pellets were inserted through shafts into side walls and administered to victims. Since a large supply of the gas was needed, and the SS did not manufacture it themselves, private firms produced the gas. These firms, previously engaged in fumigation of rodents and insects, were now put to work to destroy the Jewish "insects." At Auschwitz, on 6 August 1944 the *Referat fur Schadlingsbekampfung der Waffen-SS und Polizei in Auschwitz* ("Anti-vermin Office of the SS and Police in Auschwitz") requested increased shipments of hydrogen cyanide in order to exterminate human beings as if they were vermin.[107]

The entire, simple appearing, businesslike process of operating death camps took years to work out. The camps exemplify smooth administrative technique. Dawidowicz notes the honor bestowed upon dedicated administrative workers such as Kurt Gessten, head of the Department of Sanitation. At Belzec, a banquet was held for employees who were told by the *Obersturmbannfuhrer* that, "when one sees the bodies of the Jews, one understands the greatness of your work."[108]

WHAT have you done to us, you freedom-loving peoples, guardians of justice, defenders of the high principles of democracy and of the brotherhood of man? What have you allowed to be perpetrated against a defenseless people while you stood aside and let it bleed to death, without offering help or succour, without calling on the fiends to stop. . . .

—BEN GURION

12

FAILURE OF MULTIDIMENSIONAL LEVELS OF SOCIAL CONTROL

THE failure of social control mechanisms is the final factor contributing to genocide. Social control is pertinent to the analysis of genocide, since it might be the only factor permitting us to impede or prevent this horrendous crime.

Social control of genocide may exist at two levels—one external and the other internal. External controls are characterized by failure to act to stop genocide—the failure of authorities and the civilian population to discontinue violence, the failure of the many nations of the world to take an active stance against genocide, the failure of religious institutions to uphold their ideals, and the ultimate lack of control—authorities themselves condoning and participating in violence. Internal controls relate to factors weakening the ability of the victim group to defend itself, such as lack of a state, lack of opportunity to capitalize upon its sociocultural organizations, not realizing the intent of genocide, and physical destruction of group members.

EXTERNAL CONTROLS

The Aggressor State and Its Citizenry

Obviously in the case of the Jewish Holocaust there was no control of hostility by those in authority. The agents of authority, who theoretically control violence, were the instigators of violence against Jews,

215

since the ideology of National Socialists centered on anti-Semitism. Indeed, the Nazi party functioned by use of brutality and violence, instilling fear in those who would impede its progress. By initiating persecution and violence, the state lent legal and moral sanction to the destruction process, acting as a model for aggression. The Nazis were not checked in their hostilities against the Jews. Such crimes as genocide are germinated from radical ideas and brought to fruition by organized movements or elite forces that normal social controls do not check.

The consequence of a legitimate, powerful source of authority and social control, such as the state, embarking upon such a course of aggression is suggested in a study cited by Bruno Bettelheim and Morris Janowitz. Bettelheim and Janowitz contend:

... societal controls exercise a regulating and restraining influence only on what would be classified as "intense" intolerance, or open expressions of the desire for violence. . . .

Acceptance of external controls was not only inadequate in conditioning men to be tolerant, . . . it was not even enough to prevent them from holding outspoken views. . . . *It served only to restrain demands for open violence* [emphasis added].[1]

Thus they conclude that external control sources, that is, agencies and institutions, cannot eliminate prejudice but *can*, where intense intolerance is present, restrain people from engaging in overt aggression against a target group.

Even before mass extermination began in Nazi Germany, authorities exercised little or no control over crimes against Jews. As early as 1937 Julius Streicher designed and instigated a boycott against Jewish businesses during the Christmas season. Neither the party leadership nor the economic authorities in Berlin interfered. The customers and employees of Jewish shops were terrorized, goods thrown into the streets, and shops ransacked. This episode served as a precipitator of other boycotts that occurred sporadically over the next few months in many other German cities.[2]

When a state aborts or subverts its purpose of protecting its citizens, the breakdown of social control is complete. Hilberg relates that following the mob behavior of Germans against Jews during the *Kristallnacht* ("Night of Glass") in 1938 during which Jewish shop windows were smashed and Jewish lives were taken, there was subversion of the legal rights of individuals by the state itself. The Supreme Party Court met in February 1939 to consider the "excesses" committed against Jews by thirty men. Twenty-six of these defendants had killed Jews. Yet not one of the twenty-six party men was expelled. The court could find no "ignoble" motives in the behavior of these men.[3]

In Nazi Germany the state itself led the genocidal effort. The *Reichssicherheitshauptamt* (RSHA), the Central Security Department of the Reich, which contained such agents of authority as the Gestapo, Krepo, and the Security Service, ran the Holocaust machinery. It served as the central office of the Supreme Command of the SS (*Schutzstaffel*—the para-military formation of the NSDAP) and the Reich Ministry of the Interior. *Einsatzgruppen* forces dispatched to the East were under the RSHA, as were the death and concentration camps. If a Jew were arrested by the SS, taken away in the night, never to be seen or heard from again, to whom could one complain? The police? The state? All authorities were an integral part of the same system that channeled to Heydrich (SD), then Himmler (SS), and finally to Hitler (chancellor). The RSHA (under the SS) ran the Holocaust machinery. As Helen Fein points out, the stronger the control of the SS in a given area, the more direct were extermination actions against the Jews.

By 1941 the SS was in direct control of Jews. The RSHA established priorities, and RSHA agents, with various divisions of the SS, executed or implemented them. The primary ideological priority demanded extermination of Jews by any means available in SS zones of control. In 1941 direct extermination began outside of the Reich, and deportation to Polish and Baltic ghettos and extermination camps was initiated. In 1942 plans were laid by the RSHA to deport Jews from other occupied states.[4]

Previous to this the German citizenry could have protested Jewish persecution but in general did not. The Jewish victims had previously been defined as outside "the universe of obligation" of Germans, the dominant group.[5] People considered Jews different and did not identify with them as human beings. How was this done? Laws were passed, rights were rescinded, property was seized, ghettos were formed, and trains were stuffed with Jews who disappeared forever.

We must remember the deep divisions separating "true Germans" from the Jews. People were saturated with themes of anti-Semitism playing up differences. Himmler had likened anti-Semitism to delousing and cleanliness.[6] The people listened. Such propaganda brought social tensions and strains to their pinnacle. Norman Cohn speaks of making allowances for the Germans' traditional subservience to authority, for the harassment and strain of war, and for the growing ruthless terror being exercised against the population.[7] Laying aside the motives or causes, there remained no control of hostile actions against Jews by the citizenry of Germany.

Considering the leadership of Hitler, can we even think public opinion would affect his course of action? Hitler was sensitive to public protest against the euthanasia program of the mentally retarded because Germans expressed widespread revulsion and fear when busloads of German children were gassed at extermination centers. The process was halted by Hitler's edict. He then authorized the use of less visible means (injection of poisons). However, the gassing of German Jews was protested by very few Germans. The absence of Jews was inconsequential to most Germans.[8] There was no control exercised by German agencies of authority and none, in effect, by the German populace.

Other Nations

A strong line of defense might have been provided against the Holocaust by the imposition of controls by nations outside of Nazi hegemony, but despite the presence of warning signs of impending genocide, nations around the world failed to respond, sometimes neglecting the signs of danger and sometimes attempting to cover up mass killings of Jews.

As early as January 1936 James McDonald, high commissioner for the League of Nations refugees (Jewish and non-Jewish) leaving Germany, had clearly intimated the fate of the Jews of Germany after the passage of the Nuremberg laws. Upon resigning his post with the league in January of 1936, McDonald beseeched the league to intervene on behalf of the Jews in Germany. In his resignation letter, he addressed the Nuremberg laws; the persecution of Jews in Germany; the distribution of official hate literature in German schools; and the inability of Jews to hold government positions, be employed, keep their own businesses, or care for themselves. He pointed out systematic and increased exclusion of the Jews from all spheres of German life.[9] Ross reports:

As for the "right" of the League of Nations to intervene in the internal affairs of Germany on the issue of individual protection and rights, McDonald cited law and custom in Europe from the Congress of Vienna and the Congress of Berlin of 1878, to the Upper Silesia Convention of May, 1922, to the agreements protecting minority rights in the Treaty of Versailles and the actions of the League of Nations in 1922 and again in 1933 as a legitimate basis for intervention. He stated that the League of Nations, its member-states, and private, philanthropic, and religious organizations should join in "friendly but firm intercession with the German government, by all pacific means. . . ."[10]

McDonald felt that the league, with its covenant powers "affecting the peace of the word," should assume the full burden of intervention.[11] McDonald's foresight was simply ignored, and virtually nothing was done in response to his appeal.

Not only did the league fail to protect the Jews, but even America hesitated, faltered, or failed to take action to reduce the destructive potential of the Holocaust. Between 1933 and 1944 the American tradition of offering sanctuary for oppressed peoples was despoiled and uprooted, replaced by measures of political expedience, isolationism, diplomatic evasion, indifference, and blatant bigotry that served Adolf Hitler.[12] America did not protest when German Jews were stripped of their jobs in 1933 or their citizenship rights in 1935. Even the 1938 *Kristallnacht* resulted merely in a mild rebuke to Germany when Roosevelt simply recalled America's Ambassador for a consultation. There was neither a cutting off of trade with Germany nor new immigration laws.[13]

The accepted policy of the United States and the Allies was more than just passive. It may be considered beyond passivity when agonized cries from overseas were muffled by the Allied governments. For example, in January 1942 eight of the governments-in-exile met at London's St. James Palace and issued a declaration of accusation openly branding German atrocities. However, no mention of the Jews was made by name.[14]

Even the U.S. State Department intentionally restricted and halted information from abroad regarding the mass killing of Jews.[15] This became evident in December 1943 when Henry Morgenthau, Jr., secretary of the treasury, convinced of State Department perfidy in the destruction of the Jews, commissioned the Treasury Department's general counsel, Randolph Paul, to prepare a report documenting the eight-month delay in authorizing relief for the Jews of Rumania and France. Morgenthau had discovered duplicity surrounding cable 354, which was a message from Washington instructing Leland Harrison, minister at the legation in Bern, Switzerland, to withhold information about the tragic and desperate situation of Jews. Paul passed the project over to Josiah E. DuBois, his assistant general counsel, who prepared a report that has never been published, entitled *Report to the Secretary on the Acquiescence of This Government in the Murder of the Jews.*[16] This report, which Morgenthau corrected and renamed *Personal Report to the President,* was presented on 16 January 1944 to President Franklin Roosevelt. It pointed out, among other things, that more than a year had elapsed between the time the United States and its Allies had publicly acknowledged and then denounced Nazi Germany's policy of extermination.[17]

In addition, Morgenthau pointed out that Undersecretary of State Sumner Wells had, in October of 1942, urged Minister Harrison to forward all information concerning the Nazi assault on the Jews and then had unaccountably reversed these instructions with cable number 354.

The cable has the appearance of being a routine message which a busy official would sign without question. On its face it is most innocent and innocuous, yet when read together with the previous cables, is it anything less than an attempted suppression of information requested by this Government concerning the murder of Jews by Hitler?[18]

America's failure to act swiftly in the defense of Jews was witnessed again in 1944 when the American War Refugee Board requested that the War Department bomb the gas chambers at Auschwitz. Although during August and September of 1944 American bombers had regularly flown over Auschwitz, and although the gas chambers had already been photographed from the air on numerous occasions, and although some bombs had even been dropped there by mistake, the requests did not get official support for several months and by then it was too late.[19]

Most other nations also failed to exert control over Hitler's policies, even though there were numerous early indicators of impending doom. A memorandum reaching the British Foreign Office as early as November 1938 indicated that a senior member of Hitler's chancellery explicitly stated that Germany intended to destroy the Jews—either by emigration, starvation, or murder—and planned to expel or kill Jews in Hungary, Poland, and the Ukraine after gaining control of those countries.[20] Yet it was as late as 17 December 1942 before the first joint statement directly condemning the Nazi extermination of Jews was issued by the United States, Britain, the Soviet Union, and the governments-in-exile.[21]

Another failure by many nations to attempt to control the destruction of Jews was witnessed at the Evian Conference. Plans for the Evian Conference, a world conference dealing with the refugee crisis, were announced by President Roosevelt in 1938. Thirty-two nations were asked to help plan emigration from Germany and maybe even Austria. Fascist Italy would not attend, and Germany had not been invited.

The conference convened in Evian, France, on 6 July 1938. During the entire proceedings the atmosphere was pregnant with feelings of disharmony, fear, and confusion. Since the League of Nations already had three agencies for dealing with the refugees, Roosevelt's motives for desiring to create a new agency were suspect by members of the conference. Many believed that Roosevelt could not even influence opponents of immigration in his own country to formulate a more humane immigration policy.

One nation after another represented at the conference presented an excuse for not permitting the refugees admittance to their country. Britain, fearful of the Arabs, made it clear that Palestine was out of the question as a sanctuary. France did not wish to increase the size of her already "heavy" burden. Canada, possessing vast empty territories, did not wish to open its doors. Latin America (except for the Dominican Republic), claimed fear of German retaliation.

Eisenberg comments that the Evian Conference

... accented the spiritual bankruptcy of the nations of the world and the conspiracy of silence and passivity that prevailed toward the suffering and persecuted. The indifference of the world's rulers served Hitler well. He found in them "partners" who shared his attitude. It stiffened his resolve not to relax. . . .[22]

Unrelentingly, Polish-Jewish leaders sent appeals to Allied governments and Jewish leaders around the world pleading for reprisal against Germany. When in May 1942 the Jewish Labor Bund in Poland beseeched the Polish Government-in-Exile, warning that Hitler was going to exterminate all of Polish Jewry, there was no response until 17 December 1942, by which time most Polish Jews had already been annihilated. Forthwith, the Allied governments of Moscow, Washington, and London simultaneously issued a declaration solemnly promising that those responsible for the crimes would not escape retribution.[23]

Because Jews were offered no asylum, they were forced to remain in dangerous areas. They simply could not go to safety; escape from Nazi persecution required somewhere to go, and for the European Jews refuge was difficult, if not impossible, to find. Several European countries made some attempts to control the genocide. Jews had a better chance for survival in, for example, Denmark or Finland where there was defense of Jews by government, church, resistance, and national leaders. When there was cooperation among Gentiles and Jews to avoid Jewish isolation, most Jews were able to evade capture.[24]

In other countries there was no help, not even from resistance movements. In Poland the same partisans who aided Polish prisoners would refuse aid to Jews.[25] Jews who escaped into Spain or Switzerland were often treated, to say the least, as unwelcome and were sometimes handed over to German authorities for lack of proper identification. In 1940 Jewish refugees who had managed to escape from France prior to German occupation made the journey by ship to Mexico but were refused entry and sent back to certain doom in Europe. This same ship stopped in Norfolk, Virginia, and, were it not for the intervention of Mrs. Roosevelt, Secretary of State Hull would have turned the ship away.[26]

In December 1941, when the ship *Struma* arrived in Istanbul with over 750 refugees, it was refused permission to enter Turkey. The ship was also refused permission by British authorities to proceed to Palestine. After weeks of living in horrible, unsanitary conditions while appealing for refuge through various authorities, all passengers on board the *Struma* (save one pregnant woman permitted to leave the ship in Istanbul) later died when the ship was forcibly towed back out into the Black Sea and mysteriously exploded the following day.[27]

Russia simply did not care. There wasn't even a pretext of appeasing public opinion. Attempts to deal with Nazis for the purpose of rescuing people were not even permitted. Putting aside the issue of anti-Semitism, Russian officials seemingly lacked concern for human lives and values.[28]

Even Switzerland had no room for the Jews. Switzerland's immigration attempted to keep Jews out of the country. Eisenberg relates a story depicting what awaited many Jews who managed to get to Switzerland:

> With aching feet and an even more aching heart I have just come out of— Switzerland! Yes, you are not mistaken, I was in Switzerland, even if only for six hours. On Sunday, the twenty-second [of November 1942], I made it into Wallis with a fellow. . . . What I went through cannot be put into words. My mountaineering outfit consisted of a pair of rubber overshoes, open at the top; I had no stockings, only wrappings. We climbed up to a pass fifty-five hundred feet high, through snow twenty inches deep, and, after twelve hours of walking through snow and ice, we entered Switzerland in the western part of Wallis. For food each of us had a half loaf of bread, plus melted snow. Our feet and lips were constantly chapped. But it was impossible to stop and rest, because my shoes were always full of water and, if I stopped, there was the danger that the water would freeze. . . . a Swiss border guard caught us. He interrogated us and said we must go back. . . . in spite of all our entreaties and requests at least to spend the night there and rest, we were compelled to make the four-hour climb back up to the pass through all the snow, which was now three feet deep, even though it meant sixteen hours in the high mountains. *Without mercy we were ordered back* . . . [emphasis added].[29]

The Bermuda Conference, which opened on 19 April 1943 (the very day the Warsaw Ghetto rebellion began), was called ostensibly to resolve the "refugee question." In actuality, British and American governments were trying to appease public opinion. Rather than describe what was done, Yehuda Bauer points to what was *not* done on behalf of European Jews. No ships were set aside to save them, no food was allowed into Europe, and no negotiations about civilians were permitted within Germany. Nazis and their collaborators were issued no warnings, the Vatican was not approached, and no guarantees were given to neutrals regarding the upkeep and care of refugees after the war.[30]

Hitler himself was aware of the world's apathy regarding the Jews as early as January 1939 when he said in a speech:

It is a shameful example to observe today how the entire democratic world dissolves in tears of pity but then, in spite of its obvious duty to help, closes its heart to the poor, tortured Jewish people.[31]

Since most nations of the world made only soft utterances (and many not even that) to help the Jews, the Nazis were provided with a sense of security about their large-scale murder plans. Atrocities against the Jews were simply ignored.

Religious Institutions

Another potential source of social control of genocide is the religious institution. According to Bettelheim, the one social institution that most represents and symbolizes authority and stands at the summit of any ethical scale is religion.[32]

Supporting Bettelheim's contention is Fein's conclusion that church protest was the single common factor present in *every* instance in which individual collaboration with the state was arrested, such as in Rumania, Bulgaria, and France. In virtually *all* cases in which state cooperation was *not* arrested, church protest was absent. Church protest proved to be the intervening variable most highly related with "immediacy" of social defense movements that permitted Jews to successfully evade deportation. In virtually *all* states in which the leader of the dominant church *publicly* spoke out against deportation of Jews before or as soon as it started, the majority of Jews escaped deportation. Even in states where the native administration began to cooperate with Nazis, resistance by religious institutions (churches) proved critical for checking obedience to authority, limiting collaboration, and legitimating subversion.[33]

The Roman Catholic Church wields great influence and power over world opinion. Although covert sympathy was there, Catholic public reaction to persecution of Jews by the Nazis was embodied in a hands-off policy. The Vatican line of approach was "neutralism." Joseph Tenenbaum believes that "a fiery public indictment" from St. Peter's in Rome would have made even Hitler pause—not on the grounds of moral principles but for reasons of political expedience.[34]

The role of the Papacy is central to an understanding of the reaction of religious communities throughout most of Europe. In 1938, Pope Pius XI condemned the Nazi persecution of the Jews, saying that " . . . it is not possible for Christians to take part in anti-Semitism. We are Semites spiritually." Pius XI died on 10 February 1939.[35] Pius XII, who became Pope on 2 March 1939, had previously served as nuncio (the representative of Berlin and Munich to the Vatican) and was very friendly to Germany. After attaining his exalted office, he wrote to Hitler on 6 March 1939 saying,

We shall pray for the protection of Heaven and the blessing of the Almighty God for you and all members of your nation.[36]

By this time Hitler had already invaded Czechoslovakia, Austria, and Poland, all predominantly Catholic countries.

Later in the fall of 1943, when the Nazis in Rome were rounding up thousands of Jews for deportation, the Pope was silent. He issued no public statement of outrage or protest. Eisenberg concludes:

It is possible that the fate of the Jews might not have been improved if the Pope had spoken out, but it could not have been worsened. Lacking evidence to the contrary, we may say that the Pope's failure to protest vigorously at a time when mankind was undergoing torture and spiritual agony is in itself one of the greatest tragedies of our era.[37]

Eisenberg further points out that the church's resignation to Nazism must be judged in relation to the church success in opposing student dueling, euthanasia, and cremation (instead of burial). By contrast, the opposition of the French, Dutch, and Belgian churches must be noted. The German Catholic church never threatened to excommunicate members participating in the murder of Jews, as was the case in other European countries.

Statistics indicate that of the German churchgoing population in 1929, over 90 percent were Catholic. Approximately 43 percent of all Germans, including Hitler, were Catholics, and they comprised a large portion of the nation's leadership. In 1938 almost 25 percent of the SS was composed of Catholics. By the 1920s organized German Catholicism was denouncing the "destructive" effect Jews exerted over religion, art, literature, and political and social life. Cardinal Michael Faulhaber of Munich declared in 1933 that he held "no position with regard to the Jewish question today."[38]

In 1933 the German Protestant clergy, like the German Catholic church before them, adopted an "Aryan" clause stipulating against accepting baptized clergy of Jewish origins. By 1939 proof of non-

Jewishness was demanded from students before they could prepare for the clergy. On 17 December 1941 Protestant leaders charged:

The National Socialist leadership of Germany has given irrefutable documentary proof that this world war was instigated by the Jews. . . . As members of the German national community the undersigned . . . stand in the front line of this historic struggle which made necessary such measures as the official police recognition of Jews as the born enemies of the Reich and the world. The undersigned . . . have therefore severed all links with Jewish Christians. We are determined not to tolerate any Jewish influence on German religious life.[39]

Even in other countries, religious institutions were amiss in gestures of support for the Jews. "Caution" was exercised by the Church of England, which harbored the notion that it might be dangerous to take a frontal approach to the Jewish problem. Jews were considered to be Germany's "internal problem." On 24 January 1943 the Archbishops of York and Canterbury, supported by the Primate of Wales, issued a manifesto requesting that the British government as well as her Allies prevent the slaughter of Jews and provide them asylum. Unfortunately this did little good at this rather late date.[40]

INTERNAL CONTROLS

Looking at the Holocaust in retrospect, one might ask: Why couldn't the Jews protect themselves from the impending genocide? Such a question might subtly place much of the blame for the Holocaust on the victims themselves—the Jews—rather than the victimizers.

The criminologist Richard Quinney notes with a sense of irony that his field of study often presents the victim as the guilty party, while the perpetrator is viewed as the victim of a set of cruel circumstances beyond his control.[41] Similarly Stephen Schafer, in his theory of "functional responsibility," contends: "In a way, the victim is always the cause of a crime. . . . All crimes necessarily have victims, and, necessarily, the existence of the victim or something material or immaterial that belongs to him makes for crime and may actually produce a criminal effect."[42] Were the Jews passive, even willing, victims who aided and abetted the victimizing perpetrators?

For a target group to effectively protect itself, the potential controls it may exert upon an aggressor must come into play. If for any reason these controls are not available or are co-opted, a group is vulnerable to destruction. Four such controls are: (1) interference by the victim group's ethnic state (political self-defense), (2) mobilization of the victim group's agencies of self-defense (sociocultural self-defense), (3) realization of impending group-annihilation (psychological self-defense), and (4) physical ability to retaliate (biological self-defense). A discussion of why each of these potential controls was largely ineffective during the Holocaust follows.

Interference by the Victim Group's Ethnic State: Political Self-defense

That the Jews of the Holocaust were a nationless people proved to be the greatest obstacle to their self-defense. There was no Israel to protect Jews who were threatened anywhere in the world. No country in the world felt akin to the Jews or came to defend their existence. The fate of the Jews was in the hands of the world, but, as we have noted, the world showed little concern or mercy. Those states in which Jews had lived for many hundreds of years disowned them.

Even in America, Jews had little political influence. It did not sit well with the melting-pot image, not to mention a slumbering but potentially powerful anti-Semitic movement in the United States, for Jews to stress their ethnic identification or to support their European brethren. The American Zionist movement was still developing during this period and thus could offer little in the way of support or hope.[43]

Had a Jewish state existed, it may have intervened on their behalf—making threats, attacking, exposing, or influencing world opinion against their victimizers. No country claimed Jews as their own and most countries did not even permit them entry to escape persecution. Legislation in Germany had, in effect, made German Jews stateless; this obviously facilitates expropriation of Jewish property. In Nazi-occupied territories, many citizens were unconcerned about the fate of their Jewish nationals.

It was not to be until after the war that the Jews could emerge from powerlessness through the securing of a Jewish state.

Mobilization of the Victim Group's Agencies of Defense: Sociocultural Self-defense

If only Jews could have imagined their ultimate destiny, their sheer numbers may have provided an ability to retaliate (or rebel) with force. Yet to do this, they would have had to recognize the threat to themselves, both corporately and individually, and combined in a "cultural unity" to defend against their common enemy. Why didn't they? In the first place, the Jews of Europe did not even share a common faith in God, let alone a common culture. The Jews of Germany were highly assimilated into their native culture in comparison to other European Jews, and they looked down on Polish and other Jews. There were obvious barriers of language between Jews from Germany, Poland, Russia, Hungary, France, Denmark, and other areas. Yet these people were to find themselves side by side in the gas chambers.

Even the Jews of Germany lacked a cohesive sociocultural organization. As discussed in Chapter 11, the sociocultural organization of the Jewish communities, the *Judenrat*, was used against them.

Consequently, Jewish leaders often inadvertently helped in the destruction process through pure ignorance. For example, Germans were moving against the 70,000 Jews of Salonka in 1942. The first step was registration. Both the chief rabbi, Dr. Koretc, and the president of the community, a German Jew, encouraged Jews to cooperate with Nazi authorities, reassuring them that there was nothing to fear, the leaders feeling that compliance would actually help to save lives. They certainly could not imagine what lay ahead—that their registration lists would be used to gather Jews for deportation to death camps.[44]

These leaders were organized into the *Judenrat* to serve as an intermediate level of authority between the Nazi party and the Jewish population. This passed control of the Jews' own sociocultural organizations to the Germans. This control was established by selecting for the Jewish councils genuine leaders of the Jewish community.

Some Jews did break away from the authority of the *Judenrat*, but this simply produced a splintering of Jewish groups instead of a unifying alternative. It was such an alternative, a potential sociopolitical group of *and for* the Jews that was required if meaningful resistance was to take place. The higher SS and Police Leader Von dem Back reported that, "contrary to the opinion of the National Socialists that the Jews were a highly organized people, the appalling fact was that they had no organization whatsoever. The mass of the Jewish people were taken completely by surprise."[45]

Hannah Arendt believes that the councils did more harm than good but says, of course, that one can not generalize, since some councils were corrupt while others worked diligently to circumvent Nazi plans. According to Arendt, if the councils had blatantly refused to function, chaos would have reigned in the ghettos. Jews would have been forced to escape or rebel rather than try to exist under ghetto conditions. She knows that most would have died anyway, but perhaps, just perhaps, more European Jews might have survived. As Arendt states,

True it was that the Jewish people as a whole had not been organized, that they had possessed no territory, no government, and no army, that, in the hour of their greatest need, they had no government-in-exile to represent them among the Allies . . . , no caches of weapons, no youth with military training. . . . The whole truth was that if the Jewish people had really been unorganized and leaderless, there would have been chaos and plenty of misery but the total number of victims would hardly have been . . . six million people.⁴⁶

Realization of Impending Group-Annihilation: Psychological Self-defense

Jews had no ethnic state to aid them. Their own sociocultural organizations were weakened and used against them. Still, this does not seem to fully answer the question: Why didn't the Jews fight back? To answer this question we must first ask: did the Jews realize the impending Holocaust? Hilberg claims that the Nazis made every effort to hide their goal of destruction. The first step in self-defense against an enemy is to recognize the need for such a defense. Apparently, much of the Jews' lack of resistance to Nazi persecution came from their failure to perceive the scope of the danger. First, the Jews as a people had to realize what Hitler was doing. Jews were being murdered. But Jews had been murdered before. Pogroms were nothing new. Jews of every nation had suffered them for generations.

Judaic history is replete with persecution by oppressors. One of the most holy celebrations, the Passover, is in honor of the last plague that God brought to bear on the ancient Egyptians, releasing an entire nation from over 400 years of slavery. Obedience to God's instructions—to kill the Passover lamb and place the blood in the lintel and the two door posts and remain inside until morning—brought deliverance from the Angel of Death and their Egyptian captivity.⁴⁷ King Nebuchadnezzer took the Israelites as captives to Babylonia.⁴⁸ They suffered slavery at the hands of the Babylonians three times. Yet after long suffering, Yahweh brought the Jews out of their persecution and restored them to Jerusalem. The Jews of the Diaspora had suffered alienation from the social structures of their host countries around the world for hundreds of years.

So, religious persecution was old and familiar, as were certain forms of legal persecution. Jews had survived this before and probably believed they could survive again. Yet this persecution was to be different from all past anti-Semitic actions; it was to be a total genocide. We see that clearly now, but was it so obvious to the Jews of Germany in the 1930s?

Similarly, it was difficult for Jews to recognize and grasp the scope of the Holocaust. As Fein indicates, not just the Jews of Germany were being murdered, not just the Jews of Warsaw, or Vilna, or invaded

Russia: it was *all* Jews everywhere the Nazis held power. That realization did not come easily, but it was necessary for Jews to recognize and accept the inevitability of their ultimate death, both corporately and individually, before resistance was likely to be considered.

Perhaps one reason Jews were unable to comprehend either the nature or the extent of what was occurring was because it was not normal for people to be killed without reason. As Fein states, " . . . the very notion of a collective threat of extinction against Jews qua Jews ran contrary to western civilization's basic paradigms of crime and punishment."[49] We are socialized by both religious and civic traditions to believe that people are punished for disobedience. We believe if we abide by the law in spirit and in truth, we will be protected by the power of that very law.[50] The traditional Jewish belief in a "moral humanity" made it difficult to accept the veracity of reported Nazi behaviors.

There is a certain irony in being undone by one's high moral and philosophical plane. The assumption is often made that sophistication, based on education and intelligence, should aid an individual or group in the accurate appraisal of danger. Lazarus points out this is not always so—that accurate threat appraisal depends on situational cues that may provide warning or may provide camouflage.[51] An illustration of the latter case may be seen in the Jews' accustomed use of appeals and petitions. The Nazis encouraged this practice, even occasionally approving a few of the petitions. This occasional reinforcement encouraged the leaders and, at the same time, fettered them. They were locked into a Nazi control system of intermittent reinforcement. Such a reinforcement system produces behavior that is the most highly resistant to extinction; that is, the petitioners would maintain hope of success over long periods of time with little or no reinforcement.

The Jews who believed themselves to be free of guilt also believed that they would not be punished. "Dutch Jews initially believed that German Jews had elicited their punishment by Germany as a result of some of their own acts or attributes. The pious Jew believes that if he is faithful and observant, he will be protected by the deity."[52] It was not logical that Nazis were shooting and gassing *all* Jews. As Lazarus explains, " . . . general beliefs about one's own powers or in the ultimate providence of the world encourage hope under the worst specific circumstances. . . . such beliefs can even transcend the objective evidence."[53]

Fein describes ways in which Jews' defensive processes could permit an escape from the realization of their terrifying fate. First, if one believed that Jews were being killed, it had to be because of some action or some attribute. If the reason were reprisal for misbehavior, the blame for the punishment would fall upon the guilty—not upon all Jews.

This logic prevented Jews from an early recognition of their doom. The line of reasoning, according to Fein, is as follows:

1. Some people say that Jews are being killed. . . .
2. Killing is punishment.
3. But only bad people (saboteurs, resistance fighters, conspirators) are punished.
4. And I am not a bad person.
5. Therefore, I will not be punished.[54]

Consequently, good behavior and eliciting the good will of the oppressor would avoid punishment.

Another set of logical steps that Fein asserts permitted Jews to disassociate themselves from the group of Jews being killed and, therefore, to remove themselves from the threat is the following:

1. They are shooting another class of Jews (non-German, non-Magyar, non-Warsaw, nonurban, nonbourgeois, non-productive, non-lawabiding, etc.)
2. I am not a member of that class.
3. Therefore, they will not shoot me.[55]

The first set of reasoning, according to Fein, denied the threat to Jews as a collectivity; the second denied the threat to the individual. Both are based on finding a way to deal with painful and frightening facts. Third, and possibly the most common way of dealing with reality, was to simply deny its very existence.

This third mechanism of defense, denial, is depicted in a poignant example presented by Elie Wiesel in *Night*. Wiesel recalls how, near the end of 1942 at the age of twelve, he and his fellow Jews of Sighet, Hungary, responded to the plea of their synagogue caretaker, Moche the Beadle. Moche had been arrested and taken away by train. Upon his return to Sighet, he told everyone how the train had stopped after crossing the Hungarian border into Poland where the Gestapo had taken charge. He told how lorries had transported all the Jews to a forest where people were forced to dig huge graves. As these Jews approached the hole, they were shot in the neck. Machine gunners threw Jewish babies into the air, using them as targets. He saw a young girl, Malka, who took three days to die. Moche was there, saw it all, and lived to tell this truth. Yet, no one believed that such atrocities could be true. Jews even refused to listen to him. They said, "He's just trying to make us pity him. What an imagination he has. . . . Poor fellow. He's gone mad."[56]

Even in Auschwitz, reality was, at first, beyond comprehension. Rene Molho, a former prisoner, recalled: "suddenly everything was different. We went to the barrack. It was very cold. There was a smell of burning flesh and somebody said, 'That's people they're burning.' I was ready to slap him. 'Let's not crack up,' I said. I thought he was crazy. We saw the flames, we smelled the flesh burning, but our minds couldn't realize anything that awful."[57] Later, when the truth was evident, Molho tried, unsuccessfully, to warn others as they arrived. "I would go out where the people were coming off the trains to tell them to start something, but nobody believed me. I couldn't make them believe it, just like the others couldn't make me believe it when I came."[58]

Some people, however, accepted the reality of a massive Jewish genocide even before arrival at a death or labor camp. Not all Jews practiced the three denial processes just described. But what could be done once the reality of the genocide was accepted? "Within the context of ghetto, rebellion was an irrational act for the individual seeking his own survival alone. Only if one were convinced that the Germans intended the death of all Jews was rebellion rational."[59]

Jews had survived for generations through submission and accommodation in a world that did not want them. They had learned to adapt to and survive conflicts through a technique described by Dadrian as "submissive role playing." In brief, the argument runs as follows: historical subjugation (persecution and decimation) results in the victims becoming degraded and stereotyped by the society. Over time, the victims' self-concepts come to reflect these stereotypes, that is, they develop a negative self-image. A coercion-submission syndrome evolves in which perpetration of crimes against the victim group is accepted as a matter of course; namely, "I am a Jew; therefore, I deserve to be persecuted." The victim group may even develop traits or characteristics rendering the syndrome functional.[60]

While such defensive reactions may have been adaptive (or even essential) for survival through centuries of abuse, they were counterproductive for a Jewish response to the Nazi onslaught. It was necessary for the illusion of survival through accommodation to be destroyed before the Jews could begin to defend themselves.

What was required was the comprehension and acknowledgement of what Dadrian calls "optimal genocide." Optimal genocide is a massive destruction process relatively indiscriminate in terms of victims' age, sex, and other categories, sustained in duration, and aimed at total obliteration of the group.[61] It should be evident that accepting such a perspective, particularly when it is directed against oneself and one's ethnic group, would be both difficult and damaging. It is likely to produce the feeling of loss of control over one's own life, a state of "learned helplessness." Seligman describes learned helplessness as a condition resulting from being placed in an inescapable and unavoidable aversive situation.[62] These words do faint justice to describing the Germany of Hitler. The effects of learned helplessness are near-total apathy, withdrawal, and severe depression. Thus, should a person have the cognitive fortitude to shed his processes of denial, knowledge of the dreadful reality of his situation would probably induce the even more stultifying symptoms of learned helplessness.

Such psychological difficulties were probably exacerbated by factors related to the relocation of Jews with no say as to where or how they lived. Often they were placed in extremely high-density settings. Such extended crowding conditions have been associated with psychological withdrawal, a feeling of loss of control, and the symptoms of helplessness just described.[63] Related to this density issue is the simultaneous loss of privacy. Gove and colleagues have demonstrated that a lack of privacy is an important determinant of the negative psychological effects of density.[64]

If somehow an individual overcame these psychological barriers, many other drawbacks to resistance remained. First, individual resistance sometimes initiated collective reprisal. Sam Offen, a survivor, described from his ghetto experience how work crews left the ghetto each day in sets of ten. If someone were missing, the remaining nine were shot. A second drawback to resistance was the Nazi use of emotional blackmail; one's remaining family members would most certainly suffer hideous consequences at the hands of the SS soldiers. A third and very practical problem of resistance was that one had to have a place to escape to.[65]

Physical Ability to Retaliate: Biological Self-defense

By the time the majority of the Jews recognized the horror in store for them, it was too late for effective means of collective retaliation. The very practical matter of the physical and mental strength required to fight against an enemy must be considered.

Even before deportations of Jews began, starvation and rampant disease took a heavy toll on the Jewish community, reducing retaliatory abilities. For example, the Jewish community in Warsaw (470,000 people) experienced 44,630 deaths in 1941; the first nine months of 1942 contributed 37,462 more deaths to this figure. In the ghetto the ratio of deaths to births was about 45:1. From these statistics it has been calculated that in all of occupied Poland, 500,000 to 600,000 Jewish people perished in labor camps and ghettos. During their brief period of existence ghettos wiped out one-fifth of the Polish Jewish population.[66]

Living conditions and food supplies were terrible in the ghettos, since there was not even a pretext by the Nazis of trying to keep people alive. The administrative basis for allocating food in the camps was a ration system contrived by the Food and Agriculture Ministry, enforcing discriminatory rationing toward Jews. The standard diet for Jewish inmates consisted of watery turnip soup, supplemented by an evening ration of a bit of margarine on sawdust bread. People also ate putrid sausage and spoiled marmalade. If possible, inmates lapped up precious drops of polluted water from the wash barrack.

These living conditions inflicted sickness and epidemics; typhus, dysentery, and skin diseases were rampant. Sanitation was almost nil. In Auschwitz, which was not suitable for canalization, only fill-in latrines were available. Water was impure, and soap was in short supply. Rats ran freely through the barracks.[67]

People in the ghettos and camps were starving. Something happens to people who are sick and starving. Thinking becomes a monumental task. Sorokin, the Russian sociologist, claims that cognitive processes, including perception, become directed increasingly to thoughts and objects associated with the calamity. In situations of famine, food becomes the subject of conversation, constantly intruding into the consciousness of a starving individual, disturbing the association between the flow of ideas and images, impairing coherent and creative thinking. A person's time and energy become increasingly spent on seeking food, until the major part of one's waking hours become directly or indirectly involved in this process.[68]

People display a total lack of interest in what is going on outside of themselves, including a lack of interest in sex. When no other activity is required, the starving people automatically sit, or even lay down, exhibiting almost no movement whatsoever in an unconscious effort to conserve physical energy.[69]

Following World War II Dr. Ancel Keys conducted research on the effects of starvation. Through the use of volunteers (mostly Mennonites), Dr. Keys studied physical and psychological changes of people existing under starvation conditions. His research analyzed behavioral and personality changes due to starvation. Subjects turned inward, focusing only on the self. Today, these symptoms are known to reflect the syndrome known as Protein-k Calorie Malnutrition or PCM. The apathy and lack of energy for muscular activity that result are the body's way of conserving energy.[70]

These findings are congruent with Keys' observations of the effects of famine in the Warsaw Ghetto, 1941–1943. He described the symptoms of bradyphrenia, in which there was a pronounced slowing down of mental functions. Associative processes became sluggish, interests narrowed, and mental content became impoverished in the camps. Previously energetic young people became depressed and apathetic, losing all initiative and lying down to sleep whenever possible. They slowly but inexorably moved from life to death in a barely discernible transition.[71]

The ghetto and labor camp environments contained other damaging features, such as the crowding and lack of privacy described earlier. Noise, filth, heat, and cold added to the deplorable conditions. Also, a perceived lack of control over aversive stimuli was very destructive. Pennebaker describes the symptoms of such lack of control as including dizziness, upset stomach, and chest pain.[72] Thus the environment created by the Nazis helped beat down the Jews physically, making an aggressive reaction even less likely.

It is amazing that the Jews rebelled, even though strength and life ebbed away, but rebel they did. Once they realized their fate, their heroism was striking, though chances for escape and survival were slim. German propaganda attempted to present Jews as cowards who did not fight back. But Bauer records how the Jews resisted as they could. They fought back by engaging in forbidden activities. They offered fiery resistance to their persecutors in the Warsaw Ghetto uprising of 1943, and also in those at Vilna and Czestochowa, at Bialystok in the forests of Poland, and also at Treblinka, Auschwitz, and Sobibor.[73] And perhaps their most impressive work of resistance was their desperate, persistent struggle to survive.

Perhaps we have posed the wrong question in asking why the Jews did not fight back. Perhaps the appropriate question is how could any person suffering such a degree of physical and psychological debilitation even think of rebellion against the Nazi oppressors, let alone engage in actual physical action. We should not ask why the Jews of World War II Europe did not do more to avoid becoming victims, but rather be amazed at how even a few managed the ultimate in resistance: survival.

The Jews were powerless at the time of the Holocaust for the previously discussed reasons—no nation, inability to mobilize sociocultural agencies of self-defense, inability to perceive impending annihilation, and biological deprivation. Given this state of affairs, they were forced to rely upon others to control the Nazis. Others failed to do so. As Ben Gurion wrote in an article entitled "Before the Tribunal of History":

What have you done to us, you freedom-loving peoples, guardians of justice, defenders of the high principles of democracy and of the brotherhood of man? What have you allowed to be perpetrated against a defenseless people while you stood aside and let it bleed to death, without offering help or succour, without calling on the fiends to stop, in the language of retribution which alone they would understand. Why do you profane our pain and wrath with empty expressions of sympathy which ring like a mockery in the ears of millions of the damned in the torture house of Nazi Europe? Why have you not even supplied arms to our ghetto rebels, as you have done for the partisans and underground fighters of other nations? Why did you not help us to establish contacts with them, as you have done in the case of the partisans in Greece and Yugoslavia and the underground movements elsewhere. If, instead of Jews, thousands of English, American or Russian women, children and aged had been tortured every day, burnt to death, asphyxiated in gas chambers—would you have acted in the same way?"[4]

III

DERIVATION OF A
THEORETICAL MODEL

13

A COLLECTIVE BEHAVIOR APPROACH
TO THE ANALYSIS OF GENOCIDE

NEIL SMELSER treats collective behavior as "mobilization on the basis of a belief which redefines social action"; that is, by redefining social action, groups attempt to create a new way of life through collective behavior. This implies that collective behavior will be guided by new philosophies of life. Smelser explains that these beliefs assume the existence of exceptional forces (such as conspiracies and threats) that are operative in the universe. These beliefs involve as well an assessment of extraordinary consequences that will probably follow if a collective attempt to reconstitute social action brings about successful results. Collective behavior, in Smelser's estimation, is not institutionalized behavior, because the more institutionalized behavior becomes, the more it loses its distinctive character of being collective. Collective behavior is " 'formed or forged to meet undefined or unstructured situations.' "[1]

When social strains such as deprivation and normative upheaval exist in a society, they are indicators that there are societal problems requiring resolution. But how can social action be "repaired"? asks Smelser. A basic principle for reconstituting social action when a situation of strain exists in a society requires that sources for overcoming strain should be searched for at higher levels of social action.[2] Four components of action are: (1) values, which are general sources of legitimacy; (2) norms, which are regulatory standards for interaction; (3) mobilization of individuals' motivations for organized action in collectivities; and (4) situational facilities, skills, information, tools, and obstacles used in the pursuit of concrete goals.[3] According to Smelser:

Collective behavior is a *compressed* way of attacking problems created by strain. It compresses several levels of the components of action into a single belief, from which *specific operative solutions* are expected to flow. An episode of collective behavior itself occurs when people are mobilized for action on the basis of such a belief. Thus our formal characterization of collective behavior is this: *an uninstitutionalized mobilization for action in order to modify one or more kinds of strain on the basis of a generalized reconstitution of a component of action.*[4]

There is an "if only" mentality associated with all forms of collective behavior. Extraordinary results are promised if only certain reforms are instituted, and there are gloomy, negative predictions assuring the collapse and decay of society if sources of strain are not vigorously and quickly attacked. Reality is exaggerated by avid adherents of collective behavior movements. Smelser feels that collective behavior is irresponsible because, while searching for quick and easy cures, collectivities tend to disregard many existing legal and moral restrictions, violating the integrity and interests of many individuals and groups. He posits that "collective behavior, then, is the action of the impatient. . . . Episodes of collective behavior often constitute an early state of social change; they occur when conditions of strain have arisen, but before social resources have been mobilized for a specific and possibly effective attack on the sources of strain. This is one reason for defining collective behavior as uninstitutionalized; it occurs when structured social action is under strain and when institutionalized means of overcoming the strain are inadequate. . . . Social control blocks the headlong attempts of collective episodes to bring quick results; if social control is effective, moreover, it channels the energy of collective outbursts into more modest kinds of channels."[5]

From these conditions, Smelser derives four factors that are necessary for an action to qualify as collective behavior. It is uninstitutionalized, it is collective, it is undertaken to modify a condition of strain, and it is the basis for changing a component of social action. Restricting the definition of collective behavior to these necessary conditions prevents its use as a catchall category (as Smelser believes has occurred in the past) for diverse phenomena that do not constitute collective behavior.[6]

Along with those four necessary factors for an action to be considered collective behavior, Smelser believes that there are six determinants of that collective behavior—factors that create a condition in which collective behavior is most likely to occur. These include *structural conduciveness, structural strain, growth and spread of a generalized belief, precipitating factors, mobilization of participants for action,* and *operation of social control.*[7]

In the case of genocide, collective behavior becomes institutionalized over a realtively short span of years.

THE HOSTILE OUTBURST

A hostile outburst, particularly in the form of genocide, is a specific type of collective behavior. According to Smelser, a hostile outburst, formally defined, "is simply mobilization for action under a hostile belief."[8] Its major identifying characteristic is "its objective as revealed in its belief." Consequently, this definition of a hostile outburst is both narrower and broader than actual legal or political definitions. The definition is broader in that it encompasses phenomena that are not necessarily illegal, such as scapegoating; it is narrower in that it does not include situations such as simple disturbances of the peace and unruly displays of crowds, for example, riots.

Participants in a hostile outburst are intent upon attacking "guilty" persons or groups deemed responsible for an unsatisfactory state of affairs or a multitude of unhappy events. Consequently, outbursts of hostility may be caused by various long-standing cleavages within the society. These factors, which separate and divide groups, result from ethnic, economic, religious, racial, or class differences. An interesting point that Smelser proposes is that hostile outbursts frequently accompany large-scale social movements because hostility is often a component of belief systems that serve to guide mass movements.[9] We may appreciate the accuracy of his observation when noting that the Nazi and Pan-Turanist movements were concomitants of the Holocaust and Armenian genocide respectively.

Hostile outbursts occur when strained relations between groups lead to aggressive actions. Thus one of Smelser's focal concerns rests on the types of tensions and threats (strains) that might induce one group to attack another. Frequently, outbursts erupt when strained conditions arise in a structurally conducive setting that is "either permissive of hostility or prohibitive of other responses or both." However,

Smelser stresses that at each progressive stage of a hostile outburst there exist countervailing influences controlling hostility—for example, governmental agencies and police. Such influences might conceivably diminish the likelihood of hostilities escalating to the level of manifest aggression.[10] To determine whether a setting exists in which hostile outbursts will occur, he suggests considering the following series of questions.

1. Is responsibility clearly institutionalized so that all failures are automatically and legitimately blamed on responsible agents?
2. Is the community characterized by established hostilities among various ethnic, religious, political, or other groupings? In such cases we would expect responsibility for unsettling states of affairs to be assigned more or less instinctively to the hated group.
3. Are authorities in the community able to control hostile outbursts? Do political leaders or other important figures actively encourage such outbursts?
4. What alternative means for expressing dissatisfaction are available? Are peaceful demonstration, petition, and political influence permanently closed to the group under strain? Have such channels recently been closed?
5. What are the opportunities for communication among the group under strain? Can people interact to form a "common culture" on the basis of which they can take action?[11]

These questions have been directly and indirectly addressed in our theoretical inquiry into the Holocaust and the Armenian genocide.

It is my considered position that genocide can be analyzed on the basis of new categories I have developed in this study that are directed specifically to the analysis of genocide; consequently, Semlser's conceptual framework has been greatly modified and augmented by a new conceptual framework to create a theory of genocide.

THE VALUE-ADDED PROCESS

Smelser, following the logic of the value-added process, contends that determinants of hostile outbursts must be organized so that "earlier stages . . . combine *according to a certain pattern* before the next stage can contribute its particular value to the finished product."[12] Thus, each one of the six determinants contributes to the cumulative added effect of the next stage. As different components enter into the value-added process, the range of possible outcomes becomes progressively limited. Smelser states that "these determinants must combine, however, in a definite pattern. Furthermore, as they combine, the determination of the type of episode in question becomes increasingly specific, and alternative behaviors are ruled out as possibilities."[13]

From this point on, Smelser's analysis diverges from those new components I have specifically formulated for a theory of genocide. The following theory of genocide presents six new determinants of the value-added process. These factors, common to both Armenian genocide and the Jewish Holocaust, are the creation of "outsiders," internal strife, powerful leadership with territorial ambitions forming a monolithic and exclusionary party, destructive uses of communication, organization of destruction, and failure of multidimensional levels of social control. These different factors combine to limit alternatives to genocide.

What follows is a presentation of the author's theory of genocide. Unless specified, discussion will concentrate on some of Smelser's ideas that have been adapted in such a way as to lend themselves to this theory.

THE CREATION OF "OUTSIDERS"

A social condition structurally conducive to genocide is a history of group conflict leading to the formation of an outgroup. One primary condition culminating in the creation of such a group is a long history of being targeted as the cause of a society's problems, in effect encouraging their exclusion from the larger society. In this way a society comes to define a particular group as outsiders. The leap from defining a target group as outsiders to actually making them outsiders is bridged by intensifying aggression against them.

History of Intergroup Tensions

Outbursts of violence and hostility have historically followed lines of social cleavage. Assignment of blame is associated with generalized stereotypes that frequently stem from class, economic, racial, or religious differences. The potential number of cleavages in any society is as numerous as the many possible bases for identifying and segregating people as well as their various sources of role differentiation. For example, religious divisions have buttressed violence in ancient, medieval, and modern times, creating conflict between the East and West. Ethnic, national, regional, tribal, and racial tensions have created divisions, unequal distributions of wealth, prestige, and power; these have all contributed to segregation.

In addition, temporary cleavages such as those created by social movements can promote hostility. Nationalism, for instance, effectively divides societies into opposite camps that define each other as responsible for many evils. Temporary cleavages created by social movements may be assimilated by permanent, preexisting cleavages represented by religious, economic, or political divisions. Furthermore, cleavages that are a consequence of social movements, as shown by abolitionism, may become the basis for new divisions in the future. In effect, issues generated by social movements may instigate new structural cleavages.

To understand how structural separations are conducive to hostility, recognition of the degree to which various cleavages coincide is essential. In many societies political, economic, and racial-ethnic memberships often overlap. So any type of conflict will likely assume racial or political overtones and bring into play a multiplicity of loyalties for the involved parties. Situations in which many separations coincide provide a variety of situational strains that may become potential bases for general and frequently explosive conflict.

Social divisions generally take a substantial time to develop and often have a history of interaction, competition, and conflict between two groups. Regardless of how they develop throughout history, they are useful points of analysis for the study of collective outbursts of hostility. In this analysis they are essential starting points for the study of genocide.

Prejudices and stereotypes typically accompany the many societal cleavages. Prejudices—generalized attitudes that serve to identify a despised group—specify the kinds of threats for which this group is deemed responsible. Various types of strains in a society tend to channel hostility toward specific groups based on preexisting stereotypes and prejudices.

Once a group is viewed as different, it becomes easier to target it as responsible for societal ills. This continual assignment of blame to a specific group for society's problems creates an environment conducive to the victimization of "outsiders." This study asserts that in societies in the throes of intense social stress and upheaval, the historical structure of responsibility—the assignment of blame—and the potential for genocide are closely related. In the two cases of genocide that have been discussed, the target group had indeed been the historical scapegoat whenever the society experienced distress.

Some collective acts of aggression tend to be unrealistic, since they oversimplify causes of problems by viewing them as a consequence of the behavior of specific groups. Groups subject to scapegoating, however, are by no means random victims of sudden or uncontrollable bouts of hostility. Their victimization is at the crux of a belief system assigning responsibility for social ills to selected target groups.[14]

Intensification of Aggression Against Outsiders

Assignment of blame based on social divisions intensifies aggression toward a "responsible" group. This process of blame focuses the free-floating aggression present in society toward the responsible group. If social strain is extremely high, the generalized aggression always present is heightened, creating an optimal environment for genocide by increasing hostility against the outsiders.

Aggression eventually flows into diverse forms of hostility, such as insults, gripes, discrimination, and in extreme cases, violence. Free-floating and generalized aggression may be elicited on many possible pretexts. Such aggression could easily be channeled into hostile outbursts. If institutionalized (as it was in both the instances of genocide examined here), aggression might be further aggravated by social situations and thus more readily focused upon definite situations or events.

This process could also be encouraged by precipitating factors that lead to generalized aggression. In studying events initiating hostile outbursts, considerations of context are extremely important. Context refers to existing conditions of strain (internal strife), conduciveness (creation of outsiders), and generalized aggression within a society. A precipitating factor "confirms the existence, sharpens the definition, or exaggerates the effect of one of these conditions."[15] Generalized hostile beliefs might become crystallized and attached to certain events and objects by precipitating factors. Once hostile beliefs are crystallized and associated with an object (namely, a group), potential participants in outbursts can be mobilized for action. How these factors work and interact to lead to extremely hostile action like genocide should be considered.

The first characteristic—that precipitating factors may justify or confirm generalized hatreds or fears presently existing in a society— verifies that a questionable group has committed a threatening act in keeping with its character. Stories of sexual abuse, crime, and unpatriotic displays can stir an aggrieved group into action.

One hostile outburst might then serve as a precipitating factor for others. For example, an outburst in one locale may trigger overt aggression in other areas. Riots exemplify this. They tend to cluster into a single time period, with one riot signaling a disruption of social control mechanisms. This breakdown of control mechanisms allows latent conflicts to surface. Both hostility and the spread of hostility are contagious in nature. In fact, any rumor reporting one or more of these events can itself serve as a precipitating factor, which in turn instigates hostile outbursts. In the case of genocide, the government itself instigates acts of hostility.

Certain of Smelser's qualifying remarks about the role of precipitating factors should be examined. First, in any given outburst, more than one precipitating event may occur. This happens because there are numerous conditions of conduciveness and strain that may exist before the occurrence of a hostile outburst. Second, precipitating factors may overlap empirically with background social conditions of strain and conduciveness.[16]

INTERNAL STRIFE

Some "strains" (to be used interchangeably with "internal strife") are institutionalized and follow lines of political, religious, ethnic, racial, and class divisions. When such cleavages coincide with existing stereotypes placing blame for existing evils and/or deprivations on certain groups, strains become an inherent part of the social structure, combining with other social conditions that lead to hostile outbursts. Strain might thus become an established feature of social situations.

All deprivations can become precipitating factors for hostility, in that they can either aggravate existing strains in a society or create new ones. Those factors that coincide with existing social separations are particularly powerful in intensifying aggression toward a target group.

A heightening of internal strife in society increases the vulnerability of outsiders. Internal strife may involve either real or perceived social deprivations and/or normative dislocations requiring a society to readjust its norms. Such conditions add to the likelihood of genocide, because some groups (or political parties) will capitalize on these societal strains and use them to express hostility.

What types of strains in a society give rise to hostile outbursts? In actuality, there is a combination of strains that coalesce before a hostile outburst erupts. One type of grievance in its course of development may become assimilated to another. So in any given outburst, many different strains can converge and combine in many different fashions.[17] But two types of strain that are necessary components of genocide are real or threatened deprivation and normative upheaval.

Real or Threatened Deprivation:
Defeat in War and Loss of Empire

Internal strife occurs in a society experiencing real or threatened deprivation. Real or threatened deprivation, relative or absolute, may play a role in the genesis of hostility toward certain groups. In some circumstances, deprivation can be quite real and related to precipitating factors such as unemployment, economic competition, abrupt food shortages, falling wages, or rising prices. All of these factors are closely related to outbursts of violence. However, deprivation need not necessarily be economic. Any frustration—for example, the passage of unpopular political measures—may serve as a strain inducing hostile outbursts.[18] I believe that another type of real or perceived deprivation is defeat in war and/or loss of empire. Should both of these factors occur simultaneously, a country would undergo extreme internal strife and the tension produced by defeat might be resolved by blaming that failure upon a vulnerable group within the society.

Such events signal a failure of the larger society for which justification or explanation is required; this might be accomplished by assigning responsibility for social ills to a particular group. Sometimes there is a failure of leadership, and a search for parties perceived to be at fault is set off. Frequently, defeat in war is blamed upon an outsider group within the defeated nation. Subsequently this responsible group might be attacked.

Normative Upheaval

Strain in norms occurs during war, postwar demobilization, and rapid institutional change. Normative strain may appear in certain locales, as in a dispute involving jurisdiction during a community disaster or in the failure of a party to honor a given promise or contract.[19] What is here designated as "normative upheaval" also adds to normative strains in a society. I believe that type of normative upheaval involves a change in the status of majority-minority group members vis-a-vis one another. A society practicing institutionalized scapegoating and segregation against a minority would be particularly vulnerable to stress if there were any sudden attempt to equalize the social status of a dominant group and a minority group by changing the norms of the society. The dominant group might interpret such a change as a potential deprivation of its own privileged status.

POWERFUL LEADERSHIP WITH TERRITORIAL AMBITIONS AND THE FORMATION OF A MONOLITHIC AND EXCLUSIONARY PARTY

Powerful Leadership with Territorial Ambitions

I contend that the powerful, dynamic, charismatic leader who directs hostility toward a potential victim group in time of national crisis (such as loss of war or empire) is crucial in the genesis of genocide. Powerful leaders effectively implement genocidal policies by influencing the state machinery; they legitimize genocide by defining a particular group as the enemy. Also, if such leaders seek to expand their nation's territory, they are characterized as patriots and provide justification for removing outsiders from desired territories. Those territories might be sections of the home nation or an external acquisition of land.

Demagogues play a critical role in genocide by agitating people into action. They will frequently harangue hostile groups into overt aggression. But leadership can be exercised in other ways to accomplish the same end. Consider the following points made by Smelser.

1. A triggering act may be performed by an individual who does not intend to lead an attack. In other instances the occurrence of an act in and of itself may give rise to leadership.
2. A highly motivated, daring, and psychopathic type of person can intentionally agitate a group into action. Or behind-the-scenes leaders can be the agitators. Dispatching provocateurs by the government can also instigate hostile outbursts.
3. Organizations associated with social movements can assume leadership positions in hostile outbursts. Consequently, an initial outburst of aggression may or may not be initiated in the movement itself.[20]

Thus, behind-the-scenes leaders of bureaucratic organizations might operate independently of or in conjunction with a state leader in a genocidal process.

Formation of a Monolithic and Exclusionary Party

I must note at this point that if the government is composed of the leader's supporters who share his aspirations of destruction and who eliminate those who might present political opposition to their goals, the party becomes a political monolith. If such a single-minded group ascends to power and crushes its opposition, it might exclude from its ranks or destroy groups that differ in their ideas and ideals.

After acquiring power, social agencies or persons in control that are either unwilling or unable to avoid attacks upon victim groups in a society effectively give a green light to overt expressions of hostility. History indicates that periods characterized by hostile outbursts (I here include genocide) are frequently preceded by periods of inadequate police or military control.[21]

Yet the mere presence of military or police force does not necessarily control hostility or guarantee order. Authorities must be willing to dispatch their forces to avert destructive outbursts, and these forces must be loyal to existing authorities. However, if there is widespread permissiveness about hostility among the wielders of force, the controllers of public opinion, or prestigious authorities, hostile outbursts may actually be encouraged. On the other hand, authorities who are ineffective sometimes are so because of the general public's support of an aggrieved group or actual subversion of police activities by the public. Unwillingness or inability of those in control to act plays a significant role in instances of violent behavior, in that it officially legitimatizes and endorses hostility toward some group. It is possible that authorities might even invite aggression against a particular minority group.[22]

DESTRUCTIVE USES OF COMMUNICATION

Aggressive Ideology

An ideological system supporting the exclusiveness and superiority of a particular group is, I feel, an essential component of genocide. Ideology is a powerful tool for an aggressive leader who might employ it to reduce the inhibition of the masses in their expression of hatred toward a particular group by providing them justification and rationalization for their excesses. Ideology paves the way for plans of total extermination of the enemy, arousing the leadership and the masses to heretofore unknown levels of fervor until, finally, genocide becomes a "sacred task."

Ideologically oriented phenomena, such as value-oriented social movements, internal revolutions, nationalistic crazes, and charismatic religious movements are considered factors that accentuate violence-inducing cleavages. Dangerous value conflicts that tend to trigger violence are produced by such movements. These phenomena frequently create diametrically opposed groups, such as a radical versus a reactionary, a heterodox versus an orthodox, and one might add, a patriotic versus an unpatriotic group.

Propaganda War

What I herein refer to as propaganda war against a victim group facilitates the act of genocide. People being mobilized for action in an overt display of aggression against a group require communication that spreads destructive ideology and beliefs among the potential participants in genocide.

Communication among potential participants of hostile behavior is essential to spread negative, hostile beliefs as well as to mobilize for an attack against a certain group. Communication and consensus are prerequisites for molding individuals into crowds and hostile groups. Newspapers and other media function to communicate hostile attitudes by disseminating the types of information that escalate hostile beliefs to the point of violent action.[23]

Modes of communicating beliefs may assume a variety of forms. At one extreme is the face-to-face unrehearsed spreading of information and rumor that form peoples' beliefs. Rumors exhibit all of the components of hostile belief systems—generalized aggression, omnipotence, and anxiety. Rumors, in addition, tend to attach these components to specific situations, places, persons, and events. At the other extreme is information disseminated through organized agitation and propaganda. Between these extremes lies the press; this agency frequently spreads rumors and provocative stories, possibly adding fuel to beliefs that eventuate in hostile outbursts.[24]

Inadequate or improper use of communication facilities leads to inadequate or erroneous information and an ambiguity concerning official agencies of authority. A resultant failure of communication facilities to disseminate accurate information contributes to scapegoating. Conditions of strain in a society, complicated by incorrect information about tension-producing factors, may serve as a catalyst for hostile activities. This is illustrated by disaster situations in which communication channels are functioning improperly or in which communication is absent. The ambiguities in this situation augment the existing strains and encourage scapegoating. Sheer ignorance also promotes overt hostility, because misinterpretation of events intensifies animosities between groups.[25]

In genocide we see government at the helm of a propaganda war against the victim group. The government, with its access to mass media, social control agencies, and state agencies, is in a key position to manipulate such a war.

ORGANIZATION OF DESTRUCTION

Just as ideology prepares the leadership and masses emotionally for genocide, so the organization of destructive force paves the way physically for extermination of a target group—the final determinant in the value-added process of genocide. All other determinants for genocide—creation of outsiders; internal strife; strong leadership forming a monolithic, exclusionary party; and destructive uses of communication—must be present to reach this action phase.

Organization and Implementation of Genocide

Genocide is so massive in scope that it cannot be accomplished without a high level of advanced planning and organization. Sporadic acts of aggression cannot totally decimate a target group. Smelser contends that there may be considerable variation in the organization of an attack. At one extreme is the completely unorganized brawl that exhibits neither division of labor nor coordination; at the other extreme is a highly integrated, organized military unit with specialized roles. The degree of organization a hostile outburst possesses is a function of two factors.

First, the degree of preexisting structure must be taken into account. All groups vary in their level of formal organization. The level of organization of a hostile outburst will directly correspond to the scope of formal organization in a group. When an insurrectionary movement or a highly organized revolutionary party obtains control of the existing apparatus of violence (the army or the police), hostile behavior will be highly structured. However, if there is any weakness in a society's social control agencies, unorganized aggression may erupt sporadically.

Second, the ecological factors must be weighed. The form that hostility takes is largely dependent upon accessibility and location of objects of attack. The actual ecological distribution of aggressor groups plays a crucial role in shaping violence. In addition, accessibility to objects of attack is related to overt acts of hostility; hostile groups must be distributed in such a way that they can participate in outbursts. Additionally, the likelihood of attack is increased if people can be victimized without fear of reprisal.[26]

A breakdown in social order permits various types of deviant behaviors, such as pilfering, looting, sexual abuse, and random assaults. Because hostile outbursts often signify a threat to the existing order, deviance is frequently a concomitant of hostile eruptions.[27]

Hostility and its expression result from the build-up of specific conditions of strain, precipitating factors, etc. Once hostile outbursts begin, however, they become a sign that a fissure has opened in the social order, and that the situation is now structurally conducive for the expression of hostility.[28]

After this "fissure" has been allowed to widen for a while, the nature of aggression needed to efficiently complete genocide takes on a systematic, organized, and bureaucratic form, with the government at the nucleus of the attack. Methods of destruction become well planned and rarely, if ever, are they left to chance. To destroy the victim, a high level of organization is required, combining various governmental agencies as well as the citizenry into a machinery of destruction.

FAILURE OF MULTIDIMENSIONAL LEVELS OF SOCIAL CONTROL

The functions of social control are (1) to institutionalize respect for laws and acceptable methods of expressing grievances, (2) to reduce conditions of strain that generate hostility, (3) to minimize discrimination and prejudice that tend to intensify social cleavages, and (4) to discourage divisiveness within the ruling groups of society.[29] In potentially genocidal situations, none of these social controls is operating.

The manifestation of a single instance of hostility often excites and releases latent tendencies in the population to vent hostility and/or defy authority. Therefore, the organization and development of hostile actions are responsive to the speed and effectiveness with which agencies of social control counteract aggressive acts. Agencies of social control may or may not be able to exert any influence in this regard.[30]

Most often, agencies of control at the site of hostile outburst and elsewhere as well as the manner in which force is used play a crucial role in encouraging or discouraging hostility. However, many other factors are involved in curbing hostility. Were force the only important factor, many expressions of hostility could probably be repressed because agencies normally employed to control violence, the military and police, have superior power and organization.

Why is it, then, that such a powerful wielder of force as the police or military cannot always prevent a hostile outburst? One should view this question from two different angles. First, one must understand the behavior of those who are responsible for controlling the outburst—the authorities. Second, one must analyze the actions of those who implement the on-the-spot decisions in the military and/or the police.

Authorities need to respond both quickly and decisively when applying sanctions against hostile outbursts. Yet even this does not guarantee that aggression will be curbed. Issues implicated in violent aggression frequently involve the authorities themselves—directly or indirectly. Consequently, agencies of control may vacillate in enforcing law and order, lack impartial enforcement of justice, or be accomplices in the outburst itself. If wielders of force exhibit even a slight hesitation in their commitment to fairness, their ability to control an outburst is diminished and a green light is then given to hostile elements.[31]

Finally, I question in my analysis how it is possible that individual societies and the world, which possess numerous powerful, institutionalized levels of social control, cannot curb genocide? The answer to this question includes one or a combination of the following conditions. Either the institutionalized social control agencies are in turmoil and have ceased to be effective, or they simply ignore genocide by looking the other way, and/or they are overt or covert accomplices to genocide.

I believe that social control might never fully be able to eliminate the occurrence of genocide, but logic indicates that it could exert enough force to limit its scope. Controlling genocide requires the operation of many legitimate social control mechanisms which I delineate in the following two categories—those external to (outside of the victim group's control) the victim group and those internal to (potentially within the victim group's control) the victim group. External controls consist of the aggressor state and its citizenry, other nations, and religious institutions. These are the most powerful institutions for social control. Internal controls include the interference by the victim group's ethnic state (political self-defense), the mobilization of the victim group's agencies of self-defense (socio-cultural self-defense), a realization of impending group-annihilation (psychological self-defense), and the physical ability to retaliate (biological self-defense). Thus internal control is involved with social control through various levels of self-defense.

External Control

The Aggressor State and Its Citizenry. It is my contention that the breakdown of social control on the part of the state itself is the most destructive of all control factors related to genocide, because the state may mobilize its entire machinery (for example, the legal system, the military, and the police) into tools of destruction against the victim group; in addition, a government may allow other nations to victimize a group within its own boundaries. The reduction of tensions between the victim and aggressor groups could be greatly reduced or enhanced by the overt attitude of the state vis-a-vis the problem group. The legitimacy that the state may lend to destructive attitudes or its role in the creation or acceleration of destructive attitudes should not be underestimated.

Other Nations. Nations other than the one perpetrating the genocide may lend tacit or overt approval to genocide in the international bodies in which they participate. I hold that their own direct actions regarding the victimizers or victims of genocide also communicate approval or disapproval to others. In addition, pressure may be brought to bear upon a genocidal country by nations that threaten them with economic or military retaliation.

Neutralism, or silence, regarding atrocities against a victim group provides great encouragement to those who commit these crimes. They realize that neutralism, in effect, guarantees noninterference. Regarding genocide in another country as an internal problem of that particular country automatically defines genocide as an act for which the uninvolved government does not have to answer. It is imperative that organized religious institutions as well as nations defend human rights and values publicly and with all the power they can muster.

Religious Institutions. Religion, which cherishes human life as sacred, is considered to represent the zenith of human ideals and values. The failure to react to genocide by such a powerful and viable social control agency is, in effect, tantamount to complicity in the genocidal process. A failure to act because the victim group does not belong to a particular faith sets an example to others to disassociate themselves from human beings religiously unlike themselves—the victims. Such "different" people become unworthy of human consideration.

Internal Control

Interference by the Victim Group's Ethnic State. The nonexistence of a state representing the victim group's ethnic background can be conducive to genocide. As I see it, the aggressor state realizes it will not be opposed by an enraged government and the full force of its military. The state that would be most willing to retaliate and possibly encourage other nations to act in support of its interests does not exist. Likewise, the sanctuary and refuge such a state could provide for its ethnic compatriots does not exist.

Mobilization of the Victim Group's Agencies of Self-defense. Wherever genocide may occur, it would be highly beneficial if the victim group could call into play all of its social and cultural organizations in an attempt to control the destructive effort, impede it, or establish a means of escape for the victims. I believe the greatest tragedy a people could suffer would occur if the aggressor state assumed control of these agencies, for official and organized channels for disseminating honest information regarding victim status and any organized attempts for escape would be destroyed.

Realization of Impending Group Annihilation. Self-defense becomes infeasible if a group does not recognize its potential victimization. For victims to act defensively, a clear and present danger must be recognized. Should likely victims fail to foresee a danger and, consequently be unable to accept the reality of it, they simply cannot act in self-defense.

Physical Ability to Retaliate. Depletion of the target group's physical strength is a condition further limiting control over genocidal efforts. When aggressor governments impose conditions that drain the victim's physical and mental energies, even the desire to survive may be destroyed by the physical and psychological consequences of starvation, disease, apathy, and depression.

It is my conclusion that failure to control genocide at any one of the levels present would result in an added cost in lives. But should most or all levels of social control prove ineffective, the consequences would be devastating.

NOTES

PREFACE

1. Neil J. Smelser, *Theory of Collective Behavior* (New York: Free Press, 1962), 11, 24.
2. Ibid., 15–17.

INTRODUCTION

1. U.S. Congress, Senate Committee on Foreign Relations, Subcommittee of the Committee on Foreign Relations, Executive O, *The International Convention on the Prevention and Punishment of the Crime of Genocide*, 81st Cong., 2d Session, 1950. Washington, D.C.: U.S. Government Printing Office, 23, 24, 25 Jan. and 9 Feb. 1950.
2. Brewton Berry and Henry L. Tischler, *Race and Ethnic Relations* (Boston: Houghton Mifflin, 1978), 359.
3. Ibid., 360, cited in H. N. Brailsford, "Massacre," *Encyclopedia of the Social Sciences*, vol. 10, 191–94; "War," in J. Hastings, ed., *The Dictionary of the Bible*, 964–65.
4. A. J. Toynbee, *A Study of History* 1:465, cited in Berry and Tischler, *Race and Ethnic Relations*, 360, 361.
5. Ibid., 361.
6. Rex Weyler, *The Blood of the Land: The Government and Corporate War against the American Indian Movement* (New York: Vintage, 1982), 100.
7. Dee Brown, *Bury My Heart at Wounded Knee: An Indian History of the American West* (New York: Bantam, 1979), 106, 198.
8. Berry and Tischler, *Race and Ethnic Relations*, 361, quoted in D. D. Wallace, *History of South Carolina* 1:213.

CHAPTER 1

1. Sarkis Atamian, *The Armenian Community: The Historical Development of a Social and Ideological Conflict* (New York: Philosophical Library, 1955), 18.
2. Peter Lanne, *Armenia: The First Genocide of the XX Century*, trans. Krikor Balekdjian (Munich: Max Schmidt & Sohne, 1977), 47.
3. Christopher Walker, *Armenia: The Survival of a Nation* (New York: St. Martin's Press, 1980), 30–32, 37.
4. Ibid., 85
5. Ibid., 27.
6. Benjamin Braude and Bernard Lewis, eds., *Christians and Jews in the Ottoman*

257

Empire: The Arabic-Speaking Lands, vol. 2 (New York and London: Holmes and Meier, 1912), 14.

7. Walker, *Armenia*, 87.

8. Adda Bozeman, *The Future of Law in a Multi-Cultural World* (Princeton, N.J.: Princeton Univ. Press, 1971), 71.

9. Ibid., 71-72.

10. James Bryce, ed., *The Treatment of Armenians in the Ottoman Empire 1915-16*, with a Preface by Viscount Bryce, 2d ed. (Beirut: G. Doniguian, 1972), 617.

11. Joseph Burtt, *The People of Ararat* (London: Hogarth Press, 1926), 45.

12. Atamian, *Armenian Community*, 20.

13. Bozeman, *The Future of Law*, 73-74.

14. Edwin M. Bliss, *Turkey and the Armenian Atrocities* (Philadelphia: Keystone, 1896), 168.

15. Burtt, *People of Ararat*, 45.

16. Walker, *Armenia*, 86-87.

17. Yves Ternon, *The Armenians: History of a Genocide*, trans. Rouben C. Cholakian (New York: Caravan Books, 1981), 27.

18. Walker, *Armenia*, 86.

19. Bryce, *Treatment of Armenians*, 618.

20. Ternon, *The Armenians*, 27.

21. Vahakn N. Dadrian, "The Structural-Functional Components of Genocide: A Victimological Approach to the Armenian Case," in *Victimology*, ed. Israel Drapkin and Emilio Viano (Lexington, Mass.: D.C. Heath, 1974), 126.

22. Walker, *Armenia*, 87.

23. Henry Morgenthau, *Ambassador Morgenthau's Story* (Plandome, N.Y.: New Age, 1984), 280, 279.

24. Dadrian, "The Structural-Functional Components of Genocide," in *Victimology*, vol. 3, ed. Drapkin and Viano, 126.

25. Fridtjof Nansen, *Armenia and the Near East* (first published in Norwegian as *Gjennem Armenia*, 1928; New York: DeCapo, 1976), 267.

26. Ternon, *The Armenians*, 29, quoted in Edouard Philipee Engelhardt, *La Turquie et le Tanzimat ou histoire des réformes dans l'Empire ottoman depuis 1826 jusqu'a nos jours* (Paris: A. Cotillon) (1882-84) 2:136; Burtt, *People of Ararat*, 46.

27. Walker, *Armenia*, 88.

28. Nansen, *Armenia and the Near East*, 267; Lanne, *Armenia: The First Genocide*, 53; James Bryce, Arnold J. Toynbee, Herbert Adams Gibbons, Henry Morgenthau, Fridtjof Nansen, *An Anthology of Historical Writings on the Armenian Massacres of 1915* (Beirut: Hamaskaine Press, 1971), 91.

29. Ternon, *The Armenians*, 29.

30. Walker, *Armenia*, 89; Johannes Lepsius, *Armenia and Europe: An Indictment* (London: Hodder and Stoughton, 1897), 207.

31. C. B. Norman, *Armenia and the Campaign of 1877* (London: Cassell, Petter & Galpin, 1878), 318.

32. Atamian, *Armenian Community*, 48, 89.

33. A *piastre* was a Turkish coin of about $0.05, or 2½ d. In some regions of Turkey during the 1890s a Turkish day laborer made from two to five piastres a day, according to Frederick Davis Greene, *Armenian Crisis in Turkey: The Massacre of 1894, Its Antecedents and Significance*, with an Introduction by Rev. Josiah Strong (New York and London: G. P. Putnam's Sons, Knickerbocher Press, 1895), 119.

34. Lepsius, *Armenia and Europe*, 208-9.

35. Greene, *Armenian Crisis in Turkey*, 59-62.

36. Ternon, *The Armenians*, 66-67.

37. Walker, *Armenia*, 133-34.

38. Ternon, *The Armenians*, 62.

39. Frederick Davis Greene, *Armenian Massacres or The Sword of Mohammed* (Philadelphia: American Oxford, 1896), 191.

40. Ternon, *The Armenians*, 70–71, telegram from Charles S. Hampton, British consul at Erzeroum, 28 February, 1891, quoted by Malcolm MacColl, "L'Armenie devant l'Europe," *Revue des Deux-Mondes* (Sept.–Oct. 1896).

41. Joan Haslip, *The Sultan: The Life of Abdul Hamid II* (New York: Holt, Rinehart and Winston, 1958), 217.

42. Bliss, *Turkey and the Armenian Atrocities*, 556–57.

43. Haslip, *The Sultan*, 217–18.

44. Bliss, *Turkey and the Armenian Atrocities*, 362.

45. Lepsius, *Armenia and Europe*, 62–64.

46. Bliss, *Turkey and the Armenian Atrocities*, 465.

47. Lepsius, *Armenia and Europe*, 63–64.

48. Greene, *Armenian Massacres*, 287.

49. Lepsius, *Armenia and Europe*, 70–71.

50. Lanne, *Armenia: The First Genocide*, 85.

51. Ternon, *The Armenians*, 106, quoting L. Leclerc, "La Question armenienne," *Revue de l'universite de Bruxelles*, 1896, 523.

52. Bliss, *Turkey and the Armenian Atrocities*, 556.

53. Ternon, *The Armenians*, 106–7.

54. Greene, *Armenian Massacres*, 186.

55. James Rendel Harris and Helen B. Harris, *Letters from the Scenes of the Recent Massacres in Armenia* (London: James Nisbet, 1897), 168.

56. Ternon, *The Armenians*, 122.

57. For a further description of the massacres in these areas, see Christopher Walker, *Armenia*, Chap. 5.

58. *The Graphic*, 26 Sept. 1896. Pages unnumbered. Photo accompanying story is entitled, "The Crisis in Constantinople: Armenian Refugees on Board the SS *Douro*."

59. Michael J. Arlen, *Passage to Ararat* (New York: Ballantine, 1975), 131.

60. Diana Agabeg Apcar, *On the Cross of Europe's Imperialism: Armenia Crucified* (Yokohama: Fukuin, 1918), 21–22; Bryce, *Treatment of Armenians*, 19.

61. Apcar, *On the Cross of Europe's Imperialism*, 22.

62. Bryce, *Treatment of Armenians*, 19.

63. "Turkish Statesman Denounces Atrocities," *New York Times*, Sunday, 10 Oct. 1915; Abraham H. Hartunian, *Neither to Laugh nor to Weep: A Memoir of the Armenian Genocide*, trans. Vartan Hartunian (Boston: Beacon, 1976), 44–45.

64. E. K. Sarkisian and R. G. Sahakian, *Vital Issues in Modern Armenian History: Documented Exposé of Misrepresentations in Turkish Historiography*, trans. Elisha B. Chrakian (Erevan, Armenia, 1963; Concord, Mass.: Concord Press, 1965), 20.

65. Arnold J. Toynbee, *Turkey: A Past and a Future* (New York: George H. Doran, 1917), 42–43; Joseph Guttmann, "The Beginnings of Genocide," in *Turkish Armenocide: The Genocide of the Armenians by the Turks*, ed. Armenian Historical Research Association (Boston: AHRA, 1965), 12–13.

66. Ibid., 13, quoted in Johannes Lepsius, *Der Todesgang des Armenischen Volkes*, 4th ed. (Potsdam, 1930), 244–45.

67. Henry Morgenthau, *Ambassador Morgenthau's Story* (Plandome, N.Y.: New Age, 1984), 50.

68. Bryce et al., *An Anthology of Historical Writings*, 77.

69. Ternon, *The Armenians*, 196.

70. Walker, *Armenia*, 200–201, quoted in Henry Morgenthau, *Secrets of the Bosphorus: Constantinople 1913–1916* (London: 1918), 198–99.

71. Ternon, *The Armenians*, 196; Walker, *Armenia*, 200; Lanne, *Armenia: The First Genocide*, 118.

72. Leo Kuper, *Genocide: Its Political Uses in the Twentieth Century* (New Haven and London: Yale Univ. Press, 1981), 109.

73. Walker, *Armenia*, 201.

74. Stanley E. Kerr, *The Lions of Marash* (Albany: State Univ. of New York Press, 1973), xx.

CHAPTER 2

1. Henry Morgenthau, *Ambassador Morgenthau's Story* (Plandome, N.Y.: New Age, 1984), 112.

2. James Bryce, Arnold J. Toynbee, Herbert Adams Gibbons, Henry Morgenthau, Fridtjof Nansen, *An Anthology of Historical Writings on the Armenian Massacres of 1915* (Beirut: Hamaskaine Press, 1971), 91.

3. Christopher Walker, *Armenia: The Survival of a Nation* (New York: St. Martin's Press, 1980), 89.

4. James B. Gidney, *A Mandate for Armenia* (Kent, Ohio: Kent State Univ. Press, 1967), 27; Arnold J. Toynbee, *The Murderous Tyranny of the Turks*, with a Preface by Viscount Bryce (London: Hodder and Stoughton, 1917; New York: Tankian, 1975), 26.

5. Gidney, *A Mandate for Armenia*, 24-25; Peter Lanne, *Armenia: The First Genocide of the XX Century*, trans. Krikor Balekdjian (Munich: Max Schmidt & Sohne, 1977), 53.

6. Joseph Burtt, *The People of Ararat* (London: Hogarth Press, 1926), 46-47; Walker, *Armenia*, 47, 52.

7. Frederick Davis Greene, *Armenian Massacres or the Sword of Mohammed* (Philadelphia: American Oxford, 1896), 70-71; Dickran H. Boyajian, *Armenia: The Case for a Forgotten Genocide* (Westwood, N.J.: Educational Book Crafters, 1972), 80.

8. Burtt, *People of Ararat*, 45-47. Also see Gidney, *A Mandate for Armenia*, 25.

9. Greene, *Armenian Massacres*, 71.

10. Gidney, *A Mandate for Armenia*, 25.

11. Burtt, *People of Ararat*, 47.

12. Greene, *Armenian Massacres*, 71.

13. Frederick Davis Greene, *Armenian Crisis in Turkey: The Massacre of 1894, Its Antecedents and Significance*, with an Introduction by Rev. Josiah Strong (New York and London: G. P. Putnam's Sons, Knickerbocher Press, 1895), 114-15.

14. Greene, *Armenian Massacres*, 71-72.

15. Burtt, *People of Ararat*, 49; Bryce et al., *An Anthology of Historical Writings*, 91.

16. Burtt, *People of Ararat*, 49, quoted in A. D. Innes, *A History of the British Nation*, 902.

17. Ibid., 49-51.

18. Walker, *Armenia*, 91, quoted in Sir Edward Hertslet, *The Map of Europe by Treaty* 2(1875):1255.

19. Burtt, *People of Ararat*, 49-50; Greene, *Armenian Massacres*, 72.

20. Burtt, *People of Ararat*, 51-53.

21. Gidney, *A Mandate for Armenia*, 27-28.

22. Greene, *Armenian Massacres*, 495-98.

23. Burtt, *People of Ararat*, 53.

24. Greene, *Armenian Massacres*, 495-99.

25. Morgenthau, *Ambassador Morgenthau's Story*, 286-87.

26. Walker, *Armenia*, 64; Burtt, *People of Ararat*, 54.

27. Walker, *Armenia*, 108-9, quoted in Sir Edward Hertslet, *The Map of Europe by Treaty* 4(1875):2598-9.

28. Walker, *Armenia*, 109-10, quoted in C. B. Norman, *Armenia and the Campaign of 1877* (London: Cassell, Petter & Galpin, 1878), 263.

29. Walker, *Armenia*, 111, quoted in A. O. Sarkisian, *History of the Armenian Question to 1885*, 64.

30. Burtt, *People of Ararat*, 54.

31. Walker, *Armenia*, 111, quoted in Hertslet, *A Map of Europe* 4:2686.

32. Walker, *Armenia*, 112-14; Burtt, *People of Ararat*, 54.

33. Walker, *Armenia*, 112-15, quoted in Hertslet, *The Map of Europe* 4:2722-23.

34. Walker, *Armenia*, 115; Louise Nalbandian, *The Armenian Revolutionary Movement: The Development of Armenian Political Parties through the Nineteenth Century* (Berkeley, Los Angeles, London: Univ. of California Press, 1963), 28.

35. Gidney, *A Mandate for Armenia*, 29.

36. Burtt, *People of Ararat*, 54-55; Walker, *Armenia*, 115, quoted in Hertslet, *The Map of Europe by Treaty* (vol. 2, 1875 and vol. 4, 1891).

37. Walker, *Armenia*, 115-17.

38. Burtt, *People of Ararat*, 55; Greene, *Armenian Crisis in Turkey*, 73; Bryce et al., *An Anthology of Historical Writings*, 46.

39. Gidney, *A Mandate for Armenia*, 30.

40. Morgenthau, *Ambassador Morgenthau's Story*, 288-89.

41. Joseph Guttmann, "The Beginnings of Genocide: An Account of the Armenian Massacres in World War I," in *The Turkish Armenocide*, ed. Armenian Historical Research Association (Boston: AHRA, 1965), 5; Greene, *Armenian Massacres*, 186.

42. Greene, *Armenian Massacres*, 186.

43. Bernard Lewis, *The Emergence of Modern Turkey* (London, Oxford, New York: Oxford Univ. Press, 1961).

44. Toynbee, *Murderous Tyranny of the Turks*, 27; Bryce et al., *An Anthology of Historical Writings*, 47.

45. Akady Nassibian, *Britain and The Armenian Question: 1915-1923* (New York: St. Martin's Press, 1984) 26.

46. Morgenthau, *Ambassador Morgenthau's Story*, 116.

47. Gerard Chaliand and Yves Ternon, *The Armenians: From Genocide to Resistance*, trans. Tony Berrett (Editions Complexe, 1981, in French; London: Zed, 1983), 25-27.

48. Nalbandian, *Armenian Revolutionary Movement*, 46-48; Richard G. Hovannisian, "The Armenian Question, 1878-1923," 14, in The Permanent People's Tribunal, *A Crime of Silence: The Armenian Genocide*, with a Preface by Pierre Vidal-Naquet (London: Zed, 1985).

49. Walker, *Armenia*, 99-100.

50. Ibid., 125-26; Nalbandian, *Armenian Revolutionary Movement*, 80, cited in documents in Father Giut Aghaniants, *Divan Hayots Patmuthian* (Archives on Armenian History) 13:269; 83-85.

51. Walker, *Armenia*, 126.

52. Burtt, *People of Ararat*, 58.

53. Nalbandian, *Armenian Revolutionary Movement*, 83, cited in Great Britain, *State Papers, 1877-1878*, 3009:766, 100-101.

54. Chaliand and Ternon, *The Armenians*, 29.

55. Nalbandian, *Armenian Revolutionary Movement*, 102, cited in Great Britain, Turkey no. 1 (1889), enclosure in no. 1 *Appendix to Memorial*, 2-3; Nassibian, *Britain and the Armenian Question*, 19.

56. Nalbandian, *Armenian Revolutionary Movement*, 99-114.

57. Fa'iz El-Ghusein, *Martyred Armenia*, trans. from Arabic (London: C. Arthur Pearson, 1917), 9.

58. Nalbandian, *Armenian Revolutionary Movement*, 118-19.

59. Thomas A. Bryson, *American Diplomatic Relations with the Middle East, 1784-1975: A Survey* (Metuchen, N.J.: Scarecrow Press, 1977), 31-33.

60. Nalbandian, *Armenian Revolutionary Movement*, 122-24.

61. Ibid., 122-28.

62. Bryson, *American Diplomatic Relations*, 31.

63. Ibid., 33.

64. Nalbandian, *Armenian Revolutionary Movement*, 151-54.

65. Ibid., 163-67, quoted in M. Shatirian, as dictated to N. Hangoyts, "Hayots Hasarakan Sharzhumneri Patmuthiunits" ("On the General Intellectual Movement of the Armenian People"), *Hairenik Amsagir*, 1(Mar. 1923):31.

66. J. Missakian, *A Searchlight on the Armenian Question: 1878-1950* (Boston: Hairenik, 1950), 28.

67. Nalbandian, *Armenian Revolutionary Movement*, 166-68, quoted in *Hai Heghapokhakan Dashnaktsuthian Dzragir* (Vienna, n.d.).

68. Ronald Grigor Suny, *The Baku Commune: 1917-1918: Class and Nationality in*

the Russian Revolution (Princeton, N.J.: Princeton Univ. Press, 1972), 23, cited in *Programma armianskot revoliutsionnot i sotsialistícheskot partii Dashnaktsutiun* (Geneva, 1908).

69. Missakian, *Searchlight*, 29.

70. Burtt, *People of Ararat*, 59; Nalbandian, *Armenian Revolutionary Movement*, 169-75

71. Djemal Pasha, *Memories of a Turkish Statesman—1913-1919* (London: Hutchinson, 1922), 246.

72. Ibid., 246.

73. Nalbandian, *Armenian Revolutionary Movement*, 176-78.

74. Gidney, *A Mandate for Armenia*, 34.

75. *Supplement to the Graphic* (London) "The Riots in Constantinople," 12 Sept. 1896.

76. Gidney, *A Mandate for Armenia*, 35-36.

CHAPTER 3

1. Christopher Walker, *Armenia: The Survival of a Nation* (New York: St. Martin's Press, 1980), 190-91.

2. Yves Ternon, *The Armenians: History of a Genocide*, trans. Rouben C. Cholakian (New York: Caravan Books, 1981), 318, cited in Tarik Z. Tunaya, *History*, 199; Joan Haslip, *The Sultan: The Life of Abdul Hamid II* (New York: Holt, Rinehart and Winston, 1958), 268; Walker, *The Armenians*, 190-91.

3. Zarevand, *United and Independent Turania: Aims and Designs of the Turks*, trans. V. N. Dadrian (Leiden: E. J. Brill, 1971), xi, quoted in *Memoirs of Halide Edbin* [sic] (London, 1926), 386.

4. Henry Morgenthau, *Ambassador Morgenthau's Story* (Plandome, N.Y.: New Age, 1984), 51.

5. Henry Morgenthau, *The Murder of A Nation* (New York: Lordian Press, 1974), 62.

6. Zarevand, *United and Independent Turania*, xi, quoted in *Memoirs of Halide Edbin* [sic], 312-28.

7. Dickran H. Boyajian, *Armenia: The Case for a Forgotten Genocide* (Westwood, N.J.: Educational Book Crafters, 1972), 4.

8. Ternon, *The Armenians*, 318, cited in Tunaya, *History*, 199; Haslip, *The Sultan*, 267; Boyajian, *Armenia*, 9-10.

9. Walker, *Armenia*, 191.

10. Niyazi Berkes, *Turkish Nationalism and Western Civilization: Selected Essays of Ziya Gokalp*, trans. and Intro. by Niyazi Berkes (New York: Columbia Univ. Press, 1959), 321; Walker, *Armenia*, 191.

11. Walker, *Armenia*, 197; Richard G. Hovannisian, *Armenia on the Road to Independence 1918* (Berkeley, Los Angeles, and London: Univ. of California Press, 1967), 45-46.

12. Walker, *Armenia*, 197; Ternon, *The Armenians*, 197.

13. Walker, *Armenia*, 199; Hovannisian, *Armenia on the Road to Independence*, 45-46.

14. Morgenthau, *The Murder of A Nation*, 62; Morgenthau, *Ambassador Morgenthau's Story*, 352, 355.

15. Martin Niepage, *The Horrors of Aleppo* (London: T. Fisher Unwin, 1917), 15.

16. Haslip, *The Sultan*, 268; Ternon, *The Armenians*, 318.

17. Morgenthau, *Ambassador Morgenthau's Story*, 173-74; Feroz Ahmad, *The Young Turks: The Committee of Union and Progress in Turkish Politics 1908-1914* (London: Oxford, Clarendon Press, 1969), 159.

18. Henry Morgenthau, *Ambassador Morgenthau's Story*, 174; Charles Burney and

David Marshall Lang, *The Peoples of the Hills: Ancient Ararat and Caucasus* (New York: Praeger, 1972), 178; Djemal Pasha, *Memories of a Turkish Statesman: 1913-1919* (London: Hutchinson, 1922), 300.

19. Pasha, *Memories of a Turkish Statesman*, 243, 244.

20. Ibid., 277.

21. Fa'iz El-Ghusein, *Martyred Armenia*, trans. from Arabic (London: C. Arthur Pearson, 1917), 15.

22. Boyajian, *Armenia*, 13; Arnold J. Toynbee, *Turkey: A Past and a Future* (New York: George H. Doran, 1917), 16.

23. Boyajian, *Armenia*, 13-14; Morgenthau, *Ambassador Morgenthau's Story*, 100.

24. Ternon, *The Armenians*, 317, quoted in *United and Independent Turania: Aims and Designs of the Turks*, trans. Vahakn Dadrian (1926; Leiden: E. J. Brill, 1971), 41-43.

25. Zarevand, *United and Independent Turania*, 41.

26. Ibid., 43; Ternon, *Armenia*, 159.

27. Zarevand, *United and Independent Turania*, 43, quoted in Tekin Alp, *Turkismus und Panturkismus*, 73; "Christians in Great Peril," *New York Times*, 13 Jan. 1915.

28. Hovannisian, *Armenia on the Road to Independence*, 54.

29. Zarevand, *United and Independent Turania*, 53-54; Frederick Davis Greene, *Armenian Massacres or The Sword of Mohammed* (Philadelphia: American Oxford, 1896), 44.

30. Djemal, *Memories*, 300.

31. Arnold J. Toynbee, *Turkey: A Past and a Future* (New York: George H. Doran, 1917), 31, quoted in *Thoughts on the Nature and Plan of a Greater Turkey*.

32. Ibid., 32-33.

33. Ibid., 35-36.

34. Ibid., 31; Morgenthau, *Ambassador Morgenthau's Story*, 291.

35. Walker, *Armenia*, 203; Ternon, *The Armenians*, 170.

36. Ternon, *The Armenians*, 170; Noel Buxton and Harold Buxton, *Travel and Politics in Armenia* (New York: Macmillan, 1914), 44-45.

37. Walker, *Armenia*, 203.

38. James Bryce, Arnold J. Toynbee, Herbert Adams Gibbons, Henry Morgenthau, and Fridtjof Nansen, *An Anthology of Historical Writings on the Armenian Massacres of 1915* (Beirut: Hamaskaine Press, 1971), 45; Toynbee, *Turkey: A Past and a Future*, 31.

39. Hovannisian, *Armenia on the Road to Independence*, 195, quoting A. Khatisian, *Hayastani Hanrapetutian dsagumn u zargatsume* ("The Creation and Development of the Republic of Armenia"), 70.

40. Zarevand, *United and Independent Turania*, 43.

41. Peter Lanne, *Armenia: The First Genocide of the XX Century*, trans. Krikor Balekdjian (Munich: Max Schmidt & Sohne, 1977), 87-88.

42. Bryce et al., *An Anthology of Historical Writings*, 43.

43. Ternon, *The Armenians*, 142-43.

44. Lanne, *Armenia: The First Genocide*, 88.

45. Ternon, *The Armenians*, 141.

46. Ibid., 147.

47. Boyajian, *Armenia: The Case for a Forgotten Genocide*, 46; Ternon, *The Armenians*, 319; Haslip, *The Sultan*, 258.

48. Ternon, *The Armenians*, 147-49; Haslip, *The Sultan*, 266; Lanne, *Armenia: The First Genocide*, 88.

49. Ternon, *The Armenians*, 149; Morgenthau, *Ambassador Morgenthau's Story*, 12-13.

50. Ternon, *The Armenians*, 154; James B. Gidney, *A Mandate for Armenia* (Ohio: Kent State Univ. Press, 1967), 38.

51. Bryce et al., *An Anthology of Historical Writings*, 43; Gidney, *A Mandate for Armenia*, 39; Ternon, *The Armenians*, 154.

52. Ternon, *The Armenians*, 154.

53. Lanne, *Armenia: The First Genocide*, 93.

54. Ternon, *The Armenians*, 150–55; Toynbee, *Turkey: A Past and a Future*, 16.
55. Ternon, *The Armenians*, 151.
56. Zarevand, *United and Independent Turania*, 38–39.
57. Ibid., 36–37; Toynbee, *Turkey: A Past and a Future*, 20–21.
58. Toynbee, *Turkey: A Past and a Future*, 25–26.
59. Zarevand, *United and Independent Turania*, 38.
60. Toynbee, *Turkey: A Past and a Future*, 31.
61. Ternon, *The Armenians*, 152.
62. Morgenthau, *Ambassador Morgenthau's Story*, 23.
63. Ternon, *The Armenians*, 155–56, *Istamboul* (22 Sept. 1913) quoted by Ahmad, *The Young Turks*, 141, 156.
64. Morgenthau, *Ambassador Morgenthau's Story*, 13; Ternon, *The Armenians*, 156; Walker, *Armenia*, 236–37.
65. Morgenthau, *Ambassador Morgenthau's Story*, 14.
66. Ibid., 11–14.
67. Ibid., 14.
68. Ibid., 15–16; Walker, *Armenia*, 192–93.
69. Ahmad, *The Young Turks*, 163.
70. Morgenthau, *Ambassador Morgenthau's Story*, 18–19.
71. Ahmad, *The Young Turks*, 165; Ternon, *The Armenians*, 150.
72. Morgenthau, *Ambassador Morgenthau's Story*, 136; Ternon, *The Armenians*, 150.
73. Ahmad, *The Young Turks*, 159.
74. In E. K. Sarkisian and R. G. Sahakian, *Vital Issues in Modern Armenian History: Documented Exposé of Misrepresentations in Turkish Historiography*, trans. Elisha B. Chrakian (Concord, Mass.: Concord Press, 1965), 33.
75. Ida Alamuddin, *Papa Kuenzler and the Armenians* (London: Heinemann, 1970), 60.
76. Marjorie Housepian, "The Unremembered Genocide," *Commentary* XLII (September 1966): 55–61.
77. "Turkish Statesman Denounces Atrocities," *New York Times*, Sunday, 10 Oct. 1915.
78. Ternon, *The Armenians*, 197.
79. Walker, *Armenia*, 197.
80. Ternon, *The Armenians*, 188–89, cited in *Teskara* 68, Nov. 1914 (Archives: Library of Congress, Washington), indicating that the "destructive weapons" were deposited at the *Teshkilat-i-Mahsuse*.
81. Walker, *Armenia*, 200.
82. Morgenthau, *Ambassador Morgenthau's Story*, 116.
83. Boyajian, *Armenia: The Case for a Forgotten Genocide*, 109, quoting Johannes Lepsius.

CHAPTER 4

1. Zarevand, *United and Independent Turania: Aims and Designs of the Turks*, trans. V. N. Dadrian (Leiden: E. J. Brill, 1971), 9; Ronald Grigor Suny, *The Baku Commune 1917–1918: Class and Nationality in the Russian Revolution* (Princeton, N.J.: Princeton Univ. Press, 1972), 16–17.
2. Suny, *The Baku Commune*, 16–17.
3. Zarevand, *United and Independent Turania*, 7.
4. Yves Ternon, *The Armenians: History of a Genocide*, trans. Rouben C. Cholaskian (New York: Caravan Books, 1981), 138.
5. Zarevand, *United and Independent Turania*, 8–10, 25–26.

6. Ibid., 11-13.

7. Ibid., 26, 18, quoted in Arminius Vambery, "Constitutional Tartars" in *XIX Century*, Jan. 1906, 906; "The Awakening of Tartars" in *XIX Century*, Jan.-June, 1905, 217.

8. Zarevand, *United and Independent Turania*, 33-34.

9. Ziya Gokalp, *Turkish Nationalism and Western Civilization*, trans., ed., and Intro. by Niyazi Berkes (New York: Columbia Univ. Press, 1959), 306, 305, 307.

10. Zarevand, *United and Independent Turania*, 34.

11. Ibid., 30, 31, quoted in Ahmed Emin, *The Development of Modern Turkey as Measured by Its Press* (New York, 1914), 100-101.

12. Ibid., 47, cited in Tekin Alp, *Turkismus und Panturkismus* (Weimar, 1915), 81.

13. Ibid., 47, quoted in C. U. Clark, *Greater Rumania* (New York: Dodd Mead, 1922), 121.

14. Ibid., 36, 44.

15. Ibid., 27-28.

16. Ida Alamuddin, *Papa Kuenzler and the Armenians* (London: Heinemann, 1970), 60.

17. Zarevand, *United and Independent Turania*, 5.

18. Ternon, *The Armenians*, 156-57.

19. Zarevand, *United and Independent Turania*, 34-35.

20. Ternon, *The Armenians*, 318.

21. Ibid., 157-58.

22. Ibid., 153.

23. Israel Charney, *How Can We Commit the Unthinkable? Genocide: The Human Cancer*, with a Foreword by Elie Wiesel (Boulder, Colo.: Westview Press, 1982), 12.

24. Ibid., 24.

25. Frederick Davis Greene, *Armenian Massacres or The Sword of Mohammed* (Philadelphia: American Oxford, 1896), 185-86.

26. E. K. Sarkisian and R. G. Sahakian, *Vital Issues in Modern Armenian History*, trans. Elisha B. Chrakian (Concord, Mass.: Concord Press, 1965), 22, quoting Mevlanzade Rifat, *The Dark Folds of the Turkish Revolution*, 171.

27. Stanley E. Kerr, *The Lions of Marash* (Albany: State Univ. of New York Press, 1973), 7.

28. Sarkisian and Sahakian, *Vital Issues in Modern Armenian History*, 29.

29. Dickran H. Boyajian, *Armenia: The Case for a Forgotten Genocide* (New Jersey: Educational Book Crafters, 1972), 5.

30. Herbert Adams Gibbons, *The Blackest Page of Modern History: Events in Armenia in 1915, the Facts and the Responsibilities* (New York and London: G. P. Putnam's Sons, 1916), 26-27.

31. Johannes Lepsius, *Der Todesgang des Armenischen Volkes*, 4th ed. (Potsdam: 1930).

32. Stanley E. Kerr, *The Lions of Marash* (Albany: State Univ. of New York Press, 1978), 8-9.

33. Henry Morgenthau, *Ambassador Morgenthau's Story* (New York: Doubleday, Page 1919; Plandome, N.Y.: New Age, 1984), 304.

34. Djemal Pasha, *Memories of a Turkish Statesman, 1913-1919* (London: Hutchinson, 1922), 245.

35. Christopher Walker, *Armenia: The Survival of a Nation* (New York: St. Martin's Press, 1980), 199, quoted in Johannes Lepsius, *Deutschland und Armenien, 1914-1918* (Potsdam: n.p. 1919), xvi, from *Osmanischer Lloyd*, 26 Feb. 1915.

36. Peter Lanne, *Armenia: The First Genocide of the XX Century*, trans. Krikor Balekdjian (Munich: Max Schmidt, 1977), 101.

37. Walker, *Armenia*, 199-200.

38. Morgenthau, *Ambassador Morgenthau's Story*, 296-99, 361.

39. Kerr, *Lions of Marash*, 14.

40. Alamuddin, *Papa Kuenzler and the Armenians*, 60.

41. James Bryce, *The Treatment of Armenians in the Ottoman Empire, 1915-16,* 2d ed., Preface by Viscount Bryce (Beirut: G. Doniguian, 1972), 482.
42. Andre Mandelstam, *Le sort de l'Empire Ottoman* (Lausanne, Paris: Librairie Payot et Cie, 1917), 242.
43. Lepsius, *Der Todesgang des Armenischen Volkes,* 1930.
44. Fa'iz El-Ghusein, *Martyred Armenia,* trans from Arabic (London: C. Arthur Pearson, 1917), 45-46.
45. Kerr, *The Lions of Marash,* 14; Walker, *Armenia,* 210, citing Henry Morgenthau, *Secrets of the Bosphorus* (London, 1918), 221.
46. Ternon, *The Armenians,* 270.
47. Gerard Chaliand and Yves Ternon, *The Armenians: From Genocide to Resistance,* trans. Tony Berrett (Editions Complexe, 1981 in French; London: Zed, 1983), 62.
48. Arnold J. Toynbee, *Armenian Atrocities: The Murder of a Nation* (London: Hodder and Stoughton, 1925; New York: Prelacy of the Armenian Church of America, 1975), 72.
49. Gibbons, *The Blackest Page of Modern History,* 16-17.
50. Chaliand and Ternon, *The Armenians,* 47-49, quoting Harry Stuermer, *Two War Years in Constantinople* (Geneva, 1917).
51. Martin Niepage, *The Horrors of Aleppo* (London: T. Fisher Unwin, 1916), 15-16.
52. Lanne, *Armenia: The First Genocide,* 135.
53. Ibid., 116-17.
54. Bryce et al., *An Anthology of Historical Writings,* 79.
55. Ternon, *The Armenians,* 219.
56. Talaat Pasha, "Posthumous Memoirs of Talaat Pasha," *Current History,* 15 (Nov. 1921): 294.
57. Djemal, *Memories,* 277.
58. Ibid., 279-80.
59. Henry Morgenthau, *The Murder of a Nation* (New York: Lordian Press, 1974), 37-38.
60. Chaliand and Ternon, *The Armenians,* 84; Sarkisian and Sahakian, *Vital Issues in Modern Armenian History,* 28-29.
61. Chaliand and Ternon, *The Armenians,* 85.

CHAPTER 5

1. David Marshall Lang, *The Armenians: A People in Exile* (London: George Allen & Unwin, 1981), 20; Arnold J. Toynbee, *Armenian Atrocities: The Murder of a Nation,* with a speech delivered by Lord Bryce in the House of Commons (London: Hodder & Stoughton, 1915), 78-80.
2. Aram Andonian, "The Memoirs of Naim Bey: Turkish Official Documents Relating to the Deportations and Massacres of Armenians," in *The Turkish Armenocide,* ed. Armenian Historical Research Association (Boston: AHRA, 1965), 26; Mabel Evelyn Elliot, *Beginning Again at Ararat,* with an Introduction by John H. Finley (New York: Fleming H. Revell, 1924), 24.
3. Yves Ternon, *The Armenians: History of a Genocide,* trans. Rouben C. Cholakian (New York: Caravan Books, 1981), 270.
4. Henry Morgenthau, *The Murder of a Nation* (New York: Lordian Press, 1974), 44.
5. Peter Lanne, *Armenia: The First Genocide of the XX Century,* trans. Krikor Balekdjian (Munich: Max Schmidt & Sohne, 1977), 114.
6. James Bryce, *The Treatment of Armenians in the Ottoman Empire, 1915-16,* 2d ed., Preface by Viscount Bryce (Beirut: G. Doniguian, 1972), 385.
7. Toynbee, *Armenian Atrocities,* 28.
8. Christopher Walker, *Armenia: The Survival of a Nation* (New York: St. Martin's Press, 1980), 202-3; Henry Morgenthau, *Ambassador Morgenthau's Story* (New York: Doubleday, Page, 1919; Plandome, N.Y.: New Age, 1984), 291.

9. Toynbee, Armenian Atrocities, 32.
10. Walker, Armenia, 202-3.
11. Morgenthau, Ambassador Morgenthau's Story, 312-15.
12. Ibid., 315.
13. Walker, Armenia, 202-3.
14. Elliot, Beginning Again at Ararat, 22-24.
15. Lanne, Armenia: The First Genocide, 114; Toynbee, Armenian Atrocities, 39-40.
16. Marjorie Housepian, The Smyrna Affair (New York: Harcourt Brace Jovanovich, 1971), 27.
17. Ternon, The Armenians, 251, quoting Aram Andonian, ed., Documents officiels concernant les massacres armeniens (Paris: Imprimerie Tourabian, 1920), 145.
18. Ternon, The Armenians, 254, quoting Andonian, Documents officiels, 138.
19. Ibid., 251.
20. Walker, Armenia, 225-26.
21. Stanley E. Kerr, The Lions of Marash: Personal Experiences with American Near East Relief, 1919-1922 (Albany: State Univ. of New York Press, 1973), 14; "Exiles from Zeitoun: Diary of a Foreign Resident in the Town of B. on the Cilician Plain," Communicated by A Swiss Gentleman of Geneva, in Treatment of Armenians, ed. Bryce, 482-86.
22. Walker, Armenia, 203-5.
23. Ibid., 210.
24. Toynbee, Armenian Atrocities, 63.
25. Kerr, The Lions of Marash, 22-23.
26. "The American Mission at Van," a narrative printed in the United States by Grace Higley Knapp (1915), in Treatment of Armenians, ed. Bryce, 35; Morgenthau, Ambassador Morgenthau's Story, 297; Walker, Armenia, 208, citing Clarence D. Ussher, An American Physician in Turkey (Boston, 1917), 235-36.
27. Knapp, "The American Mission at Van," in Treatment of Armenians, ed. Bryce, 35; Morgenthau, Ambassador Morgenthau's Story, 297-98.
28. Walker, Armenia, 205-9.
29. Ternon, The Armenians, 218-19.
30. Sarkis H. Kash, Crime Unlimited (S. Milwaukee, Wisc.: Journal Printing, 1965), 57.
31. Walker, Armenia, 209-10.
32. Fa'iz El-Ghusein, Martyred Armenia, trans. from Arabic (London: C. Arthur Pearson, 1917), 18-19.
33. Walker, Armenia, 211; American Committee for the Independence of Armenia, The Joint Mandate Scheme: A Turkish Empire Under American Protection, 1919, 337.
34. El-Ghusein, Martyred Armenia, 34.
35. Walker, Armenia, 211-12.
36. El-Ghusein, Martyred Armenia, 34.
37. Gerard Chaliand and Yves Ternon, The Armenians: From Genocide to Resistance, trans. Tony Berrett (Editions Complexe, 1981, in French; London: Zed, 1983), 64, citing "Statement by Two Danish Red Cross Nurses: Formerly in the Service of the German Military Mission at Erzerum; Communicated by a Swiss Gentleman of Geneva," doc. 62.
38. Walker, Armenia, 212-13; Chaliand and Ternon, The Armenians, 64, citing "Statement by Two Danish Red Cross Nurses."
39. Walker, Armenia, 212-14.
40. "Russians Seize Port of Rizeh," New York Times, 9 Mar. 1916.
41. Dr. G. Pasdermadjian, Why Armenia Should Be Free: Armenia's Role in the Present War (Boston: Hairenik, 1918), 27.
42. Walker, Armenia, 216, quoting Misc. no. 31 (1916):291.
43. Toynbee, Armenian Atrocities, 10-11.
44. Walker, Armenia, 217.
45. Ibid., 218, quoting Misc. no. 31 (1916):291-92.
46. Chaliand and Ternon, The Armenians, 44, quoting "Extracts from a Report by a German Employee of the Baghdad Railway."

47. Walker, *Armenia*, 218.
48. Henry Morgenthau, *The Tragedy of Armenia* (London: Spottiswoode, Ballantyne, 1918), 12.
49. Morgenthau, *Ambassador Morgenthau's Story*, 303–4.
50. Walker, *Armenia*, 218–20, quoting Misc. no. 31 (1916):266–79.
51. Ibid., 266.
52. Walker, *Armenia*, 220–21.
53. "Armenians Are Sent to Perish in Desert," *New York Times*, 18 Aug. 1915.; "1,500,000 Armenians Starve," *New York Times*, 5 Sept. 1915; "Armenians Are Sent to Perish in the Desert," *New York Times*, 18 Aug. 1915.
54. "Statement of a Traveller from Kaisaria," published in the Armenian journal *Balkanian Mamoul*, of Roustchouk, in *Treatment of Armenians*, ed. Bryce, 328.
55. Ibid.
56. "Sivas: Record of an Interview Given by the Refugee Nyrad to Mr. A. S. Safrastian at Tiflis," in *Treatment of Armenians*, 320–25.
57. Walker, *Armenia*, 221; "Narrative of a Naturalized Ottoman Subject," dated New York City, 10 March 1916. Communicated by the American Committee for Armenian and Syrian Relief, in *Treatment of Armenians*, ed. Bryce, 311–16.
58. Walker, *Armenia*, 221.
59. Morgenthau, *Murder of a Nation*, 41.
60. Walker, *Armenia*, 222.
61. El-Ghusein, *Martyred Armenia*, 11.
62. Ibid., 44–45.
63. Ibid., 49.
64. Walker, *Armenia*, 223; Franz Werfel, *The Forty Days of Musa Dagh*, original version *Die Vierzig Tage des Musa Dagh* (Berlin: Paul Zsolnay Verlag A.G., 1933; New York: Viking, 1934), 268.
65. Walker, *Armenia*, 223–25.
66. Ida Alamuddin, *Papa Kuenzler and the Armenians* (London: Heinemann, 1970), 61–64.
67. Walker, *Armenia*, 225; Alamuddin, *Papa Kuenzler*, 66–67.
68. Walker, *Armenia*, 222–25.
69. Morgenthau, *Ambassador Morgenthau's Story*, 238, 240.
70. J. Missakian, *A Searchlight on the Armenian Question: 1878–1950* (Boston: Hairenik, 1950), 44–45.
71. Martin Niepage, *The Horrors of Aleppo* (London: T. Fisher Unwin, 1916), 7, 11.
72. Ternon, *The Armenians*, 250–51.
73. Walker, *Armenia*, 254–55.
74. Ternon, *The Armenians*, 251.
75. Walker, *Armenia*, 255–56.
76. Ibid., 226–27, quoting Great Britain, Public Record Office, FO 371/ 2781.201201, 7.
77. Ternon, *The Armenians*, 250–51.
78. Gibbons, *The Blackest Page*, 19; Challand and Ternon, *The Armenians*, 51; Morgenthau, *Armenian Atrocities*, 33; Bryce, *Treatment of Armenians*, 407.
79. "The Anatolian Railway, by a Physician Resident of Turkey for Ten Years," from doc. 104, in *Treatment of Armenians*, ed. Bryce, 409–13.
80. "Afiun Kara Hissar: Letter, dated Massachusetts, 22nd November, 1915, from an American Traveler," doc. 108, in *Treatment of Armenians*, ed. Bryce, 418–21.
81. Elliot, *Beginning Again at Ararat*, 39; Ternon, *The Armenians*, 251.
82. Walker, *Armenia*, 357–58; Niepage, *Horrors of Aleppo*, 22–23, 11–12.
83. Kerr, *The Lions of Marash*, 25.
84. Walker, *Armenia*, 357–58.
85. Walker, *Armenia*, 230.
86. "American Burned Alive by Turks," *New York Times*, 8 Feb. 1916.

87. "Jihad Rampant in Persia," *Missionary Review of the World,* July 1915; "The Armenians in Persia," *Outlook,* 19 Aug. 1915.

88. Ternon, *The Armenians,* 258-59.

89. Walker, *Armenia,* 230; Joseph Burtt, *The People of Ararat* (London: Hogarth, 1926), 99-100.

90. Walker, *Armenia,* 258-59; Ternon, *The Armenians,* 260.

CHAPTER 6

1. Christopher Walker, *Armenia: The Survival of a Nation* (New York: St. Martin's, 1980), 130.

2. Ibid., 171.

3. Dr. Martin Niepage, *The Horrors of Aleppo* (London: T. Fisher Unwin, 1917), 15-16.

4. Henry Morgenthau, *Ambassador Morgenthau's Story* (Plandome, N.Y.: New Age, 1984).

5. Fa'iz El-Ghusein, *Martyred Armenia,* trans. from Arabic (London: C. Arthur Pearson, 1917), 23.

6. Ibid., 45-46.

7. E. K. Sarkisian and R. G. Sahakian, *Vital Issues in Modern Armenian History: Documented Exposé of Misrepresentations in Turkish Historiography,* trans. Elisha B. Chrakian (Concord, Mass.: Concord Press, 1965), 5.

8. Joseph Guttmann, "The Beginnings of Genocide," in *The Turkish Armenocide: The Genocide of the Armenians by the Turks,* ed. Armenian Historical Research Association (Boston: AHRA, 1965), 1.

9. Frederick Davis Greene, *Armenian Massacres or the Sword of Mohammed* (Philadelphia: American Oxford, 1896), 395.

10. American Committee for the Independence of Armenia, *The Joint Mandate Scheme: A Turkish Empire under American Protection,* 1919, 37.

11. El-Ghusein, *Martyred Armenia,* 56.

12. Frederick Davis Greene, *Armenian Crisis in Turkey: The Massacre of 1894, Its Antecedents and Significance,* with an Introduction by Rev. Josiah Strong (New York: G. P. Putnam's, Sons, Knickerbocher Press, 1895), 35.

13. Arnold J. Toynbee, *Armenian Atrocities: The Murder of a Nation* (London: Hodder & Stoughton, 1915), 118-19.

14. Henry Morgenthau, *The Tragedy of Armenia* (London: Spottiswoode, Ballantyne, 1918), 14-15.

15. Niepage, *The Horrors of Aleppo,* 7.

16. Herbert Adams Gibbons, *The Blackest Page of Modern History: Events in Armenia in 1915: The Facts and Responsibilities* (New York: G. P. Putnam's Sons, 1916), 31-32.

17. Yves Ternon, *The Armenians: History of a Genocide,* trans. Rouben C. Cholakian (New York: Caravan Books, 1981), 279, 281-82.

18. Ibid., 283-84.

19. James B. Gidney, *A Mandate for Armenia* (Oberlin, Ohio: Kent State Univ. Press, 1967), 192.

20. Richard G. Hovannisian, "The Armenian Question, 1878-1923," in *A Crime of Silence: The Crime of Genocide,* Proceedings of the Permanent People's Tribunal (London: Zed, 1985), 25-26.

21. Stanley E. Kerr, *The Lions of Marash: Personal Experiences with American Near East Relief, 1919-1922* (Albany: State Univ. of New York Press, 1973), xix.

22. Hovannisian, "The Armenian Question," 26.

23. Kerr, *The Lions of Marash,* 22.

24. Gidney, *A Mandate for Armenia*, 192.

25. Stephen Bonsal, *Suitors and Suppliants: The Little Nations at Versailles*, with an Introduction by Arthur Krock (Port Washington, N.Y.: Kennikat Press, 1969), 192.

26. Peter Lanne, *Armenia: The First Genocide of the XX Century*, trans. Krikor Balekdjian (Munich: Max Schmidt & Sohne, 1977), 136, quoted in Johannes Lepsius, "Rapport secret sur les massacres d'Armenie," a French translation of the German original (Beirut, 1968), 306.

27. Mabel Evelyn Elliot, *Beginning Again at Ararat* (New York: Fleming H. Revell, 1924).

28. Hovannisian, "The Armenian Question," 24, quoting Paris Peace Conference, III, 765.

29. Ibid., 26-27.

30. Ibid., 27.

31. Ibid., 28.

32. Fridtjof Nansen, *Armenia and the Near East* (first published in Norwegian as *Gjennem Armenia*, 1928; New York: DaCapo Press, 1976), 320; Dickran H. Boyajian, *Armenia: The Case for a Forgotten Genocide* (Westwood, N.J.: Educational Book Crafters, 1972), 268.

33. Nansen, *Armenia and the Near East*, 321-23.

34. Morgenthau, *The Tragedy of Armenia*, 6.

35. Arnold J. Toynbee, *Turkey: A Past and a Future* (New York: George H. Doran, 1917), 22-23.

36. Morgenthau, *Ambassador Morgenthau's Story*, 169.

37. Ibid., 161-63, 164-65.

38. Ibid., 165-66.

39. Ibid., 168.

40. Ibid., 170.

41. El-Ghusein, *Martyred Armenia*, 11, 21-22.

42. Gidney, *A Mandate for Armenia*, 21.

43. El-Ghusein, *Martyred Armenia*, 9.

44. Henry Morgenthau, *The Murder of a Nation* (New York: Lordian Press, 1974), 41.

45. Ida Alamuddin, *Papa Kuenzler and the Armenians* (London: Heinemann, 1970), 63.

46. El-Ghusein, *Martyred Armenia*, 29-30.

47. Interview with an Armenian survivor conducted by the author in 1982.

48. Gibbons, *The Blackest Page*, 27-28.

49. Ibid., 18-19.

50. El-Ghusein, *Martyred Armenia*, 39-40.

51. Ibid., 34-35.

52. Niepage, *The Horrors of Aleppo*, 4, 6.

53. Reverend Abraham H. Hartunian, *Neither to Laugh Nor to Weep: A Memoir of the Armenian Genocide*, trans. Vartan Hartunian (Boston, Mass.: Beacon, 1976), 126-27.

CHAPTER 7

1. Theodore Abel, "Sociology of Concentration Camps," *Social Forces* 30 (Dec. 1951):152.

2. Ismar Schorsch, *Jewish Reactions to German Anti-Semitism, 1870-1914* (New York: Columbia Univ. Press, 1972), 3:1.

3. Ibid., 3:2, cited by H. E. Marcard, *Über die Moglichkeit der Juden-Emancipation im christlich-germanischen Staat* (Minden and Leipzig, 1843), 39-40.

4. Ibid., 3:5, quoted in Sterling, "Jewish Reactions to Jew-Hatred in the First Half of the 19th Century," *Leo Baeck Institute Yearbook* 3(1958):104.

5. Lucy S. Dawidowicz, *The War Against the Jews, 1933–1945* (New York: Bantam Books, 1979), 29.

6. Ibid., 30–32.

7. Ibid., 33–34, quoted in Johann Gottlieb Fichte, *Reden an die deutsche Nation* (Berlin, 1808), 488.

8. Ibid., 34–35.

9. Ibid., 36–43; Helmut Krausnick et al., *Anatomy of the SS State*, trans. Richard Barry, Marian Jackson, and Dorothy Long, with an Introduction by Elizabeth Wiskemann (New York: Walker, 1968), 6.

10. Dawidowicz, *War Against the Jews*, 47; Marjorie Lamberti, *Jewish Activism in Imperial Germany: The Struggle for Civil Equality* (New Haven and London: Yale Univ. Press, 1978), 14.

11. Dawidowicz, *War Against the Jews*, 45–46.

12. Ibid., 51–59.

13. Jehuda Reinharz, *Fatherland or Promised Land: The Dilemma of the German Jew, 1893–1914* (Ann Arbor: Univ. of Michigan Press, 1975), 79, quoted in Ludwig Hollaender "Vaterlandsrede," *K. C. Blaetter*, no. 7 (1 Apr. 1914), 149; see Sidney M. Bolkosky, *The Distorted Image: German-Jewish Perceptions of Germans and Germany, 1918–1935* (New York, Oxford, Amsterdam: Elsevier).

14. George L. Mosse, *Nazi Culture: Intellectual, Cultural and Social Life in the Third Reich*, trans. Salvator Attanasio et al. (New York: Schocken Books, 1981), xxiii.

15. Joseph Tenenbaum, *Race and Reich: The Story of an Epoch* (New York: Twayne, 1956), 6, quoted in George W. Hegel, *Philosophy of the Right*, 7, quoted in John Herman Randall, Jr., *The Making of the Modern Mind*, 1926, 431–32.

16. Lucy S. Dawidowicz, ed., *A Holocaust Reader* (New York: Behrman House, 1976), 25.

17. Krausnick et al., *Anatomy of the SS State*, 11–12.

18. Tenenbaum, *Race and Reich*, 9, quoted in Frank H. Hankins, *The Racial Basis of Civilization*, 1926, 35–36.

19. Yehuda Bauer, *They Chose Life: Jewish Resistance in the Holocaust* (New York: American Jewish Committee, 1973), 16.

20. Nora Levin, *The Holocaust: The Destruction of European Jewry, 1933–1945* (New York: Thomas Y. Crowell, 1968), 8, quoted in Thomas Mann, *Germany and the Germans*, address at the Library of Congress, 29 May 1945 (Washington, 1945), 5, 7–8.

21. Krausnick et al., *Anatomy of the SS State*, 8.

22. Dawidowicz, *War Against the Jews*, 60–62.

23. Helen Fein, *Accounting for Genocide: National Responses and Jewish Victimization during the Holocaust* (New York: Free Press, 1979), 6.

24. Levin, *Holocaust*, 43.

25. Ibid., 43–44.

26. Ibid.

27. Ibid; Dawidowicz, *War Against the Jews*, 77.

28. Levin, *Holocaust*, 60–61.

29. Dawidowicz, *War Against the Jews*, 36; Levin, *Holocaust*, 68.

30. Krausnick et al., *Anatomy of the SS State*, 32.

31. Dawidowicz, *War Against the Jews*, 88–89.

32. Levin, *Holocaust*, 69–70.

33. Dawidowicz, *War Against the Jews*, 91.

34. Levin, *Holocaust*, 70–71.

35. Raul Hilberg, *The Destruction of the European Jews*, with a new Postscript by the author (New York: Quadrangle Books, 1961), 31.

36. Karl A. Schleunes, *The Twisted Road to Auschwitz: Nazi Policy toward German Jews, 1933–1939* (Urbana: Univ. of Illinois Press, 1970), 116–17.

37. Dawidowicz, *War Against the Jews*, 90.

38. Schleunes, *Twisted Road to Auschwitz*, 216.

39. Hilberg, *Destruction of the European Jews*, 83–85.

40. Ronald Donat. *The Holocaust Kingdom: A Memoir* (New York: Holt, Rinehart and Winston, 1965), 6.
41. Dawidowicz, *Holocaust Reader*, 37-38; Joel E. Dimsdale, ed., *Survivors, Victims and Perpetrators: Essays on the Nazi Party* (Washington: Hemisphere, 1980), 330.
42. Dawidowicz, *Holocaust Reader*, 37-38.
43. Hilberg, *Destruction of the European Jews*, 31.

CHAPTER 8

1. Joseph Tenenbaum. *Race and Reich: The Story of an Epoch* (New York: Twayne, 1956), 10.
2. George M. Kren and Leon Rappoport, *The Holocaust and the Crisis of Human Behavior* (New York: Holmes & Meier, 1980), 27-28.
3. Ibid.
4. Peter H. Merkl, *Political Violence under the Swastika: 581 Early Nazis* (Princeton, N.J.: Princeton Univ. Press, 1975), 85, quoting Theodore Abel, *Why Hitler Came to Power* (Englewood Cliffs, N.J.: Prentice Hall, 1938), rep. no. 98.
5. Eugene Davidson, *The Trial of the Germans: An Account of the Twenty-Two Defendants before the International Military Tribunal* (New York: Macmillan, 1966), 22; Norman Baynes, ed. and trans., *The Speeches of Adolf Hitler: April 1922-August 1939*, 2 vols. (Oxford Univ. Press, 1942; reprint ed., New York: Howard Fertig, 1969), 2:1307.
6. World Committee for the Victims of German Fascism, *The Brown Book of the Hitler Terror and the Burning of the Reichstag*, with an Introduction by Lord Marley (New York: Alfred A. Knopf, 1933), 4.
7. Ibid., 5.
8. Joachim C. Fest, *The Face of the Third Reich: Portraits of the Nazi Leadership*, trans. Michael Bullock (New York: Pantheon Books, 1970), 23.
9. World Committee, *Brown Book*, 21.
10. Ibid., 22, cited in *Die soziale Schichtung des deutschen Volkes*, (Stuttgart: Enke, 1932).
11. World Committee, *Brown Book*, 21-23.
12. Merkl, *Political Violence under the Swastika*, 59.
13. Ibid., 514, quoting Abel, *Why Hitler Came to Power*, rep. no. 523.
14. Fest, *Face of the Third Reich*, 14.
15. Ibid., 4.
16. Merkl, *Political Violence under the Swastika*, 40.
17. World Committee, *Brown Book*, 4.
18. Merkl, *Political Violence under the Swastika*, 160, quoted in Theodore Abel, *Why Hitler Came to Power*, rep. no. 325.
19. Ibid., 55, 160.
20. Ibid., 159-60, quoting Theodore Abel, *Why Hitler Came to Power*, rep. no. 274.
21. Ibid., 167, rep. no. 199.
22. Merkl, *Political Violence under the Swastika*, 189-90, 115.
23. Ibid., 668-69.
24. Ibid., 45-46.
25. George Mosse, *Nazi Culture: Intellectual, Cultural and Social Life in the Third Reich*, trans. Salvator Attanasio et al. (New York: Grossett and Dunlap, 1966; reprint ed., New York: Schocken Books, 1981), xxxii-xxxiii.

CHAPTER 9

1. Eugene Davidson, *The Trial of the Germans* (New York: Macmillan, 1966), 22; Norman Baynes, ed. and trans., *The Speeches of Adolf Hitler: April 1922-August 1939* (Oxford: Oxford Univ. Press, 1942; reprint ed., New York: Howard Fertig, 1969), vol. 2, 1307, 1657; Adolf Hitler, *Mein Kampf* (Boston: Houghton Mifflin, 1943), 741-43.

2. Edouard Calic, ed., *Secret Conversations with Hitler: The Two Newly Discovered 1931 Interviews*, trans. Richard Barry, with Foreword by Golo Mann (New York: John Day, 1971), 66.

3. Hermann Rauschning, *Hitler Wants the World*, with a Foreword by Mark Goulden (London: Argus Press, 1941), 5.

4. Hermann Rauschning, *Hitler Speaks: A Series of Political Conversations with Adolf Hitler on His Real Aims* (London: Thornton Butterworth, 1940), 140-41, 89, 243.

5. Nora Levin, *The Holocaust: The Destruction of European Jewry, 1933-1945* (New York: Thomas Y. Crowell, 1968), 39; Joachim C. Fest, *The Face of the Third Reich: Portraits of the Nazi Leadership*, trans. Michael Bullock (1st ed., *Das Gesicht des Dritten Reiches*, Munich: R. Piper, 1963; New York: Pantheon, 1970), 4.

6. Azriel Eisenberg, *Witness to the Holocaust* (New York: Pilgrim Press, 1981), 47-48.

7. Office of the U.S. Chief of Counsel for Prosecution of Axis Criminality, *Nazi Conspiracy and Aggression: Opinion and Judgment* (Washington: U.S. Government Printing Office, 1947), 5-6.

8. Helmut Krausnick et al., *Anatomy of the SS State*, trans. Richard Berry, Marian Jackson, and Dorothy Long (1st ed., *Anatomie des SS-Staates*, Olten und Freiburg im Breisgau: Walter-Verlag A.G., New York: Walker, 1968), 130. No further source material given.

9. Ibid.; Levin, *The Holocaust*, 34-35.

10. William L. Shirer, *The Rise and Fall of the Third Reich* (Greenwich, Conn.: Fawcett, 1962), 158.

11. G. M. Gilbert, *Nuremberg Diary*, with Foreword by Sir David Maxwell Fyfe (London: Eyre and Spottiswoode, 1948), 39.

12. Krausnick et al., *Anatomy of the SS State*, 572; Levin, *The Holocaust*, 36.

13. Gilbert, *Nuremberg Diary*, xi.

14. Office of U.S. Counsel for Prosecution of Axis Criminality, *Nazi Conspiracy and Aggression: Opinion and Judgment*, 5.

15. Ibid., 4-5.

16. Lucy S. Dawidowicz, *A Holocaust Reader*, ed. with Introduction and Notes by Lucy S. Dawidowicz, quoting a letter to Adolph Gemlich (New York: Behrman House, 1976), 130.

17. Raphael Lemkin, *Axis Rule in Occupied Europe: Laws of Occupation, Analysis of Government, Proposals for Redress* (Washington: Carnegie Endowment for International Peace, 1944), 86; quoted in Hermann Rauschning, *The Voice of Destruction* (New York: G. P. Putnam, 1940), 137-38.

19. Dawidowicz, *A Holocaust Reader*, 26.

20. Levin, *The Holocaust*, 25-26.

21. Levin, *The Holocaust*, 35, quoted in Helmut Heiber, *Adolf Hitler* (London, Oswalf Wolff, 1961), 97.

22. Levin, *The Holocaust*, 35.

23. Ibid., 298.

24. Dawidowicz, *A Holocaust Reader*, 33, quoted from Hitler's last political testament, 29 April 1945.

25. Dawidowicz, *A Holocaust Reader*, 27.

26. Eisenberg, *Witness to the Holocaust*, 47.

27. Levin, *The Holocaust*, 25-26.

28. Eisenberg, *Witness to the Holocaust*, 49-50.

29. Ihor Kamenetsky, *Secret Plans for Eastern Europe: A Study of Lebensraum Policies* (New York: Bookman, 1961), 35-38.

30. Eisenberg, *Witness to the Holocaust*, 50-51; Levin, *The Holocaust*, 48, 54.

31. Levin, *The Holocaust*, 54; Eisenberg, *Witness to the Holocaust*, 50-51.

32. Levin, *The Holocaust*, 46, citing Erich Kahler, *The Tower and the Abyss: An Inquiry into the Transformation of the Individual* (New York: George Braziller, 1957), 62.

33. Lucy S. Dawidowicz, *The War against the Jews, 1933-1945* (New York: Bantam Books, 1979), 63-65; Levin, *The Holocaust*, 31; Dawidowicz, *The War against the Jews*, 65-66.

34. Dawidowicz, *The War against the Jews*, 66.

35. Levin, *The Holocaust*, 32-33.

36. Dawidowicz, *The War against the Jews*, 68. No reference to Hitler quote cited.

37. Ibid., 81.

38. Levin, *The Holocaust*, 50.

39. Ibid., 33-34.

40. Ibid., 50-51.

41. World Committee for Victims of German Fascism, *The Brown Book of the Hitler Terror and Burning of the Reichstag*, with an Introduction by Lord Morley (New York: Alfred A. Knopf, 1933), 189-90.

42. Levin, *The Holocaust*, 46-47.

43. Ibid.

CHAPTER 10

1. Azriel Eisenberg, *Witness to the Holocaust* (New York: Pilgrim Press, 1981), 48.

2. George L. Mosse, *Nazi Culture: Intellectual, Cultural and Social Life in the Third Reich*, trans. Salvator Attanasio et al. (1st ed. New York: Grossett and Dunlap, 1966; New York: Schocken Books, 1981), xxxi-xxxii.

3. Ibid., 235, citing Werner Betz, "The National Socialist Vocabulary," *The Third Reich* (London, 1955), 786-89.

4. Mosse, *Nazi Culture*, 235; Yehuda Bauer, *The Holocaust in Historical Perspective* (Seattle: Univ. of Washington Press, 1978), 9-10, citing Ariel Tal, "Forms of Pseudo-Religion in the German Kulturbereich Prior to the Holocaust," *Immanuel*, no. 3 (Jerusalem, 1974):68-73.

5. Bauer, *The Holocaust in Historical Perspective*, 9, citing Adolf Hitler, *Mein Kampf*, trans. James Murphy (London: Hurst and Blackett, 1962), 261.

6. Mosse, *Nazi Culture*, 241-42, quoted in *Kirchliches Jahrbuch für die evangelische Kirche in Deutschland, 1933-1944*, edited by Joachim Beckmann (Gutersloh: C. Bertelsmann Verlag, 1948), 32-33.

7. William L. Shirer, *Berlin Diary: The Journal of a Foreign Correspondent, 1934-1941* (New York: Alfred A. Knopf, 1941), 275.

8. Bauer, *The Holocaust in Historical Perspective*, 10.

9. Nora Levin, *The Holocaust: The Destruction of European Jewry, 1933-1945* (New York: Thomas Y. Crowell, 1968), 39.

10. Mosse, *Nazi Culture*, xxvi.

11. Joachim C. Fest, *The Face of the Third Reich: Portraits of the Nazi Leadership*, trans. Michael Bullock (New York: Pantheon, 1970), 40.

12. Adolph Hitler, *Mein Kampf* (Boston: Houghton Mifflin, 1943), 179-80, 182, 184, 180.

13. Lucy Dawidowicz, *A Holocaust Reader* (New York: Behrman House, 1976), 14, citing Victor Klemperer, *Die unbewaltigte Sprache: Aus dem Notzibuch eins Philologen "LTI"* (Darmstadt, 1966).

14. Dawidowicz, *A Holocaust Reader*, 14-15. See the pioneering work in the language

field of Naziism by Heinz Paechter, *Nazi-Deutsche: A Glossary of Contemporary German Usage* (New York, 1944), especially 10-15.

15. Dawidowicz, *A Holocaust Reader*, 15.

16. Ibid., 15-16.

17. The World Committee for the Victims of German Fascism, *The Brown Book of the Hitler Terror and the Burning of the Reichstag*, (New York: Alfred A. Knopf, 1933), 171.

18. Hugh Trevor-Roper, ed., *Final Entries 1945: The Diaries of Joseph Goebbels*, trans. Richard Barry (German ed., *Die Letzen Aufzeichnungen*, Hamburg: Hoffman and Campe, 1977; New York: G. P. Putnam's, 1978), xv-xvi.

19. Ibid., xvii.

20. Randall L. Bytwerk and Robert D. Brooks, "Julius Streicher and the Rhetorical Foundations of the Holocaust," Paper presented at the annual meeting of the Central States Speech Association, Chicago, Ill., 10-12 Oct. 1980, 4.

21. Bytwerk and Brooks, "Julius Streicher and the Rhetorical Foundations of the Holocaust"; Norman Cohn, *Warrant for Genocide: The Myth of the Jewish World-Conspiracy and the Protocols of the Elders of Zion* (New York: Harper & Row, 1967), 204.

22. Mosse, *Nazi Culture*, xxi; Bytwerk and Brooks, "Julius Streicher and the Rhetorical Foundations of the Holocaust," abstract.

23. Helen Fein, *Accounting for Genocide: National Responses and Jewish Victimization during the Holocaust* (New York: Free Press, 1979), 86.

24. Trevor-Roper, *Final Entries 1945*, xvii-xix.

25. Ibid., xxii, xxiv; Mosse, *Nazi Culture*, xxxi.

26. Levin, *The Holocaust*, 7.

27. Bruno Bettelheim and Morris Janowitz, *Social Change and Prejudice* (New York: Free Press, 1964), 247.

28. Levin, *The Holocaust*, 37-38.

29. Alexander Donat, *The Holocaust Kingdom: A Memoir* (New York, Chicago, and San Francisco: Holt, Rinehart and Winston, 1965), 13.

30. Cohn, *Warrant for Genocide*, 21-23.

31. Levin, *The Holocaust*, 18-19.

32. Cohn, *Warrant for Genocide*, 21-23.

33. Ibid., 201-2.

34. Ibid., 206-7.

35. Ibid., 203.

36. Ibid., 209.

37. Simon Wiesenthal, *The Sunflower* (New York: Schocken Books, 1976), 44.

CHAPTER 11

1. Raul Hilberg, *The Destruction of the European Jews* (New York: Quadrangle Books, 1961), 555-635. Presents concise information about the formal bureaucratic organization of the Holocaust.

2. Nora Levin, *The Holocaust: The Destruction of European Jewry, 1933-1945* (New York: Thomas Y. Crowell, 1968), 45.

3. Lucy S. Dawidowicz, *The War Against the Jews 1933-1945* (New York: Bantam Books, 1979), 73, quoted in DGFP, ser. C, 1, doc. no. 141, 253-55.

4. Leo Kuper, *Genocide: Its Political Use in the Twentieth Century* (New Haven: Yale Univ. Press, 1981), 122.

5. Levin, *The Holocaust*, 91.

6. John P. Sabini and Maury Silver, "Destroying the Innocent with a Clear Conscience," in *Survivors, Victims, and Perpetrators: Essays on the Nazi Holocaust*, ed. Joel E. Dimsdale (Washington: Hemisphere, 1980), 331.

7. Hilberg, *The Destruction of the European Jews*, 31-39.

8. Ibid., 32.

9. Helen Fein, *Accounting for Genocide: National Responses and Jewish Victimization during the Holocaust* (New York: Free Press, 1979), 65.

10. Hilberg, *The Destruction of the European Jews*, 106-7.

11. Ibid., 116-22.

12. Ibid., 122.

13. Ibid., 124-25.

14. Isaiah Trunk, *The Judenrat: The Jewish Councils in Eastern Europe under Nazi Occupation*, with an Introduction by Jacob Robinson (New York: Macmillan, 1972), 43-44.

15. Ibid., 43-44.

16. Ibid., 33.

17. Hannah Arendt, *Eichmann in Jerusalem: A Report on the Banality of Evil*, rev. ed. (New York: Penguin Books, 1982), 125.

18. Hilberg, *The Destruction of the European Jews*, 125-26.

19. Ibid., 129-30.

20. Ibid., 131-38.

21. Ibid., 148-49, 155.

22. Ibid., 174-81.

23. Ibid., 182-83. Directive by OKW/L (signed Keitel), 13 March 1941, NOKW-2302.

24. Ibid., 183-87.

25. Levin, *The Holocaust*, 290-91, quoted from a letter from Goring to Heydrich, 31 July 1941, PS-710.

26. Hilberg, *The Destruction of the European Jews*, 187-89.

27. Lucy S. Dawidowicz, *A Holocaust Reader*, ed. with Intro. and Notes by Lucy S. Dawidowicz (New York: Behrman, 1976), 83-84.

28. Arendt, *Eichmann in Jerusalem*, 106.

29. Hilberg, *The Destruction of the European Jews*, 190-92.

30. Ibid., 208-9.

31. Gerald Reitlinger, *The Final Solution: The Attempt to Exterminate the Jews of Europe, 1939-1945*, 2d ed., rev. (South Brunswick, N.Y.: Thomas Yoseloff, 1968; 1st published 1953, n.p.), 218-20, quoting PS 2992, IMT 19:457.

32. Dawidowicz, *A Holocaust Reader*, 83-84.

33. Joel Cang, *The Silent Millions: A History of the Jews in the Soviet Union* (New York: Taplinger, 1970), 7.

34. Elie Wiesel, *The Jews of Silence: A Personal Report on Soviet Jewry*, trans. and with a historical Afterword by Neal Kozodoy (New York: Holt, Rinehart and Winston, 1966), 33.

35. Dawidowicz, *A Holocaust Reader*, 83-84.

36. Hilberg, *The Destruction of the European Jews*, 141-42.

37. Joseph Tenenbaum, *Race and Reich: The Story of an Epoch* (New York: Twayne Publishers, 1956), 333, cited in Bruno Blau, "The Last Days of German Jewry in the Third Reich," *Yivo Annual* (1953):197-204.

38. Ibid., 334, cited in Blau, "Last Days of German Jewry," 202.

39. Ibid., 334, cited in Trevor-Roper, *Goebbels Diary*, 261-62.

40. Tenenbaum, *Race and Reich*, 335.

41. Ibid., 335, cited in Wilhelm Krell, "La Communaute Culturelle Israelite de Vienne," *Les Juifs en Europe*, 190.

42. Ibid., 336, quoted in *IMT* 33:534-36.

43. Ibid., 336, cited in Henri Monneray, *La Persécution des Juifs dans les pays de l'Est* (1949), 212.

44. Ibid., 336, cited in Gregory Frumkin, *Population Changes in Europe since 1939* (1951), 47-48.

45. Ibid., 338, cited in Monneray, *La Persécution des Juifs dans les pays de l'Est*, 117.

46. Ibid., 275-76.

47. Ibid., 277, cited in doc. NG-183; *Trials* 13:233.

48. Tenenbaum, *Race and Reich*, 278-80, cited in Frumkin, *Population Changes in Europe since 1939*, 108-9.

49. Tenenbaum, *Race and Reich*, 281-84.

50. Ibid., 286, quoted in Frumkin, *Population Changes in Europe since 1939*, 109.

51. Ibid., 285-86, cited in Monneray, *La Persécution*, 237.

52. Ibid., 286-88, cited in Frumkin, *Population Changes in Europe since 1939*, 44.

53. Ibid., 289, doc. no. 3824; *Trials*, 4:433-34.

54. Ibid., 289-91, cited in Hugo Valentin, "Rescue and Relief Activities in Behalf of Jewish Victims of Nazism in Scandinavia," *Yivo Annual* 8(1953):237.

55. Ibid., 291, cited in Aage Bertelsen, *October '43* (New York: 1954). No further information given.

56. Tenenbaum, *Race and Reich*, 292, cited in Valentin, "Rescue and Relief Activities . . . Scandinavia," 232.

57. Ibid., 291-92, cited in Nella Rost, "Les Juifs sous l'occupation allemande dans les pays scandinaves," in *Les Juifs en Europe, 1939-45* (1949), 128-33.

58. Ibid., 292, cited in Felix Kerstein, *Totenkopf und Treue* (1952), 180.

59. Ibid., 292, cited in Valentin, "Rescue and Relief Activities . . . Scandinavia," 231.

60. Ibid., 293-301.

61. Ibid., 301-2, quoted in doc. NG-3354; *Trials* 14:664.

62. Ibid., 302, cited in Reitlinger, *The Final Solution*, 363.

63. Ibid., 302, cited in Frumkin, *Population Changes in Europe since 1939*, 136.

64. Ibid., Tenenbaum, *Race and Reich*, 302-3.

65. Ibid., 306-7, cited in Reitlinger, *The Final Solution*, 369.

66. Ibid., 307-9, cited in *IMT* 4:355-73.

67. Ibid., 310, cited in Isaac Kabeli, "The Resistance of the Greek Jews," *Yivo Annual of Jewish Social Science* 8 (1953):286-87.

68. Ibid., 310, cited in Ben-Josef, *Heroic Figures in Auschwitz* (1950), 288.

69. Ibid., 310-11.

70. Ibid., 312, cited in report of Ambassador Emil von Rintelen, doc. NG-2582; *Trials* 13:250.

71. Ibid., 312, cited in "Rapport de Haim Benadow," *Les Juifs en Europe* (1949), 123-25.

72. Ibid., 312-13; 317, cited in Jacob Lestschinsky, *Crisis, Catastrophe and Survival* (1948), 60.

73. Ibid., 318-19; 320-21, cited in Dr. Frederic Stein, "La situation des Juifs en Slovaquie. . . .," *Les Juifs en Europe*, 216-20.

74. Ibid., 321-22.

75. Ibid., 223, cited in Frumkin, *Population Changes in Europe since 1939*, 94.

76. Dorothy Rabinowitz, *About the Holocaust: What We Know And How We Know It* (New York: Institute of Human Relations Press, 1979), 38.

77. Eugene Kogon, *The Theory and Practice of Hell: The German Concentration Camps and the System behind Them*, trans. Heinz Nordon (1st American ed., Farrar, Straus and Cudahy, 1950; New York: Berkely, 1958), 220.

78. Hilberg, *The Destruction of the European Jews*, 619-22.

79. Karl A. Schleunes, *The Twisted Road to Auschwitz: Nazi Policy toward German Jews 1933-1939* (Chicago: Univ. of Illinois Press, 1970), 257.

80. Elie A. Cohen, *Human Behavior in the Concentration Camp*, trans. from the Dutch by M. H. Braaksma (New York: Universal Library, 1953), 28.

81. Arendt, *Eichmann in Jerusalem*, 79.

82. Cohen, *Human Behavior in the Concentration Camp*, 17-19.

83. Hilberg, *The Destruction of the European Jews*, 574-75.

84. Cohen, *Human Behavior in the Concentration Camp*, 9.

85. Kogon, *The Theory and Practice of Hell*, 67.

86. Ibid., 63.

87. Hilberg, *The Destruction of the European Jews*, 611-12.

88. Cohen. *Human Behavior in the Concentration Camp*, 33-34.
89. Jean François Steiner. *Treblinka*, with an Introduction by Terrence Des Pres and Preface by Simone de Beauvoir. trans. Helen Weaver (New York: New American Library, 1979), 77.
90. Ibid., 158.
91. Hilberg, *The Destruction of the European Jews*, 578, cited in Gisela Perl. *I Was a Doctor in Auschwitz*, 61-62; also cited in Philip Friedman. *This Was Oswiecim* (1946), 69.
92. Sylvia Rothchild. *Voices from the Holocaust*, with a Foreword by Elie Wiesel (New York: New American Library, 1981), 157.
93. Hilberg. *The Destruction of the European Jews*, 580.
94. Ibid., 600-603; see 602, citing Himmler's authorization for the Dohmen experiments in a letter to Ernst Grawitz, 16 June 1943.
95. Ibid., 605.
96. Kogon. *The Theory and Practice of Hell*, 162.
97. Cohen. *Human Behavior in the Concentration Camp*, 87.
98. Kogon. *The Theory and Practice of Hell*, 163-64.
99. Cohen. *Human Behavior in the Concentration Camp*, 85.
100. Kogon. *The Theory and Practice of Hell*, 165.
101. Cohen. *Human Behavior in the Concentration Camp*, 86.
102. Kogon. *The Theory and Practice of Hell*, 166.
103. Ibid., 178.
104. Cohen. *Human Behavior in the Concentration Camp*, 43.
105. Hilberg, *The Destruction of the European Jews*, 561. Hilberg cites Judge Wladyslaw Bednarz. "Extermination Camp at Chelmno." in Central Commission for Investigation of German Crimes in Poland. *German Crimes in Poland* (1946), 107-17.
106. Cohen. *Human Behavior in the Concentration Camp*, 36.
107. Hilberg, *The Destruction of the European Jews*, 566, 571. See 572 for a listing of six camps, their locations, jurisdictions, type of killing operations, and number killed.
108. Dawidowicz, *A Holocaust Reader*, 109.

CHAPTER 12

1. Bruno Bettelheim and Morris Janowitz. *Dynamics of Prejudice: A Psychological and Sociological Study of Veterans* (New York: Harper & Brothers, 1950), 154-55.
2. Karl A. Schleunes. *The Twisted Road to Auschwitz: Nazi Policy toward German Jews, 1933-1939* (Urbana: Univ. of Illinois Press, 1970), 218.
3. Raul Hilberg. *The Destruction of the European Jews*, with a new Postscript by the author (Chicago: Quadrangle Books, 1961), 28-29.
4. Helen Fein. *Accounting for Genocide: National Responses and Jewish Victimization during the Holocaust* (New York: Free Press, 1979), 78.
5. Fein. *Accounting for Genocide*, 9.
6. Nora Levin. *The Holocaust: The Destruction of European Jewry* (New York: Thomas Y. Crowell, 1968), 314.
7. Norman Cohn. *Warrant for Genocide: The Myth of the Jewish World-Conspiracy and the Protocols of the Elders of Zion* (New York: Harper & Row, 1967), 212.
8. Fein. *Accounting for Genocide*, 26.
9. Robert W. Ross. *So It Was True: The American Protestant Press and the Nazi Persecution of the Jews* (Minneapolis: Univ. of Minnesota Press, 1980), 83-85.
10. Ibid., 85, quoted in "Letter of Resignation of James G. McDonald. High Commissioner for Refugees (Jewish and Other) Coming from Germany: Addressed to the Secretary General of the League of Nations." *Christian Century* (15 Jan. 1936):99-127.
11. Ibid., 85-89.
12. Arthur D. Morse. *While Six Million Died: A Chronicle of American Apathy* (New York: Random House, 1968), 102.

13. Fein, *Accounting for Genocide*, 168.

14. Azriel Eisenberg, *Witness to the Holocaust* (New York: Pilgrim Press, 1981), 104-5.

15. Ibid., 105.

16. Morse, *While Six Million Died*, 90-92, cited in "Report to the Secretary on the Acquiescence of This Government in the Murder of the Jews," prepared by three Protestants and signed by Randolph E. Paul, 13 Jan. 1944: from a private file.

17. Morse, *While Six Million Died*, 92-93.

18. Ibid., 94-95. Primary source not indicated.

19. Martin Gilbert, *Auschwitz and the Allies* (London: Michael/Joseph Rainbird, 1981), 345.

20. Fein, *Accounting for Genocide*, 24.

21. Morse, *While Six Million Died*, 30.

22. Eisenberg, *Witness to the Holocaust*, 104.

23. Lucy S. Dawidowicz, ed., *A Holocaust Reader* (New York: Behrman House, 1976), 291-92.

24. Fein, *Accounting for Genocide*, 325.

25. Sylvia Rothchild, ed., *Voices from the Holocaust*, with a Foreword by Elie Wiesel (New York: New American Library, 1981), 163.

26. Morse, *While Six Million Died*, 31-32.

27. Gilbert, *Auschwitz and the Allies*, 21-24.

28. Yehuda Bauer, *The Holocaust in Historical Perspective* (Seattle: Univ. of Washington Press, 1978), 84-85.

29. Eisenberg, *Witness to the Holocaust*, 113, quoted in Paul Vogt, *Armor Has No Fear* (1943).

30. Bauer, *Holocaust in Historical Perspective*, 25-27.

31. Hilberg, *The Destruction of the European Jews*, 259, quoting Hitler speech, 30 Jan., 1939, reported in the German press.

32. Bettelheim and Janowitz, *Dynamics of Prejudice*, 155.

33. Fein, *Accounting for Genocide*, 66-67.

34. Joseph Tenenbaum, *Race and Reich: The Story of an Epoch* (New York: Twayne, 1956), 69-70.

35. Ibid., 77-78.

36. Eisenberg, *Witness to the Holocaust*, 102. No further information given.

37. Ibid., 103.

38. Ibid., 100.

39. Ibid., 101-2, quoted in Friedrich Heer, *God's First Love* (1967), Chaps. 11-12.

40. Tenenbaum, *Race and Reich: The Story of an Epoch*, 80.

41. Richard Quinney, "Who Is the Victim?" in *Victimology*, ed. Israel Drapkin and Emilio Viano (Lexington, Mass.: Lexington Books, D.C. Heath, 1974), 103-8.

42. Stephen Schafer, *The Victim and His Criminal: A Study in Functional Responsibility* (New York: Random House, 1968), 79.

43. Yehuda Bauer, *The Jewish Emergence from Powerlessness* (Toronto, Buffalo, London: Univ. of Toronto Press, 1979), 58-60.

44. Rothchild, *Voices from the Holocaust*, 166.

45. Raul Hilberg, "The Nature of the Process," in *Survivors, Victims and Perpetrators: Essays on the Nazi Holocaust*, ed. Joel E. Dimsdale (Washington: Hemisphere, 1980), 662.

46. Hannah Arendt, *Eichmann in Jerusalem: A Report on the Banality of Evil*, rev. ed. (New York: Penguin Books, 1982), 125.

47. Exodus 12:21-36.

48. 2 Kings 24:10-25.

49. Fein, *Accounting for Genocide*, 316.

50. Ibid., 317.

51. Richard S. Lazarus, *Psychological Stress and the Coping Process* (New York: McGraw-Hill, 1966), 134.

52. Fein, *Accounting for Genocide*, 317.

53. Lazarus, *Psychological Stress and the Coping Process*, 134.
54. Fein, *Accounting for Genocide*, 317.
55. Ibid.
56. Elie Wiesel, *Night*, trans. Stella Rodway, with a Forward by François Mauriac (New York: Bantam Books, 1960), 3-4.
57. Rothchild, *Voices from the Holocaust*, 168.
58. Ibid., 169-70.
59. Fein, *Accounting for Genocide*, 319.
60. Vahakn N. Dadrian, "The Common Features of the Armenian and Jewish Cases of Genocide: A Comparative Victimological Perspective," in *Victimology: A New Focus*, vol. 4, *Violence and Its Victims*, ed. Israel Drapkin and Emilio Viano (Lexington, Mass.: Lexington Books, D.C. Heath, 1975), 103.
61. Ibid., 4:102.
62. Martin E. P. Seligman, *On Depression, Development and Death* (San Francisco: W.H. Freeman, 1975), see Chap. 3.
63. A. Baum, J. R. Aiello, and L. E. Colesnick, "Crowding and Personal Control: Social Density and the Development of Learned Helplessnesses," in *Journal of Personality and Social Psychology* (1978):1000-1011.
64. W. R. Grove, M. Hughes, and O. R. Galle, "Overcrowding in the Home," *American Sociological Review* (1979):59-80.
65. See various episodes of other nations aborting Jewish attempts to escape in Gilbert Martin, *Auschwitz and the Allies* (London: Michael Joseph/Rainbird, 1981).
66. Hilberg, *The Destruction of the European Jews*, 173-74.
67. Ibid., 581-82.
68. Ancel Keys, Josef Brozek, Austin Henschel, Olaf Michelsen, Henry Longstreet Taylor, *The Biology of Human Starvation*, with Forewords by J. Drummond, Russell Wilder, Charles King, Robert Williams (Minneapolis: Univ. of Minnesota Press, 1950), 2:783.
69. Ibid.
70. Eleanor N. Whitney and Corinne B. Cataldo, *Understanding Normal and Clinical Nutrition* (St. Paul, Minn.: West, 1983).
71. Keys et al., *The Biology of Human Starvation*, 793.
72. J. W. Pennebaker, M. A. Burnam, M. Schaeffer, and D. C. Harper, "Lack of Control as a Determinant of Perceived Physical Symptoms," in *Journal of Personality and Social Psychology* (1977):167-74.
73. Dorothy Rabinowitz, *About the Holocaust: What We Know and How We Know It* (New York: Institute of Human Relations Press, 1979), 34.
74. Bauer, *Holocaust in Historical Perspective*, 28-29, quoting Ben Gurion, "Before the Tribunal of History," *Zionist Review*, 22 Sept. 1944.

CHAPTER 13

1. Neil J. Smelser, *Theory of Collective Behavior* (New York: Free Press, 1962), 8-9, quoted in H. Blumer, "Collective Behavior," in *Review of Sociology: Analysis of a Decade*, ed. J. B. Gittler (New York, 1957), 127.
2. Ibid., 67.
3. Ibid., 9.
4. Ibid., 71.
5. Ibid., 72-73.
6. Ibid., 73.
7. Ibid., 15-17.
8. Ibid., 226.
9. Ibid., 226-27.
10. Ibid., 224-26.

11. Ibid., 224-25.
12. Ibid., 14.
13. Ibid.
14. Ibid., 228-31.
15. Ibid., 249.
16. Ibid., 247-52.
17. Ibid., 241-50.
18. Ibid., 245-46.
19. Ibid., 245-46.
20. Ibid., 254-55.
21. Ibid., 231-33.
22. Ibid., 234-37.
23. Ibid., 240.
24. Ibid., 247-48, 252.
25. Ibid., 245.
26. Ibid., 241, 255-56.
27. Ibid., 257.
28. Ibid., 259-60.
29. Ibid., 261.
30. Ibid., 256.
31. Ibid., 261-67.

INDEX

Abdul-Aziz, Sultan of the Turks, 26
Abdul-Hamid II ("the Red Sultan"),
  Sultan of the Turks
  Armenians, treatment of, 11, 14, 17,
    21, 33-34
  ascends throne, 26-27
  attitude toward Europe, 31-32
  Gladstone refers to, 41
  reform program, 37
  revolt against, 43, 47, 53-55, 60, 62
  rumors circulated by, 72-73
Abdul-Medjid, Sultan of the Turks, 23-
  25
Abel, Theodore, 129-30, 151, 152
Abovian (Armenian author), 33
Accounting for Genocide, 188-89
Adana, Armenia, massacre in, 17
Adil, Haci, 56
Adrianople, Treaty of, 23
Agaev, Ahmet, 66, 71
Agen, Armenia, massacre in, 14
Aggression, against outsiders
  collective behavior approach, 245-46
  ideology of
    in Armenian genocide, 65-70
    collective behavior approach, 249-
      50
    in Jewish Holocaust, 171-74
  intensification of, 11-19, 245-46
  by state
    in Armenian genocide, 110-12   .
    collective behavior approach, 251-
      52
    in Jewish Holocaust, 215-18
Agrarian League, 134
Ahmad, Ferroz, 47, 60-61
Ahmed, Oghlou, 61
Akcura, Yusuf, 56, 66, 69, 71
Alamuddin, Ida, 61, 70, 76
Alexander II, Emperor of Russia (1855-
  81), 27
Ali Merdan Bey. See Huseyinzade, Ali
Alldeutscher Verband, 134
Alp, Tekin, 49, 50-51, 69
Ambitions, territorial. See Territorial
  ambitions
American Armenia Relief Fund
  Committee, 98

American Committee for the
  Independence of Armenia, 112
American Diplomatic Relations with the
  Middle East, 36
American War Refugee Board, 220
Anatolia College, 99-100
Angriff, Der (Goebbel's newspaper), 179
Ankara, Armenia, deportation from, 99
Annihilation, group. See Group
  annihilation
Antisemitische Correspondenz, 134
Anti-Semitism, 129-44, 179
Arendt, Hannah, 191, 196, 227-28
Armenia
  destruction of
    aggressive ideology in, 65-70
    collective behavior approach, 251-
      52
    in concentration camps, 102-8
    exterminations, 83-102
    propaganda war in, 70-82
  internal strife in
    loss of empire, 22-32
    normative upheaval in, 32-42
  literary development in, 33
  outsiders in
    aggression against, 11-19
    disarming of, 19
    intergroup tensions in, 3-11
    massacres of, 13-17, 75-76
    store boycotts, 17-18
  political parties in, 34-42
  reform program in, 37
  schools in, 32-33
  territorial ambitions of, 43-52
Armenia: The Cradle of Civilization, 83
Armenia: The Survival of a Nation, 5
Armenian Crisis in Turkey, 10-11, 24
Armenians, The: History of a Genocide,
  12
Arndt, Ernst Moritz, 131
Asquith, Herbert A., 118-19
Auschwitz (death camp), 209
Austria, Jewish deportations from, 199
Aziz Bey, 62-63, 125

Bab Ali, Demonstration of, 36-37

19886146